Crime and Justice in America

(Pergamon Policy Studies-28)

Pergamon Policy Studies on Crime and Justice

Carter Hill   *THE CRIMINAL'S IMAGE OF THE CITY*

Related Titles

 PERGAMON POLICY STUDIES ON CRIME AND JUSTICE

Crime and Justice in America
Critical Issues for the Future

Edited by
John T. O'Brien
Marvin Marcus

Pergamon Press

NEW YORK • OXFORD • TORONTO • SYDNEY • FRANKFURT • PARIS

Pergamon Press Offices:

U.S.A.   Pergamon Press Inc., Maxwell House, Fairview Park, Elmsford, New York 10523, U.S.A.

U.K.   Pergamon Press Ltd., Headington Hill Hall, Oxford OX3 0BW, England

CANADA   Pergamon of Canada Ltd., 150 Consumers Road, Willowdale, Ontario M2J 1P9, Canada

AUSTRALIA   Pergamon Press (Aust) Pty. Ltd., P O Box 544, Potts Point, NSW 2011, Australia

FRANCE   Pergamon Press SARL, 24 rue des Ecoles, 75240 Paris, Cedex 05, France

FEDERAL REPUBLIC OF GERMANY   Pergamon Press GmbH, 6242 Kronberg/Taunus, Pferdstrasse 1, Federal Republic of Germany

Copyright © 1979 Pergamon Press, Inc.

Library of Congress Cataloging in Publication Data
Main entry under title:

Crime and justice in America.

(Pergamon policy studies)
Includes index.
1. Criminal justice, Administration of—United States—Addresses, essays, lectures. 2. Crime and criminals—United States—Addresses, essays, lectures.
I. O'Brien, John T., 1924—   II. Marcus, Marvin.
HV8138.C682   1979   364'.973   79-182
ISBN 0-08-023857-2
ISBN 0-08-025549-3 (pbk.)

Printed in the United States of America

Contents

v

Contents

CHAPTER

Foreword

Forecasting developments in the police, even in the most unsophisticated countries, requires the facility to forecast future events over the whole field of public affairs, as the police must adapt and modify to changes in the society they serve. While this obviously is a truism in regard to, say, the financial health of the community, which must affect the resources available for law enforcement, I wish to make a wider point, namely that to be effective the police role must harmonize with the tasks seen by the communities as most appropriate for them. The development of traffic wardens to cope with the problem of the stationary vehicle is an example of the police service taking the initiative in response to public rejection of the concept that such traffic regulation is an appropriate task for the police. However, as at any one time different sections of society assign different tasks, life is not too easy for the police forecaster!

That said, my management training encourages me to attempt this preface on the understanding that although all forecasts are wrong, it is the duty of professional advisers (and I am one) to make an attempt to foresee events, knowing that others will modify these predictions as more and better information becomes available.

The dearth of data is perhaps the main foundation for the belief that police work owes more to art than to science. The lack of authoritative police writing to which both the student and practitioner can turn for help in developing police skills has led those concerned with higher police training to rely on the exchange of ideas and experience between those most successful at innovating and developing the art of policing. The British National Police College at Bramshill has made a sound reputation in this way, as have most similar police institutions.

The contributions in this book are in that valuable tradition and must stimulate and inform, even if subsequent events follow their disconcerting habit of nonconformity with what sensible people see in the crystal ball. I am, therefore, delighted to be associated, even in this small way, with John O'Brien's project.

On the main theme of this book, certain trends in connection with crime and criminals in the United Kingdom encourage me to make some tentative projections, not least in the hope that by so doing, one increases the possibility of events following the advertised course!

The appointment of a Royal Commission on Criminal Procedure under the Chairmanship of Sir Cyril Philips provides strong grounds for predicting that the rules governing police interrogations and the rights of accused persons will be more closely defined. The consequential removal of grounds for suspicion must help and strengthen the police.

Next, there is an increasing awareness in the British police and those responsible for its management that a multi-disciplinary response to the present high level of criminality is more likely to be successful in reducing its incidence than merely increasing the numbers of regular policemen. More significantly there is a growing belief in the "caring" professions that the police have more to offer the social worker than the latter's professional training suggested. Together these changes in contemporary wisdom have combined to produce some interesting and successful case studies in which the partnerships between the police, teachers and social workers have taken many differing forms. Needless to say, these groups have been most active and effective in dealing with young offenders.

Of course, we remain baffled by the teenage recidivist, but successful schemes for identifying those who can be diverted from crime and for supporting them through their difficult years have indicated the path to follow if we are to reduce the numbers of new entrants annually reinforcing the ranks of the criminal classes.

It may be that a concentration of scarce resources to these ends implies writing off some young offenders as being beyond the capability of society to reform. This is an unpalatable prospect, but a continuing increase in the load on limited social services surely must lead to greater selectivity when deciding who is to, or can, benefit from them.

Confirmation that such a philosophy is developing in policing tactics and strategies is to be found in the current emphasis on criminal intelligence. Much higher priority is now given to monitoring the behavior and associates of professional criminals whose lifestyle confirms that they will not live peacefully within the law; the aim being to predict and thus prevent the commission of major crimes. This activity in terms of reducing crime by bringing to justice some previously immune, and thus removing the incentive to crime created by that immunity, is invaluable and more productive than great efforts applied at the scenes of crime which too often produce no return.

The problem of gaining support for the police will, however, prove more difficult if these trends develop faster than the community's understanding of the need for them. It is to be hoped that an increasing professionalism in the police service will facilitate this growth in understanding. We believe that the recent support for the police in the United Kingdom, demonstrated by a much larger increase in remuneration than that afforded to other contenders in a period of pay restraint, has placed upon the police managers a heavy duty to achieve the highest professional standards appropriate to the new value placed on the police.

It is not difficult, therefore, to forecast that the training programmes for the modern police forces in the United Kingdom must become more sophisticated, or that higher professional standards will create a demand for greater specialization in the support services. The smaller police departments will not then be able to provide competitive standards, and while the number of police forces is not likely to be further reduced in the United Kingdom, common services shared by a number of forces will certainly be a growth area.

Turning to an allied issue, the way the police respond to complaints from the public: we in the United Kingdom, having set up a truly independent review body, wonder whether the enormous resources modern police departments now deploy in this field could be diminished if police attitudes to those with whom they come into contact might be modified by an educational programme designed to give the police a more profound understanding of the pressures towards conflict in those whom it is their duty to serve. The useful beginning being made in this direction encourages me to include it in my list of predictions.

The final development I would most like to see is better training, allied to superior support services and personnel development programmes enabling the police for the first time to serve well those who need them most: the underprivileged, uneducated and deprived who presently identify the police as the enemy. I am optimistic, as policemen must be, because if the will is there, the skills exist.

To conclude, of the above, my most certain forecast is that police activity in the crime and justice field beyond 1984 will show an increase in police community involvement programmes of every kind. I believe too that as the prosecution process becomes more closely monitored, confidence in the police will increase and the most successful measure for reducing crime, a trusted police force, will result.

— SIR COLIN WOODS KCVO CBE

SIR COLIN WOODS KCVO CBE, HM Chief Inspector of Constabulary, started in the police service in 1946 as a constable in the West End of London. In 1964, on promotion to Chief Superintendent rank, he was seconded to the National Police College at Bramshill on the directing staff of the then new Senior Command Course. Later he returned to Bramshill College as Commandant, being the first serving police officer to act in that capacity.

He was appointed Assistant Commissioner in 1969 and returned to the Yard to take charge of the Traffic Department. He then transferred to take charge of the Criminal Investigation Department when Sir Robert Mark became Commissioner of Scotland Yard in April 1972.

He was awarded the CBE in the Queen's Birthday Honours in 1973 and was appointed Deputy Commissioner in May 1975.

In the Queen's Birthday Honours in 1977 he was awarded a Knighthood and on August 1, 1977 was appointed HM Chief Inspector of Constabulary.

Preface

For many years practitioners in the American system of criminal justice have been aware of their inability to plan ahead. With all of the emphasis in the public and private sectors in forecasting for future needs, they have been plagued with constant demands to ready themselves for the future. Many administrators in this system recognize the tools available to them in foretelling changes in population, business construction, urban renewal, recreation areas and even topography. The related professions deal with rapidly changing morals and mores and with slower but decisive changes in legislation and judicial interpretation. Similarly, the thrust in civil service toward selecting women and other minority group members is only beginning to be assessed. In addition, criminal justice personnel are so immersed in their everyday tasks that they cannot see the whole problem, but only their immediate needs. We also have the perennial difficulty of each function being but one part of the whole criminal justice system. Criminal justice is more than just police; it is probation, parole, corrections, prosecution, defense, the judiciary and, more recently, masses of private police who now almost outnumber the public officers.

The realization of great changes to come in the future prompted the editors to wonder what criminal justice might be like beyond 1984. Therefore, they solicited the opinions of recognized authorities in the field with regard to forecasting changes in the areas of law enforcement, correction and the judicial system, as well as allied fields.

However, anyone associated with criminal justice is well aware that it is a non-system in that there is little agreement as to theory, objectives or methodology. It is not hard to understand this when we consider the disparate disciplines involved such as law, medicine, religion, anthropology, sociology and psychology, not to speak of public administration. This polarity of professional outlook is much more pronounced in the United States than on the Continent, where there has always been a much closer relationship between law and sociology; for example, the English common law training at the Inns of Court, rather than the university as is the case on the Continent, has contributed to this dichotomy.

There is not even a common theory of criminal justice. Is the whole system designed for the protection of society through prevention and deterrence? Or is it meant to reform? There are many who believe that it must look back to the theory of punishment or desert rather than forward. Some have even advocated a double-track system combining punishment for the past with protection for the future.

This problem is well known to the researchers and practitioners concerned. But change in any system is not merely a matter of theory but also, and of greater import, the implementation of it. A theory cannot develop and progress toward an objective that is practical as well as visionary without some unified system to which all of the elements can contribute.

America has been afflicted (some would say blessed) with longitudinal and latitudinal separations of government, the former in the Montesquieuan tripartite form which rigidly maintains the divisions of legislative, executive and judicial powers. The latter is exemplified by local, county, State and National levels of administration bearing little relation to each other.

Additionally, the hope of many that Positivism would discover the answers to the questions perplexing mankind through the ages has been dashed with the realization that on the one hand science, in solving a particular problem, often creates another, whether it be with the invention of the motor vehicle or the development of nuclear energy. On the other hand, the promises of science have not led to the expected Nirvana, as shown by the base level of culture and education of recent vintage accompanying the decay of our once-proud cities. In no area of life today has science proven to be the god that failed more than in the field of criminal justice. Funding, technology, research and increased manpower have failed to stay the scourge of crime in any of its manifestations - whether organized, violent, white-collar or juvenile. The failure of all elements of criminal justice is only too obvious.

The objective of this book, therefore, is to recognize that criminal justice must become unified, if not one unit. But what do we mean by such? We have mentioned unity as to ultimate theory or objectives of the system. This area is in such a state of flux that we now hear advocates asking for a return to the once-discarded ideas of retribution and just desert. Obviously, little can be done until there are some generally accepted objectives.

What of unity as to discipline or profession? It would appear to be time to question the dominance of a technical profession such as the law in all areas of the present non-system. The administration of prosecutors' offices, courts and other criminal justice agencies by those who have little, if any, administrative training and education is something no longer to be afforded. The medical profession has long been aware that the best surgeon is not necessarily the best hospital administrator. Perhaps the legal profession should conduct similar self-introspection. It is now many years since A. E. Buck warned that the expert should be "on tap, not on top."

Should there be a profession of criminal justice generalists who are products of similar education and philosophy? Such a profession need not be as broad as that of public administration, but should probably be more inclusive than medicine, law or sociology.

What can be done with the longitudinal problem of criminal justice? The tripartite form is not so sacrosanct that probation and parole could not be combined in the executive branch of government. Why cannot the administration of the courts also be placed under the executive with a court administrator, leaving only the judicial function to the judges? Perhaps most of the criminal justice system could be moved to the executive branch of government.

As to the latitudinal difficulty, it may be politically impossible to abandon the Federal form, but certainly there could be greater concentration at the county or State level without any great impairment of local government. The system is even more aggravated in that the tripartite separation of powers duplicates itself at the various institutional levels.

The thrust of this book, therefore, is to see what can and should be done to develop a more unified system as to theory, profession, separation of powers and at the various levels of government.

At the same time, it is recognized that whatever the opportunities for, or stumbling blocks to, the unity of criminal justice, there will nevertheless be great changes in the years to come. The crisis of crime, resulting in tremendous amounts of literature, thought and research cannot have but a very great effect. There will also be the serendipitous byproducts of such great efforts.

Therefore, the various authors have based their forecasts on what they believe the state of the art will be, conditioned by their own professional education and expertise. They will endeavor to look at their particular facet of the system; but as part of the whole, and to foretell how their area may contribute to a much more unified system of crime and justice beyond the Orwellian Year of 1984.

Introduction

This book is intended for scholars, practitioners and students of criminal justice, as well as the growing number of private citizens whose interest in the field transcends the aim of mere entertainment. The editors have long been aware of the problems affecting the system, but they are equally aware that the answers to such problems almost defy solution. It is believed that this results from the inability to forecast the future form and role of the various facets making up the field. A further difficulty has resulted from the inability to forecast in a system wherein the various components are constantly acting and reacting on each other. It has been only recently that the individual practitioners have become aware of system-wide analysis and planning. The various contributors to this work have prepared their chapters with a consideration of the overall system.

The editors have chosen the authors on the basis of their exposure to the field of criminal justice, in addition to their proven expertise in a particular area.

The book has been organized to reflect five broad problem areas. The first of these deals with public law enforcement on the four levels of the American Federal system: local, county, State and National government. In addition, a particular problem is dealt with on each of these levels.

Chapter one deals with local police and the push towards consolidation. This is one of the greatest problems facing law enforcement today. The authors suggest that there are many dangers inherent in consolidation. They criticize the various arguments offered in favor of such and claim that there already exists sufficient cooperation between law enforcement agencies so as to negate the need for consolidation.

The second chapter looks at county government from the perspective of the sheriff. The author suggests that this officer should provide staff and auxiliary services to local police as an alternative to consolidation. He extols the political independence of the sheriff as opposed to the local police chief.

Thereafter the State Police are given due regard in the third chapter, wherein the author considers the evolving role of such agencies. He also offers them as an alternative to consolidation to furnish services to local police.

The last chapter of the section considers the controversial role of the Federal government from a viewpoint which suggests that consolidation will be a sine qua non for future Federal assistance.

The second problem area moves from the public to the private sector of criminal justice, the latest and most confusing segment of the system. This fast-growing area is considered in two chapters. Chapter five discusses the interaction of the public and private police and suggests that the latter should be used to augment and assist the former. This will necessitate regulation and assistance from the various governments.

The sixth chapter deals with the growth of campus and school police. The author describes the growth of such from guard forces to formal police agencies. The increase in crime, vandalism and even terrorism will require an even more professional force in future years.

The third section of the work deals with specific types of crime which are a grave threat to society. These are organized crime, terrorism, and hostage negotiations. All of these are somewhat related in that they usually encompass a broad geographical base beyond that of local police. To combat them successfully requires cooperation, if not consolidation, and above all, intelligence sources.

Chapter seven discusses the problem of intelligence in a democracy and how, when it is needed most in today's world, it is becoming ever more difficult to gather and retain. The author paints a dismal picture of the future of this critical area of law enforcement.

Thereafter organized crime is considered. The author describes how the American penal laws have been a reflection of religious mores which have placed an impossible burden on local police. This in turn, has fostered corruption. He believes that the removal of religious influences will make for a more enforceable law. He also discusses the scandalous internecine struggle between the various Federal agencies for control of narcotic law enforcement. He suggests a cost-effective program to concentrate on organized crime.

In chapter nine the author examines the problem of terrorism, and projects a continuing and growing difficulty for law enforcement unless great changes are effected in governmental cooperation, technology, legislation and other areas. Ultimately it is a problem of nationalism and ideology.

The last chapter of this section deals with a related problem of international relations and terrorism, i. e. , the taking of hostages. While this is sometimes a local phenomenon perpetrated by distraught persons, it has more serious consequences on the international level. The seizing of hostages by radical groups for political purposes is becoming ever more prevalent. The article points out that, in this area, the traditional police reaction is inadequate. Such incidents require planning, knowledge of psychology and emotional control. This in turn necessitates specialization, intelligence and technology, not to speak of training and education in this new field of police operations.

The fourth major area deals with the two complementary areas to law enforcement those of courts and correction. Chapter eleven discusses the future of courts. This recently much-criticized branch of government will undoubtedly change very much in the next decade. Plea bargaining, judicial selection and even the much vaunted adversary system itself will be given critical examination. While the form of the judicial system will change, the author believes that due process will continue to be the hallmark of American jurisprudence.

Corrections is the subject matter of the twelfth chapter. The necessary standards in this field continue to elude students and practitioners, as the author points out. Thereafter a number of other problems are considered. The article suggests that the next few years must bring solutions to many of these, since the field is now at such a critical point. He predicts that corrections will develop toward community-based facilities. Contrary to many, he believes that rehabilitation is still a viable goal. He calls for the early identification of delinquents to facilitate such rehabilitation.

Chapter thirteen is concerned with the female offender, which is another growing phenomenon in today's culture. The authors develop the thesis that biological and social factors influence women's role in delinquency. Differential treatment of the sexes is also a factor in female behavior. The authors attempt to predict the future of female crime. This will depend on the social role of women and the future legal structure. They call for a number of short and long-range reforms to reduce the female crime rate.

The fifth section of the book considers the important area of personnel in criminal justice. Chapter fourteen attempts to forecast the type of police chief required before the turn of the century. Such a forecast obviously must consider the whole field of government and the interaction of the rest of the system. The various police models of the past are looked at to facilitate the forecast, as well as the increased training and education of the future chief. The activist role of the courts will also determine the type of police chief to some extent. Lastly, the future chief will be determined by role expectation.

Chapter fifteen considers lateral entry, since mobility is a mark of any profession and law enforcement aspires to such a status. The authors recite the advantages accruing from such a policy. At the same time they explain the impediments to such. A number of surveys conducted by police agencies are examined which indicate that, while lateral entry may be the wave of the future, it is still low tide as far as this innovation is concerned.

Chapter sixteen examines the problem of minority recruitment. The author states that criminal justice agencies must be representative of, and responsive to, the communities they serve. There is also the requirement of efficiency, which must not be lost sight of. The introduction of ethnic and female minorities into criminal justice has not yet come to grips with the overriding consideration of a professional service.

The last chapter of the book considers a new area of specialization of personnel, that of ecology, in particular pollution control. The authors have given a great deal of attention to this problem, and feel that this must be a function of local police in coming decades. In spite of increasing demands for more and better police services, the authors conclude that only the police are equipped and available to control pollution. This prediction may be alarming to many police administrators but it has been arrived at after a great deal of research and consideration.

The book attempts to make predictions in many critical areas of criminal justice. The projections are based on a period of five years from now and beyond. Many other areas could have been examined. In fact, many others were considered and discarded for one reason or another. These subjects were chosen because they lent themselves to predictability and the authors chosen had the necessary sympathy for, and empathy with, the overall project. It is hoped that the book presents a futuristic picture of the new dimensions of criminal justice well beyond the Orwellian year of 1984.

I

The Public Role

Policing: Is There a System?*

Elinor Ostrom
Roger B. Parks
Gordon P. Whitaker

Many writers, in discussing the ways police are organized in metropolitan areas, have assumed that systematic ways of working together are impossible among police agencies. Bruce Smith expressed this view in a frequently quoted statement:

> There is therefore no such thing in the United States as a police system, nor even a set of police systems within any reasonably accurate sense of the term. Our so-called systems are mere collections of police units having some similarity of authority, organization, or jurisdiction; but they lack any systematic relationship to each other. (1)

---

* Prepared for delivery at the 1977 Annual Meeting of the American Political Science Association, The Washington Hilton Hotel, Washington, D. C. , September 1-4, 1977. Copyright by the American Political Science Association, 1977.
Sections of this paper are from Elinor Ostrom, Roger B. Parks, and Gordon P. Whitaker, Policing Metropolitan America (Washington, D. C.: National Science Foundation, 1977). That report was prepared with the support of National Science Foundation Grant GI 43949. Any opinions, findings, conclusions, or recommendations expressed herein are those of the authors and do not necessarily reflect the views of NSF. The work of a very able staff was involved in the data collection and analysis for this study. Technical reports prepared by Larry Wagner and John McIver were used as the basis for some of the analysis presented herein.

3

Similarly, the President's Commission on Law Enforcement and Administration of Justice summarized this image in its report, The Challenge of Crime in a Free Society:

> The machinery of law enforcement in this country is fragmented, complicated and frequently overlapping. America is essentially a nation of small police forces, each operating independently within the limits of its jurisdiction. The boundaries that define and limit police operations do not hinder the movement of criminals, of course. They can and do take advantage of ancient political and geographic boundaries, which often give them sanctuary from effective police activities.

> . . . coordination of activity among police agencies, even when the areas they work in are contiguous or overlapping tends to be sporadic and informal, to the extent that it exists at all. (2)

However, this conventional wisdom is not supported by systematic study of how police do or don't work together in metropolitan areas. Anecdotes of feuds between departments have been used in place of systematic surveys of how police services are delivered in most metropolitan areas.

An empirical description of how police work together is now possible in light of recently completed research on the delivery of police services in 80 U.S. metropolitan areas. In this research we took an industry approach to the study of police organization. This analytical approach is neutral in regard to whether systematic relationships exist in metropolitan areas. However, using this approach forces one to ask questions about the nature of production of consumption relationships in a metropolitan area rather than assume the nature of these relationships from a simple list of agencies in the area. In this paper we will first briefly describe the approach we utilized and describe the metropolitan areas included in our study. We will then present some findings on the structure of police service delivery in metropolitan areas.

THE INDUSTRY APPROACH

Instead of focusing solely on the agencies in a metropolitan area that met some basic definition of "police department," we looked for agencies producing specific public services for the area. (3) Each agency was considered in terms of what it produces or consumes, and who receives its products.

Definition of Services

In order to determine unambiguously which agencies are part of a public service industry, we must first define a group of goods or services which are considered to be the industry products. No intrinsic feature of an agency places it exclusively in one public service industry rather than another. A police department, for example, may be considered in the health industry if it provides ambulance service, in the fire prevention industry if it inspects buildings, and in the recreation industry if it sponsors a softball league. One can tell if an agency is "in" or "out" of an industry only by knowing whether it produces one of the goods or services that are considered to be an industry product.

We selected a variety of law enforcement activities that are directed to citizens. We examined the delivery of three <u>direct services.</u>

- Patrol

- Traffic Control

- Criminal Investigation (4)

These three services include some of the more time-consuming and high priority police services to citizens. For our purposes, delivery of these services involves activity by officers who have <u>extraordinary powers of arrest</u> in the conduct of the service, thus excluding private watchmen, guards, and private investigators.

We also included a number of auxiliary services that are used by police agencies in their production of direct services. These are services used by the producers of policing rather than services directed to citizens. We analyzed the delivery of four <u>auxiliary services.</u>

- Radio Communications

- Adult Pre-Trial Detention

- Entry-Level Training

- Crime Laboratory Analysis (5)

The configuration of the police industry differs from service to service. In one metropolitan area many producers of patrol may exist while there is only one producer of detention. In another metropolitan area, the pattern may be quite different. Our first effort was to identify the producers of direct services and the citizens they served.

Secondly, we determined from direct service producers whether they used each auxiliary service and if so, how they obtained this service.

Industry and Organizational Approaches Contrasted

We can illustrate the difference between the industry approach taken here and the more conventional organizational approach. Observers, using an organizational approach to study police, find that most departments having fewer than 150 full-time sworn officers do not have their own crime laboratories. These observers typically conclude that citizens served by these departments are lacking the advantages crime labs can offer to investigators.

But, in using an industry approach, we are interested in determining whether the residents served by smaller police departments are, in fact, covered by crime lab services. We ask the small, direct service producers whether they use crime lab services and, if so, where they obtain them. Most frequently we find that agencies with overlapping jurisdictions, such as county or state police agencies, provide crime lab facilities to direct service producers. Some direct service producers contract for crime laboratory services from another local police department or a nonpolice agency, such as a local hospital or a private laboratory.

Observers using an organizational approach may argue that if economies of scale exist in the production of some police services, all police agencies should be made large enough (through consolidation or merger, for instance) to gain these economies. Observers using an industry approach will ask whether these economies can be captured by organizing large, specialized agencies to produce a particular service rather than including all police service production within one agency.

In the private goods and services market we are familiar with the difference between retailers and wholesalers. We are also familiar with the differences between neighborhood, quick-service, limited selection establishments, and broad-spectrum supermarkets or department stores. There is a role for a variety of different types of firms in private goods industries. The differences among types of firms in private goods industries can be instructive when examining organizational arrangements for supplying public services. Instead of assuming that there should be only one type of agency - a large, full-service agency - serving each area, one begins with no prior assumption about any ideal form of organization, and simply asks how goods and services are being produced and exchanged. Then one develops a systematic way for measuring the structure of these relationships. Then, and only then, is it possible to begin evaluating the comparative performance of different kinds of industry structure.

Service Delivery Matrices

Once services have been defined and we have identified the producers and consumers for each service, we can depict the service-by-service structure of a police industry by constructing service delivery matrices. Measures of industry structure can be derived from the matrices.

All agencies that produce a given police service in a metropolitan area can be arranged as <u>rows</u> in the delivery matrix for that service. The <u>columns</u> in the matrix are the service recipients. For each direct service, service areas are the service recipients. We included as service areas any territory that had a resident population of at least 100, some way of making collective decisions about police services in the area, and a distinct legal arrangement with a producer of a direct police service. Thus, for each direct service, the population of the metropolitan area is divided into mutually exclusive service areas, each served by one or more producers. The service areas for one direct service may differ from the service areas for another direct service. A community of people may have one arrangement for general area patrol and another for traffic control or criminal investigation. Many service areas are cities, towns, or villages. A residential campus or military base may also be a service area.

The service recipients for auxiliary services are agencies that produce direct services. These agencies use auxiliary services in producing direct services. Thus, the columns of a radio communications service delivery matrix are those direct service producers who use radio communications. Although we found that most direct service producers use all auxiliary services, we did find some who did not require their recruits to have entry-level training, or that do not use any radio communications.

Production Relationships - the Entries in the Matrix

We use the cells of the matrix to characterize production relationships. When a producer does not deliver the service to a recipient, the cell in that recipient's column is left blank. We were not able to develop interval measures of service flow from each producer. Instead, we developed a typology of production types that differentiates only ordinally. One distinction we make is between regular and irregular production of the service. By regular production of a direct service, we mean that the producer makes the service available on a routine basis to individuals in the area it serves. Regular production of auxiliary services occurs when the service is routinely produced for the police agency being served. By "irregular" production we mean that the service is produced only in unusual circumstances. If, for example, a municipal police department investigates all reported homicides in a city, but the state police occasionally assist in homicide investigation, the municipal police would be considered a regular producer and the state police an irregular producer for that city. Although we have found some irregular production relationships for all services, our structural measures are computed excluding irregular relationships.

More important, we think, are several distinctions among types of regular service delivery. In observing police services we found that several forms of production involve simultaneous regular production by more than a single producer for any given service recipient. Three forms of simultaneous regular production are so important that we developed special ways to code and measure them. These are coordination, alternation, and duplication.

Coordination occurs when two or more producers interact in planning regular service production for the same service recipient. In many service areas homicide investigations are simultaneously conducted by several agencies who coordinate their activities. Even though two or more agencies work on the case, they maintain a single case record and share information. This is a strict definition of coordination requiring interaction in the planning and production of the service.

Alternation occurs when two agencies produce a service for the same service area, but systematically divide their production activities over space, over time, or among clientele. The production of traffic control on a freeway within a city by the State Highway Patrol, and in the rest of the city by municipal police departments, is an example of alternation in space.

Duplication in service delivery occurs when two or more regular producers supply a service to the same consuming unit without coordination or alternation.

Thus, for each direct and auxiliary service, a producer and a service recipient may have either: 1) no production relationship, 2) an irregular production relationship, or 3) a regular production relationship. If the production relationship is regular, it might be coordinated, alternated, duplicated, or independent (i.e., no simultaneous production). For each service we classify the relationship (or lack thereof) between each producer of that service and all service recipients, and enter the specific relationships in the cells of a service delivery matrix. (6)

Service Delivery Measures

From these individual service delivery matrices for each direct and auxiliary service for each metropolitan area, we can construct service delivery measures that enable us to compare service delivery across the 80 SMSAs. Some of the measures we developed are discussed below.

Multiplicity

We define multiplicity as the number of producers of a particular service in a metropolitan area. Comparison among metropolitan areas is facilitated by controlling for population size. Relative multiplicity for direct services is defined as the number of producing units for a given police service per 100,000 SMSA residents. For auxiliary services, relative multiplicity is defined as the number of producers of the auxiliary service divided by the number of direct service producers receiving the auxiliary service. This measure is an inverse indicator of the degree to which an SMSA has consolidated production of each police service. The lower the value for relative multiplicity, the greater the consolidation.

Alternation

Alternation is the proportion of service recipients in the SMSA receiving the service from two or more regular producers, where at least one of the producers alternates in time, space, or clientele. For direct services, relative alternation is the sum of the residents living in service areas receiving alternative services divided by the total population of the metropolitan area.

Coordination

Coordination is the proportion of service recipients in the SMSA receiving the service from two or more producers that coordinate their service delivery. For direct services, relative coordination is the sum of the residents living in service areas receiving coordinated services divided by the total population of the metropolitan area.

Duplication

Duplication is the proportion of service recipients in the metropolitan area that regularly receive a service from more than one producer without coordination or alternation. This measures the amount
of simultaneous production where some form of arrangement for either
coordinating or alternating the production has not been worked out
among multiple producers of the service. For direct services, relative duplication is measured by the sum of the population of the service
areas receiving duplicate service divided by the total population of the
metropolitan area.

Other Measures

In addition to those defined above, we have developed measures
of fragmentation, dominance, independence, and autonomy. These
are discussed in several recent publications. (7)

THE METROPOLITAN AREAS STUDIED

Our findings are based on data gathered in 1974 and 1975, in a
study of police service delivery in small to medium-sized metropolitan
areas. In 1970 the U.S. Census Bureau identified 200 single-state
Standard Metropolitan Statistical Areas (SMSAs) with populations of
less than 1.5 million. More than 67 million Americans, one-third of
the U.S. population, lived in these 200 metropolitan areas. We selected 80 of these SMSAs in a stratified, random sample which included
metropolitan areas in 31 states.

The 80 SMSAs include a wide variety of metropolitan area sizes,
population densities, and types of communities. Three of them have
more than one million residents. Ten have fewer than 100,000 residents. Population densities range from 32 persons per square mile to
more than 3,000 persons per square mile. Major cities are included
in this sample. Two cities have more than 500,000 residents and
another nine have between 250,000 and 500,000 within city limits.
Twenty-three cities have between 100,000 and 250,000 residents.
This study also includes the full range of other types of areas that
police agencies serve, including smaller central and suburban cities
and towns, unincorporated county areas near more built-up cities, and
rural areas.

THE PRODUCERS OF POLICE SERVICES

Direct Service Producers in Each SMSA

Most metropolitan areas have local and State producers of direct services, and many have Federal producers as well. State and Federal agencies usually supply direct services to several SMSAs. Thus, the total number of producers for the 80 metropolitan areas is greater than the number of agencies supplying those services. Municipal police departments are the most numerous producers of direct services. Table 1.1 shows a regional breakdown of the type of agency producing the direct services studied.

More than 6? percent of the producers of patrol, traffic control, and criminal investigation in the 80 metropolitan areas are municipal police. This category includes not only the police departments of cities, towns, and villages, but also township and New England town police. Agencies of this type usually supply all three of the direct services to the jurisdictions they serve.

County sheriffs' departments, county police departments, and county prosecutors' police account for about 8 percent of the producers of patrol, traffic control, and criminal investigation in metropolitan areas outside New England (Region 1). New England town police conduct these services in rural parts of metropolitan areas in those states. In many other parts of the country, county sheriffs' departments or county police have responsibility for serving much of the territory within metropolitan areas, some of which is urban, but much of which is rural. County agencies also often coordinate investigations with municipal and special district police departments and supply them with auxiliary services. Like municipal departments, most of them supply all three direct services.

State police, highway patrols, and State bureaus of investigation are another group of agencies producing direct services. State agencies control traffic on at least some highways in each of the 80 SMSAs. In half of the metropolitan areas, the highway patrol or State police also conduct criminal investigations. Thirteen other metropolitan areas in the sample of 80 receive the investigative services of State bureaus of investigation.

College and university police departments commonly supply patrol and traffic control, but fewer of them investigate crimes. We consider all campus police in a single category, regardless of the kind of governing authority responsible for the campus. State, county, and municipal colleges and universities are not the only kinds of campuses with their own law enforcement agencies. Many private colleges and uni-

Table 1.1. Numbers and Types of Producers Supplying Direct Police Services in the 80 Metropolitan Areas

Location	Number of Direct Police Producers	Percent of Direct Police Producers That Are:						
		Municipal Police Departments	County Police and Sheriffs	State Police Agencies	Campus Police	Military Police	Federal Police Producers	Other Police Producers
All Direct Service Producers	1454	64	7	7	7	6	3	6
Northeast								
Region 1	87	69	0	18	10	0	0	2
Region 2	162	82	6	3	3	0	0	7
Region 3	143	78	1	4	6	4	2	5
Midwest								
Region 5	275	74	9	6	6	1	1	3
Region 7	54	65	7	7	4	2	4	11
South								
Region 4	305	62	9	7	10	6	2	4
Region 6	182	49	10	9	10	11	5	6
West								
Region 8	48	44	8	10	6	19	6	6
Region 9	170	43	7	4	9	15	8	13
Region 10	28	68	21	7	0	0	0	4

Rows may not total 100 percent due to rounding errors.

Source: Elinor Ostrom, Roger B. Parks, and Gordon P. Whitaker: Policing Metropolitan America (Washington, D.C.: U.S. Government Printing Office, 1977), p. 9.

versities also have campus police conducting patrol, traffic control, and criminal investigation. Campus police account for almost 7 percent of the producers of direct police services in the 80 SMSAs.

Military law enforcement agencies also supply direct police services in metropolitan areas. Forty-eight base police units serve Army, Navy, Air Force, and Marine Corps installations in the 80 SMSAs. Almost all of these patrol, and more than half also investigate burglary. Investigations of homicides and of more serious burglaries on Federal military reservations are undertaken by military investigation agencies: the Army Criminal Investigations Division, the Naval Special Investigations Office, and the Air Force Office of Special Investigations. Several of the metropolitan areas have more than one installation of the same branch of the military and, therefore, have several base police producers, but only a single military investigation unit. Eighty of the 1,454 direct service producers are military units.

Nonmilitary Federal agencies constitute another group of producers. The Federal Bureau of Investigation is regularly involved in burglary and homicide investigation on Federal reservations in 26 of the 80 metropolitan areas. These are SMSAs with military or other Federal reservations. The FBI and other Federal investigative agencies, such as the Bureau of Alcohol, Tobacco, and Firearms and the Drug Enforcement Administration, conduct investigations in all metropolitan areas, but the enforcement of Federal laws is not within the scope of this study, except on Federal reservations where Federal law supplants State law as the general criminal code. Other Federal agencies producing patrol, traffic control, or burglary and homicide investigation in Federal jurisdictions include the Veterans' Administration, the National Park Service, and the Bureau of Indian Affairs. These agencies produce direct police services in a variety of combinations, usually including patrol and traffic control. Forty of the 1,454 direct service producers are nonmilitary Federal agencies.

A final type of direct service police producers are the law enforcement departments of other agencies such as housing authorities, airport authorities, park departments, state capitols, hospitals, and so on. A few of these investigate crimes, but most are patrol and/or traffic control producers. When we combine these "special district" producers, they make up about 6 percent of the producers of patrol, traffic control, and criminal investigation in the 80 SMSAs.

Multiplicity and Relative Multiplicity of Direct Services

The median number of patrol producers in the 80 SMSAs is 13. This means that half of the SMSAs have 13 or fewer patrol producers,

while half have more than 13; but a simple count of producers does
not characterize police service delivery adequately. For example, one
metropolitan area might have ten agencies that produce patrol service
for a population of one million. Another might have ten agencies, but
a population of only 100,000. The difference between the two areas is
lost if one uses only a simple count of producers. Computing the number of producers per 100,000 inhabitants of a metropolitan area (relative multiplicity) provides a means of showing the difference between
the two metropolitan areas of the example. They both would have ten
producers, but the number of producers per 100,000 population in the
first is 1.0, while it is 10.0 in the second SMSA. In relative terms,
there are many more producers in relation to consumers in the second
metropolitan area than in the first. As Table 1.2 shows, the median
number of patrol producers per 100,000 inhabitants in the 80 metropolitan areas is 5.9.

A smaller number of producers investigate homicides in metropolitan areas than conduct general area patrol: the median number of homicide investigation producers is eight. No more than four homicide investigation producers per 100,000 population operate in half of the 80
metropolitan areas. Most metropolitan areas have fewer producers of
traffic accident investigation and residential burglary investigation than
of patrol, but more producers of these services than of homicide investigation.

Considerable regional variation exists in the number of direct
service producers in an SMSA. Metropolitan areas in California and
Arizona (Region 9) and in New York and New Jersey (Region 2) generally
have the largest number of producers of direct police services. Regional variation is less for number of producers per 100,000 inhabitants.
A common pattern across all regions is that there are more producers
of patrol than of other direct services.

In general, metropolitan areas with more residents have more
producers of direct police services. By computing the number of producers per 100,000 residents, we can see whether larger SMSAs also
tend to have relatively more police service producers. We find that
this is not the case. Relative to the number of people living in a metropolitan area, there are fewer producers in the very largest SMSAs
than there are in the smallest ones. Metropolitan areas with populations from 125,000 to 249,999 tend to have the most producers of direct
services per 100,000 residents (Table 1.3).

The reason that more agencies produce patrol than the other direct
services is that smaller cities, townships, and college campuses often
organize part-time or small, full-time police agencies to supplement
the patrol capability of other police agencies responsible for providing
direct services to these areas. The municipal police departments,

Table 1.2. Number of Direct Service Producers in an SMSA who Produce Each of the Direct Services by Region

Metropolitan Areas Grouped By 1973 Population	Number of SMSAs	Multiplicity Median Number of Direct Service Producers in an SMSA				Relative Multiplicity Median Number of Direct Service Producers in an SMSA per 100,000 Population			
		Patrol	Traffic Accident Investigation	Burglary Investigation	Homicide Investigation	Patrol	Traffic Accident Investigation	Burglary Investigation	Homicide Investigation
Nationwide	80	13	11	10	8	5.9	5.3	4.7	3.9
Northeast									
Region 1	8	6	7	6	6	3.9	4.2	3.9	3.9
Region 2	4	19	18	16	13	6.0	4.6	4.6	3.9
Region 3	6	14	11	12	7	6.6	5.5	5.5	4.7
Midwest									
Region 5	16	13	12	11	8	7.2	6.4	5.6	4.5
Region 7	4	7	7	8	6	4.6	5.8	4.8	3.7
South									
Region 4	15	18	16	15	10	5.3	4.1	4.2	3.2
Region 6	14	8	7	6	6	3.6	3.2	3.3	3.0
West									
Region 8	4	5	5	7	7	4.2	4.0	4.7	4.7
Region 9	7	20	16	17	16	4.8	2.9	3.6	3.3
Region 10	2	5-21	6-20	5-20	5-20	3.9-10.5	4.7-10.0	3.9-10.0	3.9-10.0

Source: Elinor Ostrom, Roger B. Parks, and Gordon P. Whitaker: Policing Metropolitan America (Washington, D.C.: U.S. Government Printing Office, 1977), p. 9.

15

county sheriffs' departments, or State police that have authority to produce direct services for the areas continue to undertake investigations -
either independently or, in some cases, in coordination with the smaller
agencies. Where the agencies with overlapping jurisdictions conduct
investigations independently, the small patrol producers specialize in
patrol and immediate response services and do not usually conduct investigations. We will discuss some of these arrangements more fully
in a later section.

Auxiliary Service Producers in Each SMSA

Auxiliary services are used by police agencies in the production of
direct services for residents living in service areas. With the exception of radio communications, few direct service producers supply their
own auxiliary services (Table 1.4). While 68 percent of the 1,454 direct
service producers supply radio communications, only 11 percent supply
adult pre-trial detention, entry-level training, and chemical laboratory
analysis. The type of agencies producing these auxiliary services varies
considerably from the pattern found in direct service production. County
police and sheriffs are the only type of direct service producer likely to
produce detention services. State and Federal police are the only types
of direct service agencies that commonly produce entry-level training
and chemical laboratory analysis. Very few municipal police departments produce any of the auxiliary services except radio communications.

Multiplicity and Relative Multiplicity
for Auxiliary Services

Multiplicity for auxiliary services is much lower than that for
direct services (Table 1.5). The median number of radio communications producers in an SMSA is nine, for entry-level training it is four,
and median multiplicity is two for both detention and laboratory analysis. There is no more than one jail and one crime lab for approximately
every seven patrol or investigation producers in half of the SMSAs.
There is no more than one training academy for every three direct
service producers. The median is less than one radio communications
producer for each police agency using radio communications.
Multiplicity of auxiliary service producers is greater in larger
SMSAs, but relative multiplicity is less. In the median SMSA of those
over 500,000 in population, there is approximately one jail and one
lab per ten direct service producers, while in the median SMSA of

Table 1.3. Number of Direct Service Producers in an SMSA Who Produce Each of the Direct Services by Size of SMSA

Metropolitan Areas Grouped By 1973 Population	Number of SMSAs	Multiplicity — Median Number of Direct Service Producers in an SMSA				Relative Multiplicity — Median Number of Direct Service Producers in an SMSA per 100,000 Population			
		Patrol	Traffic Accident Investigation	Burglary Investigation	Homicide Investigation	Patrol	Traffic Accident Investigation	Burglary Investigation	Homicide Investigation
Nationwide	80	13	11	10	8	5.9	5.3	4.7	3.9
50,000 to 124,999	20	5	5	4	4	5.9	5.8	4.7	4.6
125,000 to 249,999	26	10	10	20	8	6.4	6.4	5.7	4.4
250,000 to 499,999	21	19	16	15	12	6.0	5.1	4.8	3.7
500,000 and over	13	29	27	28	22	4.0	3.5	3.5	3.0

Source: Elinor Ostrom, Roger B. Parks, and Gordon P. Whitaker: Policing Metropolitan America (Washington, D.C.: U.S. Government Printing Office, 1977), p. 9.

17

Table 1.4. Auxiliary Services Supplied by Direct Service Producers

Type of Direct Service Producer	Number of Direct Police Producers	Percent of Direct Producers That Supply:			
		Radio Communi- cations	Adult Pre-Trial Detention	Entry- Level Training	Chemical Laboratory Analysis
All Direct Producers	1454	68	11	15	8
Municipal Police Departments	936	66	6	6	1
County Police and Sheriffs	108	87	81	7	7
State Police	97	88	0	86	60
Campus Police	108	84	0	8	0
Military Police	81	58	17	42	12
Federal Police	40	32	8	75	65
Other Police	84	56	0	10	0

Source: Elinor Ostrom, Roger B. Parks, and Gordon P. Whitaker: Policing Metropolitan America (Washington, D.C.: U.S. Government Printing Office, 1977), p. 9.

18

Table 1.5. Number of Auxiliary Service Producers in an SMSA Who Produce Each of the Auxiliary Services By Size of SMSA

Metropolitan Areas Grouped By 1973 Population	Number of SMSAs	Multiplicity Median Number of Auxiliary Service Producers in an SMSA				Relative Multiplicity Median Number of Auxiliary Service Producers in an SMSA per Direct Service Producers Who Utilize Service			
		Radio Communi- cations	Entry- Level Training	Adult Pre-Trial Detention	Crime Laboratory Analysis	Radio Communi- cations	Entry- Level Training	Adult Pre-Trial Detention	Crime Laboratory Analysis
Nationwide	80	9	4	2	2	.86	.33	.15	.14
50,000 to 124,999	20	5	2	1	2	1.00	.50	.22	.25
125,000 to 249,999	26	8	3	1	2	.81	.33	.11	.11
250,000 to 499,999	21	16	7	2	3	.88	.35	.15	.15
500,000 and over	13	23	8	4	3	.82	.29	.11	.09

Source: Elinor Ostrom, Roger B. Parks, and Gordon P. Whitaker: Policing Metropolitan America (Washington, D.C.: U.S. Government Printing Office, 1977), p. 14.

those under 125,000 there is one jail per five direct service producers and about one crime laboratory per four direct service producers.

It is true that there are a large number of police agencies serving metropolitan areas. Most of these agencies supply direct service and radio communications. The number of detention, entry-level training, and laboratory analysis producers is substantially smaller. The roles of different types of agencies vary considerably across the 80 SMSAs.

AGENCY COOPERATION AND SERVICE DELIVERY

Conventional wisdom holds that if many police agencies exist in a metropolitan area, it necessarily follows that there must be duplication of services. Police officers are pictured as tripping over one another as they weave in and out of fragmented jurisdictions. Officers are seen as isolated from their counterparts in nearby departments and as failing to cooperate across jurisdictional boundaries.

In this section we present findings that indicate otherwise. We find little duplication of services. We discuss the ways in which police agencies in fact organize their service delivery systems to avoid duplicating each other's work. Then we examine fresh pursuit legislation which opens the boundaries between jurisdictions. Finally, we discuss the extent of emergency assistance, mutual aid agreements, and deputization among police agencies.

Although we present findings about many workable arrangements for policing among agencies, we are in no way recommending maintenance of the status quo. Police organization in each particular area can be examined to determine whether current service delivery patterns can be improved. Arrangements that work well in one metropolitan area may not work well in a different area. The recognition that policing has been organized in a variety of ways leads to the realization that many options are available for reorganizing police services delivery.

Duplication of Services

Duplication of services has been a major concern of critiques of American policing. That concern has arisen from the observation that most metropolitan areas have numerous, separate direct service police agencies. The assumption is that these agencies are duplicating each other's work. In general, our findings refute this assumption.

The work of policing is, with few exceptions, divided among the various agencies of an SMSA. Each agency is responsible for conducting a limited set of activities and for serving a limited territory.

Overlapping jurisdictions have also been viewed as indicative of duplicate service delivery. But again, the assumption is generally inconsistent with our findings. For example, county sheriffs' departments typically do not patrol in those parts of their legal jurisdiction patrolled by municipal police. Similarly, city police agencies usually do not patrol residential campuses or military bases within city limits when these special areas have their own police. It is, therefore, important to distinguish service areas from jurisdictions. A police service area is any territory with a resident population and a unique set of service delivery arrangements. Only where two or more producers conduct the same service in a single <u>service area</u> may they duplicate each other's work. Even this is unusual, however. Most producers conducting the same service in the same service area have adopted divisions of labor that eliminate duplication.

Alternation of Direct Services

In most service areas where two or more producers supply the same service, the producers have divided the work between them. The most common type of division is alternation. Service delivery can alternate in time, in space, or with respect to a specific clientele group. For example, some small municipal police departments patrol only from eight A.M. to midnight. From midnight to eight A.M., county sheriffs' departments patrol those municipalities. This is alternation in time. No duplication is involved. In such situations, county sheriffs' patrols substitute for the municipal police officers.

Alternation in space for patrol usually occurs where there is a special purpose patrol agency operating in the jurisdiction of another agency. Examples include municipal park police who patrol exclusively in the parks; school district or community college police who patrol only on campus; and special district police who patrol airports, bridges, or hospitals. The defining characteristic of alternation in space is the supply of patrol services to an enclave of another agency's jurisdiction, where the enclave does not have a resident population. Officers from the larger jurisdiction may or may not patrol the enclave; generally they do not.

For traffic patrol, a geographic division of responsibility by type of thoroughfare is often established. State agencies often patrol traffic on interstate freeways and major State highways, but not elsewhere in the jurisdiction. Municipal and county police rarely patrol freeways.

Alternation based on clientele served is exemplified by the relationship between municipal police departments and military police where municipalities adjoin large military bases. Both military police and municipal police officers may patrol the downtown area of the municipality. The military police limit their attention to military personnel, while the municipal police retain their responsibility for dealing with civilians.

For traffic accident investigation, the division of responsibility between agencies is often determined by the seriousness of the accident; i. e. , fatalities may be investigated by an agency other than the one that investigates nonfatal personal injury accidents. Also, property loss limits may determine which agency will investigate a particular accident.

Figure 1. 1 illustrates the extent of traffic patrol alternation in the 80 SMSAs. The SMSAs are ordered from left to right according to the percentage of their service areas with alternate traffic patrol producers. Above the line are bars indicating the percentage of service areas with alternate traffic patrol producers. Half of the metropolitan areas have alternation in more than 47 percent of their service areas. Half have 47 percent or less. (That is, the median SMSA has alternate producers in 47 percent of its service areas.) One-fourth of the SMSAs have alternation in 33 percent or fewer of their service areas. Another fourth

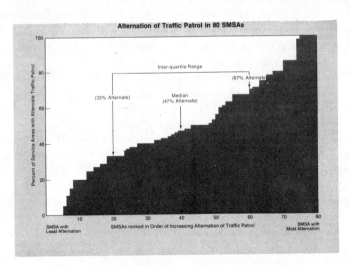

Fig. 1.1.   Alternation of Traffic Patrol in 80 SMSAs

Source: Elinor Ostrom, Roger B. Parks, and Gordon P. Whitaker:
          Policing Metropolitan America (Washington, D.C.: U.S.
          Government Printing Office, 1977), p. 16.

have alternation of traffic patrol in more than 67 percent of their service areas. (That is, the inter-quartile range is between 33 and 67 percent.) Service areas with alternate producers of traffic patrol tend to
be larger than those without alternate producers. In half of the SMSAs,
over three-quarters of the population is served by alternate traffic
patrol producers.

As shown in Table 1.6, there is more alternation of patrol, traffic patrol, and accident investigation than of burglary or homicide investigation. Legal powers and duties assigned to different types of
agencies by State law influence alternation of service delivery. In our
sample of New England SMSAs, for example, all service areas receive
accident investigation services from alternating producers because of
State policy. In Massachusetts, the Registry of Motor Vehicles investigates all fatal accidents, and in Connecticut, the Connecticut State
Police investigate all accidents on the freeways which are located in
each of the four Connecticut SMSAs. Local police agencies investigate
other traffic accidents in the SMSAs of these states.

There is usually more alternation of patrol and accident investigation of SMSAs with larger populations. These SMSAs are more likely to have airports, municipal parks, and other enclaves with specialized police forces. Larger SMSAs are also more likely to have major
freeways crossing several municipalities, each with its own local police. This creates more service areas to receive alternate service
from State police or highway patrols.

Coordination of Direct Services

Coordination occurs when two or more producers plan and execute
service activities together in a single service area. Two agencies investigating homicides or residential burglaries in the same service
area usually coordinate their work. Regular coordination of criminal
investigation typically involves performance of two related sets of
activities: one based on local contacts, the other on special investigative skills. Services such as screening crime reports, conducting
initial inquiries, and providing contacts and background information
regarding the service area are typically carried out by a service area's
own police department. Departments performing only these aspects
of criminal investigation usually participate in investigations only in
their own jurisdiction. They work with investigative specialists, who
gather and assemble physical evidence and testimony. These specialists typically work with departments in numerous service areas.

Coordination in burglary investigation occurs primarily in small
towns and in special police districts, e.g., college and university

Table 1.6. Alternation, Coordination, and Duplication of Direct
Police Service Delivery in 80 SMSAs

| Police Service | Percent of Service Areas in Each SMSA Receiving Service From: | | | | | |
| | Alternate Producers | | Coordinated Producers | | Duplicate Producers | |
	Median	Inter-Quartile Range	Median	Inter-Quartile Range	Median	Inter-Quartile Range
Patrol	21	4 - 38	0	0 - 0	0	0 - 14
Traffic Patrol	47	33 - 67	0	0 - 0	0	0 - 13
Traffic Accident Investigation	35	13 - 64	0	0 - 7	0	0 - 7
Residential Burglary Investigation	7	0 - 25	6	0 - 27	0	0 - 0
Homicide Investigation	0	0 - 15	33	13 - 70	0	0 - 0

Source: Elinor Ostrom, Roger B. Parks, and Gordon P. Whitaker:
Policing Metropolitan America (Washington, D.C.: U.S.
Government Printing Office, 1977), p. 17.

---

campuses. Most of the assistance to local police agencies in these
service areas comes from the detectives employed by county and State
investigative agencies.

Metropolitan areas vary widely in the percentage of their service
areas for which agencies coordinate homicide investigation. This
variation is displayed in Fig. 1.2. In 16 of the 80 SMSAs, no service
area has coordinated homicide investigation. These SMSAs are grouped
at the left side of the figure. All service areas have coordinated homicide investigation in nine metropolitan areas. These are at the right
side of the figure. The median SMSA has coordinated homicide investigation in 33 percent of its service areas. The inter-quartile range
is from 13 percent to 70 percent of the service areas.

As Table 1.6 shows, coordination is a more common arrangement for criminal investigation than for patrol, traffic patrol, or accident investigation. Coordination is most extensive for homicide investigation. In over half of the SMSAs, at least one-third of the service areas have coordinated homicide investigation. The median for coordination of burglary investigation is 6 percent, with an inter-quartile range from zero to 27 percent. In half of the SMSAs, 7 percent or less of the population is served by coordinated homicide investigation, reflecting the smaller populations of most service areas with coordinated investigation services.

State laws and policies are important in determining the extent of coordination of homicide investigation. County prosecutors' detectives investigate all homicides and other major crimes in California and New Jersey SMSAs. State detective bureaus have been established to investigate homicides in Massachusetts and New Mexico. In many other states, State police regularly coordinate with police in some service areas where local investigative resources need to be supplemented.

In addition to producers who regularly coordinate all investigations of burglary or homicide, there is also considerable temporary or special purpose cooperation between departments. Occasional cooperation on investigations is practically universal. Few, if any, police

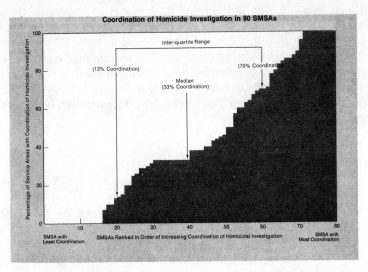

Fig. 1.2. Coordination of Homicide Investigation in 80 SMSAs

Source: Elinor Ostrom, Roger B. Parks, and Gordon P. Whitaker: Policing Metropolitan America, Washington, D.C.: U.S. Government Printing Office, 1977, p. 18.

agencies, whatever their resources, find it possible to gather all the
information and evidence they need in all cases without the assistance
of other agencies. In many metropolitan areas, special inter-agency
task forces have been established to provide continuity to the cooperative efforts of the various criminal investigation agencies working in
the area. Several SMSAs, including Des Moines, Iowa and Madison,
Wisconsin, have developed multi-jurisdictional major case squads.
The squads train together at regular intervals and are available to any
jurisdiction in the area if a major case - usually a homicide - occurs
and the local force needs the help of a specialized team. (8)

Duplication of Direct Services

Duplication occurs only in those service areas where two or more
police agencies supply the same service without alternating or coordinating their activities. As shown in Table 1.6, no duplication exists
in over half of the SMSAs for all direct services. There is no duplication in residential burglary investigation and homicide investigation
in three-quarters of the SMSAs. More duplication exists in the supply
of general area patrol than in the supply of the other direct services.
Figure 1.3 displays the extent of patrol duplication for the 80 SMSAs.
Forty-two of the 80 SMSAs have no duplication of patrol. The inter-
quartile range is zero to 14 percent. Only about 10 percent of the
SMSAs have more than one-third of the service areas receiving duplicate patrol services. In the SMSA with the most duplication of patrol,
79 percent of the service areas (but only 48 percent of the population)
are served by duplicate patrol producers. Duplication of patrol production occurs primarily in service areas with smaller populations,
and this accounts for the smaller proportion of population being served
by duplicate producers.

Duplication, Coordination, and
Alternation of Auxiliary Services

Duplication and coordination of auxiliary services are rare. Only
a few SMSAs have police agencies receiving an auxiliary service from
two coordinating producers. In more than half of the SMSAs, no duplication exists for any of the auxiliary services (Table 1.7). Where
duplication exists, it may be an advantage for training and chemical
analysis. Police agencies using two or more academies or labs have
the choice of where to send recruits or evidence. These are services
for which a choice of suppliers may be particularly useful to the agency
needing the service.

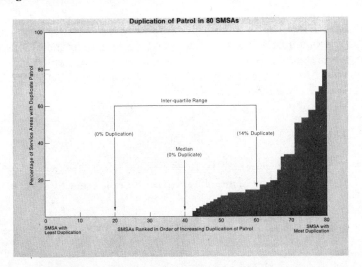

Fig. 1.3. Duplication of Patrol in 80 SMSAs

Source: Elinor Ostrom, Roger B. Parks, and Gordon P. Whitaker: Policing Metropolitan America, Washington, D.C.: U.S. Government Printing Office, 1977, p. 18.

There is some alternation in radio communications. Some smaller municipal agencies are dispatched by a civilian employed by the agency during the day-time hours. (This person may also keep police records and do other secretarial work.) In the evening hours, these agencies are dispatched by a county sheriff or a neighboring city police department. Some alternation occurs in the delivery of pre-trial detention where two agencies specialize: one holds male prisoners, while the other holds female prisoners. However, this type of alternation is not extensive. Alternation in entry-level training and crime laboratory analysis is very infrequent.

Duplication and Diversity

Although there is almost no duplication in service delivery, there is certainly much diversity in service arrangements. Diversity, by itself, is likely to be neither everywhere useful nor everywhere harmful. It may or may not lead to confusion of responsibility. Most police chiefs with whom we spoke expressed little concern about the existence of a number of patrol, traffic control, and criminal investigation producers in their metropolitan areas, nor were they concerned about those other agencies serving in their own service areas. At the

Crime and Justice in America

same time, some chiefs were concerned about ambiguities in the division of responsibilities between their own departments and others operating in the same areas. Clearly, some localities have not developed working relationships that are understood and accepted by all the agencies affected. However, such localities are rare.

Fresh Pursuit

The division of metropolitan areas into several separate police urisdictions is seen by some observers as a deterrent to effective

Table 1.7. Alternation, Coordination, and Duplication of
            Auxiliary Police Service Delivery in 80 SMSAs

| Police Service | Percent of Service Areas in Each SMSA Receiving Service From: | | | | | |
| | Alternate Producers | | Coordinated Producers | | Duplicate Producers | |
	Median	Inter-Quartile Range	Median	Inter-Quartile Range	Median	Inter-Quartile Range
Radio Communications	5	0 - 17	0	0 - 0	0	0 - 0
Detention	0	0 - 12	0	0 - 0	0	0 - 0
Entry-Level Training	0	0 - 0	0	0 - 0	0	0 - 11
Chemical Laboratory Analysis	0	0 - 0	0	0 - 0	0	0 - 7

Source: Elinor Ostrom, Roger B. Parks, and Gordon P. Whitaker:
         Policing Metropolitan America (Washington, D.C.: U.S.
         Government Printing Office, 1977), p. 20.

law enforcement. They assume that police officers have no authority
to pursue a fleeing suspect beyond jurisdictional boundaries. Because
police officers' authority is largely determined by State legislation,
we examined State laws regarding fresh pursuit both within and between
states. We found the police officers in most states have explicit authority to pursue suspects beyond the limits of their own jurisdictions. (9)
However, that authority is subject to a variety of restrictions.

Intrastate Fresh Pursuit

Thirty-nine States have intrastate fresh pursuit legislation - statutes authorizing county or municipal peace officers to pursue suspected

Table 1. 7. Alternation, Coordination, and Duplication of Auxiliary Police
Service Delivery in 80 SMSAs

| Police Service | Percent of Service Areas in Each SMSA Receiving Service From: | | | | | |
| | Alternate Producers | | Coordinated Producers | | Duplicate Producers | |
	Median	Inter-Quartile Range	Median	Inter-Quartile Range	Median	Inter-Quartile Range
Radio Communications	5	0 - 17	0	0 - 0	0	0 - 0
Detention	0	0 - 12	0	0 - 0	0	0 - 0
Entry-Level Training	0	0 - 0	0	0 - 0	0	0 - 11
Chemical Laboratory Analysis	0	0 - 0	0	0 - 0	0	0 - 7

Source: Elinor Ostrom, Roger B. Parks, and Gordon P. Whitaker:
Policing Metropolitan America (Washington, D.C.: U.S.
Government Printing Office, 1977), p. 9.

criminals across municipal and county lines. These states are shown
in Fig. 1.4.

Intrastate fresh pursuit is generally not a problem for officers
employed by State-level law enforcement agencies. Most State law
enforcement agencies have, by definition, statewide jurisdiction.
State police may pursue suspected offenders anywhere within their
state. County and local peace officers have more restricted jurisdictions. Fresh pursuit legislation is not always uniformly applicable to
these peace officers. Pursuit authority may also be limited by the
type of offense.

Of the 39 states having specific legislation on intrastate fresh pursuit, 22 authorize all county and municipal peace officers to engage in
fresh pursuit throughout their state for any offense. An additional
eight states authorize statewide pursuit under at least some circumstances. That 30 states authorize some form of statewide fresh pursuit contradicts any blanket assertion that police officers are unable
to pursue beyond their own jurisdictions. Of the nine additional states
having other forms of legislation regarding intrastate fresh pursuit,
eight authorize county-wide pursuit for any offense.

Eleven states have no legislation pertaining specifically to intrastate fresh pursuit. Lack of specific legislation does not, however,
preclude intrastate fresh pursuit activity in these states. In states
having no applicable statutues or case law, officers have the same
right to arrest another person as do private persons under the common
law. (Under common law, a citizen may make an arrest only for an
offense committed in his/her presence.) So, even in states with no
legislation or case law specifically applicable to intrastate fresh pursuit,
law enforcement officers are not helpless if a suspected criminal
crosses jurisdictional lines: the citizen's arrest right extends statewide.

Interstate Fresh Pursuit

When a suspect flees across state lines, what authority does the
pursuing officer have? Here the legislation is more specific: a majority of states have extended broad authority to the police officer as
exemplified by this statute:

> Any member of a duly organized state, county or municipal peace
> unit of another state of the United States who enters this state in
> fresh pursuit, and continues within this state in such fresh pur-
> suit, of a person in order to arrest him on the ground that he is
> believed to have committed a felony in such other state, shall
> have the same authority to arrest and hold such person in custody,

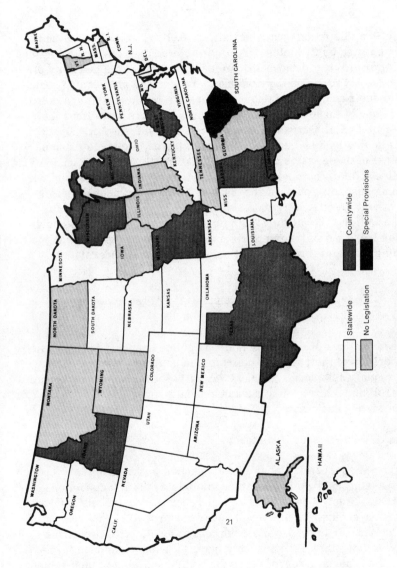

Fig. 1.4. Distribution of Intra-state Fresh Pursuit Legislation

Source: Elinor Ostrom, Roger B. Parks, and Gordon P. Whitaker: Policing Metropolitan America (Washington, D.C.: U.S. Government Printing Office, 1977), p. 21.

31

as has any member of any duly organized state, county, or municipal peace unit of this state, to arrest and hold in custody a person on the ground that he is believed to have committed a felony in
this state.

[Kansas S. A. §62-632 (1937)]

A statute like this is designated a Uniform Act on Fresh Pursuit and
has been enacted by 31 states. Ten more states have enacted variations
of the Uniform Act. Of these 10, two have broadened the authority of
the Uniform Act to include any offense. The other eight require reciprocity for their own act to authorize interstate fresh pursuit. A police
officer in any of these eight states can pursue across state lines into
any other state that has passed a variant of the Uniform Act. By 1974,
only nine states had not enacted any legislation on interstate fresh pursuit. Most of these states are located in the South, as shown on Fig. 1.5.

Police officers in most states have relatively broad powers to pursue fleeing suspects, particularly when a felony is suspected. Some
states without specific intrastate authority have used their authority
under the Uniform Act authorizing interstate fresh pursuit as authori-
zation for fresh pursuit within their own state. So the actual practice
concerning intrastate fresh pursuit may be somewhat understated.

Emergency Assistance, Mutual Aid Agreements,
and Deputization

Presumed lack of cooperation among police agencies is a favorite
topic of critics of metropolitan policing. In contrast, we find a great
deal of mutual assistance. We deal only with local producers of general
area patrol since they are the agencies usually viewed as most likely to
need emergency assistance. (10)

Patterns of Inter-Agency Assistance

Eighty-six percent of local patrol agencies in the 80 SMSAs report
that they assist other police departments outside their jurisdictions
(Table 1.8). Ninety-one percent report that they receive assistance
from other agencies. Is this assistance "reciprocal"? In almost all
cases, the answer is yes. Only 3 percent of local patrol producers
report assisting other agencies while not receiving assistance themselves. Eight percent report receiving assistance without themselves
providing assistance. Together, both types of nonreciprocal assistance
apply to only 11 percent of the patrol agencies. Ninety-three percent
of all local patrol agencies in the 80 SMSAs report providing or receiving assistance.

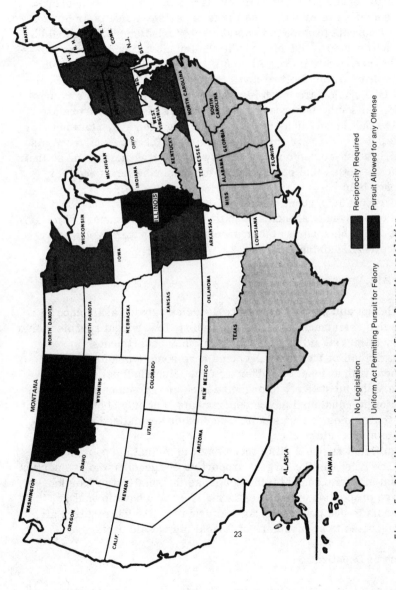

Fig. 1.5. Distribution of Inter-state Fresh Pursuit Legislation

Reciprocity Required

Pursuit Allowed for any Offense

No Legislation

Uniform Act Permitting Pursuit for Felony

Source: Elinor Ostrom, Roger B. Parks, and Gordon P. Whitaker: Policing Metropolitan America (Washington, D.C.: U.S. Government Printing Office, 1977), p. 23.

23

Municipal police departments provide assistance outside their jurisdictions more often than other types of local patrol agencies. More than 90 percent of municipal patrol agencies indicated that their officers go beyond jurisdictional boundaries to assist other agencies. County sheriffs are slightly less likely to assist outside their jurisdictions: 77 percent provide aid outside their jurisdictions. It should be noted, however, that out-of-jurisdiction for most county producers means beyond county lines. Almost all county sheriffs do assist the municipalities within their county. Special patrol producers and campus police agencies are much less likely to assist outside their jurisdictions. In some instances, the legal powers of these officers are limited to the jurisdictions of their employing agency by State law; for example, to a college or university campus. These agencies are also less likely to share radio frequencies with other agencies, and so their officers are not as likely to be aware of another agency's need for emergency help.

More than 90 percent of municipal police agencies, and about 80 percent of the county agencies, report receiving assistance. Similar proportions of campus and other special district patrol producers report receiving assistance.

Mutual Aid Agreements

Although almost all local police agencies provide assistance to and receive assistance from other agencies, fewer local agencies enter into formal mutual aid agreements with other departments.

Nearly half of the patrol agencies have some type of mutual aid agreement with at least one other agency. Municipal police departments are the most likely to organize such aid agreements. Fifty-one percent of the municipal police departments, but only about 30 percent of county agencies, campus police, and other specialized producers belong to mutual aid pacts.

Significant regional differences exist in mutual aid pact membership. The West has the largest proportion of agencies who are parties to formal aid arrangements; the South has the smallest proportion. The large proportion of agencies in the West who have formal aid agreements is due principally to California law, which requires all police agencies to be members of formal mutual aid pacts.

Patterns of Deputization

Deputization means that police officers from one jurisdiction are given police powers in a jurisdiction or jurisdictions other than their own. Almost two out of five local patrol agencies use some type of

Table 1.8. Percent of Local Patrol Producers Who
          Assistance And Who Are Members of Form
          Agreements

Percent of Local Patrol Producers Who:	Nation-wide	Type of Producer			
		Municipal Police Departments	County Police	Campus Police	Other Police
Assist Others Outside Jurisdiction	86	92	77	56	53
Receive Assistance From Others	91	92	79	87	97
Members of Formal Mutual Aid Agreements	47	51	30	32	32

Source: Elinor Ostrom, Roger B. Parks, and Gordon P. Whitaker:
         Policing Metropolitan America (Washington, D.C.: U.S.
         Government Printing Office, 1977), p. 24.

deputization arrangement. The most prevalent arrangement is a non-mutual one where one agency's officers are deputized by a second agency, but the first agency does not deputize the second agency's officers.

The officers of over one-third of the local patrol agencies we studied are deputized by other police agencies. Seventeen percent of the patrol producers deputize officers from other jurisdictions. Examination of deputization patterns for county and municipal police departments provides a clue as to why a larger number of agencies have officers deputized by other agencies than deputize officers from other agencies.

Nearly 50 percent of the county agencies indicate that they deputize officers from other agencies, while only 16 percent of the municipal agencies and almost no campus agencies deputize officers from other agencies. In many instances, county sheriffs deputize officers from the smaller municipal agencies operating within their jurisdictions. Deputization enables county sheriffs, who may have many municipal departments within their overall jurisdictions, to draw upon these departments for back-up assistance within the county as a whole.

Fewer than 20 percent of the county patrol agencies have officers who have been deputized by other departments. Sheriffs' department officers do not need to be deputized by municipalities to have powers of arrest within the municipalities in their own county. This contrasts with municipal, campus, and other local police departments, which have more of their officers deputized by other agencies. Many of these are small departments. Across the country, more than 50 percent of the departments with only part-time officers and more than 30 percent of the departments with one to ten officers have their officers deputized by another agency.

Campus police departments are most likely to have their officers deputized by city, county, or State police. This deputization may give campus police their formal police powers, since in some states college and university security departments are not empowered to authorize their own officers. Campus police are not likely to deputize others - other agencies with legal jurisdiction on a campus do not need their officers deputized.

Participation in Emergency Assistance

Only 50 percent of the patrol producers who both give and receive emergency assistance outside their jurisdiction are members of mutual aid agreements. Clearly, assistance is available in many places without formal agreements. Twenty-six percent of the agencies that report neither giving nor receiving any external assistance belong to mutual aid agreements; so belonging to a mutual aid pact is no guarantee that assistance has been provided. (Of course, there may have been no need for assistance in some of these cases.) Almost 70 percent of the producers who report both giving and receiving emergency assistance are either members of mutual aid pacts or have some forms of deputization agreement. Thus, most of the agencies reporting mutual assistance do have some formal arrangements between them, although the absence of formal arrangements does not preclude assistance.

Larger municipal police departments are less likely to give and receive emergency assistance than small departments (Table 1.9). More than 90 percent of municipal police departments having less than

Table 1.9. Assistance by Size of Producer

Type of Patrol Producer Producer	Number Reporting	Percent of Patrol Producers That:		
		Provide Assistance To Other Police Agencies	Receive Assistance From Other Police Agencies	Belong To A Mutual Aid Agreement
Municipal Police Departments By Number of Full-Time Officers	841	92	92	51
Part-Time Only	62	95	98	53
1 to 4	213	92	95	46
5 to 10	206	95	95	50
11 to 20	119	93	96	58
21 to 50	119	93	94	64
51 to 150	76	87	79	57
Over 150	46	80	61	24
County Police And Sheriffs By Number of Full-Time Officers	91	77	79	27
1 to 4	2	50	50	0
5 to 10	4	75	100	0
11 to 20	16	69	75	31
21 to 50	27	85	85	22
51 to 150	26	69	65	31
Over 150	16	88	94	50
Campus Police By Number of Full-Time Officers	93	56	87	32
Part-Time Only	3	0	100	67
1 to 4	13	31	77	46
5 to 10	36	64	92	28
11 to 20	18	61	78	17
21 to 50	20	65	95	40
51 to 150	3	33	67	33
Other Local Producers By Number of Full-Time Officers	38	53	97	32
Part-Time Only	2	0	100	50
1 to 4	11	73	100	55
5 to 10	10	60	90	0
11 to 20	8	50	100	25
21 to 50	6	33	100	33
51 to 150	1	0	100	100

Source: Elinor Ostrom, Roger B. Parks, and Gordon P. Whitaker: Policing
Metropolitan America (Washington, D.C.: U.S. Government Printing
Office, 1977), p. 26.

50 full-time sworn officers both give and receive emergency assistance.
For municipal departments with more than 150 officers, this proportion
falls to 80 percent giving assistance and 61 percent receiving assistance.
About 50 percent of the municipal departments with 150 or fewer full-
time sworn officers are parties to mutual aid agreements, while only
24 percent of the largest departments participate in such agreements.
The relationship for county departments is the opposite. Larger county
departments are more likely to both give and receive assistance than
are their large municipal counterparts. Smaller county departments
are not as likely to participate in a mutual aid agreement as are smaller
municipal departments. Almost 50 percent of the county agencies with
over 150 full-time sworn officers participate in such agreements. Department size has no relationship to assistance for campus and other
local agencies.

Cooperation, Not Isolation

We find much more cooperation among police agencies producing
patrol services than one would expect after reading many of the de-
scriptions of metropolitan policing which have appeared in national
reports. Nationwide, about 90 percent of all agencies give or receive
emergency assistance outside their own jurisdictions. While the proportion of agencies who belong to formal mutual aid agreements is
lower (nearly 50 percent of all patrol agencies), membership in such
formal agreements is not necessary for emergency assistance to be
given. Agencies operating in metropolitan areas with large numbers
of patrol producers are more likely to engage in both formal and informal assistance.

Not only do the various agencies patrolling parts of metropolitan
areas provide each other with needed emergency assistance in most
cases, but they also have generally organized their work to avoid
duplicating each other's activities. Patrol, traffic patrol, and traffic
accident investigation are conducted in alternate times or places in
most service areas that have more than one producer of the service.
Coordination of criminal investigations is common.

Overlapping jurisdictions usually do not result in duplication of
service delivery, nor do many separate jurisdictions limit fresh pursuit. Most states have legislation explicitly authorizing pursuit beyond local boun   olice agencies throughout the nation's   .

IS THERE A POLICE SYSTEM?

If a system is defined as a single, overarching hierarchical decision-making unit, then certainly the police industry in most U.S. metropolitan areas is not a system. However, the concept of a system is not limited to that of a simple hierarchy. Any collection of entities defined by a boundary and regular, predictable relationships among them is a system. The set of agencies producing specified services for a metropolitan area are a bounded collection and the police agencies included in such a collection do indeed have regular, predictable relationships among themselves in most SMSAs. Such a police industry should be considered a system.

Is this playing with words? Does it matter if a police industry is a system? We think it matters. For too long, proposed changes in the way police are organized in metropolitan areas have been made with a view toward an idealized hierarchical system, and without any careful research on current operational practices. There is certainly room for improvement in the way police services are delivered in many metropolitan areas. However, before changing from a system of separately organized service agencies to a system organized as a single unit, there should be a careful examination of the existing network of working relationships in such metropolitan areas. A large number of small police forces does not automatically mean chaos and lack of system. Nor does a single agency mean that chaos is avoided. The critical question for the organization theorist and for the reformer should be how well the system produces the intended services, and not how well it matches a standard model. We need to explore alternative models for service delivery systems. The police services industry provides us with an abundance of models for closer examination.

NOTES AND REFERENCES

1. Bruce Smith, (1949) Police Systems in the United States (New York: Harper & Brothers, 1949), p. 22.

2. President's Commission on Law Enforcement and Administration of Justice, (1967) The Challenge of Crime in a Free Society, (Washington, D. C.: U. S. Government Printing Office, 1967), p. 119.

3. The importance of separating production from consumption relationships was stressed by Vincent Ostrom, Charles M. Tiebout, and Robert Warren in "The Organization of Government in Metropolitan Areas: A Theoretical Inquiry," American Political Science Review 55 (December 1961): 831-42. A further elucidation of the theoretical approach was Vincent Ostrom and Elinor Ostrom, "A Behavioral Approach to the Study of Intergovernmental Relations," The Annals of the American Academy of Political and Social Science 359 (May 1965): 137-46. The approach taken here is described in more detail in Elinor Ostrom, Roger B. Parks, and Gordon P. Whitaker, "Defining and Measuring Structural Variations in Interorganizational Arrangements," Publius 4:4 (Fall 1974): 87-108; Elinor Ostrom, Roger B. Parks, and Gordon P. Whitaker, Patterns of Metropolitan Policing (Cambridge: Ballinger Publishing Company, 1977); and John P. McIver "The Effects of State Laws on Municipal Police Departments: Mutual Assistance in Metropolitan Areas," Workshop in Political Theory and Policy Analysis (Bloomington, Indiana, 1977), Technical Report T-20.

4. Patrol is defined as organized surveillance of public places within a specified territory and response to reports of suspected criminal activities for the purpose of preventing crime, apprehending offenders, or maintaining public order. Officers assigned to patrol also typically respond to emergencies and other types of noncriminal calls.

Criminal investigation is activity undertaken to identify the persons suspected of alleged criminal acts, to gather evidence for criminal proceedings, or to recover stolen goods. Because the agencies and the methods of investigation differ with different crimes, depending on their degree of seriousness, we specifically focused our attention on investigation of residential burglary and investigation of homicide. Residential burglary is an often encountered felony. In contrast, homicide occurs less frequently, but is generally regarded as a more serious offense.

Traffic control includes the monitoring of vehicular traffic and the investigation of traffic accidents. Because traffic patrol assignments may differ from traffic accident investigation assignments, we examined the delivery of each.

5. Radio communications is the relaying of requests for police assistance to officers in the field and the receipt of radioed requests for information or assistance from officers in the field.

Adult pre-trail detention is the holding of an adult after arraignment but prior to final court disposition of a case. Only agencies empowered to hold individuals in their facilities for more than 24 hours are included. We did not consider agencies that had temporary "lockups" as producers of adult pre-trial detention services.

Entry-level training is the department-required training of recruits for a direct service police agency. We do not disregard State requirements for entry-level training. For many departments, the State minimum is the departmental requirement. For some, the departmental requirement greatly exceeds the State minimum.

Crime laboratory analysis is the processing of evidence by persons whose testimony is accepted for presentation in court. Many kinds of laboratory analyses are required in criminal and accident investigation. We have limited our attention to the identification of narcotics and the chemical analysis of such substances as blood and hair.

6. For examples of these matrices see Elinor Ostrom, Roger B. Parks, and Gordon P. Whitaker, Patterns of Metropolitan Policing (Cambridge: Ballinger Publishing Company, 1977); John McIver, "The Effects of State Laws on Municipal Police Departments: Mutual Assistance in Metropolitan Areas," Workshop in Political Theory and Policy Analysis, (Bloomington, Indiana, 1977), Technical Report T-20; and Elinor Ostrom, Roger B. Parks, and Gordon P. Whitaker, "Defining and Measuring Structural Variations in Interorganizational Arrangements," Publius 4:4 (Fall 1974): 87-108.

7. Ibid.

8. Several of these Major Case Squads have been described in Fact Sheets available from the Workshop in Political Theory and Policy Analysis. These include: Elinor Ostrom, "The Topeka Major Case Squad"; Nancy M. Neubert, "The Major Investigative Team of Polk County"; Steve Mastrofski, "The Tuscaloosa County Homicide Unit"; Nancy M. Neubert, "A Comparison of Major Case Squads in Four Metropolitan Areas"; Staff Research Unit, Kansas City/Missouri Police Department, "Kansas City Area Metro Squad"; Eric Scott, "The

Intra-County Major Case Investigation Unit of Dane County"; and John P. McIver, "The Worcester County Fraudulent Check Association: Community Cooperation in Law Enforcement. "

9. Specific citations to legislation and further detail about intrastate and interstate fresh pursuit is available in Larry Wagner, "Patterns of State Laws Relating to 'Fresh Pursuit,'" Workshop in Political Theory and Policy Analysis (Bloomington, Indiana), Technical Report T-1.

2 The Future Shire Reeve—Tribune of the People

Johannes F. Spreen

STRUCTURE AND SYSTEM OF LAW ENFORCEMENT

This book will encompass a variety of very meaningful and thought-provoking subjects which permeate the criminal justice system. These individual subjects will be addressed by various respected and knowledgeable practitioners.

While the particular subject area of this chapter pertains specifically to the "Future Role of the Sheriff," I was struck by how many of the subject areas and issues that will be addressed in this book are involved with, and could be solved by and through, a future role of the modern sheriff as a professional executive in a new coordinated criminal justice system. That is the theme of this chapter.

The issues addressed in this book could be loosely classified into two main areas: those that are structure and system-oriented and those that are personnel and/or problem-oriented.

Policing, regionalization/consolidation, future role of state police, future role of Federal law enforcement, comparative systems, planning for criminal justice, the field of corrections, the criminal courts, the environment in criminal justice, the future role of city or local police, and the future role of the sheriff or county law enforcement are those areas which could be classified as structural and system considerations.

Community relations, the future role of police professionalism, lateral entry, future of criminal intelligence and information, organized crime, homicide investigation, terrorism, crisis intervention/negotiations, youth related problems, changing crime patterns, and leadership problems probably could be loosely grouped into the area

of personnel and/or problems (in many cases caused or aggravated by
the existing system and structure).

These issues and their classification are crucial to any meaningful study or analysis of our present system, its costs and results, and
a necessary beginning in order to make any suggestions for improvement
and change in the future.

Like the chicken or the egg, it is a problem of which comes first -
dealing with the personnel and problem areas, as we have done, or
changing the system, as we have not done.

I believe we must address ourselves to the system and structure
of law enforcement first. If we could do this, then many personnel
and other problems could be solved or alleviated as a natural consequence.

At present law enforcement does not work, at least not very well.
The police system is archaic, fragmented, overlapping, confused and
subject to bickering and jealousy over jurisdictional power.

At present the court system is costly, time-consuming, ineffective,
political in the bad sense and a hollow mockery of what it should be in
a just society.

At present the corrections system is a shambles, a stepchild, a
growth area for the cancer of crime.

Above all, the personnel in the above parts of the so-called criminal justice system are not all professionally selected or trained,
nor are all professionally dedicated. Personnel is by far the most
costly item in the law enforcement system and is growing ever more
costly.

Unless some vital changes are made in the structure of the system
and the personnel in the system, particularly at the top, nothing will
avail and we will muddle into the fearsome year 1984 - ill equipped to
deal with its unique problems - problems we cannot even begin to
anticipate now.

COST OF CONTROLLING CRIME

Today, after years of American law enforcement, we do not seem
to be doing too well at the job. Crime is the raison d'être of those in
the criminal justice system. Control of crime is costly - not controlling it is even more costly.

The economy seems to be the number one problem in this nation;
crime is number two. (Or is it the other way around?) Can the
economy flourish in a community plagued by crime? Can a healthy
economy be possible when the image of a community is one of fear?

Crime not being controlled means something to all of us - higher food bills, higher tax bills, higher business costs, etc. Crime has not been controlled and many large cities have seen an exodus of taxpayers. Smaller suburban and rural communities are coming face to face with problems of crime control and its cost.

There is no measuring of the psychic costs of crime to victims, the families of victims and even the families of criminals themselves, and to our communities and our society in general. The great dollar impact of crime (as well as the psychic impact) creates a serious economic drain on all of us.

Crime control is now facing up to budgetary constraints due to the great national movement for tax limitation that started with the passage of Proposition 13 in California. Like "guns or butter," the question is: Can we have both? Better law enforcement? Yes, but probably only if it comes at less cost. Therefore, crime control must become cost effective in many ways.

Professionalism in law enforcement offers new promise in solving many of our people problems, but it also can be costly under our present law enforcement non-system. The most promising and effective way to both more effective control of crime and improved professional personnel is to change the system and structure that is now cost inefficient and ineffective.

This weird amalgam of various local, county, state and national agencies in American law enforcement must give way to a more productive and cost effective system, one more easily and properly directed, yet still responsive to the people. This better way can focus and guide political, police, and citizen impact on crime more effectively.

It is my firm opinion, after 37 years of study and practice of law enforcement, that the catalyst and coordinator for this better, less costly, more effective crime control can and should be the county sheriff. Yes, the future of law enforcement should be directed by a modern shire-reeve, a tribune of the people - a sheriff who will be the champion of the people's rights in a more effective county-wide cooperative law enforcement, with proper liaison between local agencies of his county and state and national law enforcement agencies.

THE SHERIFF

Let's take a quick look at the ancient office of sheriff. Some interesting background on the sheriff can be found in the National Sheriff's Association publication by Truman Walrod entitled "The Role of Sheriff – Past-Present-Future".

Historian W. A. Morris, in his book on the Medieval English
Sheriff in 1300, made these observations:

The office of sheriff is one of the most familiar and most useful
to be found in the history of English institutions. With the single
exception of kingship, no secular dignity now known to English-
speaking people is older. The functions, status and powers of
the office, like those of kingship itself, have undergone change,
but for over nine centuries it has maintained a continuous existence
and preserved its distinguishing features.

Walter H. Anderson, in his "Sheriffs, Coroners and Constables,"
states:

The office of sheriff is one of antiquity. It is the oldest law enforcement office known within the common-law system and it has
always been accorded great dignity and high trust.

Thomas Jefferson pointed to the office of sheriff as being the most
important of all the executive offices of the county.
    The office of sheriff dates far back in time. His role as a peace
officer goes back at least to the time of Alfred the Great. The reeve
of the English shire was the forefather of our sheriff of today. The
shire-reeve (sheriff) has a fascinating history of over a thousand
years, but more importantly, he is still around.
    While in England, the land of his start and development, he has
been reduced in the main to a ceremonial figure, his progeny in America still rides - by car, plane, boat and still at times by horse. In the
northeastern part of the United States, due to the growth of cities and
municipal policing, he is generally and mistakenly left only the task
of jailer and server of process. In the southeastern part of our land,
the sheriff (whether or not a modern, professional lawman) is still a
rather important figure. In the western United States, the sheriff is
still a most important figure. In the Midwest, the sheriff is in somewhat a stage of transition. He is on the edge of a teeter board. His
survival or demise rests on his actions and on either the support or
non-support of the citizens he represents and serves.
    The American sheriff will either lead us into the promised land
of a future free from the blight of crime because of a new modern role
of a progressive, urban sheriff, or he will allow his opportunity to
become the key and the hope of a better law enforcement to slip by.
So we may possibly head, beyond 1984, toward state police forces with
too much power - or toward a national or military policing - or worse,
toward a "police state."

Will the sheriff exist beyond 1984? I believe the possibility is
very strong, and I believe he should. The sheriff has lasted over a
thousand years; there must be something there, something we may
have overlooked in our pell-mell push to police professionalism - a
push which has been generally centered in our large American cities.
    The sheriff's job has many functions and many responsibilities.
Unfortunately he has been shelved aside with the growth of our cities
and the rise of municipal police, so few people have adequate knowledge
or appreciation of this important office. The sheriff has a most important power - the power of posse comitatus (the power to call together
the people and resources of the community). This gives him an important role in emergency preparedness and could embrace coordination
among local police agencies.
    As regards corrections, a function growing in importance, the
sheriff has exclusive jurisdiction over the county jail and prisoners in
transit or in court. Jail administrative duties are becoming increasingly more specialized and technical. Professional correctional administrators who serve under the sheriff are becoming more common.
    Today, with our decline of cities and subsequent growth of subur-
ban and rural areas with attendant crime problems, has the time come
for the rise of the sheriff? (The sheriff is the only office holder holding the key to effectively making the criminal justice system work, inasmuch as he touches all the bases; i.e., law enforcement, court service and corrections, plus having the power of posse comitatus!)
    In America, with problems increasing in our cities, we should not
discard this important office. Rather, we should show England that
the sheriff is still a most viable figure and will be more so in the
future. The new, modern sheriff in the United States must be a person
of considerable experience, education and training. He must be an
executive type, as he is a manager of critical importance to his community.
    The emphasis for the election (or selection) of a sheriff must be
on maturity and experience, rather than just potential. Job experience
and law enforcement credentials are substantially more important
criteria than raw ambition, because a manager's or executive's function is problem solving. Making proper decisions requires "mental
capital", which takes years to acquire.
    In the sheriff we have the one individual who could make the un-
workable system work effectively and at less cost to the taxpayers.
A modern sheriff is a people's representative - the only elected peace
officer in criminal justice, the only person the people of a community
can have direct input to, and the only person with direct impact on
their concerns. Yes, the future, modern sheriff can be the key and the
hope for better law enforcement in the United States to solve the prob-

lems of the system, of the personnel in it, and thus to solve the problems of crime control.

The sheriff of tomorrow must stand before and for the people of his community as a seasoned, responsible representative with service and experience in law enforcement and criminal justice, not a newcomer to the scene or a person selected primarily for political reasons as has been the case so often in the past. He should also hold a nonpartisan office, so as to have a better chance to deal with the problems of law enforcement and criminal justice by removing the factionalism and possible favoritism that could hinder professional efforts.

PROBLEMS OF PRESENT-DAY LAW ENFORCEMENT

What are the problems of present-day law enforcement? Why does law enforcement in these United States not work?

The System

We seem to have somewhere between 40,000 police agencies (President's Commission Report, 1967) and 25,000 police agencies (National Advisory Commission on Standards and Goals, 1973). This is much too many if there is no cohesive cooperation among these thousands of agencies.

We have quite a few Federal law enforcement agencies. We have state police or state highway patrols. We have many large urban police departments with tremendous police forces. We have county police and we have the sheriff and his deputies. We have local police in cities, towns, villages and townships, ranging from cities with fairly large police forces to rural townships with single constables on full or part-time duty. Administratively, this kind of setup is pure chaos.

It is no wonder that policing has been under considerable criticism in America for a good many years, for shortcomings that any professional police officer would acknowledge; and for inability to cope with changing patterns of crime, tensions, public morals and public attitudes toward the law.

The Big Cities

There is a myriad of reasons why law enforcement and crime control is ineffective in most of the big cities of America. Part of

the problem is that some cities are just too big. Bigness does not
necessarily mean betterness. Managing a big system demands a top-
notch law enforcement administrator - one who blends that happy combination of education, training, previous experience and managerial
expertise to put such system into proper effect.

Yet even when a large municipality discovers a person with such
qualities we find that there is a factor in such cities that negates all
the above. That factor is the moving finger of time - the events that
generally can be calculated to occur to reduce the time available for
any continuity of planning, and for programs of effective law enforcement and crime control.

Tenure in office is the key problem in many of our major cities.
(In some cases, too long a tenure can also bring problems; e. g. , J.
Edgar Hoover, who probably would have continued to receive public
adulation rather than the shafts of criticism now directed at his memory
if he had retired ten years earlier.)

In the City of New York, since its consolidation in 1898, the average tenure of its police commissioners has been slightly over two years.
For such a large city, this is much too short, and causes the inability
of its top management to provide a sustained and lasting direction for
proper programs and progress. In the City of Detroit, since 1968,
there have been six police chief executives, averaging a little over
eighteen months in office. No city can really survive such a turnover
of the office of its top police executive.

There are many problems that are engendered by such a "suitcase
brigade" in our big cities. Causes, of course, are many times engendered by "politics. " Effects turn out certainly not in the best interest
of the citizens of such communities.

Smaller Cities

Are there better answers to be found in our smaller cities, where
the police chief executive's time in office (tenure) may be somewhat
longer? (Sometimes too long in certain jurisdictions, where civil
service law freezes the chief in office whether once effective or not.)

Perhaps, but here a police chief executive can be a most frustrated
individual. He must work within a system that cannot and never will
work effectively with police of many other jurisdictions. Whether
capable or not, in most cases he cannot possibly have the territorial
impact to be an effective controller of crime.

Part of our problem is the existence and the proliferation of so
many small police departments throughout our land, operating independently, sometimes almost in a vacuum. This immense fragmentation

of law enforcement and law enforcement effort is a delight to the criminal mind and a frustration to the sincere police officer and executive.

What effective law enforcement we have is due in good measure to the voluntary cooperation of concerned police executives at various levels of government. This has been in spite of the way the police function is organized in our country, not because of it. This has been in spite of the fragmentation of police into thousands of small agencies, not because of it.

America is fond of its local police departments. We want our police to be close to the people they serve. We want our police to know and to be known by members of their communities. Rapport between the police officer and the citizen at the local level is one of our chief defenses in curbing, and preventing, crime.

This is the great advantage of keeping police patrol services in the localities they serve, under local control. However, there are great disadvantages when the local agencies are too small and too fragmented. There are problems in recruiting ... training ... administrative expertise ... purchasing ... having and maintaining the right facilities and equipment for use when you need them ... sophisticated communication control ... important backup services such as evidence technicians, scientific labs and special investigators and so on.

State Police

Are answers to be found in strong State police forces? I would say, "yes - but!" Much help and support can come from modern, professional State police forces, but it would be wrong if local departments were done away with and we had only state police forces in the 50 states. It would be tantamount to a "big brother" approach and would certainly be too distant and too remote to displace local police authorities. It would not be in the citizens' interest.

National Police

While strong support should be drawn from our various Federal police agencies, one national police department would be completely contrary and abhorrent to the ideals of democracy upon which our country was founded. It would also lead to "big brother" law enforcement.

A SPECIFIC PROBLEM -
INEFFECTIVE AND COSTLY INVESTIGATIONS

Let us explore why our present law enforcement system results in ineffective and costly investigations. The American law enforcement machinery has lumbered on with very little change, in spite of a rising crime rate and a falling clearance rate over the years.

From time to time, when crime escalates, there is some public scrutiny of police agencies. Editorials may be written and answers may be demanded as to why a crime increase occurs. But in the main, we continue on with a system that many now see severe defects in. It is only when some vicious or sustained scenes of crime occur that the eyes and ears of the American public are sharply focused on what law enforcement is doing - and how it is doing it - but only for a time, and then we go back to "business as usual."

Consider the public and media attention recently given to the scene of woundings and killings known as the "Son of Sam" case in New York, or the "Hillside Strangler" cases in Los Angeles. Public attention is riveted until something is done.

These two cases concern two of the nation's largest cities, with sizable police agencies that are arrayed with tremendous resources. Still, these departments found such cases difficult to cope with. In other areas of the United States we find similar cases even more difficult to cope with. Why? Here we must examine the very basis of the system of law enforcement and protection we have created among us for our service and our safety.

In similar sensational cases, we find that this system ensures inefficiencies and ineptitude and many times results in jealousy and bitterness among law enforcement agencies - local, State and Federal. A few years ago, the Manson murders in California showed the problems of a system where the gun involved was actually being held in another police jurisdiction property unit, unbeknownst to the investigating department.

The co-ed murders in Michigan some years ago again bring into focus the problems encountered when agencies, independent and working generally in isolation, are suddenly forced into a teamwork relationship none is prepared for. A striking example of unpreparedness for a large scale, multi-jurisdictional investigation, which epitomizes police fragmentation at its worst, is the child-killer murders of Oakland County, Michigan.

THE CHILD KILLER INVESTIGATION
IN OAKLAND COUNTY, MICHIGAN

Oakland County had the misfortune of losing seven of its young
children to murder within a very short time frame. Four of these
murders are believed to be the work of the same person or persons.
    Oakland County enjoys the status of being one of the wealthiest
counties in the United States. Nestled between the cities of Flint and
Detroit, its terrain consists of small residential communities and
rural farmland. Its population ranges from auto executives to small
businessmen, to the factory worker, to the farmer, to people in various professions. The citizens of this county viewed violent crime as a
distant problem suffered by the more urban communities. The kidnapping of Jimmy Hoffa from a posh restaurant jolted but did not shake
this view.
    Law enforcement in Oakland County, as in other jurisdictions, is
extremely fragmentized. There are 43 police agencies in Oakland
County, ranging from five-man departments to the City of Pontiac,
which employs over 200 police officers. As might be expected, coordination of the police effort is virtually impossible. There is an inter-
section in the county that is policed by four jurisdictions, as well as
served by the State Police and the Sheriff's Department. Yet if an
officer from each jurisdiction were dispatched to that location, they
could not communicate en route - they would have to arrive, exit their
cars and talk face to face, as they are all on different radio frequencies.
This is not coordination, yet each police agency jealously guards its
bailiwick from encroachment by other police agencies as a king would
his kingdom. Efforts to coordinate law enforcement are met with
suspicion and disfavor by many of the local chiefs and their political
superiors.
    The problem of fragmentation became a vivid horror story in the
investigation of the child murders in Oakland County, as circumstances
placed two Sheriff's Departments, the State Police, the F.B.I, eight
local police departments in two counties, three crime labs, two medical examiners and two prosecutor's offices on the same series of crimes.
The circumstances occurred in a relatively small area.
    The first of these cases began on February 15, 1976, when a
twelve-year-old boy was reported to a local department as missing.
Four officers from that department handled the incident as a routine
runaway until the next day. When circumstances made them suspect
foul play, they intensified their investigation. On February 19, 1976,
the boy's body was found.
    On December 22, 1976, a twelve-year-old girl left her home after
an argument with her mother. On December 26 the girl's body was

found along an interstate highway in a neighboring city. In both of these cases, no crime lab was called to process the scene, even though there were two nearby State Police crime laboratories and an excellent crime lab in the Oakland County Sheriff's Department.

In January of 1977, a ten-year-old girl disappeared, and ultimately her body was also found. As the body of the girl was deposited in a very small community with only a five-man department, many problems in protecting the crime scene arose at the outset. Traffic, onlookers, response of many local departments, media, etc., created confusion. The chief of the five-man department, having no personal experience in homicide investigation, turned the investigation over to the State Police, who then requested assistance from area departments. That afternoon, thirty investigators committed themselves to finding the girl's murderer. The Oakland Task Force had been implemented.

The work of the Task Force was hampered from the start by many problems. It was discovered that one jurisdiction where a child's body was found had virtually no report, and in another jurisdiction evidence had been misplaced and mishandled. The task force had to investigate one of the slayings from the very beginning. Another agency was reluctant to submit its report to the Task Force. The dissemination of information to the press was another difficulty.

Initially, a major problem was a lack of coordination between the agencies involved. Information was not shared, offers of assistance were refused, and each investigator jealously guarded the identity of his suspects in order to be the one to crack the case. Though some of these problems were solved and others were minimized by the creation of the Task Force, some new problems were created.

In the middle of March 1977, an eleven-year-old boy disappeared. About 200 police officers and detectives from various police departments made a concerted effort to find the boy. Later in the same month his body was found 300 yards inside an adjacent county, further complicating the problems posed by fragmentation and jurisdiction.

Of course, the problem of having a couple of hundred "investigators" from many departments converge on one city to investigate one crime is apparent. Supervision of a group this size is difficult enough without compounding the problem by having individuals work together who never cooperated until the day the investigation began. Although admirable efforts were made at supervision, coordination was near-impossible; it was a case of "too much, too late."

There were occasions when one team of investigators were virtually following the trails of other investigators. During the early stage of the boy's homicide, numerous bits of information were lost forever due to inadequate reporting procedures and unfamiliarity with the cases. In addition, at this early stage, some departments were virtually using

the Task Force as a training experience for their personnel. Chiefs
were committing rookie detectives and patrol officers to investigate
the homicides and were rotating their personnel periodically to allow
everyone to participate in the investigation. Some of the officers never
had a chance to become familiar with all of the cases, yet they were
burdened with the responsibility of catching the killer.

Realizing that small police agencies could not bear the financial
responsibilities of such an immense investigation for long, a request
was made to the state for financial aid. The Task Force was awarded
funds for investigators, plus staff and office help to identify and capture
the killer. The search is still going on!

What is the Answer?

What is the answer? Ideally, one county police agency may be the
answer. One can hardly argue against the economics of the principle.
Under one agency, one can enjoy one set of procedures, one command,
and the expertise that can hardly be gained by very small departments.
Duplication of effort is all but eliminated. Preparation and presentation
of the case in court will also be more simplified and lead to conviction.

While a single county police department may be the answer, in
many areas it is a political impossibility, especially in counties similar to Oakland County. Mayors, city managers, township supervisors
and police chiefs are reluctant to relinquish their power.

As an alternative,   lity that should be considered, one that involv   peration between all
levels of law enforceme   state, with coordination
at the county level with   e responsibility for
combatting crime shoul   e who are responsible
to their citizens, unfort   barriers, while local
police do. The sheriff has county-wide jurisdiction and shares the
same responsibilities to the citizens as local police and should be the
catalyst for such coordination.

The status of the sheriff is changing. He has become a modern,
progressive law enforcement official. It is time for him to take the
lead in innovation and to coordinate law enforcement efforts in his
county. Only he has the authority to do so and keep accountability at
the local level, and he must be allowed to do so by those responsible
for funding his effort.

Let's take a look at the case at hand in Oakland County. If a major
crime unit consisting of sheriff's investigators teamed with the best
investigators from local agencies within the county had been pre-trained
and ready to be summoned to the crime scene, the investigation would

have been under one command. With expertise and talent available
within the county, experienced homicide detectives would not have mishandled evidence. Lab technicians, trained in rules of evidence, would
have properly handled the crime scenes. Reports would have been professionally written. With the responsibility on the shoulders of one
man, that man would properly coordinate investigation efforts and subsequent press releases, so the media would not be privileged to confidential police information that could impede the investigation.

Our future professional advances in law enforcement must depend
on qualified, progressive, responsive leadership at the top in order to
deal with today's sophisticated crime problems. These leaders must
work at defining and refining the roles of state, county and local law
enforcement in order to make our duplicating, fragmenting, overlapping,
costly and ineffective criminal justice system work better, be more
cost effective and most of all, be just.

The police force has never been a profession in America, and as
long as they continue to be grossly fragmented under so many political
jurisdictions they will never become a profession.

THE FRAGMENTATION OF LAW ENFORCEMENT

There has been an increasing recognition by progressive law enforcement administrators and government officials that there exists a
great amount of duplication and fragmentation within the law enforcement community.

Michigan was specifically singled out in the President's Commission on Law Enforcement and Administration of Justice - Task Force
Report: The Police, as a prime example of fragmentation in communities around the Detroit metropolitan area.

Pursuant to the passage of the Omnibus Crime Control and Safe
Streets Act of 1968, various commissions were appointed throughout
the nation to study fragmentation and charged with the responsibility
of coming up with solutions. In the State of Michigan, several different
plans have been developed in recent years. One of the plans called
MAPS (Metropolitan Area Police Services) - CAPS (City Area Police
Services) - RAPS (Rural Area Police Services) would create various
levels of agencies dependent upon population and area, and do away
with many small, local police departments.

However, this particular plan smacked of a "super police" agency
concept. The proposal could very well have taken away home rule and
the option of the citizens to choose the type of police they want to protect them. It could possibly have led to a "big brother" type of agency,

or worse, a "police state." It should be added that this plan was never adopted in the State of Michigan.

In 1973, the National Advisory Commission on Goals and Standards recommended the elimination of very small police departments. While a super agency is not the answer, there is a definite need to eliminate unnecessary fragmentation, eliminate duplication and increase efficiency and cost effectiveness of law enforcement.

In a recent issue of Law Enforcement News, Robert DeGrazia, former Police Commissioner of Boston, now Chief of Police in Montgomery County, Maryland, urged an extensive reform of the International Association of Chiefs of Police. He faulted the International Association of Chiefs of Police (I. A. C. P.) for being, in essence, a social club that perpetuated the status quo in law enforcement; that fragmentation in policing is not being reduced by the International Association of Chiefs of Police, but actually fostered. He charged that large numbers of police departments set the tone for status quo leadership within the I. A. C. P.

DeGrazia further accused the International Association of Chiefs of Police of fearing consolidation and pointed out that Departments with a handful of officers can never provide full police services or become professional.

In conclusion, DeGrazia urged that by 1985, all Departments would have no fewer than 25 members and by the year 200 no department would have fewer than 200 members. This seems a change from his previous remarks at various times that the myriad of American police departments should be consolidated into a maximum of 200 departments in the United States.

In the same Law Enforcement News issue, Ed Davis, former Chief of the Los Angeles Police Department and then President of the International Association of Chiefs of Police, bitterly defended the I. A. C. P. and the concept of personal (local) Police Departments.

He pointed out that bigness was not necessarily betterness, that it will be "the concepts of the sensitive, locally controlled police agencies that will be our salvation." Davis, in a not-too-oblique reference, stated that "an elitist approach to policing is no better than an elitist approach to any other kind of governing."

It seems to me that there is certainly middle ground here - both in the structure and composition of American law enforcement and in the caliber of personnel within it. There are two distinct and separate viewpoints possible regarding consolidation - one view of consolidation of departments, the other consolidation of services.

Consolidation Viewpoints

Consolidation has been the subject of argument for many years. On one hand, police chiefs of small departments (no doubt with some self-interest) argue that small departments provide the personal type of police services necessary and requested in the communities they protect. On the other hand, national advisory commissions and state advisory bodies, along with police administration experts, advocate that more effective, efficient and less costly law enforcement is only feasible if numerous, small, local departments are eliminated.

Over fifty years ago this problem was recognized by Raymond B. Fosdick, who felt consolidation was a necessity. In 1931, the Wickersham Commission in its report concluded that: "The multitude of police forces in any state and the varying standards of organization have contributed immeasurably to the general low grade of police performance in this country." A recent article by Peter W. Colby in State and Local Government Review points out arguments for and against consolidation.

A Chronology of Views for Consolidation

1920 - Raymond B. Fosdick (American Police Systems)

> Police consolidation for metropolitan areas would undoubtedly produce beneficial results in the United States. The increase of crime in urban districts traceable in many cases to the isolation of small police departments in heavily populated sections would seem to make necessary some form of cooperation as yet untried.

1931 - Wickersham Commission Report (quoted previously)

1936 - August Vollmer (The Police in Modern Society)

> There are more than two hundred and fifty separate and distinct police units in the Chicago region. It is no wonder that men like Dillinger and others were able to avoid the police in that section.

1940 - Bruce Smith (Police Systems in the United States)

> If every local government, no matter how weak or how small, is to maintain its own police facilities, the latter become so numerous that their interrelationships are

unduly complex and burdensome. When to sheer complexity
is added the confusion and destructive rivalries arising out
of overlapping enforcement powers, the discouragement
that so often overtakes police administrators is readily
understood.

1967 – President's Commission on Law Enforcement and Administration of Justice (Task Force Report-The Police)

A fundamental problem confronting law enforcement today
is that of fragmented crime repression efforts resulting
from the large number of uncoordinated local government
and law enforcement agencies.

Although law enforcement officials speak of close cooperation among agencies. . . there is, in fact, little cooperation on other than an informal basis.

Crime is not confined within artificially created political
boundaries but, rather, extends throughout the larger
community.

The number of departments administered and staffed by
untrained, part-time personnel is distressing.

The cost of providing basic police services is of paramount
importance in considering total consolidation. . . certain
staff, auxiliary, and field services are beyond the resources
of many departments to provide. This is also true in many
areas with regard to basic patrol services.

1971 – Advisory Commission on Intergovernmental Relations (For
a More Perfect Union-Police Reform)

Many metropolitan areas are faced with an almost hopeless
proliferation of small and inefficient local police departments. A survey of local police forces in 91 metropolitan
areas in 1967 indicated that one-fourth of all such departments employed ten or less men. . . Yet a ten-man force
has difficulty providing full-time patrol and investigative
services, not to mention the essential back-up services of
communications, laboratory and records.

1973 - National Advisory Commission on Criminal Justice Standards
and Goals (Report on Police)

Police agencies that employ fewer than ten sworn employees
should consolidate for improved efficiency and effectiveness.

There has been much pro and con among academicians, police
officials and politicians on whether or not consolidation of the numerous
small, overlapping, duplicating governments would improve police and
public service in urban-suburban areas.

The aforementioned views generally point out that small departments are costly, ineffective and cannot provide the professional,
specialized law enforcement services necessary. Consolidation should
remove jurisdictional barriers and conflict and prevent duplication of
services.

Peter Colby presents six main arguments for these views as
follows:

1. Many small municipalities cannot afford to support their own
   police force at an adequate level of funding.

2. Small police departments cannot recruit, train, and retain
   highly qualified personnel.

3. Small police departments are not sufficiently professional and
   modernized to serve the needs of their communities.

4. Supervision and administration are inadequate in small police
   departments.

5. The existence of many small forces in one metropolitan area
   leads to confusion and rivalry.

6. Formal and informal coordination among police departments
   in metropolitan areas is lacking or insufficient.

These arguments were highlighted by the Illinois Law Enforcement
Commission in a report in 1975 (Focus-75 - The Criminal Justice Plan
for Illinois)

The law enforcement agencies in Chicago and Cook County are
often ineffective because their scarce resources are spread over
too many diverse activities with no overall coordination.

However, Peter Colby, after extensive interviews with police
chiefs of 27 small departments in Cook County, takes an opposite view -
in essence, that small departments should not necessarily be done
away with, that they are able to provide the type and quality of personal services desired and needed in their communities.

Th♦ efs acknowledged that they only provide a partial rather
than ange of police services, but claimed that their partial
re at better and higher levels of personal performance and
d that specialized support services were provided by state
olice agencies.
oncludes his presentation as follows:

ll departments are accepted as an important component of
eⅡecⅡve law enforcement in metropolitan areas, the ideal organization of police services may require a mix of large and small
agencies rather than consolidation of all law enforcement and
police functions into one enormous department.

This word "consolidation" is almost a trigger word among many
police chiefs of small agencies. These chiefs, whether viewing their
jobs sincerely or as guarded sinecures, are jealous of their territories
and guard them almost as medieval lords of the past over their fiefdoms.
While there is great divergence between the views of DeGrazia,
Davis and Colby, it is my earnest conviction that the middle ground
must be spaded and fertilized to produce anything fruitful in American
law enforcement.
The author has a strong belief that small police departments in
America should not be done away with if they operate professionally:
DeGrazia's views are too drastic - 25,000 or so departments should
not be reduced to several hundred. Yet the status quo view of former
IACP head, Ed Davis, is also not realistic, but rather is self-serving.
There are different facets to the consolidation problem as viewed
by many police executives and media executives, but there is more
heat than light regarding the above. Interpretation differs. In Oakland County, Michigan, despite all disclaimers for six years that the
author did not want one county police agency, it was finally necessary
that he issue the following attestation and sign it before the media at a
press conference:

I.   I do not believe in a county police force.

II.   I have never advocated a county police department in
         Oakland County.

III.   I <u>would never</u> serve as the head of one Oakland County
       police department.

IV.   I <u>do believe</u> in local government and local rule.

V.   I <u>do believe</u> in the consolidation of police services more
       than consolidation of police departments.

VI.   As Sheriff, representing all of the people in Oakland County,
       I <u>do believe</u> I should be a law enforcement service agent
       supporting and assisting local police departments, so they
       in turn can service their citizens more economically and
       effectively.

This was absolutely necessary because even the media could not
always distinguish between consolidation of services and of departments -
and there is a whale of a difference.

It is the author's strong opinion that small police departments
should stay, but that in effect they are not full service departments.
Specialized and supportive services should be provided to them from
the county and the state. While England has reduced and consolidated
its many departments to 43 (the same number of departments within
Oakland County, Michigan), consolidation is not necessarily the best
answer here in America.

The sheriff (discarded in England) could and should be the provider
of specialized services, enabling local departments to remain under
local control and local chiefs. The sheriff also represents local control as the only law enforcement official the people of the locality
(county) can have input to and impact on due to the elective process.

As in the famous American baseball double play combination,
"Tinkers to Evers to Chance," that generally put the side out, it is the
author's view that the American Sheriff should become the pivot man in
a new criminal justice double play combination. The local department,
when specialized support is required, should contact the sheriff, who
would then provide it. If greater support and more sophistication is
still needed, the sheriff may request additional assistance from state
forces. If this were done properly and cooperatively, many criminals
would be put out - of business.

What is happening, however, is a constant struggle and jockeying
for position among our many law enforcement agencies in America.
The teamwork so necessary to really combat against crime is mostly
nonexistent.

If we could foster such professional coordination and teamwork,
then English-type consolidation would not be necessary here. Law

enforcement could remain a local option and a local service, with
strong, umbrella-type reinforcement and support - first from the
county through the sheriff, and if and as necessary from State and
Federal forces - through the sheriff as law enforcement leader and
representative of the people.

LEADERSHIP AND DIRECTION FOR FUTURE CHANGE

As we approach the year 1984, a subject of extreme importance
is the caliber of the person heading criminal justice agencies. Professionalism in law enforcement is a goal never to be achieved unless
the executive at the top is a leader and a respected professional. It
is an illusive goal, as evidenced by this quote from the Police Chief
Executive Report:

> Leadership so vitally needed for the law enforcement profession
> cannot be effectively provided under conditions present in many
> villages, cities, counties, and states of America.

The Police Chief Executive Report focused on the critical role
played by police chief executives, police chiefs, sheriffs and heads of
state police agencies. The Report addressed itself to two main areas:

1. The proper selection of qualified police chief executives for
   effective leadership, and

2. Their retention for a time long enough to develop and implement effective programs to reduce crime.

It is true that the job of the Police Chief executive is becoming
increasingly complex and demanding as new problems of complex
dimensions must be confronted. Crime continues as a dreadful burden
on the American people. In fact, its rate moves inexorably upward
and jeopardizes the safety of the individual citizen in addition to blem-
ishing the reputation and image of the community. It is this author's
feeling that crime today points out the major failure of our society -
the failure of law enforcement. The cost of crime and the cost of the
Criminal Justice system is staggering, both in economic and psychic
terms.

The Professional Leader in Law Enforcement

We must find a better way, and the professional police leader of
tomorrow must point it out. Nonprofessionals of the past in law enforcement have harvested us costly lawsuits, judicial chastisements,
limiting legislation, and adverse public opinion. The professional of
the future must be a paragon. He must be aware of the magnitude of
the moral and social responsibilities of the law enforcement role. He
must have vast knowledge, be adaptable to change, and be receptive to
new attitudes and new opportunities. He must understand his communities and must have a broad knowledge of political, educational and
social systems. The executive of tomorrow must live in a computer
world, understand communications and media relationships, be of a
scientific turn of mind, be an able manager of scarce resources, be
a personnel expert and aware of the intricacies of collective bargaining.
Such an executive is not found easily; such an executive requires a
basic rounding in educational skills as well as police work, and must,
of necessity, have years behind him.

As indicated recently in an editorial in a major metropolitan newspaper, there now seems to be a major change in the attitude of those
responsible for recruiting executives. According to information in
this article, which quotes the Wall Street Journal, there is a movement
within the business community toward hiring executives and managers
aged 50 years and older. There is now beginning to be a realization
that in selecting an individual to be the top executive of any agency, be
it private industry or government, with the multifaceted responsibilities
which are commensurate with the position, that the necessary qualities
cannot be found in a young person, irrespective of that person's initiative and drive. The qualities necessary in today's leaders require
maturity, which only comes from many years of experience. This
holds especially true for the law enforcement leader.

In addition to his professional world, the law enforcement leader
must understand and be involved with the imperfect politics of a democracy. He must live within the governmental system even though that
system leaves much to be desired.

Coordination and cooperation in law enforcement require a good
understanding of the governmental system and of practical politics.
While we can mouth "professionalism" all we wish and decry "politics,"
we cannot escape the unmistakable fact that that's "where it's at."
Politics and the particular system control law enforcement for better
or worse - generally worse.

The law enforcement executive of the future must understand
politics, have ability to deal with the power structure, and yet not
jeopardize his professionalism or compromise with crime and corrup-

tion. This requires the highest order of intelligence, of capability, of judgment - and yet some flexibility. At times he must reach decisions within himself that may require him to place his job on the line, that may require him to resign rather than compromise his professionalism. A rare combination of courage, integrity and independence must display itself in the law enforcement executive of the future. Once we select, qualify, and retain these important people in the law enforcement service, we must provide the framework for them to be effective.

Selection of Police Chief Executive (Qualifications)

The Michigan Chapter of the American Academy for Professional Law Enforcement, firmly believing that for professionalism to be effective in law enforcement it must start at the top, has accordingly adopted the following resolution for the selection of police chief executives, and a bill is being introduced into the Michigan Legislature for enactment into law.

Resolution

Every state should enact legislation that establishes minimum qualifications for future police chief executives of state, county and municipal police agencies within the state.

Minimum qualifications should be adopted for elective as well as non-elective police chief positions, and for the chief executives in police agencies of every size. These minimum qualifications should not apply retroactively to incumbent police chief exeuctives.

The Michigan Chapter of the American Academy of Professional Law Enforcement (A. A. P. L. E.) recommends and endorses the following standards for elective and non-elective police chief executive positions in the State of Michigan.

EXPERIENCE

A minimum of 4 years law enforcement experience regardless of the size of the agency.

In an agency of 30 or more full-time law enforcement personnel, 4 years of law enforcement experience, two (2) of which must be at the command or supervisory level.

In an agency of less than 30 full-time law enforcement personnel, 4 years of law enforcement experience.

EDUCATION

In an agency of less than 30 full-time law enforcement personnel, 60 semester or 90 quarter hours in Criminal Justice
or related fields, completed at an accredited college or university.

In an agency of 30 or more full-time law enforcement personnel, a Baccalaureate Degree in Criminal Justice or related fields, from an accredited college or university.

Framework for Effectiveness

Proper attitudes, professional skills, dedication, and even top
performance may be self-defeating and can frustrate and drive many
out of our emerging profession, because the system does not allow
goals and objectives to come to fruition. With that revamping of structure, there must be a revamping of law enforcement functions and the
leadership of those functions. Most importantly, we must revamp the
office and function of the sheriff (the oldest and most continuous law
enforcement and justice office in the history of the English-speaking
world).

The office of sheriff is symbolic of the development of the law enforcement function - from something citizens did for themselves to
something others were chosen to do for them. We must turn the wheel
around and allow a structure and a leader through which citizens can
again become involved in the system.

Perhaps appropriately, this chapter was started in Phoenix, Arizona. It is the author's belief that the sheriff (the reeve of the county),
the oldest law enforcement official still existing today, who went into
a decline with the rise of cities after our industrial revolution, can rise
like the Phoenix from the ashes of ineffective law enforcement to bring
new hope and better solutions to the fragmented, overlapping, duplicating, costly law enforcement system of the United States.

The author sees the sheriff as an agent of change to make an ineffective system effective, to assist in defining law enforcement roles,
to provide professional law enforcement services by contract, and to
provide effective support and sophisticated services to the many small
police departments of America.

Roles of American Law Enforcement Agencies

The problems of fragmentation are compounded by feelings of insecurity, petty piques, and jealousies engendered by widely different qualifications of police chief executives. As emphasis is increased on establishing the professional qualifications of our police chief executives and our sheriffs, we can begin to ascribe and define roles for each level of law enforcement where there is a multiplicity of agencies. This will do much to solve the overlapping jurisdictional and duplication-of-effort problems that today impede the efficient, effective, and economical delivery of law enforcement services to our citizens.

Federal Agencies and Their Roles

In essence, their work must be on a national and international range in specifically prescribed areas so that there remains the division of powers that the framers of our Constitution so wisely provided for. For instance, the Federal Government should concentrate on such national and international areas as organized crime, white collar crime across interstate lines, the growing narcotics problem with its international aspects, terrorism, etc.

State Police Roles

State police forces generally should provide supportive services from a statewide perspective to county and local law enforcement. State police should concentrate on areas such as organized crime, narcotics control, and white-collar crime from a state perspective, and leave the provision of local law enforcement to local and county authorities.

Sophisticated and costly services beyond the ability of local departments should be provided to local communities such as intelligence and investigative services, communications and records information networks, computerized criminal histories, major forensic laboratory services and statewide patrol of state freeways and expressways such as interstate and limited access highways. Mutual aid support should be provided as necessary upon the request of local communities.

Local Police Role

The local law enforcement agency should provide local law enforcement and basic 24-hour police services in the nature of preventive patrol, immediate response to citizens' calls for assistance and emergency situations, initial investigation of crimes and accidents, and if needed obtain additional supportive and investigative services from the county sheriff and through him, if necessary, from the State Police.

The County Sheriff's Role

The sheriff, as elected representative of the people of the county, has constitutional and statutory functions and should be concerned with county-wide law enforcement services involving multi-jurisdictional matters: modern, humane custody of offenders as per the laws of the state and the proper administration of the county jail; general preservation of the peace, security of the courts, patrol services for unincorporated areas either by agreement or contract; and generally specialized scientific and supportive services that can be provided from the county level. If more assistance is needed, he should request it from the State and Federal authorities in behalf of the local communities of his county.

Contract Policing

Contract policing will be the wave of the future for suburban and rural population areas. Contract policing is the term used by county sheriffs' departments for the law enforcement services provided by the sheriff's department through agreements with local agencies of government; e. g. , townships, in exchange for a pre-established annual, semi-annual or monthly fee.

The objectives of this arrangement are to provide all necessary and effective police services where costs for policing are prohibitive or taxing for the local government unit trying to finance its own force. The contractual arrangement still allows the local government unit to maintain control of the contracted force through its control of funds. Moreover, the local unit can cancel the agreement, and this can be done with or without cause.

It is a fact that all residents of the county already have the protection of the sheriff's departments, by State statute, funded through county taxation - but these services usually only include indirect technical assistance, jail services and supportive services, due to the existence of local police units in many areas and the limited manpower budget of the county force.

However, through contract policing, the local governmental unit receives not only the above-mentioned general services of the sheriff's department, but regularly assigned deputies to work directly within the local jurisdiction, often out of a local substation set up in headquarters of the township, village, etc. The contract provides the necessary funds

to hire qualified and trained deputies for the local jurisdiction. This
is at a cost savings to the contracted areas, since recruitment, testing,
training, and equipping are provided for by the sheriff's department,
plus supportive forces, including dispatchers and an established technical communications system.

On the other hand, where local units of government have, or decide
to have, their own police force, the force varies in size and quality of
operations. To begin a force, it is first necessary to plan and execute
a budget allotment, then hire a chief or director, who in turn finds 4-6
subordinates for patrol. Later, perhaps, a radio dispatcher will be
found. Training, qualifications, and technical services are dependent
upon subsequent budget allowances by the local government unit. The
duties, functions and powers of the chief or director vary from community to community, depending upon political and governmental factors.

If contract policing is agreed upon, the community or township may
experience a real cost savings, a greater potentiality for professionalism in its policing, backup forces, and the elimination of duplication in
services. The arrangement can be made by the local governing unit
which contacts the Sheriff's Department. Hearings are normally had,
and legal counsel is consulted for review of existing ordinances within
the local area before a resolution for the agreement is made and voted
upon and the contract is established.

In Oakland County, Michigan, where contract policing is operating
effectively, there are 10 townships out of 25 with contracts with the
Sheriff's Department; but the county also has some 42 local police and
public safety units, particularly in the heavily populated south end,
supported by local jurisdictions. However, in the more suburban/
rural areas of the north and west, the concept of contract policing has
steadily grown in popularity. The local agencies of law enforcement
have long been in existence in the southern half of the county, but population shifts to the northern and western sections are progressing,
making contract policing an efficient, effective, and less costly solution to the need for more and better quality law enforcement - law enforcement that is flexible and can be phased in and matched to growth.

Crime prevention and control demand teamwork, coordination and
expertise. Contract policing accentuates these qualities. An added
payoff seems to be in the important area of good police community
relations, as the contract officer realizes that the existence of his job
depends upon the proper and professional delivery of police services
to the satisfaction of the contracting community.

A PLAN FOR COUNTY DELIVERY OF
QUALITY PROFESSIONAL SUPPORT SERVICES
TO LOCAL POLICE AGENCIES

To put into effect some of the ideas presented in this chapter, the author has at present submitted a comprehensive, cost-effective proposal to better service law enforcement within Oakland County, Michigan. This could serve as a pilot program of some magnitude to overcome the problems of fragmentation by the consolidation of certain supportive services, assuring more services with limited tax dollars and providing a professional upgrading not possible in small, totally independent local police jurisdictions through the auspices of a sheriff as a service agent for professional law enforcement. It is possible that this study will become the precedent-setting model for similar efforts in other suburban communities throughout the United States. (See Appendix A)

THE SHERIFF AND LAW ENFORCEMENT
OF THE FUTURE

At the start of this chapter, we stated the premise that law enforcement does not work and throughout this chapter tried to point out why. The sheriff can be the key and the hope for law enforcement tomorrow. But that will depend on the citizens of today and the rank and file police officer in the many police departments throughout the nation. If they want a better world and better law enforcement, they must rise to the occasion, and they must properly select one among them to serve as law enforcement representative in their area. Perhaps we can learn something from the past and get our collective grit together for a better world beyond 1984.

Yes, the sheriff of yesterday and the sheriff of tomorrow will have much in common. He was then, and could be again, the leader of his county in the most important responsibilities of "conservation of the peace" and the protection of life and property. As opposed to being a power in the hurtful and oppressive sense, he should be a power in the helpful, serving sense.

To restore the greatness to this important office, it is most necessary that qualified and professional people are elected, not unqualified political hacks. It is of great significance for this ancient and honorable office that today highly dedicated and experienced persons are presenting themselves to the electorate. As the citizens learn to distinguish them from former unqualified and questionable office seekers of the past, the promise of the sheriff and his most important role of peace keeping is assured, and he can become the agent of change and the catalyst of reform and improvement in the complicated and frustrating hodgepodge that is called law enforcement in America today.

Crime is here; it must be dealt with. Laws are made by the people, and some among us must be spokesmen of the people for the proper enforcement of these laws. The sheriff is a composite of all that is necessary for coordinating a system to deal with crime and the justice system effectively - both cost-wise and result-wise.

The sheriff can be the bridge between the law enforcement world and the people of society. He can, as the people's representative, talk to them about the need for involvement in crime prevention; about obtaining their assistance and support for the development of modern police administration; for scientific advances in criminalistics; for better crime detection; for improvement in the correctional process, and so on. He can and must be an informed voice to the people. He is their representative for crime control. Likewise, he can be a voice from the people to the law enforcement world when some within that aspiring profession fail to live up to its ethics and standards. He can operate within the governmental framework on a par with his peers - the other elected officeholders in county government.

The sheriff can be the effective balance wheel between ineffective local law enforcement and too much centralized government in law enforcement matters. The sheriff, as of old, should be the "keeper or chief of his county", concerned with the peace, safety and welfare of its citizens, and responsible for a just maintenance of law and order and for enlisting responsible citizen participation in this effort. The citizen and his law enforcement representative must together shoulder responsibility for the maintenance of law and order. England has a much lower crime rate than the United States, no doubt due to a greater and more dutiful citizen involvement together with respect for law and law enforcement.

Yes, it will take a team - the concerned people of a county along with their police departments and their sheriff - to restore to the future the promise of the "blessings of liberty" and the "pursuit of happiness" in peace and security in this land. The future shire-reeve can be a modern "tribune" who can champion the people's rights - and that should include the right to relative peace, safety and security in a more effective law enforcement system.

APPENDIX A

A PLAN FOR COUNTY DELIVERY OF
QUALITY PROFESSIONAL SUPPORT SERVICES
TO LOCAL POLICE AGENCIES

Statement of the Problem

Traditionally, each police department is self-contained, with
sporadic assistance from other law enforcement agencies of an equal
or superior jurisdictional level. This has been the logical consequence
of the desire of units of local government to maintain and exercise complete control over all aspects of their legal authority. However, fragmentation of governmental entities, particularly in the large suburbs,
also inhibits the effective delivery of professional quality police services at minimum costs.

In almost all instances, this problem has been fostered by a belief
on the part of local police agencies that the use of ancillary services
could possibly result in an encroachment upon their local autonomy.
Recent criminology and police studies have, however, demonstrated
the contrary. They are in uniform agreement that substantial improvements in both the operations and costs of police support services can
be achieved through this method, virtually without any erosion of local
control. By means of a cooperative effort, with pooling of information
and personnel, local police units can realize a higher level of professionalism. The unfortunate trend in the movement of criminal activity
toward suburban areas makes this cooperative effort all the more vital.

Crime knows no boundary. When police efforts are limited in any
manner which does not also limit the criminal, the latter has a distinct
advantage at the expense of the public. In the words of the President's
Commission on Law Enforcement and Administration of Justice, the
most outstanding report in the history of American criminology: "The
geographical restriction in the apprehension of criminals often provides
them with a sanctuary from effective police activity." The availability
of quality professional police services with a cooperative inter-jurisdictional information base can only serve to enhance the ultimate effectiveness of local police agencies.

Ten years ago, the President's Commission chose Oakland County,
Michigan, as the example of a community badly in need of such a cooperative effort. Out of the whole of the United States, a chart of the
fragmentation of urban police agencies in Oakland County was utilized
as an example of a community that would directly benefit from such a

program. Oakland County represents an amalgam of 61 governmental agencies and some 43 separate law enforcement agencies. Notwithstanding this focus of national attention, little, if anything, has been done to implement the sound proposal of the President's Commission and of similar studies. As a community, we seem to be insensitive to the clear demands of crime prevention.

Given the obvious need for a cooperative effort, an in-depth examination of the present fragmentation should be undertaken, with an emphasis on various areas of police administration and operation. Inherent in such a study would be an effort to determine which support services would be more efficiently supplied on the local, the county or the State level of authority. Although our present personal belief is that the county constitutes the most effective unit of government for these purposes, future research may indicate that specific support services can be best provided by other levels of police authority. This belief is predicated upon the firm conviction that crime is a local problem which must be dealt with by strong local government. Such a study will most likely have the distinct additional advantage of becoming the precedent-setting model for similar efforts in other suburban communities throughout the United States, marking Oakland County as the leader in enlightened improvements in law enforcement. It is strongly suspected that an investigation will reveal that the social and political characteristics of both Oakland County and the State of Michigan will require customized methods to be effective in our communities.

Economically, through decreasing of the amount of overlap and duplication which presently exists in obtaining police supportive services in Oakland County, substantial savings can accrue to the citizenry. At this point, because of the lack of an appropriate data base, the savings to result from the study cannot be projected. However, it is firmly believed that substantial savings will result. A mechanism will be provided in the study to identify savings being realized.

An integral part of this study must be the follow-up implementation of its findings. Crime has been studied to death and the studies left to collect dust on some shelf. Rather than throwing additional money at the problem of crime and failing to follow through with the applications of those findings that offer solutions, this proposed project includes not only research and analysis, but implementation as well.

Specifically, the project will address the following:

1.   Administration

     a.   Recruitment of personnel

     b.   Selection and training of personnel

c. Administrative planning

d. Organized crime intelligence

e. Purchasing

f. Public information

g. Internal investigation

h. Staff inspection

i. Updated training

j. Coordination of existing pooling agreements for the emergency use of police services

k. Policy guidelines for the utilization of equipment reflecting the continual advancement in the technology of crime detection

l. Funding for ongoing special investigation teams dealing with community crises resulting from a continuing pattern of offenses (i.e., child killings)

m. Contingency planning

n. Use of systems and data processing techniques in crime forecasting and detection

2. Operations

a. Degree of coordination between overlapping and contiguous jurisdictions

b. Records of criminal activity

c. Crime analysis

d. Riot control

e. Crime scene search and follow-up laboratory analysis

f. Firearms control and use

g. Coordination of reserve officers

h. Coordination with state and federal authorities

i. Coordination of public relations problems, including media

j. Coordination of policies with regard to the prosecutor and courts

k. Allocation of specialized law enforcement functions

l. Investigation into the feasibility of contracting regular and specialized law enforcement services

m. Sources of funding for regional squads as necessitated by a series of crimes committed by the same suspect in a number of communities

n. Statutory and Constitutional impediments requiring change for implementation of program

o. Coordination of specialized operations such as juvenile, vice, narcotics, fraud, shoplifting, organized crime, etc.

p. Determination of minimum operational standards and requisite funding

q. Investigation of the procedures for use of electronic surveillance techniques

r. Coordination of techniques with respect to the preparation of evidence

s. Uniformly and effectively utilizing inter-jurisdictional communication systems

t. Coordination for the efficient security and management of detained individuals

u. Coordination with other agencies of services necessary for operational places of detention (i.e., Department of Health, Department of Special Services)

With the right leadership, Oakland County can pioneer in establishing a new and expanded role in the fight against crime and in the improvement of criminal justice - a county-coordinated role toward preventing and deterring crime.

3 Future Role of the State Police in the Criminal Justice System

William Connelie

ANTECEDENTS AND DEVELOPMENT

Police forces with statewide jurisdiction are relatively young agencies within the Criminal Justice System of the United States. They were created in most states to fill specific enforcement voids: rural policing, investigative specialists, or highway patrolling.

Although the common-law jurisdiction of the states has been a longstanding principle under the powers reserved to the states in the Constitution, policing fell to the lesser jurisdictions within the states. State constitutions authorized legislation of criminal statutes, court procedures and required enforcement by the state executive. The actual enforcement, however, fell to those traditionally established enforcement offices - the police in the cities and the sheriffs and constables in the rural areas. Law enforcement in the cities evolved into the sophisticated police departments of the present. However, the foundations for such growth were not to be found in the offices of the sheriff or town constable as they existed in nineteenth-century America.

The response to the perceived need for State-level enforcement agencies varied. The Texas Rangers were authorized under the provisional government of the Texas Republic in 1835, primarily for border patrol service. Their jurisdiction was increased later to include general police work and criminal investigation. Arizona and New Mexico also briefly established forces on the Texas Ranger model.

Massachusetts appointed "state constables" to specialized enforcement in 1865. Legislative revisions resulted in the establishment, in 1879, of the Massachusetts District Police, which later became the Division of State Police. Connecticut established a small force pat-

76

terned after the Massachusetts District Police in 1903 and this agency
soon became primarily a State detective force. (1)

The State of Pennsylvania was challenged in 1903 to respond to the
need for a State-level executive arm to enforce its own laws. The
Anthracite Coal Strike Commission presented to President Theodore
Roosevelt its report which declared Pennsylvania's role in the violence-
filled strike: "Peace and order should be maintained at any cost, but
should be maintained by regularly appointed and responsible officers
... at the expense of the public. " (2)

This challenge, and the failure of the traditional law enforcement
apparatus existing in rural areas of the state, led to the establishment
of the Pennsylvania State Constabulary in 1905. (3) This represented
the creation, not evolution, of a police organization which was to greatly influence the subsequent development of agencies for rural police
administration at the State level. (4)

Following Pennsylvania's example, other states with similar rural
enforcement problems established their own State police agencies.
Many were directly patterned after the organization in Pennsylvania,
but others developed toward more specialization of duties, especially
in the formation of highway patrols.

Our State police agencies, therefore, were formed to fill the jurisdictional void described earlier. They must now be aware, however,
that they share law enforcement responsibility in many local areas with
emerging police agencies. Although in many instances bureaucratized
and entrenched, State police agencies may not realize that their traditional role may be undergoing an erosion of responsibilities.

The population of the United States is growing, and there has been
a continuing shift of the population from the cities to the rural areas.
Such demographic movements demand change from primarily rural
agencies. The law enforcement needs of these larger population group-
ings are increasingly served by newly established municipal and county
police departments. Just as the dwellers of new population centers
demand public services, such as sewer, municipal water supply, refuse collection and traffic control, they will not settle for a police
service attuned to the needs of a farm community or small village.

The newly developed communities create increased enforcement
demands not readily met by the former law enforcement agencies.
The rural agencies must then either change and expand to fill the new
needs or modify their objectives and roles in the emerging criminal
justice system.

As communities authorize and create new agencies, the State Police has many options open to it in order to remain a vital, viable
force for meeting the constitutional objective of ensuring law enforcement to the states' residents. It may continue its traditional role of

enforcement, where appropriate, while adapting and expanding its support and provision of resources to other agencies. In addition, statewide jurisdiction and mobility ensure an important enforcement role for
State police in specialized functions of law enforcement.

THE STATE POLICE TODAY

The manner in which State police organizations emerged in the
United States did not result in a uniform style of agency in the various
states. They range from departments which perform all police investigative, patrol, and service functions to those which perform only one
of those functions. Most State police forces do have some characteristics in common, however, which have resulted in certain issues which
they must face today.

The jurisdiction of the State police forces usually encompasses the
entire geography of the particular state. This is shared with numerous
county, municipal, town and village police departments. The enforcement void for which the State Police was created is now becoming an
overcrowded theatre of operations. Since some of these agencies also
function in jurisdictions, which contain lesser governmental units, a
hodgepodge of overlapping police jurisdictions has resulted.

Many police officers can relate experiences wherein rivalry for
calls in an area resulted in three or more agencies dispatching officers
to a scene. This may be appropriate for a major crime, but not for an
auto accident, since the "extra" units might better remain on patrol,
available for other calls. Such rivalry may have as its cause the desire
by administrators to justify increases in budget or manpower or even for
self-aggrandizement. This "interdepartmental rivalry and jealousy ...
results in poor cooperation, such as withheld information and competition for recognition. " (5)

Perhaps the State-level police agency must face the fact that part
of the basis for its existence has been deteriorating. It need not necessarily be, in many of the areas it is serving, just one more level of
police jurisdiction. If, because of growth of a community, an adequate
police department now exists, perhaps it is time to change and alter
the State agency and its role.

State governments do possess the resources and size to perform
unique law enforcement functions in many instances. Although local
police agencies may be able to adequately perform most of the law
enforcement functions for their communities, some are too expensive
or infrequently used. The larger State police agency may provide these
special functions. These may include crime laboratories, highway

patrol on major highways, special investigations, and other support
or resource services.

The many recent moves by citizen groups to consider consolidation
of police services are indicative of citizen concern for the manner in
which their tax monies are spent on law enforcement. The public will
not long stand for a multilevel overlapping of jurisdictions which do not
show a demonstrably better law enforcement service. Those State police
agencies with a forward thinking attitude are assessing their role for
the future.

The Emerging Role

Present trends indicate that as local police grow and provide more
active community service, the full-service State Police departments
will find a diminishing jurisdictional base for their activities. Local and
county police agencies will emerge as the primary enforcement agencies
for most communities. This will call for a reappraisal of the State
Agency's mission, and perhaps a reallocation of resources to a support
role. Examples of this support role are present in those states which
presently perform more limited police functions. A single highway
patrol in a state provides a vital service more efficiently and better
than many local agencies. In such a manner, the State-level agency
is uniquely capable of performing many specialized functions due to its
statewide jurisdictional base.

There is a myriad of support services which are either presently
included in State Police services or which will become so in the future.
They are necessary elements of modern law enforcement and will continue to increase in importance. These activities will be best performed
at the State level, and will necessitate the existence of a police agency
at that jurisdictional level. Such a State agency will be a research and
training repository, as well as a coordinator and even supervisor of
these specialized services.

Individual, local agencies, other than very large urban departments,
could not feasibly incorporate all of these services. They usually involve high-cost, relatively infrequent utilization or a need for specialized knowledge or equipment. Particular services may also be of an
interdepartmental nature which demands the existence of an authority
superior to the local level. Additionally, several particular law enforcement functions bear a direct relationship to the State government,
or to the state as a whole, and allocation below the State government
level would be inappropriate.

Crime Laboratories

The technological advances in police work which have gained the greatest attention are best exemplified by applications of scientific knowledge. Forensic science has added immeasurably to the ability of the Criminal Justice System to pursue its objectives. Revelation of the existence of crime, the search of the scene, evidence analysis, and identification of perpetrators have all been vastly improved through the application of the scientific method.

The expense and expertise necessary to provide crime laboratories and to operate them dictates that local agencies use some central or regional facility. Logically, the need for these facilities can be fulfilled under State Police direction and control.

Police scientific laboratories supply a number of sophisticated services to investigating agencies and the community as a whole. Toxicological analyses of substances may determine the presence of poison, for example, which may then reveal that a death was caused by a criminal act. This analytical capability might also be used to assist the medical profession seraching for causes of illness.

Great advances have been made in the field of serology which have been applied to criminal investigations. Blood, hair, semen and other substances have gained increasing importance in the solution of cases. Research and advance in this area of specialization will add to the ability of the Criminal Justice System to more efficiently handle evidence and identify perpetrators.

Firearms identification and ballistics technology are becoming increasingly important within the functions of the State crime laboratory. In a society which has been prone to firearms use, both lawful and unlawful, a central source of expertise and equipment for scientific examination of weapons and projectiles is an absolute necessity.

The State crime laboratory, of course, performs many other functions designed to assist law enforcement personnel in their duties. Analysis of substances to verify violation of drug laws, examination of documents, handwriting and chemical analysis to prove or disprove impairment by alcohol or drugs, and spectrographic examination of paint chips from on a hit-run car are just a few of these functions.

It should be apparent from this brief description of crime laboratory activities that experts from many scientific disciplines must be included on the laboratory staff. It is also the case that the instruments and supplies used are very expensive and sophisticated. These factors often preclude local agencies from having their own laboratories. However, cooperation and coordination between states will provide a greater base of scientific assistance for the entire criminal justice system.

Communications

Information exchange among components of the Criminal Justice System is an absolute necessity. The mobility of criminals is not limited by the existence of town, county, state, or even national boundaries. Communications systems have been established which provide not only notification of criminal activities and the attempts to locate suspects but also supply information vital to police operation. Speedy access to motor vehicle registration data, driver information, and stolen vehicles and property has been accomplished through application of computer technology. Computers are also being used to control the exchange of messages on the various police teletypewriter networks.

The interfacing of certain computers has provided immediate access to the relevant information files and permitted the establishment of specialized data files directly related to law enforcement. National-level files provide a central data bank accessible to all the states. Individual State files are also accessible from without the state as well as by agencies within its borders.

Sophisticated and expensive electronic equipment provides for the direction of messages between agencies and access to information repositories. This resource of interstate and intrastate police communication and data retrieval is most appropriately maintained on a State level.

The police radio has become an indispensible tool for the law enforcement practitioner. In order that this tool be most effectively used, however, the range or access of the radio system must not be limited or too restricted.

Criminal mobility, police response to emergency situations, and overlapping jurisdictions all too frequently demonstrate a need for rapid communication between agencies. Such a need indicates the necessity for compatible radio communications networks on an inter-agency or regional basis. The state can most appropriately provide expensive central radio equipment and coordination. Additionally, in an emergency situation requiring multi-department response or mobilization, the effective communications component of operations would be assured and coordinated by the State agency with jurisdictional control.

Organized Crime Units

Experience with organized crime has indicated that widespread criminal activities create special problems for law enforcement. The multi-jurisdictional implications of large scale conspiracies and activities mandates a unified cooperative response among enforcement agencies.

This response is best directed under the highest authority available
within the state.

Special units with statewide authority and criminal jurisdiction can
operate much more efficiently than a number of smaller agencies restricted to their own jurisdictions. Experience has shown that a more
effective response may be made by such a State organization. The
State police agency, in addition to its flexibility in dealing with this
criminal problem, is significantly removed from much of the local
latent corrupting influence of organized crime.

Police Training

Police training and education has risen to become a science of its
own. It is recognized that the officer must possess certain knowledge
and skills to perform his duties. The supervision of personnel and the
management of police agencies also demand the acquisition of administrative expertise by supervisory and command-level officers.

Qualifications of personnel and minimum police training standards
are common throughout the United States. Uniformity of training is
more easily attained through statewide centralized training. The State
Police would be able to provide personnel and material committed to
the overall police training function of the state.

Few local agencies are equipped or staffed to provide the professional level of training which the future police role will demand. A
State-run program will be able to school police officers with a good,
coordinated collection of training aids and a highly qualified professional
staff. In addition, programs of in-service training, specialist skills,
management improvement, etc. , which would be impractical for all but
the largest municipalities, could be provided for groups of officers from
many agencies. Such a centralized service would provide uniformity,
exchange of ideas among agencies and better trained police personnel.

Pistol Licensing and Registration

There is a longstanding tradition in the United States of personal
possession of firearms. Although there has been little government interference with the "right of the people to keep and bear arms, " (6) many
states have taken steps with respect to registration.

Handgun regulation has long been considered a necessary and desirable governmental control. Growing citizen concern regarding possession of handguns magnifies this role and will probably cause an increase
in the registration of firearms.

Many states already utilize State police facilities for the administration of procedures and documents related to gun registration and
licensing of owners. Direct association with the firearms-related
function of the crime laboratory and access to computerized files and
communications assist this support service.

The important relationship of firearms licensing and registration
to the whole Criminal Justice System mandates a statewide comprehensive and accessible information system. This cannot be accomplished
by small jurisdictions which would leave some geographical areas un-
served. State police organizations possess the appropriate jurisdiction
and capability to fulfill this ever-increasing role.

Civil Defense and Disaster Preparedness

The gradual withdrawal of Federal involvement in Civil Defense
activities leaves a void which is interjurisdictional and requires State
agency-level responsibility. The State police agency will act as a
communicator and facilitator between local police and other agencies
to better prepare for all large-scale emergencies. This role applies
equally to response in times of natural or industrial disasters because
of agency access to necessary supplies, equipment and facilities.

The functions of a State police agency will include responsibility
for a statewide auxiliary police program including selection, training
and coordination. Training would also be conducted to assist local
agencies in planning and organizing for any large-scale emergency
within their communities.

State police agencies have been identified as the most appropriate
agencies to coordinate activities surrounding shipment of nuclear and
other hazardous materials, as they can best direct the proper police
response to specific emergencies because of specialized personnel
and equipment.

Criminal Records

The increasingly sophisticated nature of records maintenance and
its interfacing with computerized communications facilities indicates
the necessity for state centralization of police and criminal records.
It is neither efficient nor appropriate to the future of effective law enforcement to retain records only on a local level. Just as the communication of alarms and bulletins is necessary for improved police response,
so is access to stored information on perpetrators, suspects and subjects of investigation.

The future will prove that the State level will provide the best combination of records maintenance and access for all Criminal Justice Agencies. If it is determined in the next 20 years that a police agency is to be the appropriate storehouse of such sensitive, important information, then the State Police is the most logical agency to handle this repository.

Private Police

The criminal justice system has been expanded greatly in the past several years by many private and quasi-official agencies. Although they have existed for a number of years, private investigative, security, and police organizations have lately become more numerous and have assumed greatly expanded roles.

Security guards, private investigators and railroad police and other such occupations perform tasks that are frequently sensitive and which demand ever-increasing knowledge and expertise. The services which they provide are vital to the protection of much private property and to civil investigative activities.

The very nature of the services provided by private police agencies creates potential for abuse. There exists, therefore, a need for state-wide regulation and inspection. Many states have already established licensing of private security agencies, private investigators, and railroad police, supervised by the State Police. Such regulatory authority will continue to expand to ensure that abuses do not occur and to facilitate cooperation with public law enforcement agencies.

Specialized Enforcement

Due to the necessity for statewide jurisdiction for a particular function, certain law enforcement functions will be retained by a State enforcement agency. Among these functions is patrol of interstate highways. Traffic enforcement on limited access highways is most efficiently conducted by officers unhampered by local jurisdictional boundaries. Security for the Governor and other State officials is most appropriately performed by personnel at the State level. These duties will continue to increase, thereby requiring well trained, skilled personnel.

Criminal investigative specialists within the structure of the State police agency are available to those agencies with limited resources. The unusual crime scene search for evidence, or technically specialized investigation, is beyond the scope and ability of many small departments.

Access to a State resource pool of expertise and equipment raises the quality of response to extraordinary enforcement demands. The frequency of such demands within the larger jurisdiction of the state, along with an obligation to support other criminal justice agencies, ensures that the necessary technical competence will be maintained by the State police agency.

Other kinds of specialized enforcement activities are most effectively performed by an agency which is large enough and possesses sufficient jurisdictional authority to be available and flexible. Civil disturbances, riots, mass demonstrations and disorderly crowds create unique demands upon the law enforcement community. It is possible for the state to provide a disciplined, mobile, tactical force for these extra-sensitive situations. The ability to mobilize and respond quickly with highly trained, skilled personnel is vital in these emergencies.

The number of incidents involving hostages, terrorism and bombings continues to be a major concern for the police. The expertise necessary to deal with situations where these incidents occur calls for extensive training and practical experience. The use of sophisticated weaponry and equipment is frequently necessary. The State Police are capable of staffing and equipping special units to assist local agencies in these special police requirements.

Special Equipment

In addition to providing support in the form of personnel and expertise, the State Police also will act as a repository of special sophisticated equipment. Due to infrequent use and high cost, such equipment is not usually possessed by smaller jurisdictions. In fulfilling its emerging support role, the State Police can better anticipate the needs for these resources on a total State basis.

Aircraft of various types have proven their worth as a tool of law enforcement. Helicopters provide excellent observation capabilities for criminal and non-criminal searches. They also have a speed and flexibility of operation which has proven to be of inestimable value in enforcement activities, traffic control, rapid response to accidents and disasters and for transportation of injured persons. Helicopters and fixed wing aircraft are used for the rapid delivery of personnel and equipment to emergency or tactical situations. Proven as beneficial and even critical to certain police operations, aircraft represent a substantial investment, high operation costs, and heavy personnel commitment. As an agency committed to statewide support of law enforcement agencies, the State Police will maintain an increasing number of aircraft for such purposes.

Increased sophistication of electronic devices, photographic equipment, and the required skill in their use will continue to place great
demands on law enforcement agencies. The lawful use of electronic,
audio and visual surveillance are key factors in the exposure of criminal activities and conspiracies. Such devices, because of their sophistication and limited use, are also frequently beyond the reach of all but
the largest police agencies. As in other areas of support, the State Police can more easily obtain, maintain and operate these expensive electronic tools of effective law enforcement in the future.

There will continue to be developed expensive types of emergency
equipment which all local police agencies would like to list in their
property inventories. However, budgets of most departments prohibit
such purchases. The resources of the state, however, enable it to
assemble an inventory of aircraft vehicles, communications devices,
generators, lights, etc., for unusual occurrences. Rapid deployment
of emergency equipment will then be possible throughout the state. The
growing mobile, quick-response capability associated with the State
Police will supplement the equipment with trained operational personnel.

Contract Services

A State police agency, based on its growing experience, expertise,
and trained personnel, will be able to provide full police service on a
contract basis in situations where a local governmental authority is unable to do so. An alternative to this contractual arrangement would be
for a community to have a resident State police office to provide law
enforcement services to its citizens. Such an office would be equipped
and staffed with costs shared by that locality and the state.

Major transportation facilities such as air terminals have special
security and enforcement needs. Since many of these facilities are
owned and operated by public authorities, the enforcement responsibility
is also a public service. This service could be performed by a State
police detachment on a contract basis.

Because of construction costs, many highways were built and are
operated as toll roads under public authority. Police service on these
highways is the responsibility of that authority, but other demands are
made upon such patrols beyond traffic control. Since such highways
cross jurisdictional lines and the highway authority itself is frequently
at the State level, the State Police is the most appropriate agency to
provide police service. Such service would be supplied on a contract
basis similar to that described for the transportation facilities.

Research

Statewide authority, greater facilities and greater resources enhance the potential for State police agencies to pursue research aimed at the improvement of the law enforcement function. Communications between the State Police and all other police agencies within the state will provide the opportunity to keep abreast of law enforcement needs. This increasing awareness will stimulate further research and development projects and interstate communication of ideas and information.

White Collar Crime

An increased public awareness and enforcement effort toward the growing problem of "white-collar crime," or occupational crime, lead to the conclusion that a police agency with a broader jurisdictional base can more effectively deal with the problem. Since offenses of this nature frequently involve many jurisdictions, the statewide authority and facilities of a State police are increasingly necessary. Although corporate crime may indeed be as widespread as the national, even international, size of the corporations themselves, the State level provides an appropriate jurisdiction for response to offenses in violation of State laws. For example, many large industrial and business establishments are relocating outside of areas with large police agencies. This is creating a growing need for the availability of an enforcement agency with sufficient sophistication to respond adequately to criminal activities.

As with organized crime, specialized task forces will be organized for investigation of offenses involving the business world. These state investigative forces will have statewide jurisdiction, broad powers, and rapid communication capability for effective and efficient operation.

Support Force

The size and distribution of a State police department will permit it to function as a well-prepared, mobile backup force for local agencies. Support personnel will be supplied in the event of unusual demands upon an agency's resources, such as terroristic acts, strikes, disorderly crowds, disturbances, manhunts, disasters, etc. The availability of specialized State teams as a support service eases the burden on smaller agencies. The State police agency will have grown to provide the bulk of the total preparedness before the turn of the century.

SUMMARY

The State Police has a promising future as an integral part of the
Criminal Justice System. It might appear to some observers that a
State-level law enforcement agency is becoming unnecessary because
of a sufficiency of local police agencies. We have shown, however,
that the potential exists for a complementary rather than competitive
role for a State police. In fact, many State police departments or State
highway patrols are already functioning in such a cooperative manner
with the other police authorities within their jurisdictions.
It is probable that the Criminal Justice System will be improved
through a unification and/or coordination of its elements which will
diminish the duplication of procedures at various government levels.
It is possible, of course, that this unification might take the form of
centralization of law enforcement. In fact, many metropolitan areas
have found that centralized police departments are efficient, economical
and effective. It is doubtful, however, that people will relinquish local
autonomy over their police to the extent of supporting a centralized
State police with total law enforcement authority for the entire state.
Such consolidations would enable more effective and economical response.
However, few police administrators recommend this course because of
our cherished traditions and the ever-present fear of a police state.
Many of the benefits of a single statewide law enforcement authority can be realized in the system which is now emerging. Local police
departments, responsive to the needs of their community, will be the
primary providers of police service. The State Police will support,
supplement and complement their activities by providing equipment,
personnel and assistance. They will also continue to pursue an active
enforcement role in those specific areas for which their training, capabilities and jurisdiction make them the most appropriate police agency.
In this manner, the finest attributes of both systems can be merged into
one efficient component of the criminal justice system.

NOTES AND REFERENCES

1. Bruce Smith, Police Systems in the United States, 2nd Revised
    ed., Revised by Bruce Smith, Jr. (New York: Harper and Row,
    1960), pp. 147-48.

2. Katherine Mayo, Justice To All: The Story of the Pennsylvania
    State Police (New York: Arno Press and the New York Times,
    1971), pp. 4-5.

3. Mayo, pp. 8-10.

4. Smith, p. 149.

5. Citizens Committee on Intermunicipal Affairs, Consolidation of
    Police Services in Erie County, New York (Buffalo, New York:
    1968), p. 28.

6. United States Constitution, Amendment II.

4 The Future of Local Law Enforcement: The Federal Role

David J. Farmer

Almost ten years have passed since Lyndon B. Johnson, questing
for the Great Society and facing the reality of civil disorders and rising
crime rates, signed into law the Omnibus Crime Control and Safe Street
Act of 1968. The Act established the Law Enforcement Assistance
Administration (LEAA) as the principal Federal agency concerned with
State and local law enforcement and provided for criminal justice planning agencies in every state.

In 1960, when John F. Kennedy defeated Richard M. Nixon, crime
had been regarded as a purely local issue. (1) By 1968 it had become
a national priority. The America that could place a man on the moon
could certainly ensure the safety of its citizens on the streets. As the
President's Commission on Law Enforcement and Administration of
Justice concluded in its 1967 report, "...America can control crime
if it will." (2) On that note of confidence, LEAA was created (3) to lead
the war against crime, and it came to account for 5 percent of the criminal justice budget. (4)

Unfortunately, the rhetoric that succeeded in launching the "War
on Crime" was not as easy to achieve on the battlefield. Ten years and
six billion dollars later, there was discontent about the results and the
red tape. Although there had been many successes, there also were
numerous failures; social problems did not appear to be as tractable as
the technology of space travel. The discontent was felt particularly by
the cities, which were becoming increasingly strangled by financial
shortages and increasingly resentful of the "cooperative feudalism"
represented by Federal assistance (and the inevitable companion guidelines) in all major domestic areas.

With the election of President Jimmy Carter, reorganization and
reform of the Federal branch of government has become a top priority.

As part of that effort, the Federal element of the crime control assistance program has come under increasing scrutiny. Attorney General Griffin B. Bell has repeatedly cited what he perceives as the deficiencies of the Law Enforcement Assistance Administration, and has indicated his determination to take corrective action. A task force established by the Attorney General recently made its report (5) to Mr. Bell, with two major recommendations and offering a number of options. Following a 60-day public comment period, the administration is currently reviewing these options and several hundred proposals. Thus, the future of Federal involvement in crime control remains to be determined, and readers of this chapter should bear in mind the historical position of the author.

This chapter looks beyond this period of reassessment to 1984 and the next half century. First, what do we want to achieve in the future in the area of law enforcement? Second, how do we get to that point? These two questions, looking first toward the future and toward the goals or the ideal that we seek, are what this article attempts to explore - a perspective that takes the viewer outside the limitations of current controversies and permits a wider view. However, the ideal is not one untempered by realism. Law enforcement is part of the weave of the nation's political life, and decisions about it will inevitably be made within a context of compromise among the various pressure groups and vested interests wrapped up in the present structure, and in light of other political realities. In the same way that budgeting cannot be viewed as an "arid subject, the province of clerks and dull statisticians," (6) so decisions about the character of law enforcement will be made in an incremental and highly politicized fashion. Thus, consideration of what we want in the future might be more accurately stated as: "What can we reasonably expect?" or "Given a favorable environment, what will be the probable and desirable outcomes?" The second question then becomes "How can the favorable environment be created?"

Looking ahead to the twenty-first century, what should we expect the general shape and character of law enforcement services to be? In particular, what functions should we expect law enforcement organizations to perform? What should be the general organization of law enforcement services? What kind of personnel should staff these services? What operational systems should be used? What management systems should be used? What should be the general condition of police science? Tentative answers to these questions are offered below.

What will be the general organization of law enforcement services in 2034 - 50 years after 1984?

Two extremes can probably be excluded. First, it is unlikely that the United States will have a national police force. The geographical size and the diversity of the country are the principal guarantees against

this. Another is the nation's well-established conviction that the absence of a national police force is a barrier against tyranny. In part,
this prejudice has stemmed from J. Edgar Hoover. Conscious that
his own Achilles' heel might be that he wishes to establish the Federal
Bureau of Investigation as a national police force, Mr. Hoover consistently attacked the "national police force" straw man. He was successful, as the strength of public opinion attests.

Second, it is unlikely that the current parish-pump or atomistic
system can survive. Certainly, it should not. There are more than
17,000 police departments in the United States, ranging from one department which at full complement had more than 30,000 officers, to
entirely part-time and volunteer departments. If there is any doubt
about the confusion and the unsystematic character of the proliferation,
one need only reflect that the 1967 President's Commission on Law Enforcement and Administration of Justice reported the total number of
agencies to be 40,000. This erroneous belief was universally held
until 1975 when the statistical error was discovered and the lower figure became known. (7)

The principal intellectual advocate of localism is a perceptive
scholar, Dr. Elinor Ostrum,* whose deep understanding of the police
function must give any conscientious consolidationist pause. (8) Logic,
however, seems to argue persuasively against this proliferation. (9)
With a population of some 46 million, England has 39 police forces;
with a population of some 58 million, France has two police forces.
In comparison, the number of police departments in the United States -
with a population four or five times as great - has an Alice-in-Wonder-
land quality. Robert DiGrazia, a former Police Commissioner of
Boston and currently Police Chief of Montgomery County, Maryland,
has recommended that the country should have 300, rather than some
17,000, police departments. (10) While the precise number cannot be
predicted, it is reasonable to assume that the common sense of reducing
the number of departments will be realized by 2034.

What functions will law enforcement organizations perform in 2034?

Today, as always, police departments do what police departments
do. Their functions are many, varied, and undefined. (11) The number
and variety of these functions is indicated by the title of a polemic published by the New York City Patrolman's Benevolent Association, The
One Thousand and One Hats of Officer Jones. The confusion about definition can be seen in the absence of any definitive publication on the
subject and in the widespread public misconception of the police officer's
role. While television and popular mythology depict the police officer
as the great crime-fighter, many point out that the typical police officer

* See chapter 1

spends only a small percentage of his time on crime-related activities. (12)

It is likely that police agency functions will be more precisely defined by 2034. The growing popularity of systems thinking, general increases in the educational level of the public and of police officers, the increasing professionalism of police managers, and the development of police science (13) as well as other urban disciplines: all these factors will lead to demands for greater specificity of purpose, despite the difficulties and complexities involved. It is likely, too, that circumstances will require police agencies to take a more active role in areas other than street crime. White-collar crime, (14) for example, inevitably will grow as computers become increasingly ubiquitous. It also is probable that the service functions of police will be emphasized. (15) There is a growing recognition that the police are the only available 24-hour-a-day social service agency, and providing quality social services may facilitate greater citizen cooperation needed for crime control (both arrests and convictions). Police will also become more involved in following through on court activities, by such means as transporting witnesses to court and explaining court processes to victims and witnesses. (16)

What kind of personnel will staff police services in 2034?

In addressing this question, let us focus on each end of the spectrum - the patrol officer (or private) and the police chief. The most significant change that has been occurring at the patrol officer level in the past decade is that the officer is becoming more than just a person with white socks: now he usually has an extension school degree. Much valid criticism can be levelled against criminal justice education courses (for example, see notes on the subject in the 1976 edition of the Police Yearbook). (17) However, due to the impetus of the Law Enforcement Education Program (LEEP), a revolution has been started in police agencies, and there is no reversing the clock. The current problem, however, is that police departments have made no effective provision for the educated officer. Thus, most of the best leave for occupations that promise greater (à la Maslow) self-actualization. The grinding-down effect of a paramilitary bureaucratic organization at the patrol officer level is incompatible with education. It is likely that more effective organizational arrangements will be made for the educated officer by 2034. This process will be spurred primarily by the community need for better police service and by growing police professionalism. It will also be encouraged by the opening of police job opportunities to people, such as women, who will not perpetuate the traditional "cop" image. It is likely that this provision will include redefinition of the role of the general duty police officer to move it more toward the "community manager" concept. (18)

At the chief executive end of the spectrum, 2034 will probably see
improvements in two major areas - selection and training. Currently,
the typical qualifications for the position of Police Chief are not an advanced degree in public or business administration coupled with extensive police command experience in a variety of settings. The essential
qualifications of the successful applicant include being born and raised
in the community he serves and having spent all his working life in that
one police department. While some lateral movement does occur at the
chief level, parochialism is the rule. Compared with the English and
the French systems, we do little to prepare police chiefs for their
responsibilities. Because the job is the most difficult in the department, the position of police chief thus is usually the weakest link. By
2034, the United States will surely have its equivalent of Britain's
Bramshill, (19) providing adequate management and administrative
training to equip chiefs and other managers to use modern management
approaches such as long-term planning.

What operational systems will be utilized in 2034?

Police agencies are at the beginning of a revolution in operating
practices. The question is not whether the revolution will occur, but
how long a period is required for percolation. Research has shown the
opportunity and the need for a radical restructuring of police field service delivery systems. Three studies, two funded by the Federal Government and one by a private foundation, are particularly significant. The
Kansas City Preventive Patrol experiment, (20) despite some methodological limitations, (21) has cast significant doubt on the efficacy of
traditional preventive patrol as it is now practiced. The key words in
this sentence are "as it is now practiced." There may be a high level
of manpower saturation where crime is deterred or displaced, and a
low level where criminal activity is encouraged. But the study suggests
that, within these parameters, manpower variations are irrelevant.
The study indicates that what is usually done now by police departments
under the heading of preventive patrol does not produce the results
traditionally expected, and that police commanders have far greater
flexibility in deploying resources than they usually suppose. The Response Time Study, (22) conducted in the same city, reconceptualizes
response time, indicating that police response time alone is an insufficient concept. Citizen mobilization (the time between observation of
the crime and reporting it to the police) is a relatively large part of the
total response continuum. It also questions the belief that police departments must be geared up to respond rapidly to all calls. Rapid
response does not have great significance in making apprehensions in
most cases, and citizen satisfaction is more a function of expectations
(which can be affected by the police agency itself) than of quick response.
The study of the Criminal Investigation Process, (23) conducted by the

Rand Corporation, did not surprise informed police administrators, but it did question the popular conception of the Great Investigator. Among its conclusions: the most important determinant of whether a case is solved is the information gathered by the immediately responding patrol officers; of the remaining cases that are solved, the solutions usually come from routine police procedures. While the study's recommendations may have stretched beyond its data base, (24) the conclusions seem accurate. Taken together, these studies should result eventually in a complete rethinking and restructuring of field operations, as cities continue to experience financial pressures and as the public realizes the enormous cost of law enforcement. (25) Some departments are already beginning to change: for example, with directed patrol, (26) split force patrol (27) and the greater use of anti-crime (or blending and decoy) strategies. (28)

The direction of the operational revolution will probably be toward wider use of the systems approach in police operations. This will involve more complete and effective analysis of police problems, and identification and evaluation of alternative solutions. Illustrative examples include approaches that focus on policing prostitution not merely by arresting prostitutes but by concentrating on pimps and appropriate hotel owners; that focus mainly not on burglars but on fences; and that rely not only on preventive patrol as a method of reducing auto thefts but also on urging regulations requiring improved auto anti-theft devices, and so on. A systems-oriented approach will require, among other things, upgrading of both the police crime analysis and intelligence functions. (29) It will also include the development of more purposeful police activity: a possibility is a system for working officers similar to Management-by-Objectives but without the usual concomitant paperwork. Operations will have developed to the point where a differential response pattern will be used. Rather than responding to all calls as if they were of equal urgency, police will use a structured plan. Not all police calls require equal types of response. Some require the emergency "sirens and lights" dispatch of a police unit; some can be handled on a planned delay basis ("An officer will be there in 30 minutes.") Some can be handled over the telephone and others can involve a visit by the callers to headquarters. Perhaps some patrol officers will operate like insurance agents or detectives, responding to appointments and operating from desks rather than from cars prowling aimlessly throughout the community.

What management systems will be used in 2034?

Here the stirrings of change are being felt, but the shape of the change has not yet been adequately formulated. In the operations area, grounbreaking studies have been completed, but the management area remains uncharted, and thus the direction of changes is difficult to

predict. A number of police chiefs realize that the traditional reactive
management-by-crisis mode of police administration is inadequate, a
fact that will become even more apparent as the changes in police operations demand accompanying managerial adjustments; but the strongest
pressure for change will come when a sound police program performance
system is developed. (31) Currently the police community does not have
a meaningful system for evaluating police programs, and the result is
that police chiefs are essentially unaccountable for the quality of their
agency's performance beyond handling the public relations aspects of
sensational incidents or other problems that get out of hand.

Traditional police management textbooks owe much to the mechan-
istic view of management represented by POSDCORB, (32) discussions
of organization charts and the like. This is changing as instructors incorporate behaviorist and psychological views in police management
courses and police organizations are increasingly examined, not only
in terms of structure, but also in terms of the work-flow and the human
perspectives. Discussions about Theories X and Y and references to
Alderfer are now not uncommon in police administration. (33) New
management concepts are indeed available and will be increasingly
tailored to the police situation. An example is the matrix approach,
where department-wide policy is determined by teams of officers cutting across divisions and ranks. Also appearing anecdotally on the hor-
izon is a perspective of police management as an exercise in "interest-
group politics," along the lines described for government as a whole by
David Truman (34) in 1952 and subsequently widely discussed by others
like Lowi. (35) Perhaps the police management theory of 2034 will have
effectively synthesized these approaches. Certainly, it seems necessary.

As the foregoing indicates, police service should not be expected
to remain static. Law enforcement in 2034 should - and probably will
be - significantly different. Our grandchildren will probably look at
police organizations of 1977 with much the same wry amusement as we
have when we look at pictures of Victorian cops with tall hats and wide
moustaches. In 2034, however, the gap will be much wider than it is
between Victorian cops and police today. The 2034 projection in this
chapter may be viewed as unimaginative. It envisions no robots, nor
the inevitable computer wonders, for example, nor does it discuss
possible radical changes in the environment of police work: increasing
urbanization toward the world city, and the like. In looking toward the
future of law enforcement, this chapter has been deliberately conservative. The point is that, even assuming minimal change, dramatic advances should be expected and sought.

To reach such a level of achievement by 2034 will require significant advances in both research and action programs. While Federal
and State governments have no monopoly on either widsom or ability,

it would take a bold prophet to proclaim that police agencies and local authorities have the objectivity and capability to provide self-leadership. The change must be effected in (and by) local government, but it will require a driving force, an entity dedicated to forward movement and capable of providing appropriate leadership and support. Bootstrapping into the future is likely to slow law enforcement progress and risk the failure of achieving the more effective performance that more rapid change makes possible.

The questions, then, are whether and how State governments can give the required leadership. In the area of research, it seems inappropriate to have 50 entities attempting to sponsor or undertake research. Such an approach is possible, but it exacts a price in terms of the inefficiency of inevitable duplication and the ineffectiveness of a lack of national focus in research activity. In the area of implementation, it would be very logical and within the Constitutional framework, where localities are creatures of State government, for the states to take the lead. Given the comprehensive statewide planning on the lines contemplated in the 1968 Act, there is no substitute for effective State action in securing the implementation of criminal justice improvements. But the fact is - in both research and implementation - that no state has yet provided this leadership. This is reflected in the report of the Department of Justice study group (36) and elsewhere. (37) "Few states and local governments planned for all criminal justice expenditures at their respective levels. " (38) System-wide criminal justice planning, the report notes, has not taken place at the State level, "except on a very limited scale and only on an exception basis. " (39)

In the interests of effective law enforcement, the Federal Government should continue (and improve) its supportive activities until the states provide the appropriate leadership. Even if State-level research were significantly upgraded, the central government should continue (and improve) its research activity. As long as enough crucial states fail to provide leadership in fostering and persuading local agencies to improve their operations, continued and improved Federal activity would also seem desirable. The principal Federal thrust should be to encourage and persuade the states to take a more positive leadership stance; the Federal role would then be to support State initiatives in the reform area by such means as program, organizational, personnel and financial assistance.

This chapter has examined the future role of the Federal (or State) government in the crime control process from the viewpoint of the future of law enforcement. Other perspectives are, of course, feasible. One could begin by analyzing existing arrangements to determine strengths and weaknesses and then suggesting improvements. This is typical of many contemporary discussions about the Federal or State

government role in the crime control process, because the experience
of LEAA has been so extensively debated (40) in Congress and in the
press. This chapter has avoided this well-trodden path. Such discussions, overly influenced by present problems, often lead to the creation
of the horseless carriage rather than the automobile.

The context of this discussion has been law enforcement, concerning
only the government's responsibility for the crime control function - in
other words, the specialist viewpoint. Another discussion might choose
to consider the overall pattern of governmental involvement in the full
range of program areas such as housing, energy, environmental affairs
and other domestic issues. (41)

The future role of the Federal Government in the crime control
process undoubtedly will be resolved in the general context of issues
of intergovernmental relations and (except to the extent that special
circumstances can be demonstrated for crime control) in response to
general basic principles and pressures. Clearly, this is a valid approach, but it, too, has been widely discussed. (42)

In looking at future improvement opportunities, rather than being
obsessed with past mistakes or enmeshed in the larger question of intergovernmental fiscal relations, it is possible to put the Federal role in
sharper focus. The question is not whether the Federal role should be
abolished; rather, it is "How can it be strengthened? How can it be
increased in both quality and quantity? How can the Federal government energize the other levels of government - and, in particular,
persuade the states to fulfill their leadership role in implementation?"
Without appropriate leadership, the types of change described in this
chapter is likely to be unrealized. The prospect then would be a deterioration of the crime situation, with a corresponding decline in the
quality of American styles of living, a prospect the nation would be
reluctant to contemplate.

NOTES AND REFERENCES

1. See Gerald Caplan, "Reflections on the Nationalization of Crime, 1964-1968," Law and Social Order (1973), pp. 583-635.

2. President's Commission on Law Enforcement and Administration of Justice, The Challenge of Crime in a Free Society, (Washington, D. C.: U. S. Government Printing Office, 1967), p. 291.

3. The establishment of the Law Enforcement Assistance Administration in 1968 followed the creation by the Federal Government in 1965 of the Office of Law Enforcement Assistance (OLEA) and the 1967 President's Commission on Law Enforcement and Administration of Justice.

4. The functions of LEAA were to (a) support statewide criminal justice planning by the creation of State planning agencies (b) supply State and local governments with block grants to improve their criminal justice systems (c) to make discretionary grants (d) to sponsor and evaluate research and (e) supply money for the training and education of criminal justice personnel.

5. The Department of Justice Study Group, Restructuring the Justice Department's Program of Assistance to State and Local Governments for Crime Control and Criminal Justice System Improvement (Washington, D. C.: U. S. Department of Justice, June 1977). The study group recommended a major restructuring of the program designed to (a) refocus the national research and development role into a coherent strategy of basic and applied research and systematic program development, testing, demonstration and evaluation and (b) replace the present block/formula portion of the program with a simpler program of direct assistance to State and local governments with an innovative feature that would allow State and local governments to use the direct assistance funds as "matching funds" to buy into the implementation of national program models that would be developed through the refocused national research and development program.

6. Aaron Wildawsky, The Politics of the Budgetary Process (Boston, Massachusetts: Little, Brown & Co. , 1964, 1974), p. xxiii.

7. see President's Commission on Law Enforcement and Administration of Justice, The Challenge of Crime in a Free Society, (Wash-

ington, D. C.:   U. S. Government Printing Office, February 1967),
p. 91 for the 40, 000 figure. See the Law Enforcement Assistance
Administration, Criminal Justice Agencies, (Washington, D. C.:
U. S. Government Printing Office) for figures of 17,464 general
purpose and 987 special police agencies. The 17,464 includes
all major enforcement agencies, including state police, separate
bureaus of identification, county sheriffs and police departments
and municipal and township police departments. Special police
includes park rangers, harbor police, housing police and campus
police. Richard W. Velde, former LEAA Administrator, indicates
that the error between the 40, 000 and the approximately 17, 000
figures was clerical. A statistician had a column entitled "jurisdictions with no police officers, " and this was added to the number
of police agencies.

8.   Elinor Ostrum, et al., Policing Metropolitan America, (Washing-
      ton, D. C.: U. S. Government Printing Office, 1977).

9.   e. g., see Daniel L. Skoler, Organizing the Non-System (Lexing-
      ton, Massachusetts: Lexington Books, 1977).

10.   Remarks delivered at a Police Foundation conference on "Upgrading
      the Police, " April 1976. On this occasion, Commissioner DiGrazia
      also referred to police chiefs as "pet rocks. "

11.   Herman Goldstein, in his Policing a Free Society (Cambridge,
      Massachusetts: Ballinger Publishing Company, 1977) argues that
      "the whole reform movement in policing has been short-sighted
      in focusing almost exclusively on improving the police establish-
      ment without having given adequate attention to some serious
      underlying problems that grow out of the basic arrangements for
      policing in our society. " Among the publications which cast light
      on the functions of policing are James Q. Wilson, Varieties of
      Police Behavior (Cambridge, Massachusetts: Harvard University
      Press, 1968); Egon Bittner, The Functions of the Police in Modern
      Society (Washington, D. C.: U. S. Government Printing Office,
      1970); A. Neiderhoffer, Behind the Shield (Garden City, New York:
      Anchor Books, 1967); Al Reiss, The Police and the Public (New
      Haven, Connecticut: Yale University Press, 1971); and Ray R.
      Roberg, The Changing Police Role (San Jose, California: Justice
      Systems Development, Inc., 1976).

12. The acual percentage of time spent by police officers on crime-
    related activity clearly varies by geography and by time, and there
    are definitional and measurement problems in allocating police
    time among crime-related and non-crime related activities.
    Among the numbers which are given are 32 percent (President's
    Commission on Law Enforcement and Administration of Justice,
    Task Force Report: Police (Washington, D.C.: U.S. Government
    Printing Office, 1967), p. 121, less than 30 percent (The National
    Commission on Productivity, Opportunities for Improving Produc-
    tivity in Police Services, National Commission on Productivity,
    Washington, D.C., 1973, p. 27.) See Reiss, Albert J., The Po-
    lice and the Public (New Haven, Connecticut: Yale University,
    1971), p. 96 for his report on the Chicago Police Department that
    "only 3 percent of all time spent on patrol involves handling what
    is officially regarded as a criminal matter."

13. Contrary to some impressions, there is a body of helpful research
    in the police area. For example, see the account in David J.
    Farmer, "Fact v. Fact: A Selective View of Police Research in
    the United States," The Police Journal (Vol. XLIX, No. 2, April-
    June 1976), pp. 104-113.

14. For a general account, see Herbert Edelhertz, The Nature, Impact
    and Prosecution of White-Collar Crime (Washington, D.C.: U.S.
    Government Printing Office, 1970).

15. e.g., see San Diego Police Department, Community Profiling and
    Police Patrol: Final Staff Report of the Community Profile Develop-
    ment Project (San Diego, California: San Diego Police Department,
    1974). The Community Profile project represents a community-
    oriented approach to policing that emphasizes increasing the indi-
    vidual officer's awareness and understanding of his community and
    improving officer response to area problems. An experimental
    group of 24 patrol officers and 3 patrol superiors was given train-
    ing in methods of community analysis, decision making, patrol goal
    setting, community organization and interpersonal relations. An
    experimental and a control group spent ten months working alternating
    shift schedules on the same group of patrol beats. The major con-
    clusion of the project was that the experimental group changed their
    attitudes about patrol work and their communities. The experiment
    was however flawed by some evaluation problems, e.g., turnover
    problems in the group, lack of a community attitude survey, and the
    experimental group may have been provided with handi-talkies and
    overtime pay.

16. see Richard D. Knudten, Victims and Witnesses: Their Experiences
    with Crime and the Criminal Justice System (Washington, D. C.:
    U. S. Government Printing Office, 1977). This study documents
    victim and witness problems, and discusses implications for policy.
    Among the new approaches discussed for meeting victim/witness
    needs are victim reporting fees, equitable witness fees, and the
    concept of an office of justice advocate. A conclusion of the study
    is that "extensive victim/service programs are not needed by most
    victims and witnesses. What is needed is greater knowledge about
    the coordination of already existing community services, increased
    public and private agency willingness to service these client groups,
    designation of responsibility to some person or group for victim/
    witness concerns (probably with legal power), lessened competition
    among the various elements constituting the criminal justice system,
    and increased desire by system operatives to respond to victim/
    witness problems. "

17. David J. Farmer, "Education and Practice - Operational Relations
    and the Development of Quality Control: Remarks, " The Police
    Yearbook (Gaithersburg, Maryland: International Association of
    Chiefs of Police, 1976), p. 227-28.

18. David J. Bordua, "Comments on Police-Community Relations, "
    Law Enforcement Science and Technology II (Port City Press,
    1969), p. 118. The reference is to police as "community managers
    and monitors of social change. "

19. Bramshill is the staff training college for the British police service.

20. George L. Kelling, et al. The Kansas City Preventive Patrol Ex-
    periment: A Summary Report and a Technical Report (Washington,
    D. C.: The Police Foundation, 1974). The Kansas City Preventive
    Patrol experiment has cast serious doubt on the effectiveness of
    traditional preventive patrol. In the words of former Kansas City
    Police Chief Joseph McNamara, it has shown that "routine patrol
    in marked police cars has little value in preventing crime or making
    citizens feel safe, " and that the substantial amount of time spent on
    routine preventive patrol might be devoted to more productive assign-
    ments.

    A 15-beat segment of the city was used for the experiment. Five
    of the beats were designated as reactive: officers responded only
    to calls for service and preventive patrol was discontinued. Five
    matched beats were control areas: preventive patrol was maintained

at normal levels. Five were designated as proactive areas: preventive patrol was increased up to three times the normal levels. Victimization surveys were conducted to measure unreported crime. Community surveys were undertaken to assess citizen and business satisfaction. Reported crime and other data were analyzed. In general, the differences between the three types of beats (i. e., the three levels of patrol coverage) were not significant in terms of reported and unreported crime, of citizen satisfaction, and of citizens' perceptions of their own security.

21. It should be noted that the validity of the Kansas City Preventive Patrol experiment has been questioned. The most significant criticisms concern the location of the cars withdrawn from reactive beats when not responding to calls for service; the small sizes of the beats, presenting uncertainty concerning public perceptions of variations in patrol levels; and the small sample sizes utilized in the surveys. (For an assessment of the study, see the report of the National Evaluation Program Phase I study, A Review and Assessment of Traditional Preventive Patrol (Philadelphia, Pennsylvania: University City Science Center, 1975).

22. Bieck, William, et al, Response Time Analysis report, Executive Summary (Kansas City, Missouri: Kansas City Police Department, 1977).
Bieck, William et al, Ibid, Vol. 1, Methodology.
Bieck, William et al, Ibid, Vol. II, Analysis.
Through the use of civilian observers, analyses of the communications center's tapes, and interviews with victims and witnesses, the project has assembled a wealth of data. At the time of writing, only the data on some 949 Part I crimes have been analyzed, and the above reports refer to the Part I figures alone. The remaining data is on Part II crime calls, potential crime calls (e. g., disturbance, prowler, suspicious persons), and general service calls. Unlike earlier studies of police response time (e. g., Isaacs, 1967: Furstenberg, 1971) this study did not rely upon officer self-reporting for the data. This and the meticulous methodology give significant confidence in the results.

The results of the Part I data analysis include the findings that: arrests occurred in only a small percentage of all Part I crimes: rapid citizen reporting had a greater effect on suspect apprehension than did police response; police responded faster to calls involving serious injuries than those with minor injuries, although citizens took longer to report incidents involving serious injuries than

incidents involving non-serious injuries; citizen mobilization time
was the major determinant of witness availability; in 76 percent of
all cases, citizens encountered problems in reporting crime to
the police; in 75 percent of all cases, citizens were responsible
for the most common cause of delays: many talked to at least one
other person before calling the police; and citizens did not use
special emergency numbers for reporting only emergency calls.

Among the implications which the authors draw from their findings
are:

● Because of the time citizens take to report crimes, the application of technological innovations and human resources to reducing police reponse time will have negligible impact on
crime outcomes.

● If procedures can be developed to discriminate accurately between emergency and non-emergency calls, more productive
response-related outcomes can be achieved if coordinated
with patrol resource allocation.

● Direct rapid response to robbery incidents by other than dispatched officers may be less effective in achieving response-
related arrests than interception patrol away from the location
at which a robbery occurred.

23. The Criminal Investigation Process (Santa Monica, California:
The Rand Corporation, 1976). See also Greenwood, Peter W. et
al, The Criminal Investigation Process (Santa Monica, California:
Rand Corporation, 1977). Among the principal findings are: more
than half of all serious reported crime receives no more than superficial attention from investigators; an investigator's time is mainly
taken up in work on cases that experience indicates will not be
solved; for solved cases, the investigator spends more time on
post-arrest processing rather than the pre-arrest phase; the single
most important determinant of whether a case will be solved is the
information the victim supplies to the immediately-responding
patrol officer; of solved cases in which the offender is not identifi-
able at the time of the initial report, almost all are cleared as a
result of routine police procedures; and in many departments, investigators do not consistently and thoroughly document the key
evidentiary facts, with untoward consequences for prosecutors.

24. See National Institute of Law Enforcement and Criminal Justice, The Criminal Investigation Process: A Dialogue on Research Findings (Washington, D. C.: U. S. Government Printing Office, 1977).

25. Many still think of a police car as costing something like $3,000. This is incorrect. It takes about 5 officers to staff a police car round-the-clock seven days a week all year round, because individual officers do not usually work more than 40 hours per week and they have vacations and holidays. Considering salaries and fringe benefits, a one-person patrol car thus cost over $100,000. A two-officer patrol car costs not $3,000, but in excess of $200,000.

26. Unlike traditional patrol where officers patrol their beats entirely at their own discretion, directed patrol is structured preventive and apprehension activity - involving goal-setting and task assignment by management. Rather than a mode of merely responding to problems, the emphasis is on planned and purpose-oriented activity. See William G. Gay, Improving Patrol Productivity, Volume I Routine Patrol (Washington, D. C.: U. S. Government Printing Office, 1977), pp. 13-14.

27. Split-force patrol is an approach in patrol specialization, based on separating the call-for-service response and the crime prevention functions of police patrol. This contrasts with the traditional generalist pattern whereby police patrol officers handle all aspects of patrol. See James M. Tien, An Evaluation Report of An Alternative Approach in Police Patrol: The Wilmington Split-Force Experiment, Public Systems Evaluation (Cambridge, Massachusetts, March 1977). The experiment showed that the split-force approach in Wilmington caused significant increases in both call-for-service response and arrest productivity and for an increase in police professionalism and accountability. The report notes that the very act of forming a dedicated prevention-oriented unit leads to more efficiency, and it attributes the increase in arrest-related productivity primarily to the immediate incident-oriented investigation conducted as a result of the split-force approach. Among the other findings is that there may be an opportunity for police agencies to manage the demand of the public for police services - "inasmuch as 86% of all calls for service are non-critical in nature and citizen satisfaction is a function of expectation." The Wilmington Bureau of Police is now experimenting with this notion of managing the public demand for police services. For another form of split-

force, see also James M. Tien, An Evaluation Report of the Worcester Crime Impact Program, Public Systems Evaluation (Cambridge, Massachusetts, 1975). Worcester utilized civilians who assumed traditional police roles, and the civilians (police service aides) were deployed on patrol to respond to service calls and to assist police officers. Thus, this civilianized split-force approach involves the civilians focusing on service calls and the police on the more serious criminal-type calls.

28. See Stephen Schack, Improving Patrol Productivity, Volume II, Specialized Patrol (Washington, D. C.: U. S. Government Printing Office, 1977) for an excellent overview and see Halper, Andrew et al., New York City Police Department Street Crime Unit (Washington, D. C.: U. S. Government Printing Office, 1975), for an account of the New York experience. Blending and decoy are the two principal approaches used in anti-crime or casual clothes squads. Rather than uniformed high-visibility patrol, officers wear street clothes to blend into situations to adopt disguises to serve as decoy victims. A distinguishing feature of the New York operation is the relative size of the anti-crime operation in relation to the total patrol force. The approach has been very productive in terms of felony arrests. However, at the time of writing, a comprehensive and independent evaluation has not been made of the strategy, considering not only felony arrest productivity but also factors such as citizen satisfaction.

29. See Hobart G. Reinier, Crime Analysis in Support of Patrol, National Evaluation Program Phase 1 Summary Report (Washington, D. C.: U. S. Government Printing Office, 1977). The problem lies not only in the undeveloped state-of-the-art of both crime analysis and intelligence, but also in the problem of communicating the results of such analyses in a timely and useable fashion to operating personnel.

30. A comprehensive study of alternative police strategies for responding to calls for service is being undertaken by the City of Birmingham Police Department, and an experiment in this area is being conducted by the City of Wilmington Bureau of Police. Other departments are also experimenting with non-traditional methods for responding to calls for service, e. g., Portland, Oregon.

31. David J. Farmer, "Fact v. Fact: A Selective View of Police Research in the United States," The Police Journal, vol. XLIX, no. 2, April-June 1976), pp. 108-109. Among the deficiencies of

systems relying on crime and clearance rates is that, as is widely
understood, they take no account of unreported crime; they are
subject to manipulation and classification problems, and they lump
together major and minor crimes under the same headings. In
fact, they distort activity because they emphasize arrests. This
leads to neglect of such factors as recovering stolen property,
and gives no consideration to elements such as the fear of crime.
A sound performance measurement system must utilize the concept
of indicators - on the same lines as economists use in describing
the performance of the economy. It should also collect information on citizen perceptions of safety and of police performance, as
additional indicators.

32. As is in Wilson, O.W. and Roy McLaren, Police Administra-
    tion, McGraw-Hill, New York, New York, 1977, p. 60, "Adminis-
    tration has been classically defined by Luther Gulick in his famous
    acronym POSBCORB, which stands for the initial letters in Plan-
    ning, Organizing, Staffing (or personnel management), Directing,
    Coordinating, Reporting and Budgeting. In a text on police admin-
    istration, naturally these functions of administration and manage-
    ment are fundamental. "

33. see Huse, Edgar F. and James L. Bowditch, Behavior in Organiza-
    tions: A Systems Approach to Managing, Addison-Welsey, Reading,
    Mass. , 1973.

34. David B. Truman, The Governmental Process: Political Interests
    and Public Opinion (New York: Alfred A. Knopf, 1951, 1971).

35. Theodore J. Lowi, The End of Liberalism (New York: W.W. Norton
    and Company, Inc. , 1969).

36. The Department of Justice Study Group, op. cit. The report indi-
    cates (p. 10) that "the lessons of the past nine years of the LEAA
    program have been mixed. " On the positive side, for example,
    the Group quoted the report by the Advisory Commission on Inter-
    governmental Relations (Safe Streets Act Reconsidered: The Block
    Grant Experience 1968 - 1975, Washington, D. C. , 1977, pp. 187-
    190) that block grant funds have supported many useful criminal
    justice activities and projects and that the block grant assistance
    has established a process for crime control and improvement of
    the administration of justice. However, it does note that system-
    wide criminal justice planning has not been taking place at the
    state level, except on a limited scale. "Few state and local govern-

ments planned for all criminal justice expenditures at their respective levels. Most planned only for the 3 percent to 5 percent
of their expenditures that were derived from the LEAA program"
(p. 7). Even the planning done for the use of the LEAA block funds
often amounted to little more than a paper-work exercise required
by statute and guidelines in order to qualify for the funds. Further,
"the national leadership role for LEAA in the research and development of new and innovative techniques for responding to the crime
problem and for possible transfer to State and local governments
simply has not materialized on the scale envisioned under the 1968
Act. "

37. For example, see Twentieth Century Fund Task Force (Law En-
      forcement: The Federal Role, Twentieth Century Fund, New York,
      N. Y. , 1976) and the series of reports produced by the Center for
      National Security Studies (Sarah Carey, Law and Disorder, 1969;
      Law and Disorder II, 1970; Law and Disorder III, 1973 and Law
      and Disorder IV, 1976.)

38. The Department of Justice Study Group, op. cit. , p. 7.

39. Ibid. , p. 7.

40. See footnote 36 and 37 for references.

41. Other context choices include the decision whether to view the
      discussion from the viewpoint of the police (or other element of
      the criminal justice system) or the criminal justice system as a
      whole.

42. e. g. , see Advisory Commission on Intergovernmental Relations,
      Fiscal Balance in the American Federal System (Washington, D. C. :
      U. S. Government Printing Office, 1967), or James A. Maxwell,
      Financing State and Local Governments (Washington, D. C. : The
      Brookings Institute, 1969). Another entertaining book on the
      subject is Henry S. Reiss, Revenue-Sharing: Crutch or Catalyst
      for State and Local Governments (New York: Praeger Publishers,
      1970). Involved are such questions as - Will the Federal Govern-
      ment continue to dominate the lion's share of the country's tax
      resources, while the localities (manacled by state fiscal restraints
      such as those on property taxation) bear such a large proportion
      of the problems? Will the fiscal-needs imbalance be adjusted by
      some form of revenue sharing? Will the mechanism for money
      transfer between the layers of government be improved? Will the

relative roles of the several layers of government remain as at present? Will the system be more rational than at present? What will, or can, be done to rationalize the crazy-quilt pattern of local government - and in particular, the proliferation of governments in the metropolitan areas? Within the setting of interest group pressures and in response to the realities of accelerating problems in the variety of domestic areas, such overall questions will be addressed.

II

The Private Role:
Special Police

5 Private Security and Police Relations

Robert A. Hair

It is no small task to project the role of the security profession beyond 1984. However, I predict that the private security forces will be recognized as an integral part of the criminal justice system, maintaining a close working relationship with public law enforcement agencies.

To bolster and better understand such a statement, it is necessary to review, analyze and evaluate the present role, direction, and the contributions of private security to society. It is estimated that there are approximately eight hundred thousand people engaged in private security. It is projected that at its present rate of growth the private security sector will employ 1,400,000 people, as compared to 750,000 in public law enforcement. (1)

The estimated 450,000 law enforcement officers in the United States at the present time has not diminished the need for private security. The private sector continues to grow at a phenomenal pace, and has developed into a multi-billion dollar crime prevention industry, serving not only private enterprise, but in many instances the community as well. In 1976 approximately 6.6 billion dollars were spent on private guards, an increase of 46% in five years. (2)

Some of the basic reasons for this rapid expansion of the security industry:

- Public police overburdened and underbudgeted;
- Increasing business losses to crime;
- Increasing insurance rates;
- Federal government security requirements;
- Increasing use of electronic security devices;
- Increase in corporate and private income;
- Increased awareness of criminal activity.

113

In essence, most of the growth can be attributed to the increase in crime throughout the United States.

The indicated crime clock and Crime Index total taken from the 1976 Federal Bureau of Investigation's Uniform Crime Reports graphically and dramatically demonstrate the necessity of developing bolder and more innovative approaches in the effort to reduce crime. (See appendices A & B.)

> One holds that private security services effectively complement the public police by providing security and other related services in areas and situations where the public police do not, either because public police are not given adequate resources or because they are legally constrained from doing so. This view also holds that current controls and regulations are adequate since private police seldom abuse their powers.

> The second view holds that the private security industry feeds on fear and provides ineffective services by untrained, low quality personnel who are a danger to the public, and who in fact abuse their limited powers. This view also holds that current controls on and regulation of private police are inadequate. (3)

Experience in both the public and private sectors leads me to believe the correct view at the present time is somewhere between the aforementioned views. The private security field, particularly at the guard level, is in dire need of increased training and improved personnel screening procedures. These blatant deficiencies should not distort one's perspective to the extent that one fails to recognize the valuable role private security presently plays, as well as the increased role it can play in the future in the war on crime. It cannot be denied that were private security to be eliminated from the scene, it would make the law enforcement agency's job much more difficult, and result in increased crime and increased taxes to support the additional law enforcement officers that would be required to fill the void. There appears to be a great deal of criticism directed at the deficiencies of private security, but little action is taken to help correct them. With proper government control, assistance and direction, the private security sector could be turned into a tremendous asset to law enforcement and the community. There is a wealth of energetic, dedicated, and talented individuals in the private security profession, many of them former law enforcement officers anxious to be of service to the community and to the police. Numerous communities are now utilizing private security patrols on foot and in cars to supplement the thin blue line maintained by police. If the present trend of cutting back police

budgets, manpower and equipment requirements continues in the face
of rising crime, it will become imperative that improved means of
utilizing the services of private security be explored to compensate
for such cutbacks.

Crime prevention efforts must be a cooperative venture, not a
competitive one. Improved bridges of communication must be built
between the public and private sectors to explore, study, analyze,
evaluate and develop improved methods of utilizing the resources of
the respective sectors.

For example, having been assigned to numerous parades, stadi-
um activities, and other special events in New York City, where large
numbers of police were taken from their communities to police the
special events, I am well aware that this procedure resulted in less
protection for the communities from which they came. Consideration
should be given to studying the feasibility of developing a program
whereby private security officers could be hired to police such special
events and be supervised by police personnel. Possibly this might be
a less expensive method of policing such events, and at the same time,
one that would not deprive the communities of protection. It should
be noted that the policing of such events does not require a great deal
of skill, and, with proper training, this task should not be beyond the
capabilities of the security officer. Law enforcement agencies, in
developing plans for the future, must consider the role of the private
security sector - a force 800,000 strong cannot be ignored.

The key to reversing crime in the United States is cooperation.
The concept of public security is such that no individual can go it alone.
Below is an excerpt from an address given by Chief Don R. Derning,
past president of the International Association of Chiefs of Police, to
the National Burglar Fire Alarm Association. Chief Derning very
clearly states the importance of developing a cooperative crime-fighting effort between the public and private sectors:

> We need not only the concerted efforts of the public, the govern-
> ment, and the police, we need the help of everyone involved in
> public and private security sectors. We must find ways to free
> law enforcement officers from routine security tasks by encour-
> aging the business community to take more responsible measures
> in securing their premises. Police are in the marketing business
> too. The service they have to sell is public safety and security.
> Where your services (private security businessmen) are mandated
> by contractual agreement, ours are mandated by constitutional
> and legislative laws. Crime is, in every sense of the word,
> domestic war... And its control can only be met by the com-
> bined resources of all our private and public protective agencies ...

Having explored the general direction the private security field
is following, I should like to jump ahead in time and, based upon present trends in security, make the following predictions relating to
security in 1984:

The quality of personnel will be greatly improved due to improved
selection, training, uniform regulations, licensing procedures
and increased competition which will force fly-by-nighters out of
business.

There will be a preponderance of former law enforcement personnel in the private security sector, bringing about an excellent
mix of law enforcement and private security expertise and understanding.

There will be joint, cooperative, coordinated crime prevention
programs which will be commonplace between the public and
private police.

Security consultants will work with architects to build security
into new buildings.

Communities will hire private security forces in toto to police
their communities.

In urban areas there will be a large increase in block associations,
both residential and business, utilizing the services of the private
security sector to patrol their areas.

There will be an expansion of the perimeter patrol concept by the
private patrol sector. Liaison officers assigned from both the
public and private sectors will work together on mutual problems
and their solutions.

There will be improved required training standards for guard
personnel based on a uniform training law throughout the country.

The Federal Government will subsidize the training and possibly
the equipping of private security forces where they are assisting
in the protection of the community.

Many colleges will offer a four-year undergraduate degree in
Industrial Security, with some offering graduate degrees.

Industry will demand that top-level security personnel possess
degrees in Security.

There will be an increase in the number of private security officers deputized with some form of Peace Officer power.

Communities will form their own cooperative non-profit guard
agencies, and allow those in the cooperative to purchase the
services of guards as required.

Joint seminars and workshops between the public and private
sectors will be commonplace.

I realize that some of these predictions are bold and controversial, but I feel that the tenor of the times calls for daring action, and
when one takes such action controversy and criticism are almost a
certainty. The old way always seems better and more comfortable.

In view of the continued rise of crime against persons and property, it is obvious that the old routine approaches to stem the rising
tide of crime are failing. Police administrators must experiment
with new, fresh ideas and seek help from as many quarters as possible,
and certainly the most obvious and neglected source is the private
security sector. It is apparent that the public sector cannot cope with
the crime problem alone. Police administrators and City Managers
must rid themselves of negative attitudes and conservative approaches.
Greater imagination must be developed by the police administrators
of the nation. The British Poet Laureate, John Masefield, indicated
the value of imagination when he stated, "Man consists of body, mind
and imagination. His body is faulty, his mind untrustworthy, but his
imagination has made him remarkable." Imaginative approaches for
dealing with the crime problem must be jointly developed by both the
public and private sectors.

Even though some of the solutions offered appear way out at this
time, they should not be discarded. Jules Verne once said, "Anything
one man can imagine, other men can make real." Having spent the
better part of my life in both the public and private sectors, I am well
aware of the great talent that exists in both areas; a way must be found
to bring together these two areas of talent so that in the near future a
well-coordinated and cooperative venture against the criminal sector
will be a reality. If the future is to belong to the law-abiding citizen,
rather than the criminal, imaginative, bold approaches must be taken
to combat the criminal. In seeking proper direction for the future,
there is bound to be stumbling and even occasionally loss of direction,
and often severe criticism for sincere attempts at finding the right

direction. When this occurs, I suggest that the philosophy of an unknown author be kept in mind:

> It is not the critic who counts, not the man who points out how
> the strong man stumbled, or where the doer of deeds could have
> done them better.

> The credit belongs to the man who is actually in the arena; whose
> face is marred by dust and sweat and blood; who strives valiantly;
> who errs and comes short again and again; who knows the great
> enthusiasm, the great devotions; who spends himself in a worthy
> cause; who, at best knows in the end the triumph of high achieve-
> ment; and who, at the worst, if he fails, at least he fails while
> daring greatly.

Since the private security sector operated on a nationwide basis,
I suggest that the Federal Government enter the arena and come forth
with some imaginative and daring measures to create an improved
blend between the public law enforcement and private security sectors.
Briefly, I would like to make a case for the involvement of the Federal
Government with the private security sector.

Consider the cost of administering the criminal justice system
throughout the nation; consider the cost of making an arrest, prosecuting
the case, maintaining the correction parole and probation systems, etc.
Much of this cost could be eliminated by reducing the opportunities for
an individual to commit crime. The primary objective of the private
security sector is the prevention of crime by minimization of the opportunities for the commission of criminal acts.

The benefits to be derived from an effective private security sector are countless. It should be noted, however, that while the private
security sector is contributing to the criminal justice system in many
ways, such as guarding private and community property, conducting
criminal investigations, prosecuting criminals, cooperating with law
enforcement agencies, etc., the full potential of the private security
sector has not been realized. This is due to a lack of adequate selection, screening, and training programs, particularly at the lower level.

The crux of the problem is money. The contract security officer
is generally poorly paid, untrained, and unscreened because the client
who hires him does not want to pay the additional money required to get
a carefully selected, screened security officer, and the contract agencies cannot afford to conduct expensive training programs where low
bid is often the only criteria for getting a contract. It is essential that
the Federal Government recognize the importance of upgrading this
vast source of manpower which, if properly used, would be a tremendous

supplement to the manpower-starved law enforcement agencies through-out the country.

It is my belief that the Federal Government should, in the imme-diate future, fund the private security sector in the same manner as it has funded the public law enforcement sector in terms of training and education. Such funding can be justified on the basis of reducing crime, reducing the cost of administering the criminal justice system, and benefitting the general public.

It should be noted that the government already subsidizes seg-ments of private industry, such as railroads, buses, airlines, etc., where the interests of the public will be better served. Certainly no one can quarrel with the concept that controlled funding of the private security industry will benefit the interests of the public as much as the aforementioned funding. When one considers the continual rise in crime and the cost to society in terms of personal anguish and dollars, it be-comes mandatory that the Federal Government assume responsibility for bringing together, improving, and properly utilizing the resources available from both the public and private sectors in a joint, imaginative, coordinated effort to suppress crime.

It is recognized that at the present time private security forces are guilty of certain deficiencies, such as use of excessive force, false arrest and imprisonment, illegal search and seizure, impersonation of peace officers, trespass, invasion of privacy and dishonest, unethi-cal business practices. Not too long ago the public police were being charged with these deficiencies. A massive government-funding pro-gram which allotted monies for training and education programs for law enforcement officers, combined with restrictive legislation, did much to eliminate or reduce these evils. The National Advisory Com-mission on Criminal Justice Standards and Goals, Report on the Police, stated that "Remedies must be found for the ills that plague private po-lice. Their acceptance by public police as a productive force within the criminal justice system will be enhanced if standards of performance and regulatory controls are implemented..." (4) That improved stand-ards of performance and regulatory controls are needed to upgrade and enhance the image and efficiency of security forces cannot be disputed. The private security agencies themselves are in favor of such action. As a former member of The Private Security Advisory Council's Guards and Investigators Committee (Sponsored by U.S. Department of Justice Law Enforcement Assistance Administration) which was comprised of people in the private security sector, I am fully cogni-zant of such agencies' great concern to upgrade the security sector through the creation and implementation of proper standards and regu-latory controls.

The committee was created in response to concern over the qual-ity of services provided by private security guards and the lack of

screening, selection and training standards of <u>uniform</u> controls. In
short, the objective of the committee was the development of professional standards and the establishment of model <u>uniform</u> regulatory
legislation for the private security organizations and their personnel.
As a result of the committee's efforts, a model statute on the regulation of private security guard services was developed. (Copies of the
Report on Regulation of Private Security Services have been reproduced
for distribution by the American Society for Industrial Security, Suite
651, 2000 K Street, N.W., Washington, D.C. 20006.)

The preface of the report states that: "The purpose of the model
statute is to provide a mechanism designed to produce increased levels
of integrity, competence and performance of private security personnel
in order to safeguard the public from illegal, improper, or incompetent
actions and to serve to improve the crime prevention effectiveness of
security forces." (5) It should be noted that the proposed model statute
defines "private security" as encompassing both contract and proprietary
(in-house) security personnel and includes armored car and alarm response personnel, and recommends that any legislation with regard to
registration, minimum personnel standards, training requirements
and sanctions should apply in the areas of security mentioned above.
Thus it can be seen that the proposed statute gives a broad definition
to the term "private security."

In addressing the question of how best to implement the suggested
Model Private Security Screening and Regulatory Statute, the committee
suggested that the regulation of the private security industry be at the
State level. Regulation at this level will do much to eliminate proliferation, duplication and the inconsistencies present in the present patchwork regulation at local levels. It should be noted that this committee
and its report were the result of an earlier comprehensive report on
the private security industry published by the Rand Institute, <u>Private
Police in the United States</u>.

The formation of the committee and the resultant model statute
on private security are the Federal Government's response to the
numerous criticisms leveled at the private security industry by the
Rand Institute report. However, it my opinion, the response is not
strong enough. The Report on the Regulation of Private Security
Guard Services states: "Since 1972 The Private Security Advisory
Council of the United States Department of Justice, Law Enforcement
Assistance Administration (LEAA) has been meeting on a regular
basis to provide advisories to LEAA on the more effective utilization
of private security in the national strategy to reduce crime." (6)

As one associated with law enforcement and private security
sectors, I have failed to see any plans for the effective utilization of
private security in the national strategy to reduce crime. This is not

a criticism of the efforts of the Private Security Council, who work diligently to improve the private security field. But one must ask what happens to the advice of the Council when, many years after its inception, the private security field, for the most part, is still facing the same problems. There has been relatively little success in developing programs to coordinate the efforts and talents of both the public and private sectors. In addition, to date, very few states have adopted the suggested model statute on regulation of private security.

APPENDIX A
Crime Clocks, 1976

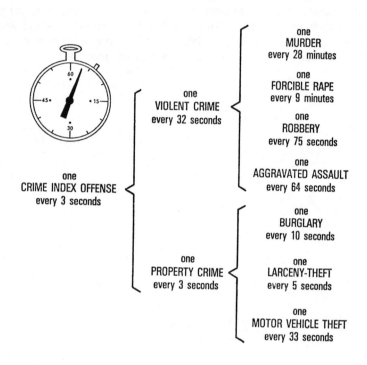

one
MURDER
every 28 minutes

one
FORCIBLE RAPE
every 9 minutes

one
VIOLENT CRIME
every 32 seconds

one
ROBBERY
every 75 seconds

one
AGGRAVATED ASSAULT
every 64 seconds

one
CRIME INDEX OFFENSE
every 3 seconds

one
BURGLARY
every 10 seconds

one
PROPERTY CRIME
every 3 seconds

one
LARCENY-THEFT
every 5 seconds

one
MOTOR VEHICLE THEFT
every 33 seconds

Source: Crime in the United States - Uniform Crime Reports,
          (Washington, D.C.: U.S. Government Printing Office, 1977).

APPENDIX B
Crime Index Total

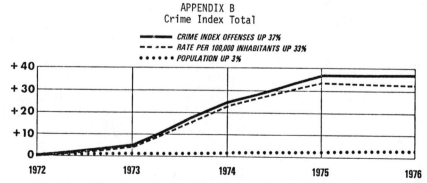

━━━━━ CRIME INDEX OFFENSES UP 37%
━ ━ ━ ━ RATE PER 100,000 INHABITANTS UP 33%
• • • • • POPULATION UP 3%

	1972	1973	1974	1975	1976

+40
+30
+20
+10
0

Source: Crime in the United States - Uniform Crime Reports,
          (Washington, D.C.: U.S. Government Printing Office, 1977).

NOTES AND REFERENCES

1. Louis J. Camin, "Some Projections For Business Security,"
    Security World 5: (2) 29, 1968.

2. "Making Crime Pay," Time Magazine, August 1976, p. 68.

3. James S. Kakalik and Sorrel Wildhorn, Private Police in the U.S.:
    Findings and Recommendations vol. 1 (Rand Corp., 1971), p. 1.

4. National Advisory Commission on Criminal Justice Standards,
    Goals, Report on Police (Washington, D.C.: U.S. Government
    Printing Office, January 1973), p. 147.

5. Private Security Advisory Council, "A Report on The Regulation
    of Private Security Guard Services including a Model Private
    Security Screening Regulatory Statute," May 1976, Preface ii.

6. "A Report on the Regulation of Private Security Guard Services,"
    Prepared by Private Security Advisory Council, May 1976.

6 Campus and School Security

John W. Powell

The fields of campus and school security are in many respects similar in that they serve a predominantly young population in an academic community dedicated to education. School security is still in its infancy but is somewhat following the same pattern as campus security during its early days. It is hoped that school security can profit by some of the mistakes made by campus security as it evolved from a low-level watchman-type operation to professional security status.

This chapter will attempt to analyze campus and school security separately, with the objective of foretelling the role each will play and the place each will occupy in the criminal justice system after 1984. It is hoped that this forecast will assist campus and school administrators in planning ahead for security needs. Preplanning to meet future security challenges cannot be stressed too strongly because any effective and successful security program must evolve over a period of time. A common failure on the part of administrators is to respond to immediate problems with crash security programs which are usually ineffective as well as expensive.

In prognosticating where campus and school security will be going after 1984, it is germane to set the tone by first describing where security has been and its present status and role. Therefore, the fields of campus and school security will be treated separately in order to provide an overview of the past and present, and to forecast what challenges each will face in the future. Finally, guidelines and direction for successfully meeting these challenges and to shape campus and school security for the mid 80s and beyond will be suggested.

CAMPUS SECURITY

Early in 1960, when I entered the campus security field as Director of Security and Associate Dean of Students at Yale University, I immediately realized that there was no reference material for me to utilize in building and reorganizing the Yale Campus Police Department (which later became known as the Yale University Police Department). There were absolutely no books, articles or other written material, and visits to several other campus security departments convinced me I would have to chart my own course to build an effective security approach at Yale.

I mention this at the outset in order to focus on the low-level and largely unprofessional approach to campus security, and on the almost complete lack of information regarding its past history and the role it has played. This was relatively few years ago, but during the interim the field of campus security has made rapid progress toward professionalism while still remaining sensitive to the academic community it serves. In my opinion, this professionalism and growth will continue in the 1980s. However, certain trends, which I will mention later, will develop with the passing years which will be dictated by the need to meet new and increasing challenges.

Let's take a look at where we have been in the campus field, where we are now and where we will be after 1984.

In the early 1900s there was very little need for campus security. During that era the university and college campus projected a "sanctuary" image that confined its population almost entirely to students, faculty and staff. The outside community did not flow onto the campus and many colleges and universities regarded themselves as autonomous islands isolated from the communities in which they were located. This sanctuary concept also fostered the feeling on campus that its population had to answer only to campus rules and regulations but not to municipal or state laws.

The sanctuary approach largely limited the campus to its own population, which resulted in very few crimes or incidents being perpetrated by outsiders. Crimes and security problems by the campus population itself were practically nonexistent. Student regulations were strict and discipline was handled by the dean of students on an across-the-desk basis. This type of no-nonsense discipline greatly reduced vandalism, thefts and similar security problems. Therefore, in the early 1900s there was very little need for anything resembling a professional security or campus law enforcement approach.

The closest thing to a security operation during this period was a watchman operation working out of the building and grounds depart-

ment. These often elderly gentlemen usually worked at night and
walked a prescribed route. They acted primarily as a fire watch,
tended or monitored the boilers, closed windows, put out lights,
checked doors to see if they were locked and otherwise insured that
campus property was protected.

The 1930s brought the end to prohibition, and about this time these
watchmen began to take on other functions related largely to student rules
and regulations. Some acted as "hall men" in student dormitories to
enforce curfews, restrictions on alcohol and strict parietal regulations.
Many of these watchmen acted as "on-the-spot deans" in that they
"preached" to the student offender but never reported him to the dean.
Gradually, they came to be known by students as "campus cops."
Alumni from this period speak about them with considerable nostalgia.
Looking back to my undergraduate days at Dartmouth College I recall
with affection our two "campus cops," "Spud" Bray and "Wormwood"
(I never knew his real name).

An excellent and interesting example of these enforcers of student
regulations who acted as adjuncts of the dean's office existed at Princeton University, where plain clothes proctors dealt exclusively with student problems and uniformed watchmen protected property. A common
piece of advice to freshmen students by upperclassmen was "don't
worry about uniformed officers but run like hell from a proctor." In-
cidently, Princeton still has proctors (traditions are hard to break in
Ivy League institutions) but now they act as well-trained and competent
plain clothes investigators.

The coming of the late 1940s and 50s brought some increases in
thefts, vandalism and particularly campus parking problems. Some
administrators felt that there was a need for at least a semblance of a
more knowledgeable security approach. In many cases this took the
form of the hiring at a low salary of a retiring local police officer and
giving him the title of chief, captain or some similar designation.
However, the security operation remained under physical plant or
buildings and grounds and its first priority was still protection of property. Many of these retiring police officers conscientiously tried to
build a better department but were thwarted by administrators who considered the security operation a necessary evil and one for which they
would provide only a bare bones-type budget (usually as a part of the
physical plant department budget).

In the late 1950s and early 1960s campus security began to emerge
in spite of administrative apathy and lack of financial and other support.
Some of the pioneers in the field displayed imagination and initiative in
providing a good measure of security with limited equipment, personnel
and other resources. Parking, petty thefts and some vandalism continued to be problems along with student highjinks such as panty raids.

However, a high percentage of campus security operations continued to answer to the physical plant director, and security personnel shared lockers and time cards with custodians and other service personnel and were often paid considerably less in salary. They also continued to work out of basements and boiler houses using discarded desks, file cabinets, lockers and other equipment. Naturally, there were no weapons, no power of arrest and very little training.

The low level of campus security during this period was clearly illustrated when I left the FBI after over seventeen years of service to become Director of Security and Associate Dean of Students at Yale University (a new title). The hiring of a professional to head a campus department at a major university was so new that it became front page news in the New York Times and other publications. It was also revolutionary to have Yale agree to my many stipulations, which included having me answer only to the president or provost, paying Yale officers exactly the same as New Haven Police Officers, having campus police personnel receive exactly the same fringe benefits as faculty and staff, and paying tuition for Yale officers to achieve degrees by attending criminal justice programs at New Haven University.

The field of campus security received its greatest impetus during the student dissent era of the late 1960s and early 1970s. This was an era of great change on campus and in some respects served to shape the future and role of campus security for the years to follow, including beyond 1984. The student dissent period brought chaos to most campuses as violence, disruption and permissiveness invaded the formerly tranquil academic communities. Disciplinary processes broke down and most administrators found themselves unable to cope with sit-ins, unreasonable student demands and violent demonstrations and confrontations. Now for the very first time the spotlight focused directly on campus security and administrators realized that, in most cases, their security forces were completely incapable of dealing with these problems or providing professional advice. And so, in many cases, student demonstrations escalated to the point where outside police agencies had to take over, often producing disastrous results.

The philosophy on campus emerged that a professional security approach was needed in preventing and controlling student problems, and to handle campus security problems without the need for outside police intervention. With this new philosophy came higher standards, salaries and qualifications for personnel. Training improved, as did departmental space. Professionals were hired to head and reorganize departments, and these professionals answered directly to the president or vice president of the institution. However, since the main problem was student-oriented, these departments, although becoming increasingly professional, projected a low profile and high degree of sensitivity

in dealing with students. This was a period of blazers replacing uniforms, unmarked patrol cars, and a change from police titles to security designations such as Security or Public Safety Officer and Director
of Security Services.

Other trends developed as a result of the student dissent era,
many of which will carry over and be expanded in the years beyond
1984. Some of these involved the use of student marshals to better
handle student problems, the hiring of younger college-educated security personnel who could relate to students and the campus community
and, for the first time, utilization of women officers.

The 1970s saw the challenge of student dissent virtually disappear
but be rapidly replaced by an even more serious challenge - crime.
There are presently no accurate statistics on campus crime other than
the FBI Uniform Crime Reports, to which only a relatively few institutions contributed. However, thefts of property, vandalism, arson and
other crimes have escalated. Of even more concern is the alarming
increase in crimes against the person such as rapes, assaults and
armed robberies, which can cause a campus population to boil over and
demand better protection and security response.

The role of any campus security department in the 70s must be
programmed toward prevention of crime and immediate, intelligent
and knowledgeable response to problems. Because crime is the challenge, campus security has changed its direction and image to better
cope with it. This has resulted in a rather rapid change to a law enforcement-oriented approach involving police powers, weapons, uniforms, marked patrol vehicles, and procedures and equipment normally
associated with outside police operations. The low visibility image of
the student dissent era has given way to the high visibility police-type
operation which would have been completely rejected a few years previously. For example, Yale University police officers, after traditionally wearing business suits while working in student areas, have emerged
in blue police-type uniforms - a move that would have caused cries of
"Gestapo" and "police state" during the 1960s.

Other important trends have emerged which will influence the
direction of campus security beyond 1984. These have included an increased emphasis on employing officers with college degrees, student
"eyes and ears" type patrols, women officers and supervisors, and increasing involvement in campus affairs. Another trend has been the
encouraging emphasis on the preventive aspects of security through
programs, posters, pamphlets, campus radio, newspapers, student
rap sessions and other means to educate the community in their own
responsibilities. The use of electronics (alarms, CCTV, access control systems, etc.) has lagged somewhat, due mainly to budgetary
considerations, but is beginning to be recognized as an important preventive measure.

Now for 1984 and beyond: generally speaking, it can be stated that the growth and professionalization of campus security since the late 1960s has exceeded any in the private security field. This progress and professionalism will continue and campus security will become an integral part of the criminal justice system. Challenges faced beyond 1984, which will largely shape the future of campus security, will undoubtedly involve not only increased crime but more serious crime, calling for a high level of performance and professionalism. These crimes could involve acts of terrorism such as bombings, arson, kidnapping, and the taking of hostages. Colleges and universities house the sons and daughters of millionaires, government officials and VIP's who could be likely targets.

The sanctuary campus of the early 1900s, which was sometimes fenced in and vehicle entry controlled, has given way to the open campus. This open campus will continue, and the outside community will be increasingly involved in campus activities and utilize campus facilities. The result will be to cause the college campus to be merely a reflection of the outside community as far as crime and security problems are concerned which will call for a law enforcement-oriented approach. Fences, walls, vehicle entry controls and other measures utilized prior to the open campus will disappear.

What about student problems? Contrary to the opinion of some campus authorities, I do not see a return to campus demonstrations or the violence of the late 1960s and early 70s. However, I do see the student continuing to assume an increasing role and voice in campus affairs and its management. I also am convinced that these students will demand a professional level of campus security to protect their personal safety and property. They will no longer be satisfied with a low-budgeted guard or watchman-type operation or a contracted security force that is only capable of handling the most routine of security functions.

The 1980s will bring about an ever-accelerating move toward the creation of professional, self-sufficient law enforcement-oriented campus departments. However, to be successful these departments must remain very sensitive to the academic communities they serve, and prevention rather than enforcement should be their goal. In order to cope with crime and the more sophisticated criminal, campus departments will have to first of all recruit capable, college educated, well motivated personnel. Salaries and fringe benefits will have to be competitive with those of local law enforcement and other fields of private security.

Criminal justice programs mushroomed during the 70s and some of these graduates will seek careers in the campus field. More and more graduates from these programs will remain as career-minded security officers on the campuses where they achieved their degree, particularly if they were affiliated with the security department while pursuing their degree. Criminal justice programs will increasingly use their own campus security department for students to acquire practical experience through involvement as part-time security personnel.

Campus departments will require a college degree, preferably in the field of criminal justice, and older campus officers will give way to these young degree-holding officers. This will, in turn, lead to these younger career-minded campus officers to replace older security administrators. No longer will colleges and universities seek to hire retiring professional security and law enforcement administrators from the FBI, military service or law enforcement agencies. Educational institutions will compete for young, proven campus security administrators and "raid" other institutions similar to the way they now endeavor to attract outstanding educators to join their faculties.

A number of colleges and universities, usually with low-level contracted or watchman-type security, have been sued as the result of rapes or attacks on students. These civil suits have contended that a college or university has a legal responsibility to provide a level of security, protection and response comparable to that existing off campus. Legal decisions will leave little doubt that an educational institution, particularly one providing student residences, has this responsibility. Naturally, this will foster the growth and progress of security on campus.

What image will the campus security department of 1984 and beyond project? To meet the challenge of crime it will have to project a law enforcement image similar to that of the police. This will entail the use of equipment associated with a police operation such as reliable FM radio communications systems, marked patrol vehicles, distinctive uniforms (which should be different than area police agencies) and the carrying of sidearms.

The carrying of revolvers, particularly after the Kent State shooting incident, has been a critical issue on many campuses, with some administrators and faculty members feeling that weapons have no place in an academic atmosphere. The 1980s will see these objections gradually disappear as students demand more protection. Professional, well-trained departments will be respected and recognized as a vital part of campus life.

The question of police authority which grants the campus officer the power of arrest and other legal powers has also been a sensitive one in the past, with some arguing that citizens type arrest powers are sufficient. The era of 1984 and beyond will see almost all campus security departments in possession of the power of citizen arrest. At

present, over 40 states have passed legislation providing police authority for campus security officers. Most of this legislation restricts this
authority to be exercised only on campus property. However, many
states grant this authority only to State institutions. By 1984 and beyond, nearly all states should pass or amend legislation to provide this
police authority to not only public but private educational institutions at
all levels.

The carrying of firearms, granting of police authority and functioning of campus police as a private law enforcement agency will also
result in mandated security training for campus security officers which
will prescribe ever increasing training standards and requirements.

Training will take on increased importance as campus departments become more law enforcement-oriented and in many respects
function as their counterparts - municipal police departments. Although states providing police authority to campus officers will require
them to undergo a minimum number of hours of training at municipal
and state training academies, the campus officer will have to undergo
considerable in-house and specialized training to equip him for his
sensitive campus duties.

A common fault of training campus officers has been to integrate
them into training classes with local police officers, which sometimes
shapes their philosophy toward regarding enforcement of laws and
arrests as their main function. This philosophy does not fit the role
of the campus officer, in which prevention and service should be the
main objective. A number of campus directors of security have spoken
about the need for "debriefing" officers after attending these police
schools so they won't be "bust happy."

So the mid 80s will see campus police training that recognizes
that campus officers must be different in their approach and philosophy
than municipal officers. Specialized training exclusively for campus
officers will be set up either within the framework of or independent
of municipal and state training academies. I would hope that this
training will revert more and more to the college campus rather than
outside police academies. Certainly, colleges and universities have
the facilities, and in many cases, the faculty to teach these officers,
although some outside law enforcement experts might teach certain
subjects. Such training would not only include the basic police-oriented
subjects (search and seizure, arrest powers, signed statements, report
writing, etc.) but would include sensitivity training, exposure to how an
educational institution functions and its purpose, and other training so
that the new officer will not only feel like an important part of the campus scene but realize that he or she works in a unique academic community demanding the utmost in discretion, courtesy and intelligence.

The 1980s may see colleges and universities coordinating this
training on one campus so that officers from multiple institutions in

that area will attend. This approach has been successfully used in teaching specialized subjects and it should prove beneficial in the specialized field of campus security.

What does all this add up to for 1984 and beyond? It means that colleges and universities, which, from a security standpoint, are merely reflections of the outside community, will become self-sufficient as far as their own security is concerned. By 1984, local police departments will largely be only able to respond to committed crimes and will welcome assistance from professional campus departments able to take care of lesser problems and the protection of property and people. The campus administrator who now feels that he can depend mainly on outside police agencies to handle campus problems should realize that as crime increases, police services to a campus decrease. Understaffed local police departments must deploy personnel where the highest rate of crime exists and use them more for response than protection or prevention. Campus administrators who have not at least started their own self-sufficient, professional security departments are not realistically facing the problem or the future.

The 1980s will also continue the trend toward the public safety concept, where all campus life dealing with environmental safety, the well-being of the population, and protection of property fall under one administrator - the Director of Public Safety. This professional will answer to the president or vice president and will administer not only the security or police department, but the parking operation, safety program, fire department and even such operations as the campus bus service and car pool.

The future will see the complete divorce of campus police or security personnel from the parking operation. Parking control will be administered by a separate parking authority with its own enforcement personnel and experts on traffic and parking matters. This is desirable from two aspects: the first that it frees the well-trained professional campus officer from routine parking control duties so that he or she can devote full time to the more important functions of protection and response; the second is that it greatly improves the security department's image in the eyes of the campus community. Students have long associated the campus security or police officer with the parking function only. In other words, the campus police have assumed the unpopular role of those who tagged and towed student vehicles. Although the campus security officer of the future will have nothing to do with administering or enforcing parking, he or she will continue to patrol, protect and respond to incidents in the parking lots. They will also work closely with and provide police support for the campus parking authority.

Parking is still a major problem on practically every campus, and after 1984 will be even more of a problem. There are numerous

reasons why this parking problem will become even more prominent
in future years, the main one being that as colleges and universities
grow, new parking areas are needed for new buildings and facilities.
Campus administrators will have to face up to the fact that parking
cannot be treated in the haphazard and vacillating manner it has been
in the past on many campuses. There will have to be well-defined
parking policies established and enforcement must be equally and fairly applied to all members of the community. One of the great failures
in the past is the unfair allocation of parking spaces so that faculty and
administrators occupy most of the desirable parking areas (or even
worse, are assigned spaces) while students and lower echelon employees are banished to undesirable areas far from the campus. Another
even more common failure is selective enforcement of parking regulations, so that students and some employees are fined while faculty
and staff tear up tickets with complete immunity.

Parking has increasingly become an important faculty fringe
benefit. Prospective faculty members and others inquire prior to
accepting an appointment, "Where do I park my car?" The 1980s will
exert additional pressure on administrators to provide desirable parking space for faculty, staff and students. However, as parking space
diminishes with growth, colleges and universities will be compelled
to build costly multilevel parking structures and charge a substantial
fee to defray some of the construction and maintenance costs. These
structures will be strictly controlled and administered by the campus
parking authority, but the security department will patrol and police
them.

An important responsibility of every campus security operation
is crowd control at athletic contests, rock concerts and similar affairs
which attract not only the campus population but an outside audience.
The larger colleges and universities usually supplement their own
security forces with local law enforcement officers or, occasionally,
contracted security personnel. The mid-1980s will call for even more
coverage at large athletic events.

The trend at athletic contests, particularly football games, has
been toward increasing fan violence. Irresponsible acts threatening
personel safety and property will undoubtedly continue and probably
grow worse. Gene Calhoun, senior official of the Big Ten Conference,
was quoted in an August 1977 issue of the National On Campus Report
as stating, "Every time I go on that field I know that some nut with an
ice pick could end my career or life."

By 1984 these athletic contests will demand not only more security personnel to control unruly fans, but routine searches of those entering stadiums to detect weapons or objects which, if thrown, could
jeopardize the safety of players, officials and fans. It is certainly

not beyond the realm of future possibility to even employ metal de-
tectors to screen those entering stadiums.

In regard to rock concerts and similar often drug-related events,
no one can forecast what will be the musical or entertainment fad of
the future. I forecast a return to a more conservative type of music
and entertainment. I do not see these concerts, which have created
major crowd-control problems on some campuses, presenting a problem in the future. In fact, by 1984, students will undoubtedly have
new musical and entertainment values and heroes. For campus security forces this could mean calmer and more orderly audiences.

Electronics will play a very large and rapidly increasing role in
the protection of property and people in the 1980s. Most campus administrators have been unwilling to spend money on electronic protection and devices, but this will have to change. The proprietary electronic protection system will replace many of the routine security
functions now performed by watchmen-guard operations. These proprietary systems are expensive at the outset but eliminate the need for
watchmen and similar personnel and, in the long run, are more efficient and economical.

When speaking of the recognition and use of proprietary electronic protection systems in the future, I am referring to the use of various types of property protection and emergency (panic) alarms to enable people to summon help. I also refer to closed circuit television,
remote control of entrance doors, card key, cypher and similar access
control systems, and other devices that are daily becoming more
sophisticated. All of these devices will be monitored by the security
department at a central console on a twenty-four hour per day basis.
This central console will not only have the capability to signal the location of alarms activated (both fire and intrusion) but will be computerized, produce a readout of activity and have the ability to videotape TV
camera output.

The head of any campus security operation of the future must
have a thorough knowledge of these devices and be involved in their
selection. He or she must also be involved in planning such security
systems for new facilities, rather than having these considered as an
expensive afterthought after construction is completed. 1984 and the
years beyond will see the recognition of electronics as an integral in-
gredient in any successful security program. In short, the 1980s will
be the age of electronic protection.

Closed circuit television must now be used sparingly on most
campuses because of the sensitive nature of the campus population,
which regards the monitoring camera as an invasion of privacy. The
advent of the mid-1980s will see this aversion to camera surveillance
disappear and CCTV be welcomed as another means of insuring better
personal safety and prompt response to emergency situations.

In conclusion, 1984 and beyond will see campus security and police departments becoming increasingly law enforcement-oriented to meet the challenge of crime. It will be an era in which colleges and universities will be largely self-sufficient in providing a level of security that will be superior, or at least equal, to that enjoyed by the outside community. This will call for high-caliber, well-trained and supervised officers. It will also demand that campus security departments be provided with all the tools needed to perform effectively such as power of arrest, weapons, police vehicles, effective communications, and increasing use of proprietary electronic, intrusion and access control systems. However, all of these tools must be utilized under the strictest of standards and policies.

The role of the campus department will embody the best of law enforcement but be tailored and sensitive to the campus community it serves. Certainly, campus security will improve its position and assume its rightful place in the criminal justice system. While doing so, it also will become a most vital and necessary part of the campus scene.

SCHOOL SECURITY

The history of school security is practically nonexistent because, in fact, it is only just beginning. By 1984 the 1970s will be looked upon as the period when school security got its start.

A few years ago I attended a conference of school security administrators, and the questions and discussion took me back to my first campus security conference in 1960. Why? Because the questions and problems were so similar to those concerning campus security administrators of the early 60s. These questions were in regard to the proper role a school security department should play, to whom it should answer, salaries and qualifications, training, and how to cope with increasing crime and student problems.

School security has also closely resembled campus security due to the fact that its need has not been recognized by the majority of school administrators. These administrators continue to deemphasize the need for security even though thefts, vandalism, arson, attacks on students and teachers and similar crimes continue to increase at an alarming rate. Many tend to "sweep these problems under the rug" and "wish" them away.

Make no mistake about it, our schools do have major and growing security problems. Senator Birch Bayh (D-Ind.), in a February 1977 speech to the National Education Association, said the "shocking trend to greater violence and vandalism" in our nation's schools is one of the most critical problems facing educators, students, parents and school administrators today. He described this acute situation as making the primary objective of public schooling "no longer education, but preservation."

In February 1977 Senator Bayh also released the final report of the Senate Subcommittee To Investigate Juvenile Delinquency, which estimated that almost 600,000,000 dollars were being spent yearly as a result of school vandalism (more than was spent on textbooks and enough to hire 50,000 additional teachers). An even more shocking statistic was that "70,000 serious physical assaults on teachers and literally hundreds of thousands of assaults on students" were perpetrated in our schools annually.

School security is making some progress, in spite of resistance and apathy on the part of many school administrators. A number of public school systems (usually in larger municipalities) have hired security professionals to organize and head their programs. An outstanding example is Broward County, Ft. Lauderdale, Florida, which in 1969 hired Joseph I. Grealy, an attorney and veteran of 29 years in the FBI, to become director of internal affairs. Grealy formulated a low-key but effective "benchmark" school security program which emphasized prevention and established close cooperation and liaison with outside law enforcement agencies. He also was the main force behind the establishment of the National Association of School Security Directors, and was its president for many years.

Where is school security headed, and what should school administrators be planning for in 1984 and beyond? First of all, there is no doubt in my mind that during the years ahead school security will be one of the newest and most rapidly growing fields in the private security sector. If I were a young man planning a career in private security or law enforcement, I would take a long look at school security and get in on the ground floor of what will be a rapidly growing profession.

By 1984, all school systems will be compelled to have some sort of security organization and program. Successful security programs will involve a combination of sensitive, well-trained personnel, electronic protection and tightened access control, and other security procedures. School security personnel will present a rather low visibility and will concentrate in trying to prevent problems through close liaison with outside police sources, as well as keeping a finger on the pulse of what's going on in their school system. They will be young, college educated officers who can relate to the school community and whose role it will be to make schools safe places in which to study and work. Many schools today rely entirely on teachers and custodians to maintain security when it should not be the responsibility of either. By the

middle 1980s school security personnel will assume the major responsibility for the security function.

School security departments will carry titles and names to dis-
associate them from the police image. Yet to be effective they should
be well-trained and have the power of arrest which should be used only
when absolutely necessary. The mere suggestion of having school
security officers carry weapons is completely rejected by school administrators today, but if problems, particularly involving crimes against
the person by outsiders, continue to accelerate, these school security
officers may some day have to be armed. However, at present I see
the arming of these officers as far away and coming only after they
have demonstrated their professionalism and value to the school system.

A very definite trend will be the hiring of well-educated and proven
security professionals to head these school security programs. Some
of these school security directors will probably be recruited from progressive successful campus security departments. They will answer
directly to the Superintendent of Schools.

School security personnel will be supplemented more and more
by electronic protection, particularly when school buildings are closed.
School administrators should be thinking about establishing their own
proprietary electronic security systems to cover all schools within
their jurisdiction. This would involve setting up a twenty-four hour per
day central monitoring console to monitor alarms and other electronic
protection and detection devices throughout the entire school system.
A minimum of security personnel would then be needed for after-hours
protection, and their responsibility would be to respond to problems
signaled by these protective devices.

Another measure which will have to be instituted in the future is
strict access control at school buildings. This will involve issuing
identification cards to students and employees and the ability to quickly
deprogram such cards when necessary. The suspended or former student, as well as students from other schools, have long presented a
serious security problem in our schools; they must be prevented from
entering. The future will see students' entry of schools through specified entrances, and their access electronically controlled by the use of
card keys or cypher access control systems (or both). Such systems
will also have the ability to immediately void a card when a student
drops out, is suspended or is no longer authorized to enter.

Another long-neglected, unrecognized component of any security
approach has been the design and construction of school buildings.
However, recently there has been some recognition that improved
architectural and design techniques can reduce the vulnerability of
school buildings. This trend will continue and by 1984 design and construction will be a major consideration in the planning of any new school

facilities. Coupled with design considerations will be planning for effective electronic security systems, locking hardware, shatter-proof glazing, and other equipment and materials that will insure a well-protected and safe building.

Present objections to CCTV which are similar to those voiced at colleges and universities will also disappear and the output of TV cameras will be monitored at a central console. These cameras will not only be used to monitor internal locations (hallways, cafeterias, etc.) but external areas of school facilities such as parking lots. Low, light-level cameras will surveil external areas at night and provide early warning of vandalism - particularly window breakage, which is a major problem. Some of these cameras will provide motion detection capabilities which obviate the need for constant viewing of monitoring screens by the console operator. In other words, the control center receives a signal when the normal picture is changed, so that the operator views the screen to ascertain the reason.

It has already been mentioned that those who design school buildings are starting to recognize that security must be considered. By 1984 the design of new school buildings will change drastically to provide safer and less accessible facilities. This will mean reducing or eliminating windows, particularly at ground level, reducing the means of climbing to roofed areas, utilizing maximum-security locking hardware (dead bolts, non-duplicating keys, etc.), planning for low-level landscaping that will not provide after-dark hiding places, and the use of effective internal and external lighting.

Other factors will also come into play which will emphasize the prevention of thefts, arson, vandalism and other acts. These will involve police community liaison programs to improve police-community relations and respect for the law. Student-parent involvement in programs designed to reduce violence and vandalism will also emerge. The students themselves will become more involved in programs to counsel their peers, and will form student advisory committees for problem solving and to secure the cooperation of students in protecting facilities and carrying out school regulations. These committees will be particularly valuable in detecting and solving potential situations prior to their becoming major problems.

The Federal Government and State governments will also increasingly recognize the security problems in our schools, and by 1984 will be funding preventive security programs to make our schools safe. The State of Florida was the first state to recognize this problem, and is funding innovative security approaches to combat crime in the schools.

In conclusion, the growth of school security will be a rapid one and by 1984 school security will have definitely arrived. It will project a thoroughly professional approach. Its role will be somewhat similar to that of campus security during the student dissent era - progressive and efficient, yet very sensitive to the community it serves.

III

Organized Crime, Terrorism and Hostage Situations

7 Intelligence beyond 1984

Joseph J. O'Brien

Man, the eternal seer and stargazer, has always concerned himself with the future. From Biblical dream interpretations to his present fixation with 1984 (already becoming 2000 A. D.) he has oscillated from doomsday gloom to euphoria. He has not always been accurate in his predictions. On some occasions he has seen himself surviving through years of plenty and abundance, while on other occasions he sees himself dying of pollution, overpopulation and overconsumption. The one thing we can be sure of, however, is that he looks to the future with great interest and concern.

The field of intelligence lends itself to, indeed feeds upon, stargazing, predictions and projections. 1984 is only five years away. Surely some fair estimate of what lies ahead can be made. To do this, however, we must look at the current state of the intelligence community.

Perhaps the most overwhelming factor affecting intelligence today is the privacy issue. One need only be conscious of the news media disclosures of the past several years alone to have no difficulty in developing a glossary of terms: political monitoring, bugging, snooping, burglary, unlawful entry, plumbers, dirty tricks, enemy lists, naked society, microfiche, data banks, credit checks, fishbowl living, big brother, life experience envelope, data collection, intelligence dissemination, dossiers, backgrounds, agent-provacateurs, infiltrators, political spies, mail covers, undercover agents, black bag jobs, information society, and surreptitious entries. The one term that might, in umbrella fashion, composite, synthesize or perhaps capsulize all of the others would be the "privacy issue" or "invasion of privacy."

The issue and problem of privacy is a very broad and expansive one. Unfortunately, positions are being taken and lines being drawn before all of the facts have been ascertained. Even as this chapter is

being read, new abuses are being alleged by sociologists, civil libertarians, and bar associations, as well as by congressional committees.

This section cannot possibly explore all of the sensitive privacy
areas relating to intelligence, nor can it resolve all of its problems.
It is its intent instead to try to document some of the more obvious
areas of concern relating to intelligence; that is to put this issue into
a more precise intelligence frame, and to capture some of the flavor
and excitement prevalent today regarding an area that will directly
effect the direction intelligence will take between now and 1984.

When did we become aware of privacy and its abuses? Appreciate,
firstly, that approximately 20 years ago computer specialists and
scholarly researchers raised the first hue and cry concerning privacy.
They warned us of the extraordinary amounts of information and data
that were being collected. They spoke of the electronic revolution,
particularly as it related to and affected the capacity and versatility of
computers. They warned us of the newly developed extraordinary increase in the capability of data banks to collect, analyze, store, and
retrieve information, adding that it would result in literally astronomical amounts of data being gathered, because such tasks were easily
accomplished with the increase of overall organizational efficiency at
minimal financial expenditure. (1)

In the spring of 1964, Vance Packard, a reputable social commen-
tator, went a step further than the sociologists and computer specialists.
He alleged that abuses directed against society and its right to privacy
were already occurring, (2) and documented them. He gave us specific
examples of how data was being allegedly misuses by personnel officers
in the corporate octopii. These officers, he stated, had investigative
backgrounds, were drawn from Federal and local police backgrounds
and could, to use the vernacular, plug back into the records systems of
their previous agencies to obtain unauthorized information for use in
their current employment.

Next, we watched former Senator Ervin's congressional investigation into the "monitoring" of the private sector by the U. S. Army's
intelligence arm. (3) Indeed, documented in his hearings were the
army's presence on campus and its infiltration of student groups. For
those who were still not aware of the extraordinary events that were
taking place or being alleged, the next horror to be disclosed in theatrical fashion on national television was "Watergate." Many of the terms
we used earlier in this chapter were first heard by the public during
those hearings, which detailed alleged criminal violations and abuses
not only by governmental agencies, but by the highest officials of government. Ultimately, the scandal would touch and destroy a president and
seriously weaken his office, perhaps for years to come.

If this were not enough to make us concerned regarding privacy
and its alleged bauses, real or imagined, then we were next exposed

to a plethora of congressional committees - as many as six functioning simultaneously - which inspected and analyzed the practices and procedures, as well as the systems, policies and histories of the components of the Federal intelligence community.

HISTORY OF PRIVACY

Few legal areas have been left as undefined as that of privacy. As a result, some assume that this concept is a modern notion. It is their belief that man's desire to seek anonymity is a refinement brought on by the conditions of the 20th century.

Research indicates that man's need for privacy begins with his origins. Studies of the animal kingdom show that privacy and the concern for privacy precedes man and can be found within the world of animals. Extensive research by Edward Hall, as well as independent study by Ardrey, (4) show animal concern for territorial dimension and flight distance; a "one-robin-to-a-branch" kind of thing. These efforts also show that animals existing in crowded habitats frequently fall victim to mysterious deaths, now believed to have resulted from heart disease brought on by the stress of a crowded environment. These studies also disclose clear indications that where crowding has occurred, animal survival has become critically threatened. Some animals have killed each other, while others, such as the lemming and the rabbit, have a documented history of mass suicides. More recent studies, as reported in the New York Times, indicate that wild animal population peaks and lows in the rabbit, deer, and mice specie kingdoms are regulated by density and weather cycles. (5)

TECHNOLOGICAL ADVANCE

Technological programs, and particularly the evolution of the computer, have been a clear plus in all disciplines as well as government and business. We are now able to make more fact-based, logical and predictable decisions than before the age of electronics through a documentation system supported by information collection, storage and retrieval. The issue of privacy raised by the computer is whether such extraordinary increase in data collection and retrieval, if not systematically controlled and monitored, would not result in an enormous power of surveillance by government over individuals. Government could control information that literally thousands of investigators could not have gathered a few years ago.

This technological progress has been due to the following developments;

a. The increased ability and likelihood of persons to move about the country has developed large public and private verification systems regarding the lending of money, credit, hiring and firing, passports, etc. The Retail Credit Corporation has over 7,000 investigators in its employ and maintains dossiers on over 42 million persons. That firm grosses over 100 million dollars annually. (6)

b. The great need today for data collection, as exemplified by the large bureaucratic organizations' need for instant information. In addition, the regulatory function of government has created a great need for specific data, as well as social scientists' increased reliance on data collection and analysis.

c. The inception of governmental programs which require more data collection, such as racial hiring and government contracts.

d. The importance of the digital computer.

e. Engineering progress in computer structuring. The standardization of computer language now allows computers to talk to each other and exchange data.

A great spotlight has been focused on alleged abuses regarding the right to privacy. It has been directed, for example, at the Federal Government, the amount of data it collects, and its ever-increasing files. In June 1975 the Privacy Protection Study Commission was established to examine the handling of all this information. Its chairman, David F. Linowes, has stated "I seriously believe that at some point in the not-so-distant future, data collection, maintenance and dissemination may no longer be merely a tool of society, but will instead become an end in itself, a force with awesome powers of surveillance and control over the lives of individuals. " (7)

According to this commission, the Federal Government maintains 6,723 different record systems containing a total of 3.9 billion individual files, or 18 files for every person in the U.S. (8) It's not necessary for a person to violate the law to be included in these files; he need only come in contact with the government.

These indices include files on current and former government employees, as well as the names of persons who have sought governmental assistance. The concern is not the legitimacy of the reason for which the records were instituted, but rather to what ultimate use they may be put, contrary to their originally stated purpose.

The computerization of these files creates greater concern. These files can be instantly retrieved and therefore become even more attractive to the searchers; not to mention the enormous amounts of information that can now be stored thanks to the computer.

An even greater concern has been pointed out by the aforementioned Linowes, who feels that "there are substantially more records

kept by the commercial or private sector than by the federal government, " (9) adding that "a preliminary staff estimate indicates that three
of the largest credit agencies in the country have a total of more than
100 million names on file. " (10) Obviously information like this, when
composited, gives an instant view or picture of the individual, his interests, hobbies, religion, political beliefs, etc. Chairman Linowes
stated in an interview in 1977 that "last year the Bell System furnished
billing records of 20,565 customers to federal agencies. " (11) The
Privacy Act, passed as a result of the Watergate abuses, does not
regulate the use of commercial data by Federal agencies. Its rules
are directed primarily at the use of personal data collected by the
Federal Government, not the collection or use of commercial data.

On June 30, 1977, the Justice Department revoked an order authorizing the Federal Bureau of Investigation to move ahead with a
computer project that had been rejected by the Ford Administration as
a threat to the individual's privacy and civil liberties. The project
would have invoked the use of the Federal Bureau of Investigation's
existing computer as a central message switching center for local and
State police agencies when they made inquiries to one another about
wanted and missing persons, as well as stolen property. Critics felt
that this would end the State system and permit the bureau to monitor
all administrative messages between local and State police agencies.
In another recent development, the FBI announced that it may soon
dispose of hundreds of thousands of files on individuals and organizations whose records were instituted because they were participants in
political protests. (12)

Former Senator Sam Ervin, Democrat, North Carolina, a longtime foe of "big brotherism, " stated that the vast network of datacollecting and exchange machines have given the government the power
to take note of anything, whether it be right or wrong, relevant or not,
and retain it forever. No longer may a man with a sign march down
Pennsylvania Avenue and then return to his home town, his identity
forgotten if not his cause. (13)

In a recent Harris survey 67 percent of those polled agreed that
Americans began surrendering their privacy the day they opened their
first charge account, took out their first loan, bought something on an
installment plan or applied for a credit charge. Only 47 percent of
those polled twelve months earlier felt that way. Those polled felt
that the Federal Government and credit companies were the two main
organizations responsible for the invasion of their privacy. This survey disclosed also that those polled had precise notions regarding what
may be or what should be placed in those files and for how long.
According to this survey an overwhelming 75 percent of those surveyed
expressed a desire for legislation that would lay down rules for the way

business and other private organizations should deal with information they have collected. (15)

In July of 1977 the congressionally commissioned Privacy Protection Study released its 651-page report, containing 162 recommendations and urging the establishment of a Federal privacy board to ensure that computer banks keep accurate and secret the mass of confidential details they hold about millions of Americans. Its recommendations impose strict limits on how the government and industry use the personal information in the nation's data banks. The proposals would give the individual the "right to know" what is reported about him in files of insurance companies, credit bureaus, schools, employers and government agencies and a right to demand correction of damaging errors. The government would have access to industry files only if provided by statute, or for a criminal investigation. It would have to notify the person involved or even issue a subpoena so he could challenge the government's request in court. "We live inescapably in an information society" the commission said, admitting that it is almost impossible for the average American to exist without giving confidential information to the government, financing and credit installations, as well as medical organizations. (16)

In 1975 a series of hearings entitled "The Nationwide Drive Against Law Enforcement Intelligence Operations" was conducted before the Senate Internal Security Committee. (17) Senator Thurmond, who presided over those hearings, stated that it was the conclusion of the committee after receiving information from several sources that "there has been a highly organized and highly effective drive on a national scale against law enforcement intelligence operations."(18) At that time 75 separate law suits had been filed against various Federal, State, and local police departments. It was further concluded by the above committee that these suits were generally undertaken to compel law enforcement agencies to divulge sensitive intelligence gathered about extremist groups or divest themselves entirely of their intelligence files and intelligence operations. (19)

Senator Thurmond also stated that the media further compounded this condition by regarding law enforcement agencies as the prime enemy of freedom rather than as their protector, whose role it is to minimize the danger posed to such freedom by the scores of extremist organizations openly committed to terrorist activities. (20)

These hearings indicated that the reaction of some law enforcement agencies might well have been to disengage from intelligence operations or to reduce them, obviously feeling concern and uncertainty with regard to their own rights and responsibilities. The hearings further suggested that some agencies have reduced their files and/or curtailed their monitoring of extremist groups of the left and right.

If the above conclusions are reasonably well-founded, they come at an unusual period in the country's violent evolution.

HISTORY OF INTELLIGENCE

Harry Rowe Ransom traced the history of intelligence to Bible records which show that Moses was instructed to send out what in essence were intelligence officers "to spy out the land of Canaan." (21) He found additional references in Sun Tzu, a Chinese military theorist who wrote "On the Art of War." Sun Tzu attributed a wise sovereign's ability to achieve results beyond that of the ordinary man to his "fore-knowledge." (22) Ransom speaks also of the well-organized intelligence system of the Mongols. (23) He comments further on the highly developed intelligence apparatus which evolved in sixteenth century England. (24)

Mythos tells us of the ancient city of Syracuse in Sicily, which installed an artificial S-shaped cave, where were incarcerated misdemeanants and felons whose conversations, and hoped-for confessions, were overheard through holes in the cave walls. (25) For a more vivid, technical example of intelligence and privacy invasion one need only look at the figure of J. E. B. Stuart, the "intelligence officer" of the Civil War. His ability to develop information regarding enemy movements has often been mistakenly related to the traditional role of cavalry. Records of the Confederate States, however, reveal that he maintained a wire-tapper (wireless-tapper) on his staff who cut into the Federal lines freely and often. (26)

Legal Problems

Some of the specific legal problems affecting the intelligence community at this time are the Freedom of Information Act and the Privacy Act.

The United States Information Act, enacted in 1967, enables the release of secret and confidential information to the public. The act substitutes the "need to know" with the "right to know" as the test for access government records. Under its provisions an individual, newspaper, interest group or corporation can file requests with a government agency for a document and the agency has ten days to comply. Nine areas of exempt categories were established, some of which are the following: classified national security documents; information exempted by other laws; trade secrets; confidential commercial information; personal information on individuals.

In 1976, approximately 150,000 requests were received for information. These requests have placed heavy burdens upon the agencies involved. (27) In addition, in 1975, 120,000 man-hours were expended by the Justice Department alone to process some of these requests. In 1976, that figure rose to 600,000. (28) Such requests caused the F.B.I. to bring in 400 agents from the field to man a six-month assault against a massive backlog. This effort was described by former FBI Director Clarence Kelly as a multi-million dollar effort to clear the paperwork. (29) It was estimated in the July 1977 issue of Police Officer's Journal that this effort would, according to Director Kelly, cost 6.5 million dollars. (30) Since the act's inception in 1967, twenty million dollars has been reportedly spent by Federal agencies in compliance with its provisions. (31)

The Privacy Act gives the individual the right to inspect many of his own records maintained by Federal agencies, correct inaccuracies and to a limited extent control the use of these records. It imposes upon the agencies of the Federal government a "code of fair information practices," setting standards for the collection, maintenance and dissemination of personal information which these agencies are legally bound to follow. It gives the individual no right to inspect the records of state or local government agencies or private agencies. This act deals solely with the personal records of individuals and not of corporations or businesses. (31a)

In addition, as mentioned earlier, the intelligence community across the country is described as having been besieged by law suits wherein the litigants claimed their rights were violated by intelligence activities. In hearings of September 1976 before the Senate Subcommittee on Internal Security, Captain Justin Dintino, Commander of the Intelligence Bureau, New Jersey State Police, detailed the following problems in connection with recent legislation effecting the Intelligence Sector. (32)

1. "Liaison with Federal law enforcement agencies has been reduced. These agencies fear that informants who have provided reliable criminal information will be identified when the individual gains access to his records."

2. "Less criminal information is being exchanged because agencies are apprehensive about what information they can safely release to other agencies. In addition law enforcement agencies that were about to institute intelligence units were chilled against it."

These hearings of September 1976 touched on the significance of terrorism in this country today. Regarding this phenomenon, Chief Edward Davis, Los Angeles Police Department, stated "If the price of liberty is eternal vigilance, then abandonment of the intelligence function must be regarded as a first sign of impending death for American freedom. " (35)

Francis J. McNamara, former head of the now abolished Subversive Activities Control Board, stated further in those hearings that many law enforcement intelligence-gathering agencies are now disbanding their operations in direct contravention of the recommendations of seven successive Presidential Commissions, including; (34)

The President's Commission on Law Enforcement and Administration of Justice - 1963;

The President's Commission on the Assassination of President J. F. Kennedy - 1963;

President's Commission on Crime in the District of Columbia - 1965;

National Advisory Commission on Civil Disorders - 1967;

National Commission on the Causes and Prevention of Violence - 1968;

President's Commission on Campus Unrest - 1970;

National Advisory Commission on Criminal Justice Standards and Goals - 1971.

All of the above commissions urged the establishment of Federal, regional and local police intelligence units.

Critics of law enforcement intelligence-gathering agencies argue that the operation of such agencies on a local level can have a "chilling effect" on the right of free speech and legitimate dissent. The counter-groups argue that the increased terrorism is in itself an argument toward supporting intelligence units to investigate and monitor terrorist acts.

In 1976 there were 1,570 bombings in this country, and there is no indication that this figure is declining. A more recent concern is the belief, held by some, that terrorists will invade nuclear installations and steal explosive materials to construct "kitchen nuclear bombs. " (35) These two items alone, some believe, justify the use of intelligence units.

TERRORISM

Terrorism continues to be a key word in the jargon of intelligence officers. Most agree that terrorism has been with us since the earliest recorded moments of history. In recent years, however, we have seen a much greater amount of terrorism, as well as an increase in the amount of exposure given it by the news media. Resultingly, the terrorist concern has mounted in the past several years.

Instant electronic communications and televiewing of such events during and immediately after they occur has created an enormous awareness on the part of all sectors on both the national and local level. Large cities, however, have been the particular geographic targets, where news coverage and population are the greatest, as well as the fact that key corporate offices and diplomatic locations are headquartered there. This is not to mention the presence of the many diverse national and political groups and ideologies that such cities attract. The incidence of terrorist attacks has increased and has become a major concern of police officials, who only a few decades ago need not have directed the enormous amount of energy toward handling them that their counterparts today must.

Some believe that revolutionary bombings are a new thing. In 1600, however, Guy Fawkes attempted to blow up the Parliament of the British Government with several thousand pounds of black powder. Nearly 400 years have passed since Guy Fawkes, and the day of the crude, unsophisticated explosive has given way to devices which contain larger amounts of explosives obtained throughout clandestine channels, and which use highly technical electronic timing mechanisms. Today's bomber demonstrates great imagination in the construction of long-delay, remote control and boobytrap fusing systems. (36)

It is significant to note that the author of this description of today's bomber was Sergeant Terrence McTigue of the New York City Police Department, who on September 10, 1976 was very seriously injured while dismantling a bomb planted by Croatian terrorists in a locker at Grand Central Station. His assistant, Police Officer Brian Murray, was killed in that tragic incident.

The terrorist problem has been facilitated by at least three factors:

Modern transportation and communication.

New methodology and techniques in weaponry.

Large media exposure.

Terrorist activity has increased in this country over the past decade. This increase is particularly manifest in the most recent years. The following is a summary of bombings for the years indicated:

Year	Number of Bombings
1972	1,962
1973	1,955
1974	2,044
1975	2,074
1976	1,570

Dr. William Kintner, Professor of Political Science at the University of Pennsylvania and an authority on terrorism, in testimony before the Senate Committee on Internal Security of the U.S. Senate, Washington, D.C., June 18, 1976, pointed out the "chaotic" condition existing with regard to police intelligence. "Domestic Law Enforcement," he stated, "is operating with a drastically reduced capability." (37) Dr. Kintner discussed how this depletion in intelligence has come about, and mentioned the effects of Watergate, followed by widespread apathy toward police intelligence and an organized campaign of legal harassment against intelligence units. (38) He warned that the protection of the First Amendment does not mean prohibition against intelligence-gathering about activities to inflict mass violence on our communities which could take innocent lives. (39) Dr. Kintner's first requirement, in coping with terrorism, is adequate police intelligence, without which, he said, the most dedicated police force in the world would be unable to protect its community. (40)

In testimony during the Senate Subcommittee Hearings on October 23, 1975, four bomb experts, described by Senator Thurmond as four of the country's top experts on terrorist bombings, agreed that an intelligence unit was absolutely vital to the successful investigation of terrorist bombings. (41)

Terrorism has taken on new dimensions. Innocent people are now frequently the victims. The experience of the Munich Olympics in 1972 dramatically proved this. The terrorists' ability to disrupt society has increased with the evolution of technology and has been further amplified with the advent of instant publicity.

The term itself, however, still escapes precise definition by the experts. Ambassador Lewis Hoffacker, Special Assistant to the Secretary of State, speaking on programs dealing with terrorism, stated that "Intelligence is one of our more valuable resources in this self-defense endeavour." (42) Terrorists, later to be called patriots, set off a revolution that would make this a free nation; racist violence has been going on in the south for over 100 years. Today, however, the threat is much greater. The FBI has recorded over 700 incidents of guerilla-type violence in the past six years. These incidents include sniper attacks, bombings, arson, bank robberies and ambush murders in which 83 police officers and civilians were killed and 284 injured.

Technological Terrorism

        Another development relating to intelligence is the increased concern by some surrounding technological terrorism. In a report released March 2, 1977, (43) it was warned that the possibility of attack by terrorists armed with nuclear, biological, or chemical weapons "is very real and ought to be realistically and urgently faced. " (44) To deal with this, the government panel recommended legislation that would permit police disruption of the activities of a suspected group, detention of citizens without arrest and forcible searches without warrant. (45) The report stated it is now possible for terrorists with "reasonable resources and talent to make an atomic weapon with about half the power of the Hiroshima bomb. " (46)

        The report also mentioned the danger of biological weapons. One truck could disseminate bacteria to a medium-sized city, and the resulting medical care problems would be catastrophic. Anthrax or crypto-coccosis could be surreptitiously released in the air circulation system of a domed stadium, and more than 70, 000 persons could be infected within an hour. The report added a key recommendation that law enforcement be given the power to gather intelligence on individuals and groups that might become involved in violence or civil disorders, adding that the gathering of such intelligence has been drastically cut back following exposure of abuses by the C. I. A. and F. B. I. Regarding civil disorder and terrorism, the report stated, "the relative peace of recent months is a false calm and we must see in the current social situation an accumulation of trouble in the future. There will surely come a time when once again socio-economic conditions will generate violent reactions. " (47)

        The report predicts that the nation will experience a slight increase in terrorism and a new wave of violent political protests. It urges government officials to plan for citywide curfews and provide for temporary suspension of some legal activities; advocates the use of court injunction to block potentially violent demonstrations; and, as a last resort, recommends the use of military forces.

        A recent news article vaguely alleged the presence of a secret document warning of social upheaval and revolution by the year 2, 000 that may destroy the United States unless drastic steps are taken to curb the energy crisis. (48) Another recent news article alleged that a secret congressional report entitled "Nuclear Proliferation and Safeguards" prepared by the Congressional Office of Technology Assessment warned that mankind is threatened by a shocking lack of nuclear safeguards. (49) It stated that any jack-of-all-trades technician and a single knowledgeable researcher could put together a primitive but effective atomic bomb. The essential ingredient of plutonium could be stolen from nuclear arsenals. It stated further that an intact atomic bomb could be stolen even in the U.S. by 8-20 terrorists, adding that the psychological value of a successful theft would be considerable. (50)

Recently, a group of this nation's leading molecular biologists met in a public forum at the National Academy of Science to discuss the needs for guidelines for D.N.A. recombinants research. The research, some feel, could be a boon to mankind, but it could also transform a benign bacteria into a dangerous killer. A recent news article questioned, "how much more dangerous would they (Hanafi Muslems) have been had they not been armed with guns and machetes but with death-dealing bacteria or a nuclear device or dangerous byproducts like plutonium powder?" (51) This article stated further that "the greatest danger facing the world today is that physical science and technology have advanced so much faster than social, psychological and political science that we are rapidly reaching the point of potential self-destruction." (52)

Currently, we are told there are no plans to protect the country from biological attack. The army has spent millions in ways to defend its own troops against that type of warfare but not to defend the population. The Public Health Service says its agency has no such plans.

It should be noted that since 1969 there have been 170 threats and acts of violence against atomic plants. This has resulted in the implementation of elaborate security measures, which in turn resulted in the following:

a. An increase in the security forces at those locations.
b. Semi-automatic weapons assigned to security forces.
c. Additional surveillance and alarm systems.
d. The implementation of new lock systems whenever a person leaves employment. (53)

Doctor Douglas DeNike, a specialist on Nuclear Terrorism, has stated that "the probability of a terrorist attack on a nuclear facility is increasing by about 20 percent a year." (54)

Despite round-the-clock security forces and magnetically coded I.D. cards, U.S. Security Officers concede that the present system is not foolproof. The U.S. Air Force plans to utilize voice patterns, fingerprints and handwriting in a new sophisticated identification security method. A visitor to a secured location would first have to punch out his I.D. number on a pushbutton panel. He would then have to speak into a

machine. If the machine accepted his voice pattern, he would go to a
second area where he would be obliged to write his signature. If his
signature was accepted, he would move to a third booth and his fingerprints would be taken. If they were accepted he would be permitted into
a high-security area. (55) It is estimated that the above security combination would screen out all but one of 125,000 of the would-be intrud-
ers. (56)

The subject of terrorism cannot be discussed in the intelligence
context without an appreciation of how it is affected by the news media.
Andrew Young, United States Ambassador to the United Nations, upset
by the news handling of the Hanafi Muslem siege in Washington, D.C.,
suggested that the Supreme Court might "clarify the Constitution's First
Amendment to inhibit newspapers and television from creating a climate
of violence." (57)

Robert A. Baron, Purdue psychologist, has stated, regarding the
seeing of violence on television, that "it not only gives unstable people
the idea of doing the same but also teaches them exactly how to go
about it." (58) Michael Spioto, 1st Deputy Police Superintendent, Chicago Police Department, adds that "overpublicizing crime tends to
bring the kooks out of the woodwork." (59) There appears to be a con-
census that expectations of media coverage encourage terrorism.
Stuart H. Leery, Managing Editor of the Chicago Sun-Times, has
stated that "the press must start thinking more about the way people
like terrorists are using us. We have become part of the story." (60)
Terrorism and its mass viewing have become part of the entertainment
industry.

Dr. David Hubbard sees terrorism as it relates to airplane hijack-
ing as "the spread of a rapidly mutating virus," adding that "the terrorist scenarios get more and more bizarre as one unstable individual
takes clues from some earlier widely publicized event. (61) The chief
target of all terrorists is the T.V. audience but by acting as a conduit
for the terrorist incident it excites other embryo terrorists. For every
one that gets ended five get started." (62) In a recent statement the
Freedom of the Press Committee held that "the council rejects as un-
thinkable any notion that because such activities may be contagious,
they should not be reported." (63)

In April 1977 Richard S. Salant, President of C.B.S. News, issued
a set of guidelines for network journalists to follow in covering "terrorists holding hostages" situations. (64)

PRIVATE SECURITY

Another area of interest regarding the future of intelligence is the developing role of private security. That role has always been significant. During the Civil War a famous private detective, Allen Pinkerton, was named as Chief of Intelligence for the Northern Armies. (65) In recent years law enforcement agencies and private security organizations have begun to close ranks and are now increasingly riding under the united criminal justice banner.

Indeed, the basis of this book is in part predicated on such considerations, that is, the unification of all police agencies within the criminal justice setting. Considering the enormous need the intelligence community has for raw data in the public security and terrorism section, it is obvious that intelligence information from all sources, including private security, can be of great value. Surely as regards terrorist acts, both those perpetrated and those feared, the security director of the corporate installation can be a significant source of information. As terrorism has escalated, these directors have become increasingly more professional. Their requests for intelligence guidance will increase and will become more and more sophisticated. The private security sector has become increasingly more important as its sphere of responsibility has spread from building and plant security to personal security (bodyguarding) for its employees. In recent years these personal security services have been extended from the superstar of the silver screen to the corporate executive and now may include even his family and staff, both here and abroad. Agencies such as Wackenhut, Pinkerton's and Burns International Security have divisions capable of implementing a variety of detailed personal security plans. (66) These plans have increased geometrically in the past five years.

The point must be made that such cooperation with private security agencies, though necessary and rewarding, could result in sensitive dissemination problems for police agencies in general, and may well become (if not judiciously handled), a legal nightmare for the intelligence community which is already breathing heavily under the strain of class actions, as well as hues and cries from sociologists, civil libertarians and officially sanctioned investigative committees. It should also be noted here that the security industry itself has come under investigation regarding the privacy issue. (67)

Also, in a separate development on April 21, 1977, a newspaper account detailed the intent of the American Civil Liberties Union to file a lawsuit charging that top officials of Honeywell, Inc. conspired illegally with the Federal Bureau of Investigation in the early 70s to infiltrate religious and political groups that opposed Honeywell's production of

antipersonnel weapons. The suit would allege that the F.B.I. provided
information from paid informants to a confidential source within Honeywell not only to head off possible disruptions of the company's annual
meeting of stockholders, but also to prevent any attempt by anti-war
groups to obtain publicity or to embarrass Honeywell's officials. (68)
    In another development, polygraph (lie detector) tests by private
industry are coming under closer scrutiny. The American Civil Liberties Union estimates that 300,000 tests were administered in the public
sector last year. (69) Trudi Hayden, Director of the ACLU's privacy
project, stated "even if the polygraph were totally accurate, and we
don't believe that, and even if it had not strayed into issues like sexual
preference and drug abuse, which we have been told it does, we would
still be opposed to such tests." (70) In a recent related event, the Privacy Protection Study Commission gave Congress a 651-page volume
containing 162 recommendations for imposing strict limits on how the
government and industry use the personal information stored in the
nation's data banks. One recommendation was to make it illegal for
an employer to force an applicant to take a lie detector test.
    Again, the private security industry itself is coming under in-
creasing publicity. (71) This focus is likely to be disturbing to the
private sector. As the alleged abuses by private security mount, law
enforcement agencies, and particularly the intelligence community,
will have to reassess their relationship with private security. This
consideration becomes even more dramatic with the increase in the
number of seminars, workshops and symposiums which invite members
of both law enforcement and private security to come and share experiences.
    As the public fear of terrorism and its awareness continues its
upward spiral, the large corporation will be forced to direct even
greater attention to its property. On August 3, 1977, two bombs were
placed in mid-Manhattan office buildings, killing one person and in-
juring several others. A report carried by the New York Times indicated that 100,000 employees left their New York offices in the pre-
cautionary aftermath. (72) Large corporations gave the rest of the
day off to their employees at enormous financial cost. How often can
these corporations do this? How often must they do this? What will
the security director's role and input be in these costly decisions?
His role will continue to expand with the increasing fear and panic of
terrorism as his "right to know" directly effects his decisions concerning terrorism, escalates.

PROJECTIONS

As this country moves hopefully into a brave new future afforded by the start of its third century, we see crime on the increase, burnt and tarnished cities, wars, racial unrest, unequal opportunity, expanding technology, spare body parts, flights to the moon, meals in pills and a satellite communication system. Based on the previous pages and their evaluations, the following are this author's projections regarding the national trends for intelligence beyond 1984.

There will be a continued awareness and sensitivity on the part of the private sector regarding the role and activities of the intelligence community. We may expect an ongoing concern and continued monitoring of intelligence on the part of civil libertarians and sociologists, among others, demanding tighter controls over intelligence agencies. Hopefully, as the intelligence community successfully displays its integrity and good intent, this pressure will decrease.

There will be a maintenance of emphasis on the part of law enforcement agencies regarding the legalistics involved in intelligence. This will be marked by a greater utilization of legal advisors, frequently drawn from the private sector, as well as a continued concern for legally precise guidelines regarding the gathering and dissemination of intelligence data. We will see a continued judicious attitude regarding this gathering and dissemination.

By 1984 and beyond we will see the establishment of the intelligence role as a true police specialty. This will be brought on by increased terrorism on the one hand and the continued proof of the importance of intelligence in countering terrorism, asassination and community unrest on the other. This could be hampered temporarily by an economic crunch which would result in the curtailment of monies spent on police services in general. It will surely be hastened as some news media point out the alleged horrors of intelligence and then turn the coin to develop a fertile news source by taking a more supportive posture regarding intelligence. This in itself will be hastened as terrorism continues to rock and shock the masses, who in turn will ask, "What should be done?" and "Who is to do it?"

There will be a greater emphasis on the selection, training and development of the embryo intelligence officer. Intelligence files will be generally reduced to stay within the accepted view of what these files should include and reflect. A greater emphasis will be placed on accuracy and relativity than on volume. There will be increased precision regarding what can and should be filed.

We will see greater utilization of public information, including official documents and newspaper reports. A natural development here will be an increased emphasis regarding research analysis and library science, hopefully filling the need for a more scholarly and professional gathering and use of intelligence data. We can expect a greater concern for formal training in analytical techniques. As regards terrorism, we may expect new groups, inspired by the publicity and recognition given to terrorist acts, to utilize similar tactics to push their own demands.

News media will continue to be the exposure vehicle for terrorism. Unfortunately any curtailment or reversal of that trend could result in the creation of and a need for even greater displays of attention-getting tactics by terrorists.

Terrorism will continue in its upward spiral. Bombs will remain a major instrument of disruption, with an increase in the expertise of the makers. Terrorist acts will continue in their successful pattern. The availability of small, powerful weapons, as well as the theatrical way in which the media handle terrorist acts, will help to continue these depredations. Kidnappings and other terrorist acts directed at VIPs and dignitaries, as well as community and civic leaders, will increase. This will be true especially at major transportation facilities. A whole new security style and science is developing here, with private corporations seeking out former representatives of local police agencies to head or institute a wide range of security services. It's to be expected that intelligence units will lose some of their senior personnel to this developing national security interest.

Energy and utility plants, particularly because of the publicity given them as feared targets, will continue to be items of concern, especially because they are a means of dynamic community disruption.

In another development the nuclear threat, currently being voiced, seems to be overrated but the publicity already given it makes it an obviously attractive target for its news value, as well as the terror it would create. Nevertheless the amount of force, precision and expertise required to surmount the current trends in plant security seems to offset any seriously effective effort.

By 1984 terrorist organizations will have had ample time to effect strong coalitions between groups on an international basis. These affiliations will be monitored by the intelligence community.

By 1984 a greater controlled cooperation between police agencies will also have been forged as a result of terrorism. This need will have outweighed any current inhibitions that may exist against information flow. Professional cooperation will extend to the private security agencies as terrorism at private facilities mounts.

After 1984, a greater and more sophisticated cohesion of intelligence units will develop, utilizing common schools and an interchange of personnel and equipment, either directly or through retirement. There will be a greater exchange of intelligence techniques via books, professional articles on intelligence, seminars, schools, symposiums and college courses, all dealing with intelligence and the judicious use and implementation of techniques relating to this field. This effort will be largely brought on by the growing national threat of terrorism and the need to monitor and counter its national effectiveness.

By 1984 and beyond, technological advancements will have affected the intelligence community through the increased use of sophisticated computers, detecting devices, communicational techniques and electronic identification systems.

In the area of social control, such things as curfews will be considered, as well as more effective methods of control regarding crowds and public assemblages. There will be a continued interest in the development of specialized units, hopefully as effective as the Hostage and SWAT units have generally been. They will involve the use of round-the-clock, instant response teams to fill the need for a terrorist counterattack group, perhaps styled along the same lines as those recently used abroad. This need is likely to be filled by a government agency's utilization of a military force, with local intelligence officers acting as consultants.

It is not a promising picture, but it is believed that Americans will have to surrender a small portion of their freedom to guarantee the retention of the remainder.

NOTES AND REFERENCES

1. Alan F. Weston, Privacy and Freedom (New York: Atheneum
    Press, 1967), p. 298.

2. Vance Packard, Naked Society (New York, 1964), p. 87.

3. Samuel Ervin, Uncle Sam is Watching You (Washington, D.C.:
    Public Affairs Press, 1967), p. 3.

4. Edward Hall, The Hidden Dimension (New York: Doubleday &
    Co., Inc., Anchor Books, 1967), p. 7.

5. Hope Ryden, "They Count Horses Don't They?" New York Times,
    August 17, 1977, p. A-21.

6. Richard Harwood, "Is Your Name on a Secret Dossier?" Washing-
    ton Post, May 29, 1966.

7. Philip Sanford, "What's Happening to Your Privacy?" Parade,
    Staten Island Advance, February 27, 1977, p. 24.

8. Ibid.

9. Ibid.

10. Ibid.

11. Ibid.

12. "FBI Set to Discard Files" Daily News, February 10, 1976, p. 6.

13. Jeffrey Antevil, "Snooper Sleuth" Daily News, February 6, 1972,
     p. 137.

14. "Americans Feel Threatened by Data Files," The Police Officers
     Journal, May 1977, p. 45.

15. Ibid.

16. Privacy Protection Study Commission Report, July 1977.

17. The Mindszenty Report, Cardinal Mindszenty Foundation (St.
     Louis, Mo., January 1977), p. 1.

18. Senate Internal Security Subcommittee Hearings, The Nationwide Drive Against Law Enforcement Intelligence Operations, Washington, D.C.: U.S. Government Printing Office, September 18, 1975.

19. Ibid.

20. Ibid.

21. Numbers 13:20 quoted by Harry Rowe Ransom in Central Intelligence and National Security (Cambridge: Harvard University Press, 1958), p. 45.

22. Sun Tzu, "On the Art of War," as quoted by Harry Rowe Ransom in ibid, p. 45.

23. Michael Prawdin, The Mongol Empire (London: G. Allen, 1940), p. 254, quoted by Ransom, Ibid.

24. Garrett Mattingly, Renaissance Diplomacy (Boston: Houghton Mifflin, 1955), p. 260, as quoted by H. R. Ransom, Ibid., p. 47.

25. Deputy Commissioner Jas. Taylor, "All About Eavesdropping," New York City Police Dept. Handbook, 1974, p. 2.

26. Heros Von Borche, Memoirs of The Confederate Wars of Independence, p. 168.

27. Warren Weaver Jr., "U.S. Information Act Difficulties Despite Successes," New York Times, August 8, 1977.

28. Ibid., p. 16.

29. "400 FBI Agents Will Handle Demands for Filing Info," The Police Officers Journal, June 1977, p. 21.

30. Ibid., p. 21.

31. Weaver, op. cit., p. 16.

31a. U.S. Privacy Act of 1974, Title #5, U.S. Code, Sect 552a, effective September 27, 1975.

32. Senate Internal Security Subcommittee Hearings, "The Nationwide Drive Against Law Enforcement Intelligence Operations," statement made by Capt. J. Dintino, New Jersey State Police, September 9, 1976.

33. The Mindszenty Report, op. cit., p. 1.

34. Senate Internal Security Subcommittee Hearings op. cit., The
    Nationwide Drive Against Law Enforcement Operations, pp. 7-13,
    September 18, 1975.

35. Ibid., pp. 4, 5.

36. Senate Internal Security Subcommittee Hearings, Terrorist
    Activity, statement by Sgt. Terence McTigue, NYC Police Dept.,
    October 23, 1975 (Washington, D.C.: U.S. Government Printing
    Office, 1975), p. 505.

37. Senate Internal Security Subcommittee Hearings, Threats to the
    Peaceful Observance of the Bicentennial, statements made by
    Dr. William R. Kintner, June 18, 1976.

38. Ibid.

39. Ibid.

40. Ibid.

41. Senate Internal Security Subcommittee Hearings, Terrorist
    Activity, October 1975 (Washington, D.C.: U.S. Government
    Printing Office, 1975), pp. 526-27.

42. Ambassador Lewis Hoffacker, speech made before the Mayor's
    Advisory Committee on International Relations and Trade, the
    Foreign Relations Assn. at Louisiana, New Orleans February 23,
    1974, entitled "The U.S. Government Response to Terrorism, a
    Global Approach."

43. "Disorders and Terrorism" (Byrne Report), Report to the Task
    Force on Disorders and Terrorism-National Advisory Committee
    on Criminal Justice and Standards & Goals, Washington, 1976.

44. "Latest Worry Terrorists Using High Technology," US News and
    World Report, March 14, 1969, p. 69.

45. Ibid.

46. Ibid.

47. Op. cit., Disorders and Terrorism (Byrne Report), p. 2.

48. Jack Anderson, "Energy Crisis May Bring on a Revolution," Staten Island Advance, April 5, 1977, p. 9.

49. Jack Anderson, "Lack of Nuclear Safeguards Signal Worldwide Danger," Staten Island Advance, March 14, 1977, p. 9.

50. Ibid.

51. James Wiegart, "Terrorism a Grim Look into the Future," New York Daily News, March 14, 1977, p. 26.

52. Ibid.

53. Tony Brenna, "Security to Guard Atomic Plants from Terrorists is Still Shockingly Weak," Enquirer, March 18, 1977, p. 22.

54. Ibid.

55. Peter Gwynne and Stephan Michaud, "Fail Safe," Newsweek, January 17, 1977, p. 42.

56. Ibid.

57. "Terrorism and Censorship," Time magazine, March 28, 1977, p. 57.

58. Ibid.

59. Ibid.

60. Ibid.

61. William Hines, "Hostage-Taking: The Newest Wave," Staten Island Advance, March 10, 1977, p. 1.

62. Max Lerner, "Terrorist Theatre," New York Post, March 14, 1977, p. 27.

63. "D. C. Terror Incident Leads to Demands for New Counter Measures," Law Enforcement News, April 19, 1977, p. 3.

64. Les Brown, "CBS Issues Guidelines on Terror," New York Times, April 15, 1977, p. c-28.

65. Op cit., Ransom, p. 49.

66. "Executives and Stars Buying Private Protection," Police Times, May 1977, p. 6.

67. "Privacy Protection Study Commission Report" as quoted in When Private Eyes Poke into Your Affairs, US News and World Report, February 7, 1977, p. 34.

68. Michael Jensen, "ACLU Suit Says Honeywell Conspired With FBI," New York Times, April 21, 1977, p. d-1.

69. Anna Quindlen, "Polygraph Tests for Jobs-Truth and Consequences," New York Times, August 19, 1977, p. b-1.

70. Ibid.

71. Striking Back at the Super Snoops, Time magazine, July 18, 1977, pp. 16-18.

72. "100,000 Leave New York Offices Over Bomb Threats," New York Times, August 4, 1977, p. b-6.

8 Organized Crime and Justice beyond 1984

Ralph Salerno

The initial reaction to the challenge of attempting to describe any situation as it will appear some years hence is that the assignment will be a difficult one to fulfill. As a methodology for an approach begins to formulate and develop there comes the realization that the goal will not be as difficult to reach as was originally imagined. Organized crime particularly lends itself to this kind of study in that it is influenced by broad social patterns, has been so in the past, and will probably continue to be so in the future. The importance of "outside" influences has proven to be frustrating for policemen and other criminal justice personnel who do not like to recognize the very limited impact that their investigations, prosecutions, sentencing, attempted rehabilitation and supervision on probation and parole has been able to make on the phenomenon we call organized crime.

At this time, new patterns of change are developing which will influence the future. In this chapter the writer will attempt to avoid advocacy and limit the record to an objective analysis of the past which has brought us to where we are; an accurate recording of the emerging changes; and a reasonably educated guess as to the future, with an emphasis on "educated" and a limited dependency upon "guess."

The United States is currently engaged in a trend which follows a British precedent. The major difference is that the United States will probably take fifty years to accomplish what was done in England in one fell swoop. In 1960, the British government completed a review and reform of its penal laws which can best be characterized as a purging therefrom of matters which, perhaps, never should have been placed there at all. ** The Parliament had developed an awareness that em-

---

** Based upon conversations with the Honorable William Rice-Davies, M. P., chairman of the Parliamentary committee which conducted the study and made recommendations to the parent body.

bodied in the penal law were attitudes and positions which reflected successful lobbying over the years by church, parental and other groups for the purpose of trying to influence and control social conduct as a matter of law. The result had become that lawmakers, policemen, prosecutors and the courts were engaged in the implementation of religious positions, and thus were imposing upon the general society the social attitudes of various segments of that society.

The reform was a decision by government that it was improper to allow such vested interest groups to pass on their own concerns, interests and responsibilities to government functionaries, particularly when done as a matter of penal law. Without endorsing or refuting any particular code of conduct, the legislators simply removed such matters from the area of criminal sanctions requiring the efforts of criminal justice personnel.

Turf Accountants were a long-established English tradition. They could legally service the wagering instincts of persons of substance who were able to establish a line of credit. Bets on horse races and other matters of interest, often placed by telephone, were accepted, and at regular intervals the accounts were balanced by the remittance of a check representing winnings or a billing for the amounts lost. In 1960, widespread legalization of gambling took place for the more affluent who might enjoy gaming clubs and casinos, and the government decided to "give the little fellow a whirl" by permitting cash betting shops to service bets on horses, football and other events which might be of interest to the average citizen. One very important consideration in the deliberations of the research committee was the result of a poll conducted of every Chief Constable in England, soliciting their views on the subject of gambling legalization. The British police did not suffer from a traditional problem of police corruption arising from gambling enforcement, such as has been the case in the United States throughout the twentieth century. Some minor problems had begun to appear on the British scene, and this probably influenced the unanimous vote in favor of legalization, with licensing, regulation and enforcement given over to other agencies of government.

As a part of the sweeping reform, drug maintenance for addicts became a fact. The government was neither approving drug abuse nor offering an unrealistic hope of "curing" the addict. The decision was to allow certified addicts to be able to maintain themselves at a reasonable legal cost, avoid the exorbitant costs of illegal drug markets, and not be forced to engage in criminal activity in order to obtain the funds necessary to supply their "habit."

Sexual conduct was dealt with. The law would allow consenting adults, in privacy, to establish their own norm. Prostitution was not legalized, but the law would take action more vigorously when it was

conducted in the form of obvoxious public behavior such as open street
solicitation. England, then, dealt in one move with what later came to
called, in the United States, "victimless crimes." In the invervening
years there have been some slight modifications from time to time.
The maintenance of addicts in a private doctor-patient relationship did
not work out to the satisfaction of those monitoring the program. They
held the concept of maintenance to be a valid one, but changed the
mechanics involved so that the drugs were obtained through government
clinics. There has been no strong demand for a reversal of the total
reform, and the public appears to be content with the current status of
things.

A distinct advantage to reform in England is that there is a single
criminal code, whereas in the United States we have fifty-one of such
when the Federal statutes are added to those of the individual states.
It is probably that by 1985 (25 years after Parliament's action) the
United States will have moved slowly, erratically and much less prag-
matically toward the British model. Our country, with a larger and
more diverse population, jealously guards the prerogatives of State
law from Federal encroachment. It is reluctant to perceive that, although we speak highly of Constitutional separation of church and state,
it is governed by penal statutes replete with provisions concerning
divorce, abortion, gambling, drinking, drug use and sexual behavior,
which too are the results of successful lobbying by church groups over
the years. It represents a case of individual churches imposing their
religious standards on the total population by means of government law
and enforcement of the statutes. Not too many Americans are pleased
by the fact that what literally thousands of husbands and wives elect to
do in the privacy of their bedrooms is, under penal statutes, felonious
and calling for years of imprisonment on the law books of the states in
which they reside.

This American dichotomy (some observers offer the word hypocrisy)
has been a boon to organized criminal enterprises for many decades.
Anything that can be done to reduce the contradictions will have an effect
on organized crime. Changing values and lifestyles will probably give
impetus to the sluggish American movement, and the demographics involved will help too. As the population shifts out of the Northeast toward the Sunbelt States of the South, Southwest and West there will be
a greater comingling of ideas and values. Thus, the polarization of the
past between the North and the South or the East and the West will be
reduced with the diffusion of people among these geographical areas.

ALCOHOL

The history of American ambivalence concerning the consumption
of alcohol can be traced back to the immediate post-Revolutionary period.
The imposition of a tax on alcohol by our emerging nation gave rise to
the Whiskey Rebellion in the state of Pennsylvania. It required our first
president, George Washington, to send troops to quell the rebellion. In
the years that followed the Federal and State governments increased
regulation and taxation, and not always as a producer of revenue. Often
the legislation was a form of government disapproval of alcohol consumption, and the law and its enforcement was expected to reduce such consumption. This form of disapproval was often inspired, and always supported by, groups who were opposed to the consumption of alcohol on
religious or moral grounds.

Ultimately, in some areas of the nation, principally in the South,
such groups were able to induce government to take its disapproval beyond restriction, regulation and taxation into total prohibition. By the
beginning of the 20th Century prohibition was a growing movement at the
State and local level encouraging the suggestion of national prohibition.
Following World War I, added impetus led to the ratification of the 18th
Amendment and the enactment of the Volstead Act for enforcement, and
the era of National Prohibition was ushered in. The nation was said to
have embarked on a "noble experiment," but the results, certainly upon
the criminal justice system, were disastrous. No better description can
be given than that of Elmer Irey, who was Chief of the Enforcement
Branch of the U.S. Treasury Department. In his book, The Tax Dodgers
(Greenberg Press, 1948) he states, "the most extraordinary collection
of political hacks, hangers-on and passing highwaymen got appointed as
prohibition agents. As I think back upon prohibition enforcement, I am
astonished that so many agents did remain honest. Certainly, they, and
the law they were enforcing, were held in high contempt across the land. "

Anyone who has studied organized crime in its modern era comes
away convinced that it was in the Prohibition era that those criminals
who rose to leadership positions among the gangs of thugs involved in
importation, manufacture and distribution of illegal alcohol first developed the sophisticated techniques of political involvement, corruption
and evasion of the sanctions of criminal law that have been their trade-
mark ever since. The proponents of the legislation could not be satisfied that they had curtailed consumption of alcohol because there was
much evidence to the contrary; and the opponents of the movement
could not be happy that the Constitution of the United States (which we
like to refer to as "sacred document, ") was being ignored, contravened
and villified. It did not take long for any objective person to acknowledge

this attempt to control social behavior by law had failed, but little objectivity was to be found on either side of the issue. By 1928 repeal of the amendment was a political issue in the presidential primaries and election, with diehard defenders characterizing Catholic Al Smith, the democratic nominee, as the tool of "rum and Romanism."

Those states which had earlier imposed prohibition had never stamped out the production of "moonshine" and "red-eye" whiskey, and the conditions that had prevailed there spread throughout the country. Home manufacture of beer and "bathtub gin" became rampant, and for those with more expensive tastes alcoholic beverages were imported from Canada, Europe and the Caribbean. The literature of that period and motion picture films describing the era seem to have concentrated on New York and Chicago and the colorful exploits of Al Capone, Dutch Schultz and Waxey Gordon. They would lead to the erroneous conclusion that organized criminal groups took over the alcohol industry only in the Northeast. Two headlines from the San Francisco Chronicle during 1928 give evidence that the Far West was equally affected:

"McDonough Brothers, bail bond brokerage house, described as a fountainhead of corruption, controlling manufacture and sale of illicit liquor, wine and beer in the North Beach area and Mission District."

"Underworld vengeance against a gangster who played the double role of hijacker and bootlegger cost the life of Jerry Ferri, age 37, local beer baron and former Chicago racketeer."

A report of homicides during the 1920s compiled by the Los Angeles Police Department reads, in part, "Darwin Avenue, a street on the north side of Los Angeles, was known as 'Shotgun Alley', because of the bootleg and gang wars in that vicinity."

Repeal in 1932 returned the situation to State and local law, so that prohibition of the sale of alcohol continued in many jurisdictions. As we entered the 1970s (four decades after Federal repeal) it was still illegal to serve drinks by the glass in most of Texas and Kansas. Legislators from various parts of Florida, when at the State capitol in Tallahassee, would have to engage in the demeaning practice of "brown bagging." That is, they could bring a bottle of liquor into a restaurant (usually in a brown paper bag), be served the glasses and ice into which they could pour their own liquor. The governor of the state of Mississippi was embarrassed at a country club where he was dining with friends when lawmen conducted a raid and found him and those at his table being served alcoholic beverages illegally. Americans suffered the suggestion that their right to vote might be purchased or inveigled from them by

several ounces of alcohol, and thus there were laws which kept liquor
stores and bars closed on Election Day. Even in states which permitted
the sale of alcohol, this was often done under the subterfuge that the law
permitted such sale of liquor in restaurants as a part of serving food.
Regulations required that receipts from the sale of alcohol be limited
to a minor part of total income. Just about every neighborhood bar in
the United States would find it impossible to meet the terms and conditions in the law, so that what often happened in fact was that the law was
overlooked and law enforcers corrupted, with an attendant "scandal"
every few years, which would be thereafter ignored. In Wichita, Kansas,
a country club which was relocating donated its clubhouse and adjacent
land to the State university. The building was to be used as a faculty
clubhouse and the lovely restaurant and bar would continue to operate,
as it had, under a club license. (A club license is the means employed
by the more affluent to evade the intent of the law where public bars
are prohibited. It is often used to continue segregation of the races.)
There was some embarrassment when the university learned that a
club license could not be obtained for a premises located on State property. It became necessary for the faculty to form a non-profit corporation, all for the purpose of being able to serve alcoholic beverages.

The trend today is toward the gradual disappearance of prohibition
of the sale and consumption of alcohol. In Dallas and Houston, Texas,
liquor can be served by the drink. The governor of Mississippi, who
was chagrined and discomforted, signed into law a statute permitting
local option choices rather than the State ban which had prevailed.
North Carolina has finally permitted package liquor stores, and legislators in Tallahassee can order a cocktail with dinner just as they could
for years in Miami, Orlando, Tampa and elsewhere.

The work of the Presidential Commission on Law Enforcement and
the Administration of Justice helped to place the consumption of alcohol
in a better perspective. In its 1967 report the Commission indicated
that in 1965, two million arrests, or one out of every three in the nation, were for the offense of public drunkenness. Patently, a tremendous percentage of the resources of the criminal justice system were
being poured into this bottomless pit. The Commission recommended
that drunkenness per se, without any other attendant violations of law,
not be treated as a crime, but as the social/medical problem that it is.
This suggestion has been widely implemented, with the commensurate
saving of system resources for more important usage.

This general trend toward reform will continue so that beyond
1984, very little relating to alcohol will be a criminal justice problem.
Regulations and taxation will continue as a substantial revenue producer
without any guise of governmental approval or disapproval of alcohol
consumption. Hours of limitation will slowly disappear, with supply

and demand exercising the logical control. We will come to realize
that if bar patrons all go home at 10:30 P.M., then eleven will automatically become the closing hour. On the other hand, if there is a consumer demand during twenty-four hours of the day, it is capricious and
arbitrary to set a closing time of midnight, 2 A.M., 4 A.M. or any
other specific hour. The repeal of prohibition greatly reduced the role
of organized crime in liquor manufacturing, distribution and sale. If
there are no hours of limit, organized crime will not be able to operate
the "after-hours clubs" which now abound. **

In summary, the criminal participation in this industry has always
been greatest when the laws and regulations are unpopular, unrealistic
and therefore, largely unheeded. The corruption of public officers is
commensurate with inordinate regulation. Beyond 1984 we will have
learned a lesson from attempts to control alcohol, and we will be utilizing this lesson in other areas as well.

GAMBLING

Gambling is another area of public conduct where current efforts
toward reform are often met with the criticism that we are seeking to
legalize an activity only because of a failure to stamp it out by law and
law enforcement efforts. This is putting the cart before the horse. Our
nation began without any such laws, and reform today is the strong suggestion that:

1. We never should have had any laws.
2. Their stated purpose, whether right or wrong, has failed.
3. Greater evils have resulted therefrom than the evils that were
   originally supposed to be addressed.

Therefore, the changes taking place today are the correction of
error which was introduced into the original status quo.

Gambling was not a prescribed activity in the Colonial days of
America. George Washington's diary tells of how many pounds he won
"playing at cards" and how many pounds he lost betting on the horse
races in Maryland. The Father of our Country was not confessing in-

---

** The Detroit riot of 1967 which did irreparable damage to that city
was triggered when two police officers attempted to serve a sum-
mons at a "blind pig" in the black ghetto. A "blind pig" is the
name given in Detroit to a premises which engages in the sale of
liquor at a time when regular licensed bars are prohibited from
doing so.

discretions or wrongdoings to his diary; these were legal and accepted
activities. Lotteries paid for a student dormitory at Yale and for improvements at Harvard and King's College (later Columbia University)
at times when these were all strongly Church-related institutions of
learning. Lotteries were conducted to purchase artillery for the defense
of Philadelphia and to support the troops of the Continental Army during
the American Revolution.

Anti-gambling legislation, particularly against lotteries, began to
appear in the 1830s. Researchers are easily able to identify the role
of church groups in this successful political movement. In his 1977
study, funded in part by L. E. A. A. , Professor Robert Blakey of Cor-
nell Law School's Institute on Organized Crime cites:

> Episcopal and Presbyterian churches too, escalated their opposition
> to the games. Methodism, condemning all forms of gambling, gained
> adherents throughout the 1830's and 40's. Pennsylvania, inspired
> by these reform movements and its Quaker traditions, banned all
> lotteries in 1833, even those which might otherwise be specially
> chartered by the state.

> By 1834 New York, New Jersey, Massachusetts, Connecticut, New
> Hampshire, Maine, Vermont, Ohio and Illinois had all joined in
> prohibiting lotteries. In 1842, Congress enacted a ban on federal
> lotteries. Texas and California banned the games in their first
> state constitutions. By 1862 few states lacked an anti-lottery law.

What is frequently overlooked by researchers is the parallel interest
of businessmen in this movement. Blakey's research indicates, "The
very success and respectability of the colonial (lottery) games invited
English interference. The Lords of Trade in England had long opposed
lotteries on the ground that they dissipated wealth. " It cannot be entirely coincidental that anti-gambling legislation beginning in the 1830s took
place with the advent of the Industrial Revolution, which would change
the states from an agrarian community to an industrial nation. Factory
owners and wealthy businessmen of that era would often, themselves,
serve in the legislative bodies of the time. In addition they would probably serve on the boards of elders of their churches, and thus be in a
position to influence the "invitation" to a Protestant clergyman to become
the pastor of the flock. Thus they could influence legislation directly,
or indirectly by inspiring clergymen whose employment and advancement
in church hierarchy they could control.

While the enactment and enforcement of such laws was always her-
alded with a religious fervor that was seeking to protect the moral fabric
of the nation, it was seldom, if ever, that the service to economic inter-

ests was openly identified. In order to get a proper perspective of the period of about 100 years ago, inspect the values reflected in legislation:

1. Gambling was an evil that had to be protected against by law.
2. Statute law was not considered strong enough to achieve the goal; the matter was most frequently controlled by provisions of state constitutions.
3. Child labor was not considered an important evil. It was legal for a 14-year-old child to be employed six days per week for up to 72 hours per week in a factory or in a coal mine. Whoever influenced legislation did not demand enactment of child labor laws.
4. Lack of education was not considered evil. There were no compulsory education laws that might take children out of the factory and mining work force and into the schools.

The total body of law more than 100 years ago was fostered by persons who were complacent about human slavery, de facto for black people, and with a slight veneer of compensation for poor whites, usually recent immigrants. In the past century we have come to recognize the need for emancipation, child labor and education laws, but some still cling tenaciously to concepts of gambling and drinking that were a product of that era.

In keeping with our tradition, even when a countermovement began, it was not as a social change as much as a response to the economic pressures of the Great Depression. In 1931 the state of Nevada legalized many forms of gambling, and during the remainder of that decade many states decided to allow pari-mutuel wagering on horse races at tracks licensed by the state, which would in return exact a hefty percentage of the gross as tax revenue. In fact, many states, including California, Illinois and New York, have long enjoyed greater revenue from pari-mutuel wagering than has Nevada from its almost total legalization of casino gambling. In New York the income from pari-mutuel wagering is in excess of $200,000,000.00 per year. These early beginnings of legalization remained alone for quite some time, despite the evidence that the realm of illegal betting had been taken over by organized criminal groups throughout the United States.

Seeking an area to make up for the loss of the goose that laid golden eggs (which was Prohibition) the crime syndicates had capitalized upon the vagaries of our gambling laws as against the instincts of sizeable numbers in the population. Senator Estes Kefauver, in his public hearings during 1950 and 1951, established that control of illegal betting on horse races (the most pervasive form of gambling up to and during the 1940s) had been effected through the crime cartels control of the racing wire services. The racing wire service provided information on races throughout the country, changes in jockeys, post positions, odds, last minute scratches of horses scheduled to run, and, of course, the eventual identification of the horses that ran first, second and third and the payoff prices of these winners. With blatant hypocrisy, newspapers whose editorials commented on crime and government and citizenship regularly published the charts and results of race tracks located many hundreds and sometimes thousands of miles away, with the full knowledge that the readers who demanded this information had no legal way of betting on the events in the city where the newspaper was published. Yet these readers demanded the data in order to expedite their bets with illegal bookmakers who often corrupted the police and others in the criminal justice system.

One result of Kefauver's congressional investigation was the suggestion that where State and local authorities had failed to stamp out illegal gambling, the Federal Government would be able to do so. The Federal jurisdiction would, once again, be based upon the taxing powers of the Congress. Legislation was enacted which required the purchase of a $50 tax stamp by anyone engaged in the business of wagering, and in addition the Internal Revenue Service was expected to collect a 10 percent excise tax on the gross amounts involved. Clearly, whatever had been learned about the Treasury Department's success or failure in alcohol enforcement was being ignored. The most modest estimate is that the 10 percent excise tax should have yielded at least 2 billion dollars per year. The largest amount ever collected by the government was 6 million (or about 3 percent of what should have been the anticipated revenue). All data tends to indicate that the amount of money wagered illegally in the United States continued to grow. There is some evidence that smaller, independent bookmakers were frightened out of the market by the involvement of "the Feds." Thus, the net result was that a bigger gambling jackpot was being divided by a smaller number of entrepreneurs (mainly organized crime), so that the Federal Government had done the big crime syndicates a significant favor (once again)!

Some opponents had opposed the law, saying that it was a guise under which the Federal Government would compel bookmakers to identify themselves to the national government, and with these records being open to State and local police, the registrants would then become vulnerable to arrest under State penal provisions. Ultimately, the Supreme Court of the United States ruled exactly this way, declaring the $50 tax stamp to be in violation of Fifth Amendment rights in that the registrants were being compelled by law to give evidence against themselves.

The Treasury Department has always prided itself on an ability to collect taxes that are largely voluntarily paid by most Americans. The

1953 anti-gambling tax proved that the organized crime groups did not come within this category. In 1961 the spectre of Federal gambling enforcement was increased when the Federal Bureau of Investigation was given jurisdiction for the crime, rather than the tax violation of interstate gambling. Those who suggested that it was now all over for the gambling combines were again terribly disappointed. Their alibi, after almost a decade of F. B. I. jurisdiction, was that interstate violations were not enough, that what was required was legislation that would enable the F. B. I. to move against gambling combines of some size even if operated entirely within the boundaries of one state. The response was found in the Organized Crime Control Act of 1970, which established a Federal crime (under instate commerce provisions of the Federal Constitution) if the gambling activity involved five or more persons, a gross of at least $2,000 per day, and a continued activity which exceeded 30 days. The same statute called for the establishment of a National Gambling Study Commission, which was to be formed two years after the enactment of the 1970 law.

Among the findings of the National Gambling Commission, reported in 1976, was the fact that Federal Government tax policies had inhibited legal gambling (State licensed and/or operated entities) with no evidence or any reduction of illegal activities. By 1977, throughout the United States, it could be found that criminal justice priorities for gambling enforcement, prosecution and sentencing had reached an all-time low, at both the Federal and State levels, because of the demand for greater priority against more serious crimes.

During the 1960s, beginning with the state of New Hampshire and closely followed by New York, New Jersey and others, state lotteries proliferated until fourteen states in the northeast quadrant of the U.S. were operating some form of lottery. In addition, New York and Connecticut authorized off-track betting on horse races to be operated by local government. There was also an expansion of pari-mutuel wagering on dog races and Jai-Alai games. Most of these changes had been introduced with the dual aim of gaining government revenue and competing with organized crime activities. Blakey's analysis is that it is difficult to achieve both aims in that they counteract each other. He suggests that if revenue is to be the prime consideration, then the ability to compete with criminal enterprises is lessened. This appears to be true, in that the State lotteries take a 40 percent profit after 15 percent has been used for operating costs, and there is little evidence of successful reduction of illegal lotteries. Blakey recommends that government should narrow and define its objective as being toward one goal or the other. The National Gambling Commission makes the same observation, indicating that the legal forms of gambling could be more competitive with a more enlightened tax policy.

There are two exceptions to the general rule of unsuccessful competition by legal entities. The New York City Off-Track Betting Corporation did, even by concession of persons opposed to the concept, reduce illegal wagering on horses with bookmakers by almost 50 percent. This gain was greatly reduced when the demand for higher revenue received higher priority. In 1975, financially beleaguered New York City imposed an additional surtax of 5 percent on winnings, over and above the 18 percent taken out of the gross. This caused a 25 percent decline in total handle (which represents a net loss of revenue).

The other exception may be in lotteries designed expressly to compete with the illegal numbers game. By mid-1977, Massachusetts had a legal numbers operation which seems to be affording competition to organized crime although it is too early for a complete analysis of the total effect. In New York, an even more interesting point of view is manifesting itself. Early in the year, an announcement was made regarding the preparation of a New York State Lottery "numbers game." When it seemed a long time coming, a reporter for the New York Post asked John Quinn, the lottery commissioner, about the delay. He was told that the lottery was ready to go but that the approval of the governor (Hugh Carey) was being withheld because of "political considerations." Quinn said, "It's a political decision rather than a lottery decision. There are socio-economic factors. The Governor has to make a tough decision. I recognize that." The newspaper article explained that one consideration was the avowed opposition to a legal numbers game from politicians of Harlem and East Harlem, the heart of the city's vast numbers racket. The Black and Hispanic numbers operators are convinced that a carefully structured legal competition can destroy "their" game. Whether the constituency being represented by the minority politicians is the community as a whole or only the best interests of the illegal gambling czars is an interesting question.

A 1976 statewide referendum in New Jersey approved the licensing of gambling casinos in Atlantic City. This ended the mainland exclusive that had been held for so long by the state of Nevada. Operators in that state quickly hedged their bets by lobbying successfully for the removal of a ban which had forbidden Nevada licensees from having a proprietary interest in casinos elsewhere. There can be no question that this move will keep customers from traveling to Nevada from eastern population centers. An early financial success in Atlantic City will also spur the present demand for legalized casinos in Pennsylvania, New York, Massachusetts, Florida and elsewhere. More casinos will subdivide the eastern market, which Atlantic City will initially enjoy. After a few years only the strongest competitors will survive.

The trend toward further legalization of gambling will continue in the United States for some time. After 1984 the picture will look something like this: State lotteries, off-track betting and casinos will be added by more states. Pool cards on football, baseball, basketball and hockey will be legalized, probably as government owned and operated enterprises. The possibility of legal wagering on individual team sports will come about eventually through the research and development products of major computer companies, which see further legalized gambling as an emerging future market for their technological production.

In time, both government-owned wagering entities and private sector licensees who pay taxes to government will come to realize that the greatest limitation upon their success will be the illegal gambling operations of organized criminal groups. At that time, the "legals" will become a constituency calling for stronger action from the criminal justice system than has been the case. Arrest, conviction and serious penalties for gambling violations will become fact, even though the serious penalties will take the form of financial sanctions rather than jail sentences. Even as the liquor industry has become one of the most successful and powerful lobbying groups in every State capitol and in Washington, D. C. , the legitimate gambling industry will successfully lobby for strong action against its competitors. The judiciary will come to impose stronger gambling penalties on those who interfere with the government's attempt to raise revenue through wagering operation and taxation in order to meet the demands for service to the public.

A long time after 1984, when the social stigma has been removed from gambling, and illegal competition has also been removed, wagering will take its place among other high-risk activities such as investment in the stock market and will receive the same social approbation. It may be possible that after several generations, private sector corporations will induce government to phase itself out of operations and simply collect revenue through taxation of gambling.

Through this period of change, gambling will lose its allure for organized crime. When gambling was almost 100 percent illegal it afforded criminals the opportunity to gain revenue, the rationale for the corruption of public officers, and the support of much of the citizenry. When there is a legal alternative, Americans will accept it, even if the offering does not duplicate every advantage of the illegal system. The gift to organized crime of having proscribed gambling will be removed, and we will discover that the criminals cannot compete on even terms with legitimate inventiveness, engineering and business acumen. This will be a better place for gambling.

NARCOTICS, DRUGS AND CONTROLLED SUBSTANCES

The drug scene in the United States involves substances which are cultivated, grown and processed outside of the United States and then brought into the country; it includes legally manufactured pills, liquids and powders, and it includes a highly mobile society of persons who may engage in some form of use or abuse of the chemicals involved. Because of these many factors, the Federal efforts at control are of paramount importance because of the limited ability of states and political subdivisions thereof to have a meaningful impact on the total problem.

The major Federal concern came originally in the Harrison Act, passed by Congress in 1914 as a tax statute. Thus enforcement was vested in the Bureau of Narcotics, a subdivision of the Treasury Department. The Federal jurisdiction was cloaked in a masquerade of Federal taxing powers rather than as a straightforward criminal concern. Drug abuse, when it seemed to be limited to musicians and ghetto minorities, did not have a high priority. For example, in 1950, with a police force of about 23,000 persons, some 20 were assigned to the Narcotics Squad of the New York City Police Department (less than 1/1000 of manpower resources).

During the 1960s, concerns about drug abuse became a white middle-class issue, and in 1962 President John Kennedy called a White House Conference on Narcotics and Drug Abuse. One of the conference results was the establishment of The President's Advisory Commission on Narcotic and Drug Abuse, mandated to study the problem in depth and report to the president in November 1963. The final report was received by President Lyndon Johnson, who had succeeded his recently assassinated predecessor. The recommendations tended to suggest that as much as drug abuse was a law enforcement problem, the issue was deeply involved with social and medical problems which called for action on the part of the comparatively new Department of Health, Education and Welfare. Because 1964 was a presidential election year any real action was deferred until 1965.

Effective February 1, 1966, the terms of the Drug Abuse Control Amendments of 1965 took effect. In reality they opened a series of bureaucratic empire-building maneuvers, in which government agents and agencies fought almost as fiercely among themselves as they did the basic problem. The amendments sought to control the improper use of tranquilizers and hallucinogens and jurisdiction was given to a newly created Bureau of Drug Abuse Control (BDAC) within the Food and Drug Administration of H.E.W. This bureau began with 200 agents and announced a goal of 500 agents by 1970. The Federal Bureau of Narcotics, which had never grown to number more than 250 agents in the Treasury

Department, immediately began to feel threatened by the budget resources allocated to B. D. A. C. The threat became even more realistic when personnel were recruited away from the Treasury agency to H. E. W. with the lure of higher salaries that the new agency's budget allowed.

At operational levels the competition became fierce and there was no coordinated effort against dealers who might handle an entire range, from heroin and marijuana through hallucinogens and tranquilizers. Informants, who could sell information about the same culprit to both agencies, were often the principal beneficiaries. Federal agents from both agencies often observed and maintained surveillances on suspiciously acting characters who in reality were from the other agency. This ridiculous situation continued until about 1968, when B. D. A. C. , its jurisdiction and agents were taken from H. E. W. and the F. B. N. was taken from Treasury, and both merged into the Bureau of Narcotics and Dangerous Drugs, which became a part of the Department of Justice. The merged organization was hardly a happy, coordinated force. Those who had departed F. B. N. for B. D. A. C. were considered "deserters" who had "abandoned" the older agency for higher G. S. ratings and salaries. In the merged unit these "deserters" became group leaders of resentful former colleagues. Men might be working for superiors with much less seniority and experience than themselves who had advanced through actions their agents considered to be disloyal.

This was not the entire range of Federal enforcement dissension. The enforcement section of the Treasury Department did not relish the loss of the Federal Bureau of Narcotics. It had established a record of having incarcerated more major organized crime figures than all other agencies combined. To overcome this loss, Treasury sought to increase the narcotics capabilities of the Custom Service and thus capitalize on the public concern about drugs.

An opportunity to do exactly that took place in 1969 with the advent of the Nixon Administration, when G. Gordon Liddy became the second in command of Treasury enforcement. A major supplementary budget was obtained to increase the narcotics section of Customs, and Myles Ambrose, a former executive director of the New York-New Jersey Waterfront Commission, was placed in charge. Once again, recruitment took the form of proselytizing and raiding experienced officers away from B. N. D. D. with promises of pay increases and upgraded status. ** The battle went beyond budget and personnel when Customs sought to become the first line of defense against imported drugs not only by guarding the nation's points of entry, but by obtaining jurisdiction of the overseas offices (and informant networks) that had been established over many years by the old Federal Narcotics Bureau. This was strongly and success-

_____

** The writer knows of one agent who moved three times, always with a grade and pay increase.

fully resisted by B. N. D. D. , but the bureaucratic infighting, typical of
Washington D. C. , became fierce.

Egil Krogh was the Nixon staff aide with oversight interest for the
White House over law enforcement matters. About nine months after
the increase of Customs' narcotics capability, he suggested that still
another agency was needed. There came into being the Office of Drug
Abuse Law Enforcement (ODALE) and Ambrose was shifted from Customs to take charge of the new unit, which he staffed with agents from
Customs and B. N. D. D. ODALE established a narcotics "hotline" with
promises of reward money for useful information, but this program was
a colossal failure. It established as its target the drug dealers with the
greatest community visibility of affluence, or roughly dealers in ounces
and quarter kilos. The result was three highly competitive Federal drug
enforcement organizations vying for budget, headlines, White House interest and noteworthy arrests. For the next several years around the
United States, if one were to ask State and local narcotic agents how they
got along with "The Feds, " the answer was always the same. "It is a
pleasure to work with them because they have all the money for informants and for 'buys' of narcotics and for equipment. " The only problem
is one must spend 50 percent of his time trying not to get caught in the
crossfire going on between B. N. D. D. , Customs and ODALE.

The situation led, as might have been expected, to excessive zeal,
particularly on the part of ODALE agents who were led to believe that
they were the chosen troops of the White House. Several unfortunate
cases attracted national notoriety when doors were kicked in, people
pulled out of bed and guns placed to their heads - and other excess -
before the embarrassed discovery that the Federal agents were at the
wrong address. The ensuing uproar in the press led to the demise of
ODALE, which came in a rather unique fashion. ODALE agents and
some Customs agents, together with B. N. D. D. , were merged together in
a superagency of more than 2, 000 persons which was to be known as the
Drug Enforcement Administration. Chosen to rule over this seething
cauldron of discontent was John Bartels, an attorney who had headed the
first Organized Crime Strike Force in Newark, New Jersey for the
Department of Justice, with a reasonable degree of success.

The task taken on by Bartels was certainly not an enviable one. The
clear-cut "French connection" that brought Turkish heroin into the United
States after processing by French Corsicans in and around Marseilles
had presented a reasonable limited target. For quite some time it was
known that about 80 percent of the heroin entering the United States followed this route. The yield of the poppy seed turned into morphine base
would be shipped to France, purified in clandestine laboratories and then
continued through various channels into the major markets of the U.S.
It was often suggested by the less than learned that all we had to do was

get the Turkish government to cut off the poppy crop, and/or the French
government to break up the laboratories, and our drug problems would
be resolved. These simplistic solutions overlooked important facts;
that poppies can be and are grown in many parts of the world other than
Turkey; and that a heroin laboratory can be established anywhere that
$2,000 worth of equipment and a chemist can be brought together. (This
was later clearly proven when the Turkish crop was severely diminished
and the laboratories around Marseilles were no more, all without any
reduction of supply to the U.S. from other sources.)

Even before the French connection was dissolved, the merchants
of heroin had demonstrated an ability to be flexible and adapt to change.
At one time the route had been a direct one from France to New York
City, the major market. When enforcement had made that route somewhat more difficult the heroin would be routed to Montreal and other
parts of Canada for trans-shipment across the border into the U.S. In
its last stages the route became a dog-leg from Europe to South America
and then north to the United States. As the Turkish crop diminished new
sources of supply built up. Asian heroin, particularly from the Golden
Triangle of Laos, Cambodia and Burma began to appear. The increased
movement of ships, aircraft and personnel to and from the Viet Nam
theatre of war was very helpful to the marketing plan. Asian heroin
would also be shipped into Vancouver, British Columbia (which has
more than half of all of Canada's heroin abusers), and moved south into
the U.S. Asian heroin began to appear in large quantities in Amsterdam,
Holland, some for local use in Europe and some for further shipment to
America. Still another source, which eventually became the major one,
developed in Mexico. (By 1976 D.E.A. estimated that 80 percent of the
heroin siezed by the agency came from Mexico.)

There were further complexities. One was the reappearance of
cocaine. The Narcotics Task Force of the Presidential Commission on
Law Enforcement and the Administration of Justice, in 1966, gave six
lines to a description of cocaine, which read:

> This drug is included as a narcotic under Federal and other laws
> but, unlike the opiates, it is a powerful stimulant and does not
> create tolerance or physical dependence. It is derived from the
> leaves of the coca plant cultivated extensively in parts of South
> America. At present it is not the major drug of abuse it once was.

By 1975, less than a decade later, it had surpassed any previous
level it had ever attained as a major drug of abuse. When it first re-
appeared it was the drug of choice of the more affluent, principally the
jetset society and persons in the entertainment world. In a comparatively short period of time the tiny gold and silver spoons that are often used

to ladel a cocaine dosage began to appear as a favorite piece of jewelry, worn as an adornment around the neck of the middle-class young, including college students. Finally, it began to show up as the sign of drug abuse of pimps, prostitutes and the inner city minority poor.

The reappearance of cocaine, joining heroin as a major drug of abuse, and the new sources of supply brought about another complexity. At one time enforcement agencies could concentrate on a limited number of white syndicate members, principally Italians and Jews, who had established the credentials to deal with the French Corsicans for heroin. Now, many Blacks, Hispanics and Orientals were able to move into middle management of the drug market and to act as importers. Spanish-speaking criminals now find it easier to make contacts and connections in Mexico and South America than before, and Orientals can play a much greater role in the Asian sources of supply. The number of people within the United States who can make a foreign contact for a multi-kilo importation of cocaine and heroin has probably increased by a factor of more than 25. Instead of being able to concentrate on about 100 suspected major importers, the number for law enforcement to deal with is closer to 2,500, with many importers not known at all.

To deal with this convoluted miasma, John Bartels had a single, larger than any prior, agency, but it was an organization fragmented by years of internal dissension and a decade of jurisdictional gerrymandering and abrasive competition. The final straw, which eventually toppled Bartels, was representative of all that had preceded it. Vincent Promuto was a former lineman for the Washington Redskins professional football league who had retired from the sport with a law degree. Popular with the public, the press and with a number of politicians, he was appointed to a $35,000 per year post as Communications Director of D. E. A. on the basis of a "White House recommendation." His appointment was resented by many on the supervisory levels of the agency. He quickly became a matter that generated controversy, and part of the in-house backbiting and rumor mongering that was part of the status quo. ** At one point (January 1975) syndicated columnist Jack Anderson wrote "The nation's top narcotics officials have been so busy investigating one another that they haven't had much time to cope with the dope peddlers." Anderson indicated that Bartels had complained privately that his staff had used investigations to blackmail one another.

Andrew Tartaglino, who had begun his Federal career many years earlier with the old Federal Bureau of Narcotics, now held a top-level

---

** During this period of turmoil the agency's Acting Deputy Administrator, the Chief of Enforcement and Director of Public Affairs all were investigated by the D. E. A. and the F. B. I. without any evidence being uncovered that would corroborate the allegations and charges.

agency position as Deputy Director. He pushed for investigation of charges that Promuto associated with high-level Washington D. C. gamblers. When Bartels seemed satisfied that the charges were not sufficient for any action and ordered the investigation closed, Tartaglino would not accept the directive and was transferred to meaningless duties. The matter began to be reported in the press, the Department of Justice had the F. B. I. look into the affair, and Senator Jackson of Washington, chairman of the Senate Permanent Sub-Committee on Investigations (who was warming up for a run in the presidential primaries) decided to investigate too. Rumors were leaked to the press that charges of obstructing justice might be brought against Bartels. The matter subsided when Bartels resigned and Promuto was dismissed for allegedly misusing his telephone and travel privileges. **   The total effect on the agency was traumatic.

In early 1977 President Jimmy Carter appointed Judge Griffin Bell of Georgia Attorney General of the United States. Both indicated an agreement that problems of drug abuse and the crime arising therefrom represented the single most important factor in the nation's crime picture. The new attorney general ordered a feasibility study of the value of merging D. E. A. with the F. B. I. , and another uproar began. The International Association of Chiefs of Police strongly condemned the suggestion. Two Harvard professors, James Q. Wilson, who has given much study to crime and law enforcement, and Mark Moore, who had been a principal consultant to D. E. A. , both wrote to the president opposing the merger on the grounds that the F. B. I. would become "contaminated." No one in either agency seemed to favor the proposal. It is most probable that though there might be some token joint investigations by agents of both units the idea for this shotgun wedding will be abandoned.

Such has been the sad past history of attempts to stanch the flow of heroin and cocaine into the U. S. The current picture is not encouraging to the objective viewer. In mid-1977 the facts are these. It takes approximately 6 tons or 12, 000 pounds of heroin to supply every addict in the United States for one year. There is no hard estimate for cocaine because the number of users is impossible to ascertain, and the degree of usage is unknown. Most of the supply of these drugs comes from Mexico and South America. These same geographical areas have been

---

**   In August 1977 the Civil Service Commission ruled that Promuto's dismissal was arbitrary and unreasonable. The government paid him one year's back salary and offered him his position back. He indicated he was pleased that his name had been cleared and that he would resign to go into private practice.

major contributors to the swelling number of illegal aliens entering the
United States. Giving an illegal alien an average weight of 150 lbs. (or
about 70 kilos) and knowing that a kilo is 2.2 pounds, it would seem impossible to stop 6 or 12 tons of drugs from coming into the country when
we cannot prevent so many tons of people from getting in. The estimated
number of illegal aliens in the U.S. in mid-1977 is given as "somewhere
between 3 and 8 million." President Carter has recommended that those
aliens who can prove they have been in the country five or more years be
allowed to remain as registered resident aliens.

The law enforcement effort is further complicated by important international considerations which should prevent the reoccurrence of
simplistic remedies which would begin with "We should force the government of Mexico to..." News reports indicate that our State Department
would recommend strongly against any effort to clamp down on illegal
Mexican aliens and their continued entry into this country. It is suggested that the United States is currently acting as an economic escape hatch
which allows some poor Mexicans to come to the U.S., earn a living and
send some money home to needy relatives. To stop this would add to the
economic woes of Mexico and might contribute to the instability of the
present government. There is an insurgent movement going on in Mexico
now. A revolution could place a new government on our 2,000 mile border which might be much less friendly than the current government.
The conclusion becomes that any "get tough on drugs" movement proposed by D.E.A. that would include making it difficult for aliens to illegally enter our country would be overridden by the State Department
considerations.

After 1984, we will arrive at the logical conclusion that there is
no way to cut off the supply of heroin and cocaine. We will then concentrate on trying to reduce the demand. It is quite likely that the Federal
Government's effort will concentrate on research for drug antagonists,
some reasonable form of "cure" of dependencies, and maintenance of
addicts under conditions which should reduce their need to commit
crimes to raise the funds necessary for illegal purchase, in markets
where heroin and cocaine sell at consumer level for a price 200 times
greater than the value of gold. **

SUMMARY

After 1984, having reached an understanding that it is impossible
to control public behavior through penal and/or tax laws, we will remove

---

**   Gold is selling for about $140 per ounce. One kilo of heroin or
      cocaine brings in more than $1,000,000 in consumer sales.

from such laws the provisions which made gambling, drugs and alcohol the attractive activities they have been for organized crime. This level of pragmatic reality will divest organized crime of a great deal of the public endorsement it has had in the past. This, together with greater study, will allow us to know that arrests and convictions may be a correct means of attacking organized crime, but the true measure of the effectiveness of our efforts will come from measuring the dollars they earn rather than how many arrests we make. The target will then become to reduce the dollars and increase the risk involved in these businesses. There will be fewer but better cases made against organized crime figures. They will be directed against major figures (once we no longer need large numbers of convictions for impressive statistics). Better understanding will lead to better sentencing. Judges and parole authorities will realize that organized crime figures are beyond rehabilitation, and this will no longer be a consideration in their sentence or treatment in prison. It will have taken us much longer to get there than our British cousins, but after 1984, organized crime will begin to become a tolerable problem that no longer needs the highest priority.

Current trends suggest that in a decade or so a number of changes will take place in statute law and in public and police priorities.

1. Much more gambling will be legalized, both in the private sector and in government-operated entities. The effects of the Proposition 13 Movement (cut taxes, less government spending) will help to accelerate casino gambling and the legalization of sports betting. State lotteries and off-track betting systems will proliferate.

2. The futility of suggesting that we can stop illegal drugs from entering the United States from Mexico, South America, Asia or from being manufactured domestically will finally become apparent to all. Public attitudes will become such that we will maintain those who might have to commit crime to support drug habits, and ignore those who are wealthy enough to purchase their drug of abuse without committing crime.

Government will monitor the problem as a public health matter rather than with the law enforcement approach which has predominated for so long.

3. The current soft attitudes toward pornography and prostitution will continue and even increase. The limit of government concern will be to safeguard children and limit these activities only when they are conducted in a publicly obnoxious way. The "crime" approach to both pornography and prostitution will dwindle, and perhaps disappear.

4. Penal law will eventually reach the Constitutional mandate of separating Church and State. Many "crime" laws will be administratively ignored or legislatively removed from the statute books, as we realize that they were placed there in the first instance only because

of the successful lobbying of one or more religious groups who have
thus imposed their religious beliefs on all others.

5.   Police "Public Morals Divisions" will diminish and perhaps
disappear with the long overdue recognition that it should not be the role
of the police to enforce morality. Higher priority demands will further
accentuate this movement of personnel to other duties.

6.   Churches and the family unit will acknowledge that their own
responsibilities cannot be abdicated or assigned to the Criminal Justice
system, so that the evils that were perceived in any of the foregoing
activities will have to be addressed by the first two institutions rather
than assigned to the latter.

9 Political Terrorism
Frederick J. Cavanagh

Terrorism is perhaps one of the most difficult words to define in any language. Much of the problem is caused by the political, ethnic and religious differences existing between nations, and in some instances, between the peoples populating each nation. Consequently, within our contemporary societies, the terrorist in one nation is admired as a liberator in another nation. Even efforts on the part of the United Nations have failed because of this divided feeling among nations. In recent months, efforts to define terrorism have been subjected to further confusion by the appearances of articles, books and mass media presentations using such terms as "guerrilla," "revolutionary," "terrorist," "insurgent," and "rebel" interchangeably. Today, the public and many members of the branches of government, including our law enforcement components, are unsure of the real meaning of terrorism.

Terrorism in our times is so specialized that we can no longer place trans-national acts of violence in the same category with the criminal acts of the modern day "Bonnie and Clyde" gangs such as the Symbionese Liberation Army (S. L. A.). We must recognize that there are various forms before we are able to successfully contain terrorism. Terrorism, then, may be defined in general terms, as the use of force and/or fear in order to attain a utilitarian goal. Specifically, there are two types of terrorism - criminal and political.

Criminal terrorism is the use of force and/or fear in order to secure the money and property, or to take the life of, another. On the other hand, political terrorism is the use of force and/or fear to bring about political change. The methods of the criminal and political terrorists may be the same but the utilitarian goals are quite different. Too often this distinction is blurred because of the disprop-

tionate amount of media coverage devoted to the activities of our
modern-day criminal gangs.

For example, the S. L. A., one such gang, was in reality never
more than a small coalition of sexually promiscuous, drug-oriented
college students who recruited older, hardened and uneducated criminals into their organization. This pitiful group of rebels, having arrived on the campus scene too late to participate in the rioting, revolutionary 1960s, supported its members by committing acts of criminal
terrorism which allegedly included murder, bank robbery and petty
thefts. The operations of the S. L. A. were quite similar to those of the
Ma Barker, Alvin Karpis, John Dillinger, and "Pretty Boy" Floyd
Gangs, their criminal terrorist counterparts of the 1930s.

However serious the activities of the criminal terrorist may seem
to be, our law enforcement agencies are strategically able to eventually
apprehend them. However, the real problems for law enforcement
agencies, both now and in the future, are to be found in attempting to
control political terrorism. The task of controlling violent activities
which transcend local, state and national boundaries is a mission
which is virtually impossible to accomplish. Unlike profit-oriented
criminal terrorism, political terrorists are rebels with a cause and
with a belief that the cause justifies the deed, no matter how cruel or
onerous it may be.

The very nature of political terrorism inhibits detection. Almost
invariably, the existence of a political terrorist organization is not
known until it commits its first overt act against society. At this stage
it is, in all probability, operationally unfeasible to attempt agent infiltration despite wide-spread acceptance of this procedure. However,
political terrorism is not a movement in toto or of the whole organization, as is the case of criminal terrorist activities. On the contrary,
the overt activities of political terrorists represent only one phase of
a revolutionary movement and occur only after the revolutionary organization has attained an advanced stage of underground growth and development. An understanding of the formation and development of a revolutionary movement and the positions occupied by its political terrorist
arm is vital if we are to successfully combat this worldwide problem.

REVOLUTIONARY GROWTH DYNAMICS

The birth of a revolutionary movement starts with the seeds of
discontent nurtured by an autocratic government either unable or unwilling to consider the complaints, reasonable or unreasonable, of

certain segments of the populace. Because the growth of a movement takes place in a covert or hidden environment, its existence remains unknown to the recognized government. The multi-varied activities of the movement are likened to a colony of ants growing steadily underground, while only the terrorist actions and those activities designed to create agitation and unrest among the citizenry are conducted aboveground. The successful growth culminates with aboveground guerrilla warfare. These various and accelerating stages of growth may be shown as follows:

1. Unhappiness with the nation's political, economic or social conditions.

2. Creation of wider discontent for government through lies, propaganda and ridicule.

3. Development of a public acceptance of the validity of the cause. Generation of a core of believers, no matter how small.

4. Limited agitation through labor unrest and student demonstrations. Infiltration of government agencies and national organizations.

5. Solicitation of money, arms, equipment from sympathetic foreign nations. The acceptance into the movement of foreign agents as propaganda and training consultants.

6. Recruitment and training of sympathizers as active members. Formal listing of sympathetic followers.

7. Infiltration of the national labor unions, national students groups, the clergy, and other nationally recognized groups.

8. Creation of national front organizations.

9. Intensification of expansion and recruitment for the revolutionary movement's front organization.

10. Expansion of cells or units into all areas of the country.

11. Large-scale dissemination of hard-line propaganda psychologically designed to intensify dissatisfaction with the government and to plant the option of revolt in the minds of the people.

12. Above and belowground activities to force the government to spread its resources to the point of ineffectiveness. Simultaneous strikes, rioting, demonstrations on a nationwide level.

13. Highly concentrated activities, covert and overt, designed to cause further erosion of morale in all levels of government. Revolutionary infiltrators in government contribute to indecision-making.

14. Rapidly accelerating political terrorist activities against government installations to indicate strength of the revolutionary movement.

15. Intensification of recruitment and training for guerilla warfare.

16. Small-scale, sporadic and positional guerilla warfare.

17. Widespread and mobile guerilla warfare.

During its growth and development, the revolutionary movement may undergo certain internal changes which reflect the success of its progress, effectiveness and internal leadership problems. In addition, the activities of its political terrorist units (or cells) are adjusted to reflect the reactions of the population to their acts of violence.

Certain other covert and overt activities take place during the course of the movement's final thrust toward the assumption of national governmental control. Others permeate each phase of the movement's growth. Some of these activities are conducted by the terrorist unit or the foreign agent consultants, others by members of the movement's hierarchy. They are as follows.

a. Selective assassinations of controversial national personalities, opponents of the revolutionary movement, government leaders, wealthy and influential members of the established society, leaders and members within the movement who have lost power or have inhibited the movement's growth, and infiltrators.

b. Kidnappings of the wealthy and members of their families, and leaders of government and industry, to secure ransom money for the movement.

c. Selective sabotage designed to damage or render useless the
economic vitality of the nation, the government (military and
police), depots and information centers, transportation, communication and industrial production centers, bank and other
commercial information centers.

d. Infiltration of the cabinet of the government; the state department; the military; large national and local police departments;
government intelligence units; and the industrial, commercial
and scientific research establishments.

e. Development of a governmental structure capable of assuming
power when the recognized government falls. It is comprised
of some of the movement's hierarchy, sympathizers with some
measure of national popularity and foreign agents of national
origin.

THE REVOLUTIONARY MOVEMENT'S
INTRASTRUCTURE

All operations and activities of the revolutionary movement,
whether conducted above or underground, are all functions of a well
organized and efficient bureaucratic structure. The intrastructure is
built on a series of units (or cells) rising through sections (or branches)
to geographically designated areas (or districts), then extending out to
states (or zones) ending at national and/or international headquarters.
The membership is comprised of four types:

a. The Leadership Group, composed of full-time, completely
dedicated members and the nucleus of the revolutionary
organization.

b. The Regulars, who perform assigned organizational duties
and attend covert meetings while maintaining their overt
roles in society.

c. The Reserve, who generally do not attend meetings on a
regular basis, but are used on special missions while maintaining their overt roles in society.

d. The Irregulars, who do not attend meetings and are not
formal members, but can be relied upon to perform certain

legally acceptable assignments, such as participating in mass
demonstrations, passive resistance and in failing to assist the
recognized government.

Another group, incapable of being measured, is comprised of
differing members of society who are partial to the cause because of
racial, economic, ethnic or religious heritages. Yet this latter segment of society, unorganized and law-abiding, is potentially a reser-
voir for future revolutionary recruitment and financial support.

The revolutionary movement is a bifurcated operation wherein the
various parts operate simultaneously. While the political terrorists
are conducting their open acts of violence, the main revolutionary
movement is in the process of covertly infiltrating the heart of government. In addition, the underground organizational operations participate in the recruitment, training, and assignment of members; in the
solicitation of money and supplies; in the establishment of safe houses
for terrorists on the run; in the development of supply locations for the
conduction of terrorist activities; and in the maintenance of psychological activities designed to generate and maintain public support against
the recognized government. The role of gathering and analyzing intelligence for dissemination to political terrorist sections is also one of
the duties of the underground organization.

The Unit (or Cell)

This basic component of the revolutionary organization is comprised of a leader and unit (cell) members. The leader assigns duties,
observes and evaluates unit members, acts as the link with the Section
or Branch leaders and participates in committee activities. Members
of a cell or unit are given information on a "need to know" basis and,
depending on the nature of the unit's activities, may not even know the
identity, background or residences of fellow unit members. This unit
(cell) compartmentalization affords members the ultimate available
protection from detection when participating in dangerous and illegal
activities. This procedure also inhibits law enforcement infiltration
and renders any infiltration virtually ineffective in combating the terrorist activities of a political revolutionary movement.

There are basically five types of Units:

a.   An Operations Unit made up of a leader from three (3) to
     seven (7) members. The members generally know each
     other by aliases and operate as a unit, collecting money,
     distributing propaganda and performing ancillary political
     duties.

b. The Intelligence Unit has a high degree of compartmentaliza-
    tion in order to protect the other units. Within the Intelli-
    gence Unit, the leader avoids direct contact with the other
    members of the unit. The members of this type of unit
    generally do not know fellow members and contact is main-
    tained through a mail drop, known messenger or an unsus-
    pecting nonaffiliated person. The unit leader maintains con-
    tact with the section or branch leader by means of a known
    messenger or mail drop. Inter group direct contact is mini-
    mal.

c. The Auxiliary Unit is comprised of a unit leader, assistant
    unit leaders and members. The size of this unit varies and
    depends on the intensity and success of underground efforts
    in the areas of recruitment, training and miscellaneous ad-
    ministrative work assignments. Primarily, this unit serves
    as a staging area for the screening of recruits, for interested
    or suspect members, and for the performance evaluation of
    newly activated members. In a growing revolutionary organi-
    zation, this unit is the largest of the four in individual size,
    but not necessarily in the numbers of units. It is to this unit
    government (military, intelligence, police) infiltrators
    are initially assigned.

d. The Specialization Unit is highly compartmentalized and is
    comprised of a unit leader and as many as eight (8) members.
    Unlike the leaders of the preceding units, the cell leader is
    generally an important member of the revolutionary move-
    ment's hierarchy, a situation which is generally unknown
    to his or her cell members. The members of this unit
    are specialists in assassinations, sabotage techniques,
    demolitions, armaments, electronics, investigative techni-
    ques, photography, mechanics, forgery and many other fields
    of criminal and anti-criminal behavior. The members of
    this unit are not known to each other unless assigned together,
    and then only by fictitious names. Members of this unit
    generally work alone or are assigned because of a particular
    expertise to a Special Operations Unit.

e. The Special Operations Unit is comprised of a unit leader,
    two assistant unit leaders and up to ten members. This is the
    unit specializing in acts of political terrorism. The unit
    acts as a team, with each member known to one another. The
    primary purpose of this unit is to terrorize.

Unit (Cell) Variations

There are basically two types of variations in a unit, depending
on the unit activities. They are as follows:

a. Twin Units. These are developed for the purpose of acting
    as a backup for an active Intelligence Unit. The Twin Unit is
    available to continue the gathering of information in the event
    that the activities of the primary Intelligence Unit are un-
    covered by the government. The Twin Unit is also used to
    evaluate and verify the reliability of intelligence data and
    their sources.

b. Chain Units. These are primarily developed for the Opera-
    tions Unit when it is functioning as the manufacturer of arms,
    ammunition, printing or other tasks requiring a large number
    of production workers. They are also employed when the
    Operations Unit is required to distribute propaganda materials
    and provide supplies and safe houses during escape and evasion
    situations.

POLITICAL TERRORISM

Historically, few revolutionary underground movements have re-
frained from using political terrorism in order to attain their goals.
While some measure of popular support is always present in any society because of some discontent, revolutionary movements have
never completely relied on the "discontented," or on the concept that
their cause was so worthwhile that popular support was assured. On
the contrary, the underground leaders assume that the "people" population are generally not interested in rushing to the "barricades" in
order to bring about what the movement considers to be "beneficial
change." It is this public attitude which forces the revolutionary
movement to employ terrorism. Brutal methods are used to generate
the publicity needed to propagandize the cause and the existence of the
revolutionary movement dedicated to its accomplishment. The use of
political terrorist units is visible proof to the people that the revolutionary movement has some offensive and retaliatory power.

Origin of Political Terrorism

The origin of terrorism is buried beneath the dust of antiquity. In all probability it was used by primitive tribes to secure power and control over fertile land areas containing the life-sustaining necessities of food, wood and water. However, the use of terror to bring about political change is a comparatively new phenomenon which is largely the creation of Nineteenth Century European anarchists. The concepts of political terrorism, as we confront them in our era, were developed by such writers as the Russian anarchist Peter A. Kropotkin and his German counterpart Johannes Most.

In 1848, Kropotkin wrote "A single deed is better propaganda than one thousand words." This concept remains as one of the primary reasons for the commission of violent and seemingly useless acts by political terrorist units. Kropotkin's writings were attempts at philosophically justifying revolutionary movements and the use of terroristic acts against the leaders of recognized governments.

Johannes Most, on the other hand, devoted his writings to the compilation of terroristic tactics and training guidelines. In New York City during 1884, he published a manual of training entitled, "Revolutionary War Tactics." This guide included terrorist tactics for use in large cities; the manufacture and use of nitroglycerin and other chemicals used in explosive devices, the use of arson and poisons, and the use of letter bombs on the opponents of a revolutionary movement. Most is credited with being the first to refer to police officers as "pigs." He also expressed the view that the killing of a police officer could not be considered a crime because they were inhuman.

One of the most active nineteenth-century revolutionary groups practicing political terrorism were the Russian Narodniki. Originally this group, comprised of many young people, mostly well-educated, were Socialists advocating agrarian reform. Their efforts resulted in a series of trials during 1878, which meted out some severe sentences but gave the movement worldwide publicity and a larger following. Influenced by a hardcore terrorist element from within and frustrated by the failure of peaceful efforts, the Narodoniki, in 1879, elected to pursue their objectives with violence. During the same year the Narodoniki hierarchy met and sentenced Tsar Alexander II to death. After numerous attempts had failed, a five-person political terrorist unit accomplished their task with a crude anti-personnel bomb in 1881.

The Narodniki were actually precursors of the Russian Revolution of 1917. Their efforts united a large segment of the population in a cause. They developed strength for the revolutionary movement from the popular support; and they consequently weakend the Tsarist government to the point of being forced to institute some social reform. The very fact that the Russian ruler was unable, or unwilling, to go far enough, provided a reason for the continued existence of an organized revolutionary movement. This movement continued, its ranks filled with succeeding generations of Russian revolutionaries, ultimately toppling this autocratic regime in 1917.

The economic conditions of the nineteenth-century Irish were quite similar to those of the Russian peasant. Bound to the land by an agrarian economy, they were beholden to a generally absent landlord, who was unfamiliar with their problems, or unwilling or unable to do anything to correct them. Religious and legal restrictions, in addition to a disproportionately heavy tax rate on their farm tenantships, created the proper environment for revolt. Their conditions reached a level of intolerance when the Irish lost one-half of their eight million population to migration, disease and starvation during and immediately following the Potato Famine of the 1840s. The fact that the British Government learned of the blight too late and then misjudged the seriousness of the problem did little to alleviate the fear that the situation was a British effort to decimate the Irish Race. It was in this climate of hatred that the first effective Irish revolutionary organization came into being.

The Irish Republican Brotherhood (I. R. B.), also known as the Fenians, was a secret society at its inception, dedicated to the cause of Home Rule. However, repeated failures to pass this quasi-independence legislation in the English Parliament increased the I. R. B. 's base of popular support and changed their goal to that of complete independence. Encouraged by increased membership and a large sympathetic following, the I. R. B. geographically positioned political terrorist units throughout the country and initiated selective bombings, assassinations and arson attacks against government officials, landowners and their families and properties.

Unlike previous Irish revolutionary organizations, the I. R. B. was well structured and well run. It managed to accomplish the following:

a.   It kept alive a righteous cause of existence.

b.   It generated wide support from the populace.

c.   It developed financial support through foreign front organizations formed among the recently-migrated Irish.

d.   It propagandized and received some worldwide sympathy through newspaper articles written in the newly-formed Irish-American newspapers.

e. It assisted in the formation of its successor, the Irish Republican Army (I. R. A.).

Many national revolutionary movements throughout nineteenth-century Europe originated within secret societies that employed political terrorism. Sicily, in its efforts to displace the French-controlled Neapolitan monarchy, had the Mafia; Italy, the Camorra and the powerful Carbonari; France, the Charbomiers; Serbia, the Black Hand; and Spain, the Disinherited. All of these revolutionary movements developed active and sympathetic followings among their national populations because their causes were based on needed social and economic reform. At this time in history, the effects of the Industrial Revolution had disrupted the centuries-old role of man in an agrarian society, and the recent success of the French Revolution became an encouraging example of how political violence could displace the "divine right" of autocratic kings.

All of these secret societies were effective in disrupting the functions of their recognized governments. Some, having forced some measure of reform, died. Others successfully toppled their governments or gave birth to twentieth-century revolutionary movements. A few, the Mafia and the Camorra, having fulfilled the righteousness of their cause, degenerated into secret criminal and profit-oriented organizations.

Early twentieth-century revolutionary activities were generally the extension of movements set in motion during the preceding century. Many were destined to continue until their goals were accomplished. The assassination of Archduke Franz Ferdinand, the immediate cause of the First World War, is credited to the Serbian Black Hand. The Russian Revolution of 1917 and the Irish Revolution of 1921 are other examples of successful movements having roots in the Nineteenth Century.

The events in Spain during the 1930s represent a unique change in revolutionary movements and what now appears to be the precursor of an international policy currently in vogue. It is the policy of nations openly aiding that movement which is idealistically compatible with the philosophies of the assisting nations whereby the assisted country is more likely to fall under their orbits of influence.

During the Spanish Civil War the Loyalists, on one side with the support of Communist Russia, fought the Republicans, supported by Fascist Germany and Italy, in a war which rapidly escalated from the level of political terrorism through positional guerilla warfare to a full-scale military conflict. Other Spanish revolutionary organizations such as the Federation of Spanish Workers and the Disinherited, both

of whom had carried the momentum of revolution until the moment of
conflict, were quickly massacred by both the Loyalists and Republicans.
Today other revolutionary movements are present in Spain in the form
of separatist groups. The Catalonian Separatists and the Basque
Separatists have active special operations units which have killed at
least thirty people, including political leaders and police officials,
since 1976. Each organization's purity of purpose and national identity through independence has popular support among Spaniards of
Catalonian and Basque ancestries.

The current problems between Israel and the Arab states center
on which national group should control Palestine. The Jews base their
rights on being indigenous to the area, the Palestinian Arabs on having
lived in the region for hundreds of years.

During the First World War, the British Army had seized Palestine from the Turks. Subsequently, in 1917, the British government
issued the Balfour Declaration, which implied that the region should
be used to establish a national homeland for the Jews. After the
League of Nations made Palestine a mandate of Britain in 1923, hos-
tility between the Jews and Arabs accelerated. The situation grew
more volatile as the number of Jewish immigrants greatly increased.
Much of this migration was the result of European Jews attempting to
escape the terror of Adolph Hitler's persecutions. Between 1918 and
1948, over one-half million Jews migrated to Palestine and caused
the resident Arabs to wonder if the Jews intended to take over their
country and displace them. In order to defend themselves from the
consequent Arab raids on their settlements, the Jews formed the
Haganah as a covert defensive unit in 1937. However, as the Arab
raids became persistent and the Haganah maintained a defensive posture, a split within the Haganah's ranks resulted in the formation of
the Irgun. The members of this group were pledged not only to re-
venge further Arab attacks on their settlements but also to actively
pursue the creation of a Jewish nation. The political terrorist arm of
this movement was known as the Stern Gang. When repudiated by some
segments of the Palestinian Jews because of their harsh terrorist tactics, the Stern Gang left the Irgun and continued as a separate revolutionary movement. It was effectively eliminated by the British Army
forces in 1942. A few survivors helped form its successor, the Freedom Fighters of Israel (F. F. I.) in the same year.

The Irgun, still smarting from the bad publicity of the Stern Gang,
and from David Ben-Gurion's inactive Haganah, paused for a reorganization. The two leaders, Isaac Yotzernitsky and Friedman-Yellin,
decided to pattern the new Irgun after the I. R. A. In so doing, it
developed intelligence units; an underground newspaper; auxiliary units

for new recruits; and a series of operations units in order to manufacture arms and ammunition. With the F. F. I., concentrating on
selective targets for arson, bank robbery, assassination and bombings,
chaos and terror became a way of life. Finally the British, unable to
maintain law and order, confronted with other areas of insurrection
throughout the Empire and greatly shocked by the assassination of
kindly Lord Moyne, the British Resident Minister, returned the Palestinian problem to the United Nations. In 1948, by resolution in the United Nations, the new nation of Israel emerged when the region was
divided between the warring factions. However, this did not solve the
problem.

In the interim period of time we have witnessed three wars between Israel and a consortium of Arab nations. Today we find Palestinian Arabs, under the banner of the Palestinian Liberation Organization (P. L. O.), conducting the same type of terrorist activities
against Israel as the Irgun did against the British authorities thirty-
five years ago - and for the same cause. Will the Jewish-Arab issue
ever be solved? Mankind is more likely to find the solution as to
"which came first - the chicken or the egg?" The logical disposition
of the Palestinian problem rests on a mutually independent government for both peoples, who live in peaceful coexistence.

In the span of time following the Second World War and up to the
start of 1978, the legitimate world governments have been subjected
to thirty-seven revolutionary conflicts. Some of these insurgencies
originated externally and had little popular support among the people.
A number of nations, including Angola, Laos, Yemen, Chile, Peru,
Thailand and Cambodia have experienced more than one revolutionary
incursion. Others, such as Rhodesia, Zaire and Ethiopia, are in a
continuous state of mobile guerilla warfare. Actually, during the
thirty-three years there is no period of time which has been free of
revolutionary movements and their accompanying acts of political
terrorism. There may be variations in the terminology used to describe the units within their infrastructure, but they are basically
structured and function as previously described. See p. 8

A Change in Tactics

Events in recent years suggest new tactics have been introduced
in the operations of political terrorism. These changes in tactics

suggest that perhaps several world governments control numbers of
different-named terrorist units and deploy them against international
targets. There are also suspicions that these culturally diverse terrorist units are part of an international revolutionary movement.

A description of international terrorism according to the Task
Force on Disorders and Terrorism (1) is as follows:

> International terrorists may be broadly classified as minority
> nationalist groups, Marxist revolutionary groups, neo-Fascist
> and extreme right-wing groups, and ideological mercenaries.
> National liberation movements show considerable organization,
> with long-term planning and well-defined objectives. Generally,
> they receive support from private sympathizers and encourage-
> ment, training, materials and occasional safe haven from sympa-
> thetic governments. There is considerable evidence that terror-
> ists are receiving sympathetic training in Cuba, the Soviet Union
> and Eastern Bloc Countries. These terrorists have been em-
> ployed mainly where guerrilla warfare is ostensibly being waged
> to overthrow a legitimate government, but they are obviously
> available for attacks against other targets. The existence of
> such terrorist organizations poses a grave threat not only to per-
> sons and property, but also to international relations.

The world has witnessed a steady increase in the number of terrorist units since the 1960s. At the present time, one can count fifty-four
such groups. Governments' efforts to determine their relationships
to specific revolutionary movements has not been very effective and
at times has been very frustrating. This is partly due to their growing numbers and to the trans-national characteristics of their activities.
There are also an increasing number of instances where units, formerly believed to be diverse, are now participating in joint operations.
Some of the most active international terrorist organizations are the
following:

a.   Irish Republican Army, based in Ulster and in the Republic
     of Ireland, seeking the merger of Northern Ireland with the
     Republic of Ireland.

b.   Baader-Meinhof Group, based in West Germany, violent
     terrorist nihilists.

c.   Japanese Red Army, based in West Germany, Japan and
     Lebanon. This group has conducted joint operations with

the Baader-Meinhof Groups, the Carlos Groups and segments
of the Popular Front for the Liberation of Palestine (PLFP).
Fanatical and determined, they may be hired for special
operations.

d. South Moluccans, based in Holland, seeking independence
from Indonesia.

e. Monteneros, based in Argentina, seeking social reform.

f. Croatian Separatists, based in West Germany and United
States, seeking an independent Croatian Republic within
Yugoslavia.

g. Basque Separatists, based in Spain and France, seeking
independence within Spain.

h. F. A. L. N. , based in New York, seeking Puerto Rican independence from the United States.

i. Popular Front for the Liberation of Palestine (P. F. L. P.),
based in Lebanon, Iraq and Libya, seeking independence
within Israel. Well financed by Arab nations.

j. Carlos Group, based in Latin America and France. Terrorist nihilists who are probably for hire by well-financed revolutionary groups.

Political Terrorism in the United States

Violence is not new to a nation conceived by revolution. During
our some two hundred years of existence, succeeding generations of
our citizenry have lived through periods of racial, ethnic and religious
strife. Even scattered incidents of terrorism have occurred infrequently, but they invariably have represented a spontaneous or retributive,
non-revolutionary response to social injustice. The beliefs and acts
of violence committed by contemporary groups such as the Students
for a Democratic Society (S. D. S.), the "Weather Underground" (W. U.)
and the New World Liberation Front (N. W. L. F.), have never captured
the imagination of the American people. While the politics of peaceful dissent are encouraged and even flourish in a democratic society,
the opportunity for peaceful change also exists. It is therefore most
unlikely that the democratic process of the United States Government

would be usurped by political terrorism. The real annoyance may be
found in the acts of violence perpetrated by small groups with limited
goals and by foreign-based terrorist units using our streets to resolve
their foreign problems. These activities could result in significant
disruption to our economy should they be directed against our industrial
and commercial centers and result in the loss of jobs and production.
It is these areas of fragile vulnerability that must be safeguarded.

Controlling Terrorism

Man's sophisticated methods for self-destruction increase in
proportion to the development of his technology. We have developed
biological, chemical, nuclear and electronic weaponry capable of
causing widespread death and destruction. It is likely that terrorists
will, at some time in the future, secure these inhuman instruments
and direct them against nations of the world.
Terrorism must be outlawed by the United Nations and punished
under international law if it is to be effectively controlled. It is
facetious to believe that national law enforcement agencies with limited
territorial jurisdictions and limited resources can combat transnational
terrorists capable of being in safe-countries within hours after their
acts of violence.
However, some changes in local and national law enforcement
attitudes, and the implementation of certain procedures, could lessen
the impact and discourage the current acts of domestic violence. The
following recommendations are strongly suggested:

1.   Free exchange of information between government and local law
     enforcement agencies.

2.   A continuous evaluation of the private security procedures in use
     at commercial, industrial, nuclear, and military sites.

3.   The use of sophisticated electronic and sensor detection devices,
     developed for use in the Vietnamese War, but not yet released by
     the government for general use.

4.   Inventory control over the manufacture, distribution and storage
     of weapons, explosives and ammunition. These procedures are
     imperative for military installations and for the widely dispersed
     National Guard Armories.

5. The creation of F. B. I. and states-based anti-terrorist teams maintaining open communication, liaison, strategically located throughout the country, and capable of conducting joint operations.

6. Strong, legally sound Federal legislation prohibiting and punishing domestic political terrorism.

7. Propagandizing the support and control of political terrorist movements by foreign powers, as well as their acts of violence and violations of human rights.

8. Reducing or eliminating legitimate social and economic injustice when they appear in our society.

9. Government security supervision of all research capable of developing instruments of destruction.

10. Recognition that political terrorism is only one segment of a larger, more dangerous underground revolutionary movement which may be supported and controlled by a foreign government.

11. Warn all foreign nations that any terrorist activities instigated by their government will be considered an act of aggression.

While these suggestions are not offered as a panacea for political terrorism, their implementation would aid in the preservation of our domestic tranquility; for it now appears that political terrorism with the tacit, open or surreptitious support of many foreign governments will increase during the coming years.

THE FUTURE OF TERRORISM

While it is generally agreed that meaningful measures to control political terrorism in the future must originate in the United Nations, this august body has accomplished little to alleviate the problem. An examination of the report submitted by the Ad Hoc Committee on International Terrorism during the 28th Session in 1973 (General Assembly Official Records, Supplement No. 28, A-9028, 1973) reflects the failure of that committee to even reach an agreement on the definition of international terrorism. Five years have passed since the submission of the committee report, but that first crucial definitive step has yet to be taken.

However, an examination of the member nations comprising the
U. N. Ad Hoc Committee on International Terrorism creates serious
doubts about the sincerity of their efforts. It now appears that some
of the nations serving or having served on this committee are now
suspected of supporting and encouraging political terrorist operations.
Other member nations, while publicly decrying these subversive activities, covertly serve as safe-countries and even provide supplies,
training, weapons, ammunition and money for ideologically compatible
revolutionary movements.

Jack Anderson (2), the internationally syndicated investigative
reporter, quoting from a classified Central Intelligence Agency document, states in substance, that Libya, South Yemen, Iraq, Red China,
North Korea, Tanzania, Zambia, Mozambique, Botswana, Algeria and
Cuba are actively engaged in supporting foreign revolutionary activities. Other nations, such as Argentina, Paraguay, Chile, Guatemala,
El Salvador and Uruguay, quietly tolerate domestic terrorist activity
presumably designed to keep their governments in power. It is interesting to note that Algeria, South Yemen, Tanzania and Zambia served on
the United Nations Ad Hoc Committee on International Terrorism.

However, these nations are not the only members of the U. N.
who foster the terrorist activities of revolutionary movements. According to John Barron:

> Since the late 1960's ...the Politburo has come to appreciate
> that even uncontrolled terrorism can contribute to the Soviet
> objectives of debilitating foreign societies. It does so by divert-
> ing resources from constructive national pursuits, provoking of-
> ficial repression, providing a pretext for physical damages...
> Hence the KGB now lends clandestine aid to some terrorist
> groups that are not under total Soviet domination. Brian Crozier,
> director of the London-based Institute for the Study of Conflict,
> states that at any given moment several hundred Africans are
> undergoing guerilla training in Soviet camps. Though most
> trainees apparently are targeted against South Africa, Rhodesia
> and the Portuguese colonies, defectors report having seen
> natives of Nigeria, Kenya and Tanzania in the camps around
> Odessa. (3)

Further evidence of the Soviet Union's posture on terrorism is
revealed in the remarks of Leonid Brezhnev, Chairman of the Polit-
buro, on June 27, 1972, after concluding the SALT I Agreement with
the United States. He stated that the establishment of detente with
the United States "in no way signifies a possibility of weakening the

ideological struggle" with the Western nations. "On the contrary, we should be prepared for an intensification of this struggle. " He firmly proclaimed that the Soviet Union would continue to support "all revolutionary forces of our time. " (4)

The prediction of future terrorism in the United States is pointed out by former U. S. Senator Strom Thurmond (S. C. Dem) during the July 30, 1975 hearings conducted by the Subcommittee of the Internal Security Laws. Thurmond states that:

Terrorist bombings by Puerto Rican Revolutionaries in this country and in Puerto Rico have attracted much attention because bombings are spectacular. But information gathered by the Senate Internal Security Committee over the past several years points to the conclusion that the bombings may have concealed a much more important aspect of the Puerto Rican situation if the word of the Communists means anything. What this evidence suggests is that International Communism has been using Puerto Rico has a bridgehead to infiltrate, disrupt and ultimately bring about revolution in the United States. (5)

As they struggle for world power and supremacy, the two ideologies, communism and capitalism, have increased their competition among the Third World nations. Their political intrigues, often supported by political terrorism and fueled by economic maneuvering, have generated frequent revolutions and the consequent rise and fall of emerging political leaders.

However, as the opposing ideologies introduce modern technology into their orbits of influence, the Third World will become more aware of alternatives to living . Their industrialization will bring education, modern medicine, better pay, time-saving devices and the other symbols of "the better way of life. " A leadership cadre will develop and with it a desire for "true" independence. Internal leadership struggles for power and externally-motivated revolutionary movements, accompanied by their attendant acts of political violence, will occur until a strong leadership emerges. These conditions will result in general discontent and provide the "purity of cause" for the formation of revolutionary movements. At this point in time, it appears that political violence will be a way of life among the Third World as it emerges into the 21st Century.

Externally motivated political terrorism will also increase in Western Europe as the "post-industrial" society develops during the last 20 years of the 20th Century. This new society is one in which a shrinking population containing fewer numbers of highly technical workers will be forced to support a steadily increasing number of elderly and retired people. The increased taxation, combined with the lower economic growth rate, will create a corporate profit problem. The result will be increasing confrontation between militant labor unions and industry. Strikes, violence, rioting and all the weapons of labor-management struggle will create frequent government crises. The problem will be compounded by the loss of factory jobs to a large Third World low-paying labor force. It is very possible that the standard of living in Western Europe may be the same as that of the Iron Curtain countries by the 21st Century. These conditions in Western Europe will result in general discontent and may well provide the "purity of cause" necessary for the formation of revolutionary movements.

As the 21st Century approaches, it appears that many of the world powers are unwilling or unable to control political terrorism. Some nations may feel that the concept of political terrorism is an adequate substitution for a formal forceful intervention or a declaration of war. Unless or until all nations agree on methods of control, these senseless acts of violence will be a way of life in most areas of the world in our lifetime.

NOTES

(1) National Advisory Commission on Criminal Justice Standards and Goals, Disorders and Terrorism (Washington, D.C., U.S. Government Printing Office, 1977), p. 12.

(2) Jack Anderson, "The Terrorized Sit" Winsted Evening Citizen, Winsted, Connecticut, July 6, 1978.

(3) John Barron, KGB: The Secret Work of Soviet Secret Agents, (New York: Macmillan Co., 1974).

(4) The Brezhnev quotations appeared in the Washington Post, June 28, 1972.

(5) Terrorist Activity. Hearings before the Permanent Subcommittee of the Internal Security Laws of the Committee of the Judiciary, U.S. Senate (Washington, D.C.: U.S. Government Printing Office, 1974).

BIBLIOGRAPHY

Anderson, Jack. "The Terrorized Sit." Winsted Evening Citizen,
    July 6, 1978.

Archer, Jules. Resistance. Philadelphia: Macrae Smith, 1973.

Barnet, Richard J. Intervention and Revolution. New York: The
    World Publishing Co., 1972.

Barron, John. KGB: The Secret Work of Secret Agents. New York;
    Macmillan Co., 1974.

Bassiouni, M. Cherif, ed. International Terrorism and Political
    Crimes. Springfield, Ill.: Charles C. Thomas, 1975.

Clutterbuck, Richard. Living with Terrorism. London: Faber and
    Faber, 1975.

Guevara, Che, and Gerassi, John, ed. Venceremos. New York:
    Simon and Schuster, 1968.

Hyams, Edward. Terrorists and Terrorism. New York: St. Martin's
    Press, Inc., 1974.

Mc Knight, George, Mind of the Terrorist. London: Michael Joseph,
    Ltd., 1974.

Report of the Commission to Consider Legal Procedures to Deal with
    Terrorist Activities in Northern Ireland. London: Her Majesty's
    Stationery Office, 1972.

Report of the Task Force on Disorders and Terrorism. Washington,
    D.C.: U.S. Government Printing Office, 1976.

Terrorist Activity. Hearings before the Permanent Sub-Committee
    of the Internal Security Laws of the Committee of the Judiciary,
    U.S. Senate, Washington, D.C.: U.S. Government Printing
    Office, 1974.

Terrorism. Hearings before the Committee on Internal Security,
    U.S. House of Representatives, 93rd Cong., 2nd session,
    Washington, D.C: Government Printing Office, 1974.

Wilkenson, Paul. Political Terrorism. London, Macmillan Press,
    Ltd., 1974.

10 Police Response to Hostage Situations

Harvey Schlossberg

Since the 1972 Munich Olympic massacre, the importance and far-reaching effects of both national and international terrorist situations which involve the holding of hostages has been brought into sharp focus and gained world attention. The need has clearly been demonstrated for a complete response system by the police. The traditional approach, i. e., meeting force with a higher level of force, was clearly ruled out by the Munich police response and gave way to an understanding that there was a greater need for focusing on human behavior not only in terms of its effect on hostages and the criminal, but on the police as well. The program, which is encapsulated in this chapter, represents a brief and ever-simplified view of one which requires intense training and leans heavily on psychotherapy for its practitioners. It was at the now famous "Williamsburg Siege," an incident marked by 47 hours during which time the police admirably used no weapons and came off with a successful conclusion, that the philosophy got its first field test. Just as the traditional police approaches seemed dwarfed by the overwhelming complexity of a hostage situation, so too are the traditional psychiatric approaches. The primary guiding philosophy of the entire program has always been that human life has to be our main concern since property can be replaced and criminals can be caught, but never can we give back lost life. The psychiatric model, requiring that an individual who is seeking help be in a controlled atmosphere, is based on the principle of a one-on-one relationship. The hostage situation takes place in an ever-changing environment complicated by imputs from various sources, e. g. the press, neighborhood troublemakers, well-meaning instigators, etc. The traditional police approaches that are available can generally be broken down into three types.

The first could best be described as an assault tactic. This is a rather simple method whereby several police officers are designated as an assault team and at a given command charge into a place. Of course, this is quite dangerous, both to the hostages and the police. For example, in the confusion or because of a change of clothing or misperception, the assault team may find it difficult to distinguish between the criminals and the hostages. On the other hand, it is not uncommon to find booby traps set for the unsuspecting rescuers.

The second approach involves the use of selected sniper fire. Again, this approach is not very complex. One merely selects a high-velocity gun with high power scope and matches it with a good sharpshooter. Unfortunately, the same difficulties as described earlier still remain, i.e. difficulty in distinguishing between hostages and criminals. In addition, we have the anxiety of a life-or-death decision to confound the shooter.

The third course of action involves the use of chemical agents. Chemical agents present a variety of problems, not the least of which is that they may not be non-lethal in some cases. For example, an individual in an aroused state can breathe more gas before it has an effect than a relaxed individual; body weight and general physical condition could influence the outcome of a gas situation. In addition, gas is not predictable; it cannot tell the difference between friend or foe. Finally it is subject to the elements, i.e. change in wind.

A fourth approach which has been added to the response repertoire is called "contain and negotiate." This approach is preferred because it is not violent and, unlike the others, it is reversible. It is important to point out that we have not reached the point where we can scrap the other approaches, and we may have to utilize them at some point; however, since they have risks to all the combatants, they should be only resorted to as a last and final selection. The negotiator is a synonomous term for therapist. He must wear blinders both in terms of reality and judgmental system. He must disregard the turmoil that is occurring all around him. With little or no information about his client, he must proceed on a therapeutic course which is usually conducted while looking down the wrong end of a firearm. The starting point is to consider the whole scene as a kind of situational occurrence. This means you deal only with what is happening in front of you, nothing more. You don't read into it, and you don't add to it. You deal with only what is presented to you. Since very little, if anything, is known about the criminal's developmental or social history, most of the more sophisticated psychiatric theories prove useless. Police officers are probably most experienced in this kind of situation; that is why we train officers rather than resort to mental health professionals. The only problem with policemen is that they are seen as men of action. The community looks to policemen who will come down and make things all better, the "good daddy" concept. We see this in situations requiring continual police intervention. That is, the policeman is called to the scene because of some sudden change (crisis) with which people cannot cope. The presence of the officer, in and of itself, has a calming effect. Tempers cool down, anger is assuaged, yet frequently all that the police officer has done is record information and has been physically present. The unconscious process involved is that "daddy is here, he will make everything better." Therefore, the panic reaction is reduced and the individuals involved successfully resolve their own problem. Unfortunately, the policeman comes from the general population. The minute he puts on that uniform he says "Gee, I have to make things right." When we get down to a hostage situation, what happens is there is a man with a gun, holding hostages, and threatening his masculinity or his ego. He is saying "I am the boss" and the officer is saying "I have the uniform, I am the boss." The result is that the situation escalates and builds up to a confrontation because police feel pressure to do something.

In fact, we do not have to do something. Built into our approach is the philosophy that we do not have to do anything. The burden for action has to be switched to the criminal. He has to make the first move. He has to initiate action. This represents a role reversal and requires intensive training. A term I like to use to describe this situation is 'dynamic inactivity'; that is, police presence is sufficient to have an effect on a situation and does not require a performance.

There are two basic premises which underlie the entire hostage program. The acceptance, or rather the understanding, of these premises is absolutely essential to the proper police response in a hostage situation. The first is that the hostage, in and of himself, has no value. That is, as a person, the value of the hostage is rather as a device or tool for gathering an audience or attracting attention to oneself. The taking of a hostage can be seen as a creative act - namely, if one is unable to attain needs through legitimate channels, then he can cry, stomp his feet, and scream; he will be ignored. But let him put a gun to someone's head and the whole world takes note. Therefore, the taking of a hostage is viewed as creative problemsolving since within seconds one goes from obscurity to international fame. The second principle is that it is just as much in the criminal's interest as it is in the police interest not to let a hostage situation become violent. It is a given fact which is understood, unless the criminal is psychotic, that in any violent confrontation the victory will go to the establishment authorities because of manpower and equipment. Therefore, if a hostage is killed, the criminal will have to remain be-

hind and deal with the consequences of his act. The psychotic is usually too disorganized to put together a hostage situation. In addition we
must accept the fact that in our society there are people who will kill
and we will not be able to prevent it; but most hostage jobs are structured or created to attract attention or find a way out of having to kill.

Hostage situations can be broken down into three basic types.
There are hundreds of different hostage situations. No two are the
same; every one is different. They all have their unique qualities,
but we have, for the purposes of handling them, felt that they can be
force-fitted into three general categories.

The first one is called "the professional criminal": the professional criminal in the sense of a man who gets up in the morning, is
shaving and looking into the mirror and says to himself "You know, I
could use some money today. I know what, I'll go down and knock over
the A&P." "Professional" should not be considered in terms of experience but rather in purpose; that is, the purpose of his crime is to
get money. He goes into a place and something horrible happens. He
gets caught in the act. A teller in a bank or a clerk in the store sends
an alarm. Perhaps a policeman walks in the door by mistake. A civilian sees him and calls the police. He gets caught. He takes a hostage, but the hostage for him means only one thing. It means escape.
He uses the hostage as a shield and what he is really saying is "I'll
trade you my freedom for this guy's life." These are the most common situations, and they really are the easiest ones to handle, because
you do not have to make too many decisions. Either you can get a shot
at him, you can trip him, you can grab him - or you are going to have
to let him go. He doesn't let you decide anything else. What we want
to do is contain him, and with that in mind we have developed procedures for locking people like him into a small area; we do not want
them to escape. The immediate reaction is, of course, panic, and
with panic the desire to run. The results of panic can either be to run
or attack. Perhaps the best way to describe panic is to picture walking down a long dark hall when out of the shadows a figure springs
shouting "surprise." If he attacks, the outcome will be fatal and usually over prior to its becoming a hostage situation. If we can help the
criminal over the panic to run, then he may realize the nature of the
consequences and possible outcomes and finally will surrender.

The second kind of situation is the so-called "psycho." While
this kind of person is a "psycho" I do not want you to be misled. To
start with, the definition of such, which is a little unfamiliar and may
be confusing, has to be understood if we are going to be able to deal
with this type of person. I do not see any behavior as abnormal. All
behavior is normal for what a person feels, sees, and bases on the way

he structures the world around him. If you could put yourself into a
person and see and feel the world the way he is experiencing it, you
would do the exact same thing as he does. For example, if you go into a mental institution and an individual is rolled up in a ball and banging his head on the wall, he is not crazy. Rather, his behavior is
meaningful, understandable and pleasurable to him. Imagine you thought
you had spiders crawling all over your head; maybe banging your head
on the wall is a good way to get them off. Often a person goes into a
situation that begins like a regular crime; he holds up a bank or a
store. The only difference is, he manages to get caught. He arranges
for himself to get caught. There is something different in the quality
of the demands he makes. Let me give you an example. A man goes
into a bank to commit a hold-up. The bank is crowded. He stands on
line waiting his turn to get to the teller. The only difference is, he has
a shotgun in his hand. He is standing on line with a long gun in his
hand, out in the open.

The teller does not send an alarm. He does not see anything unusual about it. A woman walking by, in front of the bank, looks in and
sees the man on line with a shotgun. She says "Gee, that does not look
right, maybe I should call the police." She dials 911. The police arrive at the scene. The man is still waiting on line. He has about
three more people to go before he gets up to the teller. When the police walk in the door, he announces "This is a stickup" and he takes
the three people that are in front of him on line as hostages. He does
not say to the teller, "Put all the money you have in a bag and give it
to me." What he says to the policemen who come in the door is, "I
want one thousand pizza pies."

Admittedly, this is extreme, but the point of it is that the quality
of that demand is somehow different than what you would normally expect. His next demand after the pizza pies is "one million dollars."
Now he is in a bank that is loaded with money and he is asking two uniformed, radio-car police officers for one million dollars. He ignores
the reality of the situation and is obviously responding to some internal stimuli.

The idea behind what he is doing, is not to get the money, because
if it were, he would have gone in and announced, "This is a stickup,"
taken the money and have been gone long before the police had gotten
there, or he would have attempted some kind of escape. Asking for
pizza pies, or for political prisoners to be released, or the mayor, or
the governor, is a different kind of request. The missing element is
escape; that is, what is demanded is not wanted, but rather there is
pleasure in running the situation. In reviewing the clinical evidence
resulting in interviews with these types of people, one is confronted

with an array of diagnostic labels ranging from paranoid-schizophrenic
to latent homosexual, but it becomes clear that these labels have no
real meaning beyond clinical classification. It serves us better to examine their behavior and lifestyle; something characteristic can be seen
running through their whole life pattern. They are basically the kinds of
guys in everyday life you call losers. Everything they do in life fails;
they have no friends, they cannot form relationships with people, they
are afraid of women. If they are married, they are in the process of
getting a divorce because they have no sexual life. They cannot hold
a job. They are the kind of people that, if they were to ask you what
time it was, you would look at your watch and inadvertently give them
the wrong time; everyone does.

    This type of person stages the entire situation, with hostages as
a kind of last attempt to prove that he has power, or to prove his
masculinity, or to prove his ability to get out of the world what he
wants. It is a very desperate kind of move, a very last attempt at
settling and proving, once and for all, whether or not he can succeed.
Frequently he has, associated with it, a suicidal component.

    Basically he is confronted by two psychological dynamics. Let
us separate them out: he is confronted by frustration and conflict.
Now these two dynamics are not important in handling the situation,
but they are important in understanding what is going on. In addition,
one of the things we found is that the police officer goes through the
same exact process that the criminal goes through. Frustration is
simply wanting something and not being able to get it. You would not
grow and develop if you were not frustrated. You learn how to get
out of the world what you wanted by being frustrated. We have to
think of it in terms of levels. We all have a different level to which
we can be frustrated. It goes back to that early phase of learning how
to handle the world. If you have never had any frustration, you would
go to pieces, you could not handle frustration. If you have had a very
frustrated life, then you can tolerate more frustration. For many
years we thought of frustration as existing in what used to be called
the "frustration-aggression hypothesis." That is, if you are frustrated, if you cannot get what you want, if something is blocking you from
what you want, you get angry. If you get angry, you get aggressive,
so that frustration automatically leads to aggression. But we believe
that it is not that clear-cut. There is a little process that happens in-
between. When people become frustrated, because frustration is so
elementary to life, they automatically start doing something. They
start going into problem-solving, or reasoning, or creative thinking.
They try to get what they want. If that does not work, then they move
into the aggressive stage. If we have closed all the areas of problem-

solving for an individual, there is nothing that he can do, no way that
he can get what he wants. At that point, he becomes aggressive and
takes what he wants. You notice that I said that he has to think that
there is a solution. He has to believe that there is a solution because he will keep working until the last door is closed. We, in a
sense, are involved in keeping him in that problem-solving phase,
creating an atmosphere conducive to keeping a person working on a
problem. Why? Because as long as somebody is working on the problem, then he does not get aggressive. If he does not get aggressive,
he is not going to hurt anyone. It is that simple a relationship. This
is important because if we fail, and problem-solving stops, people
then move out of the problem-solving phase into the aggressive phase.
There are really only two basic ways to handle agression in our
society; you can turn it in against yourself of you can turn it out against
the world.

The important is the way that the dynamics work in an inadequate personality. He is saying to himself, "I can't get anywhere. I can't succeed
in life. Nothing works out right for me. If only they would have given
me the right opportunities. If only they would have permitted me to go
to the right schools. If only they would have presented me with a
chance. They don't deserve to live." In the extreme "I am going to
kill them," it becomes a homicide. The same individual could also
say to himself "I can't amount to anything. I can't get anywhere. If
only I would have taken advantage of the opportunity. If I would have
applied myself, if I would have studied. I don't deserve to live." And
in the extreme, it is a suicide.

The important is, if we stay in problem-solving, in a hostage
situation, then we never have to worry, is really basic to life. It is a
motivating force. Because it is energy, you have to think of it in terms
of levels. A certain amount is good. It moves you, it makes you alert,
makes you creative, makes you think, makes you problem-solve. But
if you have too much of it, it starts spilling over and disrupts behavior
completely.

Without going into the specifics at this point, basically the ranges
of anxiety can be seen in all of its states from mild, moderate, severe
to panic, with a kind of fluidity allowing easy movement within and
among the stages. Needless to say, the police intervention would have
to match the appropriate state and its corresponding ability for the
individual to problem-solve. In understanding what occurs it is very
important to fully understand anxiety and the way in that it differs from
fear. Both are important for survival and both are, for the most part,
anticipatory response mechanisms which prepare the individual to meet
an impending danger. As you know, both are important survival mec-

hanisms; without either, one would not survive the perils of our complex society. Of course, with anxiety there is an obvious absence of an object, while fear gets one ready for a real environmental attack, as by a wild animal. On the other hand, anxiety is free-floating and will attach itself to any object present in the context of a situation. In a hostage situation what happens, of course, is that the most obvious object for this anxiety to attach itself to, and the anger to displace itself on, is the police. Therefore, from their original role as passive interceptors, the police become the active objects of the situation and can get caught up in the spiral of the activity. Because anxiety is important for survival, one of the side effects is the heightening of awareness of the senses. The criminal becomes supersensitive. He can read the expression on your face. He watches every move you make. He can hear the hammer go back on a gun three blocks away. He is really attentive to every single action. Now his interpretations may be all wrong. That does not matter. The point is, he is watching very carefully and he is very tuned into the situation. He is making all kinds of decisions based on what he is processing. The higher the anxiety, the more likely his interpretations are wrong. The idea, then, is to reduce his anxiety so he can perceive the situation accurately. In addition, as anxiety goes down, he becomes less aware and less sensitive. He is not as tuned into things. He starts making errors and mistakes, because making them is normal. He is not watching everything that is going on. In that is this guy homicidal or suicidal? The second psychological element we spoke about, was the conflict. Conflict is wanting something and not wanting something at the same time. It is an ambivalent feeling of love and hate. Well, in a hostage situation, it is a little more serious but the same thing is happening, a power conflict. Here is a man who has never experienced any kind of power or success. All of a sudden he is an important guy. The hostage is begging him "Please don't kill me." He has life and death - godlike power. The police are out there; 300 policemen asking him to come out, be good, don't hurt anyone, "you are important." The press is calling him on the telephone. They want to find out what kind of war hero he was. He has fantastic power. The only trouble is, he has never had it before. What is going through his mind is "Gee, this feels great. I had better get out of here before I get hurt. No, I'll stay a little longer. No, I had better go. No. Stay. Go. Stay." And he is being pulled back and forth. And of course, fear of punishment overrides the entire situation. Implied is that somehow he will get punished after this is over, i.e. prison, mental institution, or in his imagination, even worse. If frustration, conflict and fear of punishment are together, what they produce is anxiety. Now the anxiety period of relaxation

with everything calming down, we can more effectively deal with him.
We can talk to him more easily and he can go into problem-solving.
Also, as anxiety runs down, he is starting to get tired. He is getting
sleepy and begins relaxing. What this means for us is that many hostage situations have ended just this way; that is, the criminals and
often the hostages just fall asleep. The negotiations teams are designed, really, as therapists. They spend weeks learning crisis intervention therapy; it is basically a form of psychotherapy. We are dealing
with people having high anxiety states. The negotiating teams help
compress time factors in the holding of hostages that these jobs would
normally have to run, because one of the best treatments for anxiety
is time. If we analyze the current medical model, or the psychoanaly-
tically oriented model, it becomes apparent that whether we use drugs,
electric shock, or hospitalization, the key feature in any treatment regime, is basically time. Therefore we treat this man who is holding
the hostages by treating his anxiety with time. And we compress the
time, and seek to utilize the time by using a negotiator.

The third type of hostage situation, in addition to the professional
criminal and the psycho, is the group. There are really two types of
groups. If you read the sociological literature, you see that there are
hundreds of groups, but for our purposes, there are basically two
kinds. There is a loose, unorganized, spontaneous kind of group
which we sometimes call a mob, and there is a tightly organized group,
with a leader, goals, aims, etc., which frequently we call a fanatical
or terrorist group.

The loose kind of group is the kind that you have in a prison takeover. There is really no leader and no structure. It is something
that develops spontaneously and grows as the situation goes along. The
fanatical group is comprised of people from our society who feel that
they are not getting what they are entitled to, not getting their fair
share. Someone is trying to take it away from them; they have been
exploited; they are being taken advantage of. If this should sound
familiar, it is what is called our inadequate personality, only now it
is a group of inadequate personalities. The real problem, if you can
think about it, can be conceptualized as, what would it be like if you
were the most inadequate guy in an inadequate group? That is, the
group members are busy playing for each other and trying to impress
each other. This is true of the political left or right, either extreme.

Sometimes, therefore, what develops is what we call the "Kami-
kaze Personality," which simply means that they think the only way
out of the situation is to die. It's tragic, but this sometimes happens.
The only way they can get out of the situation and save face is to give
up their lives. They don't want to, but they are forced into it in order

to maintain peer acceptance. The way that we deal with a group is the
same way that we deal with an individual. We set up negotiating, we
lock them in and we try to resolve the crises that they are going
through, with the use of our crisis team.

Often we cannot solve their problem. For example, a group that
takes hostages here and wants a country in the Middle East to release
political prisoners allows us no way in which to solve that problem.
After thinking about it they may come to realize that what they are
asking for is unrealistic. It should be apparent, however, that the
system I am describing is an anxiety-reducing system and one of the
key elements missing in a militaristic group is anxiety. It is for that
reason that we will frequently encounter difficulty in using crisis intervention techniques unless we first change the nature of the situation by
environmental manipulation. Another important principle which we
utilize as part of our crisis intervention is transference. This is
really a distortion of the term transference, but I think it describes
the intensity of a relationship which begins to form between the criminal and the hostages, and the negotiator and the criminal. Part of the
explanation for this is certainly the need for affiliation under stress
and the desire to constantly verify feelings against a standard. Some
explanations of the identification with aggressors, identified after
World War II in concentration camps, could explain this phenomenon
as well. Of course the time factor is important again here since the
longer the period of time that people are pressed together under stress,
the more likely it is that these relationships will form and the more intense they will be. In the absence of contrary information, the relationship is positive. It can be negative, but if it is, we are usually helpless
in changing the direction. But the absence of information sometimes
suggests that hostages are family or friends, who are a greater risk.
These transference reactions can take place within a matter of minutes.
Much of what happens can be understood in terms of brainwashing, need
for conformity and acceptance as well as group pressure. Without a
proper understanding of some of the basic research in social psychology,
it is difficult to comprehend the process. There are two points I should
like to make supporting this view. The first is that the extraction of a
pledge from the criminal not to hurt the negotiator is usually respected.
Is it because in our society we have learned from the movies that even
the savages respect a white flag of truce, or perhaps that the formation
of a new society under stress conditions provides us with new ground
rules as defined by the current situation? The second example is that
the hostage situation provides a stage for the hostage taker. Immediate
violence would not provide a long center-stage performance, so that the
push is constantly to prolong it and therefore the criminal is desirous
of using time in common with the police.

Imagine you are standing with a hostage. The police are called
and they arrive on the scene. The police walk over to you and say
"What's going on here?" You say, "I've got a hostage here, I want a
million dollars, I want a trip to Europe." etc. " The police then say
"Gee, that's very interesting. " They turn around, they get back into
their police car and then they drive away, leaving you standing there.
What value is that hostage to you? The hostages are taken in order to
create an audience. Frequently the criminal will ask for the mayor,
the governor, the wife. When they are making that kind of request,
they are asking for that audience to be present to show them or impress them. If you provide that audience, what you are going to do is
to trigger things off. The negotiator serves as a substitution for the
hostage, not physically, but rather symbolically. Up to this point, if
the criminal is desirous of something, he must put pressure on the
hostage. The negotiator takes the pressure away by saying "Can I
help you?" so the criminal will switch his attention from the hostage
to the negotiator. Basically the negotiator sets himself up as a
"significant other. " A significant other is one who makes an offer to
help, and the person to whom the help is offered believes, in fact, that
he can help. This relationship permits the hostage holder to "venti-
late" that is, to express all his pent-up anxieties. The process involves verbal interaction in order for the criminal to put his thoughts into
order and, as a result, this often slows him down and frequently permits him to hear them for the first time. This is done in a "safe"
atmosphere and with the help of the negotiator whose presence aids
him to reevaluate his circumstances.

This chapter represents, of course, a very over-simplified
schematic presentation of the procedures for the psychology of police
response and tactics for hostage situations. It must be bolstered by
training in order to reduce the shock to the officers handling the situation. It further requires intensive training in some of the general
principles of psychology, particularly those applicable to an understanding of crisis intervention theory, i. e. the role of the significant
other permitting ventilation and the reestablishment of a state of
equilibrium. As with any therapy, the technique is frequently no better
than the therapist.

In terms of predicting the future for negotiations, it is clear that
we will have to develop additional strategies, especially since current
methods and theories are becoming more readily available to the
criminals. This is being accomplished via textbooks devoted almost
exclusively to the art of negotiating, and through the mass media, not
only in terms of news reporting, but even in dramatic productions
which are remarkably accurate. The terrorists, in particular, have

become involved in so many more volatile and complex issues which
present them with intense frustration and ultimate escalation of their
reactions that solutions to problems seem to become more and more
elusive - and therefore negotiations will have to revolve more and
more around police and psychological strategies rather than realities.

Perhaps the biggest challenge will be to keep the individuals who
practice negotiations from becoming too technical and specialized.
This will most likely be accomplished by gradually and systematically
training all law enforcement officers in the dynamics of human behavior. Perhaps in the long run, someday, a specialty and prerequisite
for law enforcement work would involve training similar to that of a
psychological technician; much like the relationship of first-aid training to medicine.

Nevertheless, just in evaluting the state of the art of negotiating
today, it is clear that many psychologists, psychiatrists and social
scientists are becoming very involved in the theory and scientific
study of both negotiations and the personality types which they will
have to deal with. Their study has gone beyond armchair speculation
and the gathering of empirical data and will probably shortly evolve
into a research model. One area now avoided which will get much
more attention in the future is that of the impact on the victim of a
hostage situation. In the near future, the effects on victim involvement will be analyzed, with emphasis on the possible defenses and
strategies which may be proven effective if marshalled by the victim
to assist in his release. In general terms, we have just begun to
understand some of the very surface characteristics and dynamics of
police response to hostage situations. We must recognize that the police do not stand alone and that whatever changes do occur in police
response, equal and opposite reactions will occur in the behavior of
the criminals involved.

IV
Law, Courts and Corrections

11 Criminal Courts of the Future

Neil Chamelin

INTRODUCTION

What will the criminal courts of the United States look like in the year 2000 and beyond? How will the criminal courts operate? The answer to these very significant questions depends on an analysis of many variables both within the without the criminal justice system. A great many social trends and phenomena must be examined before any forecasting can reasonably assess the future of the criminal courts. These questions cannot be answered by an isolated study of the history of the criminal courts in the United States; nor can they be answered simply by looking at quantitative measures and data on the growing backlog of cases, the increase of court administrators, arrest statistics, cleared cases, numbers granted probation, or numbers of persons incarcerated for criminal violations. Neither can the future of the criminal courts be projected without examining the likely growth or increase of crime in the coming years. As was emphatically pointed out by the National Advisory Commission on Criminal Justice Standards and Goals in 1973:

> The crime problem is likely to grow rather than diminish in the coming decades. By the year 2000 the population of the United States is expected to increase by 50 percent. This increase will mean a corresponding increase in the amount of crime. Increased social change, moreover, is likely to contribute to national instability - and more crimes - during the next thirty years. Technological advances and rapid urbanization also will heighten the vulnerability of our society to criminal activity, making the act

of the offender more harmful to personal and social interests and
the offender more likely to escape apprehension.

These worsening crime trends have generated mounting dissatisfaction with America's system of criminal justice. While all
components of the system have been criticized, it is becoming
apparent that, as the Nation's crime-consciousness grows, the
role of the courts in crime control is becoming the center of controversy. (1)

A more specific analysis of the Commission's position reveals
that a number of major long-range sociocultural trends will have an
impact on the criminal justice system and, specifically, the courts.
A brief look at the implications of some of these trends as reported
by a recent major research study is in order. (2)

The population of the United States will continue to grow during
the foreseeable future. This will result in an increase in the teenage
and young adult population within the age grouping normally associated
with high arrest rates. There will also be a greater rise in the population of black youth as compared to white youth. This increase will
be reflected in higher unemployment rates for all youth, but particularly blacks between the ages of 16 and 19 years. It is expected that
crime rates will continue to increase within this youthful age category,
particularly for acts of violence.

American society is continually becoming more industrialized and
is moving toward an era that has been labeled post-industrial, where
there will be more emphasis on occupations which are service, research and education-oriented. Those who lack the education or the
opportunity to get education, coupled with rising unemployment rates,
possibly suggests an· increase in crime. All of this, together with
increasing urbanization, particularly among black and particularly involving black youth, is also suggestive of increased criminal activity.

Sociological trends also indicate that there is a continuing decline
in religion and need for spiritual well-being on the part of the American
public, and an increase in man's desire for material gratification; and
expectations for social institutions to meet these materialistic needs.
The general implication of this is an anticipated increase in overt de-
fiance of legitimate authority, including an increase in law violations
and disrespect for law enforcement institutions, along with continued
increased challenges to regulation of moral conduct.

There will also be a continuing increase in the growth of science,
and technology and reliance upon automation of the production of goods
not to speak of the computerization of information-type activities which

will necessarily require a more highly educated population, thus resulting in a greater disadvantage to those who do not have the necessary level of educational achievement. This will also create additional problems for the criminal justice system through the increased use of scientific and technological advancements by offenders to violate the laws of society.

This country is experiencing an increased growth in economic affluence, which is also producing a greater handicap for those who cannot or have not achieved the necessary level of competence to keep up. Many individuals may well turn to criminal activity as a means of sheer survival within the system.

Another sociocultural trend reflects a wider participation of different groups within the mainstream of American society, particularly a gradual increase of participation and leadership by blacks and females. This inculcation into leadership roles will cause greater expectations for equality in jobs, education, housing and political representation, including jobs within the criminal justice system. Failure of society to meet these expectations at a sufficient rate to satisfy needs may result in some individuals turning to criminal activity, including an increase in female offenders.

Each of these sociocultural trends, and numerous others, will not only have an impact on crime and crime rates, but will have a dramatic impact in the operations of the criminal justice system, including the courts.

THE NEED FOR CHANGE

Many members of the general public and personnel within the criminal justice system view the courts as that portion of the criminal justice system where the majority of the problems now lie. The public perceives that court decisions, particularly those of the United States Supreme Court, are creating situations which prove beneficial to individuals who violate the laws of society and, at the same time, present severe limitations to law-abiding citizens and the police. Many feel that the processes of justice are too slow and too lenient; that the courts are the bottleneck of the system and the prime reason for what is viewed as high rates of recidivism. Again, as noted by the National Advisory Commission:

Two premises underlie the report of this Commission. The first is that crime in America is seriously interfering with the Nation's ability to attain economic, political, and social well-being for all its citizens. The second is that no attempt to alleviate this problem can succeed unless dramatic improvements are made in the ability of the courts to perform their critical role in the criminal justice system. (3)

Many suggestions for reform have been made. Some have been implemented. Much more must be done. The fact is, the criminal courts are, and will continue to be, a focus for change in the criminal justice system. How successful they will be depends on a number of variables.

Resistance to change on the part of judges and other personnel in the judicial branch of government is perceived as being one of the greatest barriers to be overcome. Historically, attorneys and judges, probably the most educated members of the criminal justice system, have been viewed as being the most resistant to outside input to bring about changes. Barriers have been encountered by those attempting to work with the judicial system to bring about changes. Efforts to foster change by using available money through the Law Enforcement Assistance Administration showed the initial reluctance of the judiciary.

The relationship of the judiciary to the law enforcement and corrections components of the criminal justice system leads many to believe that there is an attempt by the judiciary to assume the administrative responsibility of the entire criminal justice system. This produces some strained relationships which too often cause stumbling blocks in the effort to bring about change. Perhaps the three most critical and significant areas in which it appears the courts have intervened in the operation and supervision of other components of the criminal justice system are: 1) implementation of the exclusionary rule, 2) rights of the confined, and 3) implementation of equal employment opportunity/affirmative action programs and other personnel practices of criminal justice agencies. These and other issues will be explored in the remainder of this chapter.

COURTS AS CHANGE AGENTS

In recent decades, there has been a major shift in the role of the criminal and appellate courts regarding their relationship with other components of the criminal justice system. The change has been gradual in some areas, but has not escaped attention. The checks and balance system that earlier marked the relationship of the courts to police and corrections has apparently gradually eroded to a point where many view the courts as a supervisory component of the system rather than an equal check and balance element. Although the trend began in the 1950s with the appointment of Earl Warren as Chief Justice of the United States Supreme Court, it was not until the early 1960s that a noticeable impact began with the Court's decision in Mapp v. Ohio, which imposed the exclusionary rule on the states. The effect of that holding was to rule inadmissible in a criminal case evidence searched and seized unreasonably in violation of the Fourth Amendment to the United States Constitution. The subsequent decisions following this line of reasoning have, for the most part, placed the courts in a position of dictating policies and procedures to be followed by law enforcement agencies. In essence, the courts began establishing a pattern of not only reviewing policy decisions of law enforcement agencies, but went a step further and began establishing those policies. The trend continued right up through the end of the 1960s with case decisions such as Escobedo v. Illinois and Miranda v. Arizona.

In the area of corrections, the courts have begun to impose policy decisions on correctional agencies through a line of cases dealing with the rights of offenders. Recognizing and accepting this trend, the National Advisory Commission on Criminal Justice Standards and Goals, in its 1973 Report on Corrections, noted the need for establishing standards related to the rights of offenders. These areas include: right of access to the courts; access to legal services and legal materials; protection against personal abuse; healthful surroundings with adequate medical care; protection against unreasonable searches; right to nondescriminatory treatment; rehabilitation, retention and restoration of rights; the need to establish rules of conduct and disciplinary procedures as well as procedures for non-disciplinary changes of status and grievance procedures for inmates; free expression and association; the right to exercise and practice religious beliefs; adequate access to the public; and remedies for violation of rights of offenders.

As noted earlier, the third major area of court intervention in the practices of other components of the criminal justice system has been in the area of regulation of personnel and employment practices. Since the passage of the Equal Employment Opportunity Act of 1972, which imposed the equal employment requirements of Title VII of the Civil Rights Act of 1964 upon public agencies, hundreds upon hundreds of court cases having clearly shown the intention and implementation of court-imposed procedures for the operation of criminal justice agencies. Numerous cases can clearly point out where courts have not only found discrimination in the employment practices of agencies, but have resolved these problems by actually imposing and supervising personnel practices at the first-line operational level of the agencies.

Few can deny that these changes brought about by court rulings have been needed for the improvement and proper operation of various components of the criminal justice system. The effect is not questioned. Rather, the method by which the courts have gone about accomplishing their objectives has been severely criticized. The courts are no longer simply reviewing policy decisions of other components of the system and requiring agencies to modify practices until an acceptable method has been achieved. Instead, the courts are themselves making the changes. The impact has been to make the courts appear to be supervising the operations of the police and correctional authorities. If this trend continues, it will have a dramatic effect on what the criminal courts look like in the year 2000 and beyond.

There is some indication that the Supreme Court's position on the exclusionary rule is easing up and tending toward abolition. The ultimate effect of this, if the trend continues, will be to completely do away with the exclusionary rule and its prohibition on the admissibility of evidence in criminal cases. It will be replaced by increased civil liability on the part of officers who flagrantly violate the provisions of the Fourth Amendment. The ultimate result could be that evidence obtained by unreasonable searches and seizures will be admissible in criminal cases against offenders but that individual officers and police agencies will assume civil responsibility for their conduct. There is no similar indication of an easing on the part of the courts in their supervisory role dealing with the rights of offenders or with personnel issues and equal employment opportunity questions. Until present practices and past effects of discriminatory practices can be totally abolished within public agencies, it is unlikely that the courts will relinquish their present hardline approach to insuring implementation of equal employment opportunity programs. Likewise, until the courts are convinced that inmates in correctional institutions are being offered certain guarantees consistant with humane treatment, it is likely that the courts will continue to exercise supervision in this area.

Consequently, although there may be some easing of the court's assumed role as supervisor of other components of the criminal justice system in some areas, it is likely that the change will not be drastic in the foreseeable future.

LEGISLATIVE CHANGES

Despite the need to overcome certain barriers of resistance to change within the judiciary, changes can be made from external sources that will produce results. Among others, the legislative branch of government has an impact on the operations and quality of the judiciary. Specifically, legislative enactments can bring about reform of the substantive criminal law as the structure of courts systems.

One "solution" often heard is simply to increase the number of judges through legislative fiat. Such a suggestion is meritorious in instances where the only problems faced by the judiciary are related to workloads. Normally however, overcrowded dockets are symptomatic of problems far beyond quantitative analysis and solution. They are suggestive of complex issues of a qualitative nature not as easily resolved.

Overburdened court dockets and crowded court case loads will continue to grow as crime continues to increase during the remainder of this century and beyond. More than half of the arrests made by police and a substantial portion of court cases involve offenses which are, at the most, marginally related to the severe crime problem we continue to face in this country. All State legislatures have been encouraged by national study commissions to revise and appropriately modify their criminal codes at least once each decade. A number of states have undertaken these major revisions. Some have not yet begun.

Every ten years is probably not often enough for major code revisions. Without attempting to inject personal bias and prejudice, there are many criminal laws still enforced which should be legalized, decriminalized or, at the very least, subjected to administrative disposition through tribunals rather than tying up the criminal court systems. These offenses, in the long run, only temporarily delay a continual pattern of behavior on the part of some individuals, not necessarily constituting serious criminal offenses, but occasionally disturbing the peace and tranquility of some of the populace. As noted, some states have moved in this direction, and have seen some minor impact on criminal court systems as presently structured. However, whatever relief is provided the court systems through the reform of substantive law will be short-lived. The ever-growing crime problem will quickly fill with court cases of a more serious nature the void created by legalization or decriminilization of certain acts. The system itself must be reformed.

Lower court systems are often not sufficiently financed or staffed to handle the overwhelming workloads demanded of them. The majority

of Americans who come in contact with a court do so at the lower
level in State systems. Coping with the sheer volume of work in
these understaffed, underfinanced, and sometimes under-qualified
courts has produced a situation of "assembly-line justice" which is
likely to continue unless vast changes are made. The unification of
State courts into an organized system financed and administered at
the State level could provide some relief, particularly for the lower
courts, where the problems appear to be most pronounced. A unified
system can produce a better-operated court system with appropriate
financing, personnel assignments, and adequate administration to
better meet the prescribed roles of the judiciary.

REFORM OF COURT MANAGEMENT
AND JUDICIAL PROCESSES

The sociocultural trends examined earlier, combined with the
known increase in court case loads, will likely result in more requests
for jury trials in years to come. Court systems must be able to cope
with the sheer volume of cases without sacrificing individualized due
process. Coping will require a massive attempt to divert many cases
from reaching the trial stage. Community and police projects on diversion now underway must continue and must be increased substantially. But the courts must get more involved in diversion programs
also. They must help find ways to keep individuals out of the courts
without sacrificing or neglecting the judicial function. In other words,
nolle processing, or dismissing serious criminal cases, is not the
answer to overcrowded court dockets; court resources must be utilized only for offenses of a serious nature. If present trends continue,
the whole due process concept in the American system of jurisprudence
will possibly falter. The volume has produced an untenable assembly-
line process for disposing of criminal cases, particularly in the lower
courts. Individualized due process is on the decline. To save our
system, streamlining of court processes and better management is
needed.

Plea bargaining has been a partial salvation in the past; but will
it work in the future? The National Advisory Commission on Criminal Justice Standards and Goals recommended total abolition of plea
negotiations by 1978 as a course of action to improve the judicial
system. That time frame has already passed, while plea bargaining
remains a very viable part of judicial processes. Not only is the
commission's recommendation unworkable, it is absolutely absurd.

Even if all of the recommendations and suggestions for streamlining
and improving the flow of cases through the judicial process work to
their optimum, it is unlikely that court systems will experience a
great deal of leisure time. As unacceptable as plea negotiations are
to some who believe in the basic tenets of American jurisprudence,
the practice must remain as an integral part of the system. Without
it, total collapse is imminent. This is not to say that plea bargaining
in its present form is ideal. The commission's recommendations to
formalize, recognize, publicize, insure fairness, raise visibility,
and provide structure and review of such procedures is much more
palatable and workable as a means of diverting cases from full and
formal trial processes.

Other suggestions for streamlining judicial processes go directly to the heart of the adversary proceeding as we know it. It has been
suggested that less strategic and tactical role-playing and "oneups-
manship" would help speed up the judicial process if it were replaced
by more sharing of information, factfinding and the willingness to provide discovery to the litigants in a criminal case. In other words, it
has been suggested that the adult criminal process follow a similar
philosophical format that characterized the initial juvenile court concept as developed in the late nineteenth century - that being to examine
the facts and circumstances surrounding the nature and seriousness
of an offence, and the needs of the offender, and to dispose of the
case in a manner beneficial to all without invoking the formal processes of trial. Even though this concept sounds ideal and workable, this
writer has doubts about the efficacy or acceptability of such a system,
given the historical and constitutional philosophies around which the
adversary processes of the American judicial system is built. It is
doubtful whether the concept will receive a great deal of support from
any quarter.

Regardless of whether some or all of these ideas are accepted or
implemented, better management is necessary if the judicial system
is to survive. A great deal of time is currently wasted both in pre-
trial and trial processes. Efforts to speed up the trial, the selection
of juries by involving the court directly in questioning prospective
jurors, the cutting down of allowable continuances, providing for more
speedy trials, better scheduling of cases, operation of courts on a full
day with reasonable recesses rather than on "banking hours" can all
help expedite the processes of justice and perhaps bring the case loads
within managable limits.

One of the greatest boons to the betterment of court management
has been the creation of the "court administrator" concept. Court
administrators serve as behind-the-scenes, non-judicial managers of

the business of operating a court system. They can assume general
management and overall administration of the courts, including handling all personnel matters, dealing with financial aspects of maintaining the court system, managing and maintaining space and equipment
requirements, public information and speechmaking, preparing administrative reports, preparing and maintaining calendars of court
cases, and managing and operating the data processing system for
support of court operations. In sum, court administrators are business managers for the judicial branch of government and, by performing their functions, free judges to spend a great deal more time in
their primary function - judging. It is anticipated that the court administrator concept will continue to grow and will become more acceptable with each passing year, so that within the foreseeable future the
business of running the courts will be in the hands of competent professional administrators who, working for judges, will be better
equipped to handle administrative responsibilities, thus freeing judges
to spend more time on the disposing of criminal cases.

The use of the computer will continue to play an increasingly important role in the judiciary. The proper use of computers can not
only help support the administration and management functions necessary to operate a court system effectively as a business enterprise,
but can also provide a great deal of support to speed up case processing. Legal research, case histories of offenders, preparation of
transcripts and procedures for selection of juries are examples of
some possible uses.

                              JUDICIAL SELECTION

Over the next thirty to fifty years there is likely to be a gradual
shift in the processes for qualification and selection of judges. As
much as has been written on the advantages and disadvantages of both
the elective and appointive methods for selecting judges, and the emphasis placed on selection processes like the Missouri and California
Plans that combine the best features of both the elective and appointive systems, it is likely that election of judges will gradually disappear
from the American scene. The growing complexities of operating and
functioning within the judicial system will require individuals to be
selected on merit. The requirement for individuals to possess the
background and competency to perform effectively as members of the
judiciary will not only bring about the demise of the elective system,
but will probably result in specialization in the handling of particular

types of cases. As a consequence of this specialization, it is most likely that the requirement that judges be attorneys will become universal. Right now many states, particularly at the lower court levels, are struggling with this requirement.

Emphasis will be placed on the need for continued legal training and education for members of the judiciary. As specialization becomes a reality, judges will be required to participate in programs which enhance their skills to perform in particular specialties and, until the court administrator concept becomes universally accepted, the need for judges to be adequately trained in organization and management principles to improve their ability to operate court systems will be emphasized, if not mandated.

CONCLUSION - WHERE DOES IT ALL LEAD?

The criminal justice system cannot control the trend of increasing crime. The system, particularly the courts, must be able to cope, but coping will require major changes in the present quality of the administration of justice. Legislative bodies must do what they can to help restructure court systems and areas of responsibility. The role of the courts must be reexamined in terms of their relationship with other components of the criminal justice system. The resistance to change must be overcome. Better management techniques must be incorporated in the operations of court systems. The system must be streamlined. There must be a return to the concept of individualized due process and a demise of the assembly-line, bureaucratic approach that is now gradually taking over our judicial processes. Judges must be selected on a basis of their qualifications to perform in a specific area of responsibility. Will these changes occur?

Some of the changes are already in the process of occurring. The identification of the problems in the courts as they relate to the administration of justice have become much more publicized than in the past. Thus, merely recognizing the problem exists is one step forward. In recognizing the need for change, court personnel are becoming less and less resistant to outside input. The apparent trend toward easing the impact of the exclusionary rule shows some indication on the part of the courts of the need to appropriately define their role with respect to other criminal justice agencies. Criminal law reform is underway in the legislatures of many states. Unification of court systems has been attempted by a number of jurisdictions. Management is gradually getting better. The court administrator concept is, and will continue to be, more widely acceptable. Recommendations to streamline a number of operating processes are being studied and implemented on a gradual basis. Modification in judicial selection will be slow in coming, but will take place. Areas where resistance will remain concern the alteration of the adversary proceeding to more of a fact-finding, information-sharing process, and the future of plea negotiations. It is doubtful whether these two major issues will receive much acceptance in the foreseeable future.

Thus, efforts are being made to bring about necessary changes in the quality of the administration of justice, but the changes are not occurring as fast as the problems continue to increase. Crime is on the increase; analysis of major sociological trends using historical data and extrapolation techniques to forecast major social ramifications clearly indicates that crime will continue to increase, although there may be periods of fluctuation. Sociocultural developments are contributing factors to the incidence of crime; thus, it is clear that courts alone cannot control the increase. For that matter, the criminal justice system cannot control the forecasted increase and cannot have impact on the sociocultural trends themselves. Consequently, the criminal justice system, particularly the courts, must be able to cope with the increase of crime. Coping today with current crime problems is a most difficult task.

The quality of the justice system is largely controlled by its structure, roles and philosophies. The judicial component of the criminal justice system must be streamlined, but quality must never be sacrificed for quantity or for the sake of a system that operates smoothly on paper. Legislative bodies must do what they can to help restructure court systems and their areas of responsibility. The role of the courts must be defined in terms of their relationship with other components of the criminal justice system. The resistance to change must be overcome. Better management techniques must be incorporated in the operations of court systems. There must be a return to the concept of individualized due process and a demise of the assembly-line, bureaucratic approach that is now gradually taking over our judicial process. Judges must be selected based on their qualifications to perform in specific areas of responsibility. Will these necessary changes occur?

Some of the changes are already in the process of occurring. The identification of problems in the courts as they relate to the administration of justice have become much more publicized than in the past. Thus, merely recognizing that problems exist is one step forward. In recognizing the need for change, court personnel are becoming less and less resistant to outside input. The apparent trend toward easing the impact of the exclusionary rule, as indicated earlier in this paper, shows some indications of the need to appropriately redefine the judicial role with respect to other criminal justice agencies. Criminal law reform is underway in the legislatures of many states, unification of courts systems has been attempted by a number of jurisdictions, and management is gradually getting better. The court administrator concept is, and will continue to be, more widely acceptable. Recommendations to streamline a number of operating processes are being studied and implemented on a gradual basis. Modifications in judicial selection procedures will be slow in coming but will take place.

This writer believes that there will be resistance to several areas of proposed change. The alteration of adversary proceedings to more of a fact-finding, information-sharing process is a significant departure from the heritage of the American judicial system. That fact alone - change - will mean great resistance will be encountered. This writer believes it doubtful whether much acceptance or agreement to proposals to abolish plea negotiations will be forthcoming in the foreseeable future. The adverse reactions shown to the recommendations of the National Advisory Commission on Criminal Justice Standards and Goals in the mid-1970s - recommendations to abolish plea bargaining - were, undoubtedly, the most controversial recommendations of the Commission report.

Despite these areas of resistance, efforts are being made to bring about necessary changes in the quality of the administration of justice, but the changes are not occurring as fast as the problems continue to increase. Much more must be done.

NOTES AND REFERENCES

(1) National Advisory Commission on Criminal Justice Standards and Goals, Courts (Washington, D.C.: U.S. Government Printing Office, 1973), p. 1.

(2) California Commission on Peace Officer Standards and Training, The Impact of Social Trends on Crime and Criminal Justice (Cincinnati: Anderson Publishing Co., 1976), pp. 25-264.

(3) NAC, Police, p. 1.

12 The Field of Correction

Vernon Fox

Corrections in the modern sense began in the late 1700s, after
the Industrial Revolution, to replace earlier harsh and bloody punishment. In England, Parliament passed the Penitentiary Act in 1775
under the sponsorship of Sir William Eden and John Howard, who had
published his famous book, State of Prisons, in 1777. In America, the
Quakers in Philadelphia established a penitentiary in 1790 that emphasized solitary confinement, hard labor, and moral re-education through
Bible reading. This was followed in 1815 by the establishment of
Auburn system in New York that emphasized silence, congregate
labor by day, solitary confinement at night, and corporal punishment.
The American experiment attracted world attention. Probation was
begun in Boston by a volunteer, John Augustus, in 1841, and Massachusetts provided tax funds to pay for probation in 1869. Parole
developed gradually from Captain Alexander Maconochie's ticket-of-
leave at the Norfolk Prison Colony in Australia in 1841, to the Irish
system developed by Sir Walter Crofton in 1854 that provided a system of incarceration by stages and gradual release and, finally, to
the United States, when the indeterminate sentence and the reformatory movement began operation in Elmira, New York, in 1876. The
juvenile court began in Chicago, in 1899. All these movements became part of the total correctional system in America.

The effort of the Quakers and other groups in America was intended to make corrections humane. The religious emphasis in the
attempted correctional treatment dominated the prisons in the 19th
century. Education appeared minimally at Cherry Hill in 1844 in
Pennsylvania, in 1876 at Elmira in New York, and had been widely
accepted by 1931 when Austin McCormick published the first book on
it. (1) In the 1930s and after World War II, the clinical team of psy-

237

chiatry, psychology, sociology, and social work were brought into the
prisons. None of these programs has ever been adequately implemented.

STANDARDS AND GUIDELINES

The first attempt at establishing standards and guidelines in
American corrections was the "Declaration of Principles" adopted and
promulgated in the first meetings of the organization now known as the
American Correctional Association in Cincinnati in 1870. (2) These
37 principles were considered to be "articles of faith" that could not
be legislated nor enforced. All of the principles are considered by
correctional leaders to be valid today, but many have still not been
implemented after more than a century. Many have been adopted in
varying degrees by different jurisdictions. The public has remained
generally apathetic about the field of corrections and, in fact, still
tends to admire almost to the extent of hero worship many outlaws of
the old "Old West" in the late 1800s, such as the legendary Jessie
James, Harry Longbaugh ("The Sundance Kid"), Robert Leroy Parker
("Butch Cassidy"), and many others.

The first time the public became aroused enough to take action
was when five men dressed as policemen from Al Capone's gang lined
up seven of George "Bugs" Moran's mobsters and killed them in a
garage that served as Moran's bootleg headquarters on North Clark
street in Chicago. In 1929, the National Commission on Law Obser-
vance and Enforcement was appointed by President Herbert Hoover to
study the "entire question of Law Enforcement and organization of
justice." It was best known as the "Wickersham Commission" after
its chairman, Geroge W. Wickersham, a former Attorney General.
The Wickersham report was published in 1931.

In 1939 the Attorney General's Survey of Release Procedures con-
sisted of five volumes covering probation, pardon, parole, and prison.
In 1965, Congress passed the Federal Prisoners Rehabilitation Act,
The President's Commission on Law Enforcement and Administration
of Justice was appointed, and the Joint Commission on Correction
Manpower and Training was initiated. The report of the President's
Commission on Law Enforcement and Administration of Justice was
published in 1967 with a cover report and nine Task Force Reports
covering the entire field of Criminal Justice. The Joint Commission
on correctional Manpower and Training produced many publications,
with its final report, A Time To Act, published in 1969. The National
Advisory Commission on Criminal Justice Standards and Goals publi-

shed recommendations in 1973 that covered the entire field of criminal justice. Thier recommendations in corrections examined the 129 standards included for that field. The American Correctional Association accepted 79 of them, modified 40 standards, changed the implementation date on nine standards and rejected the one standard that suggested that courts should retain jurisdiction throughout the correctional procedure. (3)

The American Correctional Association published a Handbook of Case Work and Classification Methods for Offenders in 1933, having been edited by Edger H. Doll at the training school of Vineland, New Jersey. The first edition of Manual of Correctional Standards was published by the American Correctional Association in 1947. The second edition was published in 1959. The third edition was published in 1966, and subsequent attempts at revision have been frustrated by disagreement in some areas. While the third edition of the Manual is still in effect, another book, Correctional Classification and Treatment: A Reader, was compiled by the Committee on Classification and Treatment of the American Correctional Association in 1975. (4)

The United Nations' Section on Social Defense has attempted to gather information about correctional systems around the world. There are many United Nations publications, probably the most consistent being the International Review of Criminal Policy. On November 6, 1974, the United Nations General Assembly passed resolution 3218, indicating that torture should be forbidden in correction systems around the world, and adopted the UN Standard Minimum Rules for the Treatment of Prisoners. The implementation of these rules has not been uniform.

It is obvious that correctional leaders, practitioners, and professionals have been attempting to improve prisons and correctional services since the adoption of the penitentiary concept in 1790. Looking forward past 1984 to the completion of two full centuries of trying may provide opportunities for speculation for the future in corrections based on the past. History can be used to plan for the future so that it will not have to be relived.

PROBLEMS IN PROGRESS

Four principles and interrelated sources of resistance to change in corrections are 1) the conflicting theories regarding effective measures, 2) the social organization necessary to administer correctional programs, 3) characteristics and ideologies of correctional personnel, 4) organization of correctional clients as they relate to each other and to the correctional personnel. (6) There is disagreement as to whether all offenders should be treated alike or whether they should be handled individually. Custodially and legally oriented personnel tend to hold to criminal justice demands that every one be given equal treatment. On the other hand, treatment personnel from the helping professions, such as psychiatry, clinical psychology, and social work, espouse the approach that each person should be treated in accordance with his needs. The social organization in prison and other correctional settings is a functional balance between correctional personnel and correctional clients. If the clients resist programs to the extreme, resentments could lead to riots, and in any case, the program would be counterproductive and ineffective. Correctional personnel tend to be conservative in attitude. Many old-line correctional officers have seen many offenders come back repeatedly, have seen little evidence of the effectiveness of case work, and are reluctant to change their roles as custodial officers. Correctional case workers tend to point to their large case loads and extensive amount of paperwork and are admittedly unable to demonstrate much effectiveness in changing behavior. The correctional clients themselves are notoriously resistant to change in correctional programs. Once they become accustomed to learn to "play the game" or "play the nods," they become disturbed when this orientation is changed. In addition, they are not sure that many caseworkers, counselors, and psychologists are not punitive. "Treatment" has sometimes been considered to be synonymous with humanitarianism.

There are other impediments to penal reform that include problems of 1) deterrence, 2) the doctrine of least eligibility or less eligibility, or whether the cost of caring for offenders should exceed the remuneration given to the least of the law-abiding citizens, 3) the limitations of rehabilitative goal, and 4) ethical and other problems in conducting research in the field of corrections. (7) There is no evidence that the death penalty, long-term imprisonment, or other punishments deter others from committing major crimes. The effectiveness of the deterrence is generally limited to minor transgressions, such as traffic offenses. The question has been asked whether the criminal justice system should not be scrapped if it cannot deter other major crimes. In a lecture at the University of Chicago in 1928, Richard E. Park expressed the same sentiments regarding the criminal justice system and said, "We might as well dance!" The doctrine of least eligibility has been fundamental in welfare and correctional programs, holding that welfare recipients and correctional clients should not receive more than self-supporting and law-abiding citizens.

This does not carry over into the health field to suggest that an ill or hospitalized person should not receive more medical assistance than healthy citizens. The efficacy of the doctrine of least eligibility in the field of corrections has been questioned in several quarters as being unrealistic and counterproductive to the correctional goal. Certainly, it costs more to keep a person in a maximum custody institution than it would to send him to one of the best universities in the land. The limitations of the rehabilitative goal are primary that more control is taken over by offenders for treatment purposes than would be taken simply for confinement purposes and, further, not enough is known about the multiplicity of causes to develop a foolproof program - not even as much as medicine, which has greater specificity in many areas, but has not even attempted to develop a broad theory of the "cause of disease." Yet corrections is expected somehow to develop the "cause of crime" so that it can be controlled. The problem of research is ethical in terms of the invasion of privacy of an individual and release of confidential information, and inability to control the many uncontrollable variables that enter into a criminal event.

Crime is not a unitary phenomenon. If a series of blank maps were obtained and the incidence of crime plotted on one, the incidence of welfare recipients plotted on another, and the incidence of health problems plotted on another, the configuration would be similar. These indices and others are only symptomatic of causal breakdowns. Consequently, crime is only a symptom, probably the most visible symptom, of this social breakdown, but cannot be successfully studied in isolation.

During the quarter century following World War II, a fervent attempt was made by correctional administrators and practitioners to implement the rehabilitative model by psychiatrists, clinical psychologists, social workers, and other treatment-oriented personnel. Budget requests designed to implement this goal were made in almost every jurisdiction in the country. The almost uniform reaction to these budget requests were recommendations for cuts by the budget director or commissioner, further cuts by the executive who presented the budget to the legislatures and the Congress, and debate in legislative and congressional committees ending in passage of appropriations bills that generally deleted the request. Correctional agencies were fortunate if they received what they had received during the previous fiscal year. In fact, several legislatures cut back staff in the 1970s at a time when prisons and other correctional caseloads were increasing! By the mid-1970s record high prison populations were reached without an increase in staffing and, in fact, a reduction in some jurisdictions. In the meantime, correctional leaders who had been giving lip service to the rehabilitative ideal were publicly lamenting that "all we are doing is warehousing, deep-freezing, and processing people. " This led the American Correctional Association to use "Body Crunch #1" as the theme for the 106th Annual Congress on Correction held in Denver, August 20-24, 1976.

In the meantime, evaluation research depicted the rehabilitation idea as a failure! The famous "Martinson Report" (8) concluded, on the basis of a survey of evaluation research in Corrections between 1945 and 1967, that the majority of correctional programs showed neutral results, a few showed negative results, and a few showed positive results. Meetings of national organizations and literature in the correctional field were characterized by bitter debates that resulted in some personal animosity between correctional administrators, practitioners, and academicians in the correctional field. A national survey made by Corrections Magazine in 1975 (9) has indicated that 63 percent of correctional administrators say that some rehabilitation programs do work and another 15 percent argue that there is not enough evidence to abandon the rehabilitation concept, making a total of 78 percent of the correctional administators still favoring treatment programs. Only 12 percent wanted to abandon parole and go back to flat sentencing.

Complicating the problem is the fact that most evaluation research can not possibly control all the social and personal variables involved in a crime-generating situation. The individuals who perform the treatment functions are much more important than the system they use. Some persons can make almost any method work because of their empathic skills, while other inept persons "screw up the gold standard. " Further, different personalities and different problems require different approaches. All treatment programs cannot be the same for all people, any more than a medical doctor in a hospital can order appendectomies for all new admissions. Under either system, there would be some successes, but the failure rate would go up because of the attempt at applying the same methods to everybody.

Another problem is that too complete acceptance by clients, administrators, or other observers may result in too high expectations from any particular treatment approach. When it fails to meet expectations, disillusionment with the treatment approach results in its rejection as a failure.

Intervention by the courts in adult and juvenile procedures has further crippled implementation of the rehabilitative goal. It was litigation by inmates, for example, that eliminated the use of behavior modification in correctional programs. As a result, the Law Enforcement Administration ceased to fund experiments or programs using behavior modification in 1976. Many other suits brought by prisoners

upheld the "right to treatment," while others upheld the "right to refuse treatment" under First and Fourth Amendments. This succes-
sion of litigation that increased nationwide from 500 per year in the
1950s to 15,000 in the 1970s has become time-consuming for correctional administrators. Even more important, the judgments asked in
litigation against State correctional administrators commonly reached
into the millions of dollars. Commissioner William D. Leeke, of the
South Carolina Department of Corrections and President of the American Correction Association, has indicated that by 1976, litigation
against him has requested judgments in excess of $3,000,000 - and
South Carolina is not one of the larger jurisdictions!

The combination or underfunding, understaffing, overcrowding,
and intervention by the courts in matters beyond the control of correctional administrators has placed correctional administrators and practitioners into a "Catch-22" position. (10) They cannot get funds, they
cannot improve their programs as they would like, and yet they are
subject to court orders and political criticism that has shortened their
occupational survival. (11)

THE CROSSROADS BEFORE 1984

Resolving the current dilemma of corrections has attracted the
attention and efforts of correctional administrators and scholars. Because of the intense concern by the public in this field through fear of
crime, moral judgments, social anger, and other forces, political
leaders have responded with similar concerns. The action by Congress
in this field through the 1960s into the 1970s is a collective manifes-
tation of this concern and effort.

Various solutions have been proposed by persons interested in
the field. Keopotkin called for the abolition of prisons as long ago as
1887. Wilson questioned the need for prisons in 1950. (12) Martin
called for their abolition in 1954. (13) Menninger has indicated that
imprisonment is inhumane and ineffective, calling for other methods
to be found in the correctional field. (14) The American Friends Committee (Quakers) have indicated that the 200-year old experiment of
imprisonment grew out of attempts by the Pennsylvania Quakers to reform the old harsh methods of corporal and capital punishment and
they, too, have called for alternative methods. (15) The National
Advisory Commission on Criminal Justice Standards and Goals indicated in 1973 that the major adult institutions operated by the states
represent the least promising component of corrections. (16)

The National Council on Crime and Delinquency began a campaign
in 1972 to establish a moratorium on the construction of new prisons.
There are at least 600 organizations interested in prison reform and
the abolition of prisons. (17) In a study by the National Clearinghouse
on Criminal Justice Planning and Architecture in 1977, Illinois was
told to close its four largest prisons - Menard, Statesville, Joliet,
and Pontiac. (18) Corrections Magazine devoted one full issue in
1975 to "Deinstitutionalization." (19) It is obvious that there is a
strong movement among correctional administrators, practitioners,
and students of the field to deinstitutionalize and to dismantle the traditional correctional system.

On the other hand, there are other writers who want to lock everybody in prison who might be dangerous to society. One writer goes so
far as to want to imprison all offenders for punishment and then, if
they are still considered to be dangerous, ship them to a distant island.
(20) Wilson wants to lock up all criminals to make the streets safe.
(21) There are others equally "hard-nosed" regarding the field of corrections who say that offenders escape the full impact of official
punishment in the modern system of corrections. (22)

More balanced views are also available in the literature. Hawkins
contends that small, homogenous countries like Sweden and Switzer-
land can eliminate prisons in favor of community-based alternatives,
but the large, heterogeneous countries like the United States needs
prisons for a few dangerous people; but that they are now being over-
used. (23) Norval Morris contends that prisons are needed, but they
should hold only the most dangerous offenders for the public safety
and not exceed 100 in population. (24) This represents a more moderate view between the total abolition of prisons and imprisioning every
offender for punishment.

Parole has been attacked. Fogel suggests the abolition of parole
in favor of flat sentencing where some good time could be earned and
not forfeited for misbehavior, as well as some other embellishments.
(25) Maine was first to abolish it in 1975 as of March 1, 1976, but
parole will continue for those sentenced under the indeterminate law.
California, Indiana, and Illinois followed suit in 1977, but how long
parole will exist is still in discussion. Florida considered flat sentencing and abolition of parole in 1976 and 1977, but did not follow
through when projections of resulting prison populations indicated that
it would be very costly. The underlying debate is centering around
whether a rehabilitative program can realistically be set in a justice
base. Legally oriented people want everything treated alike, while
treatment-oriented people want to use the time available to do what
can be done to help the offender adjust to society. The idea of abolish-

ing parole has not flourished widely, has appeared in a few places, and the results can be studied in the future. Attorney General Griffin Bell called in June 1977, for the passage of Senate Bill (S-1437) to revise the Federal criminal code, including abolition of parole. The call for parole boards to assume new roles, such as serving as a review board to handle inmate complaints or grievances, has been present for some time, (26) as had the call for their abolition. (27)

Probation continues to be unchallenged, partially because it is considered to be a local function and serves local people. Even though probation may be "provided" by the State, it is the local judge who works with probation in his jurisdiction. The juvenile court has incorporated more due process as a result of Supreme Court decisions in the 1960s, particularly the Gault decision in 1967 (In re Gault, 387 U. S. 1, 18 L. Ed. 2nd 527, 1967.) The basic tenets and purposes of the juvenile court remain the same, although addition of counsel to all procedures has resulted in longer hearings and administrative ways to work with delinquents, reserving juvenile court action for only the serious cases. The jail has resisted essential change throughout the centuries, but recent recommendations by official commissions for State operation of jails indicate concern.

A new "Radical Criminology" was introduced at York University in England that broadened the perspective of crime as a result of the capitalistic social and economic order. (28) Since crime is really a problem of capitalistic society, according to this view, the world must be freed from the dehumanizing conditions and contradictions of capitalism, including the brutality of class oppression, exploitation and domination. (29) The view holds that a democratic future through a "rediscovered" Marx will tend to be more humane and equal than is the present brutally repressive and bureaucratic government as an extension of the white, middle-class power. (30) This humane relationship between equals is seen as finding its way into corrections through the relationship between correctional worker and offender being negotiated as equals for the welfare of the state and all of society.

In any event, dissatisfaction with imprisonment and the traditional correction systems is well documented. (31) On the other hand, prison populations are rising to record highs, with about 285,000 people in prison in January 1977. This paradox is difficult to explain. Without doubt, corrections is at a crossroads in the late 1970s and early 1980s.

CORRECTIONS BEYOND 1984

The perspective that includes the past history of corrections, the present dilemma, and extrapolation from development in other fields of social and mental health concerns can provide a base for projection into the future. Ancient and medieval societies responded to crime by enslavement of the offender, assigning him to public works, execution, or exile. There was no imprisonment for punishment. Between the 14th and 18th centuries, English and other European societies developed harsh and bloody corporal and capital punishments. Ingenious devices for torture were developed. Workhouses for minor offenders began in the 1550s. The penitentiary movement generated by the Quakers in Philadelphia in 1790 marked the beginning of the institutionalization of major offenders that had started about two decades before. It is interesting to note that the beginning of institutionalization for offenders coincided with the Industrial Revolution (circa 1750) when technology permitted sufficient productivity to permit keeping nonproductive and criminal people in a humane manner. The beginnings of humanitarian treatment of offenders did not begin until the late 18th and early 19th centuries.

The beginning of the serious study of criminology and its practical application in corrections was in 1764 with the publication of Beccaria's famous Essay on Crimes and Punishments, representing the Classical school of criminology that ignored the offender and let the punishment fit the crime. In 1876, Lombroso responded to the emphasis on biology of his time and represented the Positivistic school of criminology that essentially ignored the crime and focused at first on the individual offender as a "born criminal," but later centered on the social and behavioral sciences, holding that criminal behavior is learned.

The issues in corrections in the 1970s are the same as those embodied in the history of corrections, particularly the etiology of crime, the focus on punishment and/or rehabilitation, and institutionalization. If the criminal is born, then his incapacitation or elimination for the protection of society is the only logical policy. If criminal behavior is learned, then rehabilitative programs to change attitudes, self-concept, and generate aspiration and motivation in line with society's norms is the only logical policy. The role of institutionalization, only two centuries old in the history of man, has been severely questioned on the basis as to whether an offender can be taught to live in society by removing him from it.

Institutional treatment of public charges, particularly welfare

recipients, the mentally ill, and the major criminal offender have
followed similar patterns, and in that order, separated roughly by a
half-century to a century in time. Welfare recipients and debtors were
first sent to workhouses in the 1950s because they were lazy and had
to learn to work. Their deinstitutionalization began with the Elizabethan
Poor Law of 1601, although county poor farms remained in the United
States into the 20th century, until welfare programs in the 1930s took
them out of institutions altogether. The mentally ill were first treated
in the United States at the Philadelphia Almshouse in 1732, followed
by the construction of mental hospitals throughout the county. After
World War II, a strong movement toward their deinstitutionalization
through community mental health clinics and more efficient furlough
plans received impetus from the National Institute of Mental Health
through grants and technical assistance. These hospitals still exist,
but the movement is toward community treatment as soon as possible.
Major offenders were institutionalized roughly from 1790 and the prison population has risen consistently since then. A record high prison
population of 285,000 was reached in January 1977, and no abatement
appears in the immediate future. In the meantime, there are persistent calls for deinstitutionalization from prison administrators, practitioners, and academicians with contacts in the field, while the punishment and prison approach is sponsored by university-based writers
without practical experience in the field of corrections. This paradoxi-
cal situation merits further examination.

Some logical predictions for the future of corrections were made
by Richard McGee in 1969 (32) and remain valid, as follows:

1. Fewer offenders will be confined for long periods in custodial
   institutions.

2. Institutional programs will place greater emphasis on preparation for release and less on escapes and economic production.

3. New correctional institutions will be smaller.

4. There will be less of a sharp dichotomy between incarceration and parole or probation supervision.

5. Probation services will be expanded to include hostels, group
   homes, training programs, job placements, sheltered workshops, psychiatric services, and specialized counseling.

6. Post-institutional supervision or parole will exhibit changes
   coming closer to probation.

7. The character, composition, and function of parole boards
    will change to include better people for other decision-making
    tasks. As a matter of fact, they may disappear.

8. New forms of disposition from courts as substitutes for con-
    ventional sentencing will be developed.

9. Community-based programs will make more use of related
    community services, both public and private.

10. More and more attention will be given to developing informa-
    tion systems, making use of computer technology to assist in
    decision-making tasks.

11. Empirical research methods will be employed to assess the
    effectiveness.

12. Professional competent assistants will be provided at all
    levels so the long-term needs for public protection will be
    better served.

Summarizing the historical trends and the direction of thinking of
knowledgeable writers who have meaningful contacts and relations with
the field of corrections, it is obvious that the direction corrections is
going, despite a few systems going other directions and rising prison
populations in the 1970s, is toward retaining the rehabilitative goal
and deinstitutionalization in favor of community-based programs. This
combination has been successful in Sweden and other places where it
has been tried. Rehabilitative programs in the community are available to programs housed in the community. Halfway houses, community correctional centers, work release, study release, drug and alcohol
programs, ex-offender organizations for self-help in social adjustment,
and other community-based programs can be of positive and effective
use in working with offenders. (33) The institutional setting, however,
really militates against rehabilitative programs that are considered to
be effective when they can counterbalance the ill effects of the institution itself.

Public policy is a balance between economic goals and social goals
as seen by the political leaders. This means that politics are more
governing than the other phases, since interpretations must be made by
policy makers. These interpretations are frequently made on the basis
of personality, religious and moral values, and other factors before
economic and social considerations are reached. The political, econo-

mic, and social concerns, in that order, must be addressed before any
public policy programs can be implemented. In the Vietnam adventure,
for example, political concern governed over economic costs and social
counterproductivity. Similar concerns contributed to the landing on the
moon, military occupation of Germany and Japan, long-distance busing
to achieve school desegregation, and almost any public policy activity,
both domestic and foreign.

In corrections, the political concerns center around "law and
order" slogans of political candidates and leaders, "crime fighters,"
calls for "stiffer penalties" and "mandatory sentencing," and similar
searches for simplistic solutions to complex problems that really get
in the way of economic efficiency and social values.

Corrections beyond 1984 will emphasize community-based corrections and the rehabilitative goals and will deemphasize institutionalization and punishment. This is the obvious resultant of the consensus of
the majority of correctional administrators in the field and of the writers
who have had meaningful contact with the field. It will take some effort
to get past the slogans for punishment and confinement as simple solutions, but the expense of costly and ineffective institutionalization will
eventually prevail, as the cost of welfare has recently attracted the
attention of politicians for its reform.

CONCLUSION

Corrections beyond 1984 will maintain the historical trends experienced in the past and the logical processes of protection of society
by emphasizing community programs to improve the attitudes and self-
concepts of offenders and to give them sufficient hope for the future
that they do not regard themselves as "born to lose." The old formula
in crime prevention, M + O = C (Motivation + Opportunity = Crime)
holds in the criminal justice system. Corrections is concerned with
the motivation, while police and other agencies are concerned with
opportunity in terms of security systems and patrol patterns. If corrections does not work with the motivation of offenders, the field would
be abdicating its function and doing a disservice to the very society it
purports to protect. The work of corrections focuses on the individual.

Community-based correctional programs offer the greatest hope
for success in the field of corrections beyond 1984. This includes welfare services and family counseling for the pre-school counseling in
the elementary school for the early school child, voluntary police
supervision and juvenile courts counseling for youth coming into con-

tact with the law, group homes and halfway houses for juveniles and
adults who need to be removed from their homes but not from the community, and specialized programs available in the community for a
variety of problems. Small prisons will be needed control dangerous
offenders, but these should be programmed to treat the dangerous offender and to learn from him through research. The dangerous offender can be identified and treated. (35) The vast majority of offenders
however, are not dangerous, and can be handled in the community. In
fact, the probation caseloads today exceed the persons in prisons and
correctional institutions and on parole at the juvenile and adult levels.

    Early identification and attention can reduce the delinquency and
crime problem. School social workers report that they can assess
the basic personality of children when they arrive at school in kinder-
garten or the first grade. By the time they get into the third grade,
they can predict the children who will have behavior problems. Many
child development experts indicate that basic personality, including
emotional problems, has been established by three years of age. (36)
It is "all over" by then. It becomes ridiculous to expect miracles
from corrections beginning treatment at 16 years of age, but it has been
done successfully by basing correctional treatment on the strengths
the individual has developed attempting to assist in problem areas. It
is best done in the community where existing facilities and programs
can be used. Correctional programs are evaluated according to what
is most effective, least costly, and does least damage. Community-
based correctional programs for juvenile and adults meet these criteria. Community-based corrections and the rehabilitative goals
appear to have enough logical and other support to convince political
concerns to implement them as public policy in corrections beyond
1984.

NOTES AND REFERENCES

1. Austin H. MacCormick, The Education of Adult Prisoners (New York: Osborne Association, 1931).

2. "Declaration of Principles adopted and promulgated by Congress" in E. C. Wines, ed., Transactions of the National Congress on Penitentiary and Reformatory Discipline Help at Cincinnati, Ohio, October 12-18, 1870. (Albany, New York: Weed, Parsons and Company, Printers, 1871), pp. 541-47.

3. Response of the American Coreectional Association to Correctional Standards as Originally Proposed by the National Advisory Commission on Criminal Justice Standards Goals, (College Park, Maryland; American Correctional Association, May 1976), 53 pp.

4. Leonard J. Hippchen, ed., Correctional Classification and Treatment: A Reader (Cincinnati; W. H. Anderson for The American Correctional Association, 1975), 303 pp.

5. World Implementation of the U.N. Standard Minimum Rules for the Treatment of Prisoners (Washington, D.C.: American Bar Association, 1975).

6. Donald R. Cressey, "Sources of Resistance to Innovation in Corrections," Offenders as a Correctional Manpower Resource, (Washington, D.C.: Joint Commission on Correctional Manpower and Training, June 1968), pp. 149.

7. Norval Morris, "Impediments to Penal Reform," The University of Chicago Law Review (Summer 1966), vol. 33, no. 4, pp. 627-56.

8. Douglas Lipton, Robert Martinson, and Judith Wilks: The Effectiveness Of Correctional Treatment (New York: Praeger, 1975).

9. "Editor's Notebook: Rehabilitation?" Corrections Magazine, vol. 1, no. 5, May/June 1975, p. 2.

10. Joseph Heller, Catch Twenty-Two (New York: Simon & Schuster, 1961). Joseph Heller Catch Twenty-Two (New York: Modern Library, 1966), paperback. Joseph Heller, Catch--22, (New York: Dell Publishing, 1976), paperback. This is a comic novel

that has sold over 8,000,000 copies about members of the 256th
Bombing Squadron set on a tiny Mediterranean Island during
World War II. Members could be discharged from service for
insanity, but when a member came out of combat and pleaded insanity, the administrative decision was that anybody who tried to
get out of combat service by any reason, including insanity, must
be sane. Therefore, nobody was released from duty.

11. "Correctional Administrators Face Increasing Job Insecurity as
    the Positions Become Hot Seats," Corrections Digest, November
    12, 1975, p. 1.

12. Joseph Wilson, Are Prisons Necessary? (Philadelphia: Dorrance
    Press, 1960).

13. John Bartlow Martin, Break Down the Walls (New York: Ballan-
    tine, 1954).

14. Karl Menninger, The Crime of Punishment (New York: Viking
    Press, 1969).

15. American Friends Service Committee; Struggle for Justice (New
    York: Hill & Wang, 1971), p. v.

16. "The Future of Institutions" in Corrections (Washington, D.C.:
    National Advisory Commission on Criminal Justice Standards and
    Goals, 1973), p. 349.

17. Mary Lee Bundy and Kenneth R. Harmon, ed., The National Pri-
    son Directory; Organizational Profiles of Prison Reform Groups
    Groups in the United States (College Park, Maryland: Urban
    Information Interpreters, April, 1975). Mary Lee Bundy and
    Rebecca Glenn Whaley, ed., The National Prison Directory:
    Organizational Profiles of Prison Reform Groups in the United
    States (College Park, Maryland: Urban Information Interpreters,
    May 1976).

18. "Abandon Four Biggest Prisons, Illinois is Told by New Study,"
    Corrections Digest, vol. 8, no. 12 (June 8, 1977), pp. 2-3.

19. Corrections magazine, vol. 2, no. 2 (November/December 1975).

20. Ernest van den Haag, Punishing Criminals: A Very Old and Pain-
    ful Question (New York: Basic Books, 1975).

21. James Q. Wilson, Thinking About Crime (New York: Basic Books, 1975).

22. Andrew Von Hirsch, Doing Justice (New York: Hill and Wang, 1976), p. 129.

23. Gordon Hawkins, The Prison: Policy and Practice (Chicago: University of Chicago Press, 1976).

24. Norval Morris, The Future of Imprisonment (Chicago: University of Chicago Press, 1974).

25. David Fogel, "...We Are the Living Proof...": The Justice Model for Corrections (Cincinnati: W. H. Anderson, 1975).

26. F. Lovell Bixby; "A New Role for Parole Boards," Federal Probation, June 1970, pp. 24-28.

27. Herman Schwartz, "Let's Abolish Parole," Reader's Digest, August 1973, pp. 185-90.

28. Ian Taylor, Paul Walton, and Jock Young, The New Criminology (London and Boston: Routledge & Kegan Paul, 1973).

29. Richard Quinney and John Wildeman, The Problem of Crime: A Critical Introduction to Criminology, Second Edition (New York: Harper & Row, 1977), pp. 171-72.

30. Michael Harrington, The Twilight of Capitalism (New York: Simon & Schuster, 1977).

31. Robert Sommer, The End of Imprisonment (New York: Oxford University Press, 1976).

32. Richard A. McGee, "What Past Is Prologue," The Annals - The Future of Corrections, vol. 381 (January 1969), pp. 9-10.

33. Gary R. Perlstein and Thomas R. Phelps, ed., Alternatives to Prison: Community-Based Corrections, A Reader (Pacific Palisades, California: Goodyear Publishing, 1975); Paul H. Hahn, Community Based Corrections and the Criminal Justice System (Santa Cruz, California, Davis Publishing, 1975); Vernon Fox, Community-Based Corrections (Englewood Cliffs: Prentice-Hall, 1977).

34. Bruno M. Cormier; The Watcher and the Watched (Montreal and Pittsburgh: Tundra Books, 1975).

35. See Robert Lindner, Rebel Without a Cause (New York: Grune and Stratton, 1944). Also, Harry L. Kozol, Richard J. Boucher, and Ralph R. Garofalo, "The Diagnosis and Treatment of Dangerousness," Crime and Delinquency, vol. 18, no. 4 (October, 1972), pp. 371-92.

36. Burton L. White, The First Three Years of Life (Englewood Cliffs: Prentice-Hall, 1975), p. 264.

13 The Female Offender: The 1980s and Beyond

Jacqueline Boles
Charlotte Tatro

Women are making headlines in sports, science, law, and crime. Why? Can we expect this trend to continue? Changes in sexual mores, technologies of family planning, economic changes, as well as the women's liberation movement, have combined to make it possible for women to participate more fully in the economy of this country. Most women believe this is beneficial to all women, yet there are costs: increased risk of illness associated with work stress, for example. "Is the increase in crime among women one of the costs of women's liberation?" This chapter will examine the participation of women in crime with a view toward identifying those trends which presage the future.

PROFILES OF FEMALE OFFENDERS

Recently, in a large city court sixteen women were brought before the judge. Seven were charged with prostitution, three with shoplifting, and five were arrested for possession of illegal drugs. One woman allegedly had killed her husband during a family fight. Like their male counterparts, women offenders differ widely in their motivations, seriousness of their offenses, and their social and personal resources. However, based on arrest statistics, it is possible to describe the typical female offender. Presently, the typical female arrestee is not a presidential assassin or the leader of a militant underground movement. Rather, she resembles Lois. Lois is white, 23, and has a high school education. She and her husband were arrested in their house trailer in a suburb of a large city. She was charged

with receiving stolen goods. Her history includes drug use and one
prior arrest for prostitution. In her defense she claims she didn't
know the television sets were stolen. "Besides," she said, "her husband said it was okay." Lois, and many of the thousands of female
offenders like her, see their role as women who "go along with" their
men. They see no alternative to the lives their husbands, fathers, or
boyfriends choose for them.

The majority of future female offenders will, more than likely,
not be Ma Barkers or Nancy Ling Peerys. Instead, they will resemble
Lynn, who is 31, white and college-educated. She is a computer pro-
grammer with five years' experience. She is single but an active
dater. Lynn worked for a large bank and was highly regarded by her
employers until they discovered that she had defrauded the bank of
over $40,000. Her justification for her crime was simply that she
could use the money, and she said, "It was fun outsmarting the bank
examiners."

FEMALE OFFENDERS TODAY AND TOMORROW

Arrest statistics indicate that female criminality is increasing
dramatically. Presently, the percent increase for all crimes for
women is higher than for men. For example, for the years 1960 to
1975 the percent increase for all women was +101.7 and only +22.8
for men (Uniform Crime Reports, 1976). The increased participation of women in some serious offenses has been dramatic. Between
1960 and 1975 the percent increase of women arrested for murder
was +105.7; robbery, +380.5; stolen property, +727.2; and narcotics,
+1,011.9 (Uniform Crime Reports, 1976). However, for the same
period arrests of women have declined for the following: manslaughter
by negligence, sex offenses excluding rape and prostitution, gambling,
offenses against the family, drunkenness, vagrancy, and suspicion.
Despite the substantial increase in arrests of women in crimes of
violence, most arrests are for non-violent property and drug offenses. For example, in 1975 there were 1,707 women arrested for
murder and 185,984 for larceny (Uniform Crime Reports, 1976).
Twice as many women were arrested for disorderly conduct as for
narcotic violations. Rita Simon (1975) in her excellent study of female criminality arrives at the following conclusions: the average
increase in the proportion of women arrested for serious crimes is
greater than the average increase in the proportion of women arrested for all crimes; the increase in female arrest rates among serious

offenses was caused almost entirely by women's greater participation
in property offenses, especially larceny. Simon (1975:47), using
Uniform Crime Reports data for 1972, presents the rank order of arrest offenses for females.

Table 13.1. Rank Order of Offenses For Which Female are Most
Likely to be Arrested

Offense	Percent of All Female Arrests- Simon	Rank Order	Percent of All Female Arrests Atlanta	Rank Order
Larcent-theft	20.2	1	14.5	3
Drunkenness	9.8	2	26.3	2
Disorderly conduct	8.5	3	29.4	1
Narcotic Drug Laws	6.0	4	7.8	4
Other assaults	4.1	5	2.4	9
Drunken driving	3.8	6	3.8	6
Prostitution	3.4	7	7.0	5
Liquor laws	2.7	8	1.6	11
Embezzlement and Fraud	2.4	9	.3	19
Aggravated assault	2.0	10	2.6	8

Table 13.1 allows us to compare Simon's findings with arrest data from Atlanta, Georgia, for the same year. Clearly, most offenses for which women are currently arrested are related to property crimes and drug abuse. This general trend is expected to continue. Simon predicts that by the 1980s men and women will be arrested equally for fraud, embezzlement and larceny; by the 2010s the proportion of men and women arrested for forgery and counterfeiting should be equal. Thus, she predicts that in the future the majority of arrests will continue to be for property offenses, but the female offenders will be more skilled and sophisticated.

. . . that women's participation in selective crimes will increase as their employment opportunities expand and as their interests, desires, and definitions of self shift from a more traditional to a more liberated view. (Simon, 1976:35).

ETIOLOGY OF FEMALE CRIME -
BIOLOGY AND ROLE

Stereotypes of Female Criminals

Female criminality has always fascinated the public. Magazines like True Detective usually feature articles about murderesses or girl friends of notorious bank robbers. Female criminals have been stereotyped, not only by the press, but by social workers, criminologists and others who have studied and written about them. Wilson and Rigsby (1975) have characterized the stereotypes of the female criminal as: Lady Macbeth, Mother Goose, and Poor Pitiful Pearl. Devious Lady Macbeths drive their husbands and lovers to crime while they (cleverly) stay in the background and reap the rewards. Both Lombroso and, more recently, Otto Pollak pictures female criminals as devious, cunning, and deceitful (Smart, 1977).

In Mother Goose there is a rhyme about a little girl who, when she was bad, was "horrid." Thus, women like Hildegard Lackert, nicknamed Bloody Birgetta by the inmates of a notorious death camp where over 250,000 were exterminated, are thought to represent the reverse side of women's ordinary kind, nurturing nature. Finally, there is poor Pearl who is more to be pitied than feared. She is a victim of circumstances, having been exploited by parents, boyfriends and husbands.

The Freudian View

Like many stereotypes, there is some truth to these characterizations, but they are superficial and do not go beyond surface considerations. Freud pioneered the study of female consciousness and sexuality, but however significant the initial insights, Freudian theory persists in the "anatomy as destiny" dogma. Though the Freudian theories vary somewhat, there are some commonalities. Most Freudians believe that a woman's body is the major determinant of her personality and behavior. For example, Eric Erickson (1964) analyzed the uses of play spaces by young children and concluded that because of their sexual anatomy, boys emphasize erectile, projecting, and active motifs (a Windmill, for example); whereas girls' use of space emphasizes protective, passive, and expectant motifs (a house enclosed by a fence). Women are, then, by nature concerned with inner space, and their destiny is in their wombs.

Further, Freudians attribute a variety of psychological parthologies to women including masochism, narcissism, penis envy, and passivity, largely because male anatomy and behavior are seen by them as the standard against which female anatomy and behavior are judged.

> Freud himself sees women as anatomically inferior ... The root of their inferiority is that women's sex organs are inferior to those of men, a fact universally recognized by children in the Freudian scheme. The girl assumes that she has lost a penis as punishment, is traumatized, and grows up envious and revengeful (Klein, 1973:16).

This conception of woman as a biological and psychological inferior permeated thinking about female criminality; prostitution is a case in point. The typical Freudian explanation (Greenwald, 1970) focuses on the arrested psychosexual development of the prostitute so that the act of prostitution is seen as a result of repression of early sexual love for the parent.

In the last few years there has emerged a considerable body of research on the female: her sexuality, the development of her gender identity, and her roles in contemporary society. A consideration of this research will aid in the understanding of the causes of female criminality.

Biological Factors in the Female Gender Role

Unfortunately, concepts related to the study of sex roles are not
well defined and vary somewhat from study to study. Here gender
identity is defined as the sense of self that one has as either a male
or female. (1) "I am a female" is a statement about gender identity.
Gender role is all of the activities and attitudes which express for oneself and others one's own gender identity. "I am supportive and loving
toward my husband and children" is an expression of gender role.

All societies hold expectations about how males and females ought
to behave. Currently in America, it is acceptable for males to brag
about their sexual prowess - but not for females. All of us as men
and women express our gender identity somewhat differently because,
even though there are sex role stereotypes (men don't cry), everyone
has had a wide variety of experiences, so that one's actual behavior
is a reflection of an interplay between societal expectations and stereotypes and our own individual beliefs, attitudes, and values.

Table 13.2 is a schematic, very abbreviated, dotline of the process of gender identity and role formation. The five primary sources
of gender identity are: chromosomes, hormones, external anatomy,
internal anatomy, and gender assignment and rearing; gender assignment and rearing being the most important. When a child with external male genitalia is born, the physician says, "It's a boy." The
nurse brings the baby to the mother and says, "You have a boy." In
most cases the parents believe that "it" is a boy and raises it accordingly. (2) As the child grows, he is socialized by his parents, relatives, peers, teachers, and the mass media so that he will behave
appropriately. Children gradually internalize social expectations
about appropriate sex role behavior, and, as adults, they express
their gender roles according to their individual conceptions about how
these roles should be played.

Presently, researchers from the biological and social sciences
are trying to discover to what extent our sex role behavior is biolo-
gically determined, as opposed to learned.

Recent research indicates that the process of fetal development
is more complex for males than females:

Nature's plan, in a nutshell, is that the embryo will become a
female unless two 'extras' make it a male. The first is the Y
chromosome, which turns the unisex gonads into testes ......
The second requirement is the male sex hormone testosterone...
As far as endocrinologist can tell, the anatomical development
of the female fetus does not require the female hormone. All
that is necessary is the absence of male hormones (Tarvis and
Offir, 1977:104).

There is some evidence to indicate that the significantly higher number of physical, psychological, and social problems that boys have
may be related to the fact that "it is easier for nature to make a female. "

There are four sexual functions which are sex-linked and immutable: impregnation, lactation, menstruation, and gestation. Except
for these, sex role expectations are alterable.

As long as the four basic reproductive functions are allowed for,
however, no particular gender stereotype is unalterable. A
society has almost unlimited choice of role design or redesign
... Nothing - nothing - of the differences between the sexes is
immutable ordained along sex lines (Money and Tucker, 1975:
39-40).

Yet much of the research on female criminality has attributed the
etiology of criminal behavior to physiological factors. For example,
Cowie, Cowie, and Slater (1968:171) actually propose a chromosomal
explanation of female delinquency:

The chromosomal differences between the sexes starts the individual on a divergent path, leading either in a masculine or femi-
nine direction ... It is possible that the methods of upbringing,
differing somewhat for the two sexes, may play some part in
increasing the angle of the divergence.

There are several behavioral characteristics often assumed to be
innate in women and are given as "causes" of female criminality.
Women are frequently described as passive and emotionally dependent
- like Poor Pearl. For example, in Konopka's study of delinquent
girls, she says,

While these girls also strive for independence, their need for
dependence is usually great - and almost completely overlooked
and unfulfilled. The need for support seems to exist in all adolescent girls (Konopka, 1966:40-41).

The passive and dependent female is portrayed as helpless, unable to
act without social support. She cannot act independently and creative-
ly in new situations (Deutsch, 1944; Bardwick, 1971). Studies of
dependency in children produce conflicting results (Maccoby and
Jacklin, 1974). Some show little girls as more dependent than boys;
however, Goldberg and Lewis (1969) point out that boys are socialized

Table 13.2. Development of Gender Identity and Roles Formation

Sources of Gender Identity	Gender Identity	Gender Role
chromosomes	"I am a male"	"I must support my family"
hormones	"I am a female"	"I love children"
external anatomy		
internal anatomy		
gender assignments and rearing		

to act more independent than girls. At present no evidence links any innate factors to either passivity or dependency.

Men are generally perceived as more aggressive than women. Dozens of studies show males of all ages engage in more physical aggression, fantasy aggression, verbal aggression, and play aggression than females do. The differences show up as soon as children begin to play with each other, at the age of two or three and last into adulthood (Tavris and Offir, 1977:54).

Both hormonal and socialization differences between the sexes account for the proclivity of males for aggression (Maccoby and Jacklin, 1974); yet, there are situations in every society when aggression is either prescribed or proscribed for both men and women. Males may, indeed, be predisposed to act aggressively; that is, the threshold for eliciting aggressive responsive in men is probably lower. Yet women do act aggressively, and there are situations when aggression from women is socially expected and approved, i. e., defending herself from rape or protecting her children from harm.

As with aggressivity, a lower threshold for releasing dominance behavior is associated with the male (Money and Tucker, 1975). Male styles of relating and male games focus on power strategies. For example, men prefer zero-sum games, such as chess, in which one player wins and the other loses. In contrast, women, partly because they are generally physically weaker than men, have developed ways of relating which emphasize cooperation and compliance (Maccoby and Jacklin, 1974; Leventhal and Lane, 1970). Little girls usually prefer to play games where "everyone can win and be happy." As adults women are more apt to prefer mixed-motive games in which players cooperate rather than zero sum games. Women, of course, learn to play and enjoy both zero sum games and games which emphasize cooperation.

In sum, of the characteristics discussed, only aggressivity and dominance are linked to innate differences between the sexes. Adler (1975) points out that the only differences between the sexes which are linked to the overrepresentation of male offenders are: strength, size, aggressivity, and dominance. Further, these four characteristics represent biological differences between men and women, but their roles in crime causation are not clear. The percent of total arrests for homicide and aggravated assault is about the same for men and women (3) and has remained relatively stable for twenty years (Simon, 1975). Further, even though physical size and strength are important in activities like hand-to-hand combat, the great bulk

of criminal activity does not demand either large size or great
strength. Burglary, auto theft, and even robbery can be performed
by women as well as men. However, there are differences in the
socialization experiences of males and females which may account
for some of the differences in criminal activity between the two sexes.

Social Bases of Sex Role Differences

There is no society in which boys and girls are reared the same.
From infancy boys and girls are treated differently. From the time
they began to talk they also begin to form their gender identities. They
learn that their culture has different expectations about them depending on their sex. As they grow, they model their behavior after their
same-sexed parent, their peers, and other adults around them. They
are rewarded when they behave in sex-appropriate ways and are punished or ridiculed when they behave inappropriately. Girls in American
society are given much more latitude in behavior than boys. It is al-
right for a young girl to act like a tomboy; a boy who acts like a sissy
will be ridiculed and harrassed. For children in industrialized societies the mass media present larger-than-life models for children to
emulate. The male models are usually more vivid than their lack-
luster female counterparts; consequently, boys can learn more about
being a man from the mass media than girls can learn about being a
woman. All societies, using their available resources, attempt to
prepare children for their future adult roles.

The differential socialization experiences of girls and boys are
offered as partial explanations of differences between the sexes in
both number of and types of crimes committed. Both sex stereotyping
and socialization experiences are important determinants of adult
behavior in men and women. Numerous studies of sex stereotyping
fairly consistently show women to be passive, emotional, submissive,
dependent and having interpersonal values (caring, nuturant, etc.)
and males as active, independent, dominant, and rational (Balswick
and Ward, 1977). Sex stereotypes are important because they guide
our expectations about how men and women should behave, and, consequently, how they are taught.

Most research shows that women are reared to be more dependent, emotional (that is, showing emotion), and nuturant than males
(Maccoby and Jacklin, 1974). Women are not raised to be as independent, achievement-motivated, and assertive as males. However,
girls are also socialized to both value and cultivate both their physical attributes and their interpersonal skills. Girls learn early in life

that their life chances depend on how successfully they can market
their most important attributes , i. e. , their physical attractiveness
and their interpersonal skills. Girls spend most of their youth learning how to "be and act pretty."

From the research studies surveyed, we can conclude that: (1)
the formulation of an individual's gender identity and role is a result
of the interactive effects of biological and social factors; (2) except
for the four reproductive functions, there are no sex-typed behaviors
which have exclusively innate causes; (3) sex role stereotypes appropriate to each culture are taught to and internalized by children; and
(4) the differences in male and female gender roles may account for
some of the sex differences in crime rates.

ETIOLOGY OF FEMALE CRIME - SOCIALIZATION

Criminologists have given little thought to the sex variable even
though it explains more variance in crime rates across cultures than
any other (Harris, 1977). Harris (1977:3) argues that most general
theories of crime and delinquency are "... no more than special theories of male deviance." Theories of female criminality are treated
as special cases or exceptions to the general theories, and most explanations treat female misconduct as extensions or variations on the
female gender role.

Differential Opportunity and Socialization

There are more men than woman arrested and in prison. Any
satisfactory theory or female (or male) criminality must try to explain those facts. The opportunity structure and differential socialization are frequently used either separately or together to explain
sex differences in misconduct.

Women have been assigned to certain physical spaces and structural positions. Female territory encompasses the home, yard,
shopping center, and general office space in commercial and government organizations. Women are housewives, mothers and workers.
In 1974, 39 percent of the labor force were women. Seven out of ten
employed women work full time, and more married women and more
women with children under school age are working than ever before.
(4) Though women are employed in all occupational and industrial
sectors, they are concentrated in a few: 77. 8 percent of all clerical

workers, 91.1 percent of bank tellers, and 69.6 percent of all food
service workers are women. In fact, women are heavily concentrated
in the "people service, food service, and office service" occupations.

The effect of the opportunity structure on female misconduct is
twofold. First, because women spend much of their time in and around
their homes, their opportunities for committing crime are less than
for males. Second, the types of crimes committed by women are related to their structural positions in the labor force. Women have
ample opportunities to commit such offenses as shoplifting, petty
larceny, theft by taking, fraud, etc. They have fewer opportunities
than men to engage in major stock swindles, price fixing, or hijack-
ing interstate trucks.

The effects of women's socialization experiences are also twofold. Women's socialization experiences lead them to be more com-
pliant to others' expectations than men; therefore, they are more apt
to be law-abiding if the significant others in their lives value law-
abiding behavior. Women are also taught the inter-personal relations
skills which are useful in certain types of criminal activity, especially
fraud and theft. A woman can convince a sympathetic male that she
must cash a check to feed her child. Recently, a female employee of
a discount store was able to convince 38 men during one week that
she was giving them a "special deal" on television sets. The men
paid her in cash and on Friday evening they arrived at the rear of the
store to pick up their sets; the woman and the sets were not there.

It is artificial to separate opportunity from effects of socialization. For everyone, including female offenders, the opportunities
seen, made and used are related to one's particular learning experiences. The opportunities women have are related to their structural
positions in society as well as their gender roles. Examples from a
few studies will clarify these interrelationships.

Frequently, girls are arrested for status offenses like curfew
violations and "being ungovernable." Girls who are taken into custody
for the above offenses are usually described as "ungovernable, unman-
ageable, incorrigible, and beyond control" (Greene, and Esselstyn,
1972). The specific behavior, whether or not it includes an actual
law violation, is almost always sexual (Armstrong, 1977).

Adult women are arrested for a variety of activities also related
to sex; the City of Atlanta, Georgia enforces six separate ordinances
related to prostitution alone. For the last twenty years, nationally
women have accounted for over 70 percent of all arrests for prostitution and commercial vice (Simon, 1974). There are several explanations for the differential arrest of girls and women for sex-related
offenses. In this section the socialization experiences and opportunity

structure which may predispose women and girls toward sex-related offenses will be discussed.

Gray's 1973 study of teenage prostitutes showed that the process of becoming a prostitute involved certain types of childhood experiences and the knowledge that prostitution offered a viable alternative to unstable family conditions and/or poverty. Gray (1973:409) says, "Prostitution existed as a concept in the minds of most of the girls by the time they were eleven years old." These girls perceived the economic and social advantages in prostitution. These young women became prostitutes because they believed prostitution offered them several advantages and few disadvantages. Their previous socialization experiences facilitated their perception of prostitution as an acceptable occupation.

In a study of exotic dancers Boles and Garbin (1974a:1974b) traced the process by which 51 women chose the occupation of stripping. Each of the features (stars like Sally Rand and Gypsy Rose Lee that travel a circuit) had personal contacts in show business; many of them grew up in show business and had strippers as members of their families. Seventy percent of the house girls (local girls who strip in clubs) had been go-go dancers, and 20 percent had been waitresses. Thus, most of the strippers had learned the norms of the entertainment business, especially the strip club variety, before they began actually performing as strippers. Most of the women became strippers because they saw it as "solving" a personal or professional crisis. For example, one feature started stripping because she could not get work as a belly dancer, and stripping was the only way she could stay in show business. A house girl gave this reason: "My marriage broke up, and I was tired of the wife and mother bit; I wanted a whole new life" (Boles and Garbin, 1974a:321).

The prostitutes in Gray's study and the strippers in Boles and Garbin's study were primarily young women with little education from working-class families. Given their personal and social attributes, for these young women stripping and prostitution looked like the best opportunity for a better life.

The choices made by prostitutes and strippers apparently result from the confluence of social learning and opportunity. Many of the general theories of crime causation, i.e., social reinforcement, differential opportunity, etc., adopt the point of view of the offender: the motives, experiences, and influences which led the individual or group to adopt criminal behaviors. The roles of law, police enforcement strategies, senting procedures and other societal controls in crime causation are often ignored.

The Role of Law and
Social Control Mechanisms

Criminal laws are enacted to serve several purposes; in general,
they are supposed to deter morally disapproved behavior and punish
wrongdoers. Generally, we assume that if we enact a law prohibiting
murder and make the punishment for its violation severe and sure, we
will not see many murders. The Aztecs violently disapproved the use
of alcohol, and they stoned anyone (except the very old) who appeared
on the street even slightly inebriated. By all accounts they successfully discouraged alcohol use.

However, laws may also be enacted for purely symbolic purposes.
Governments affect the distribution of values through symbolic
acts as well as through instrumental ones. The struggle to control symbolic actions of government is often as bitter and as fate-
ful as the struggle to control its tangible effects (Gusfield, 1963:
167).

Sex laws in general, and prostitution laws in particular, serve to define a moral community. Most sex-related legislation speaks to the
symbolic significance of these laws.

The sheer bulk of legislation relating to sexual matters might
well form the object of an independent study itself, since it seems
to evince almost a collective obsession on the part of legislators
with such activity. (Davidson, et. al., 1974:887).

Many sex-related criminal statutes are not meant to actually deter;
laws prohibiting adultery, fornication, seduction and B-drinking are
rarely enforced. The effect of laws regulating prostitution is negligible. Geis (1972:200) belittles the effectiveness of New York's prostitution laws: "The lesson seems quite clear. Neither under the first
rather stringent law, nor under the second more moderate law, nor
under the present, even more stringent law, has prostitution apparently changed very much in New York."
The purpose of these laws is largely symbolic in that they define
a moral community which is opposed to the "immoral" behaviors codi-
fied in the laws.
Sex-specific laws apply to only one sex. In England the only sex-
specific law is one that defined infanticide as a female offense committed only by women who have not recovered from the trauma of child-
birth (Smart, 1977). In the United States the vast majority of all our
laws are designed to be sexless. For example, in the Georgia code

the pronoun "he" is used throughout with the understanding that "she"
may be interchanged with "he" at any point.
   "Sex-related offenses are those crimes which may be committed
by either sex but which in practice appear to be committed more by
one sex than by the other" (Smart, 1977:8). There are numerous sex-
related offenses. More males steal automobiles and rob banks; more
women are shoplifters. However, there are many (usually sex-related)
offenses for which girls and women are arrested because the presump-
tion of the criminal justice system that these are "female" behaviors
and offenses. Prostitution is perceived as an offense committed by
women, as arrest figures demonstrate. Yet most prostitution laws
are written so that the customer is a party to the illegal act. Why
aren't the customers arrested?
   Prostitution-related criminal statutes have been attacked on several constitutional groups: violation of free speech, equal protection,
due process, and unconstitutional vagueness (Davidson, et al., 1974).
In most appellate courts the constitutionality of these statutes has been
upheld. The differential arrest of women over male customers and
male prostitutes has been deemed selective but not discriminatory
(U. S. v. Wilson, 1975; Black v. State, 1975). One Louisiana judge's
argument illustrates this thinking.

> The court states the record does not support the fact that male
> prostitution is prevalent and constitutes a social evil detrimental
> to public welfare just as does female prostitution, and a court
> may not suppose male prostitution is a problem of such signifi-
> cance that the legislature should proscribe the practice as a
> crime (State v. Devall, 1974).

The criminal justice system, in practice, associates sex offenses with females when judging youthful offenders. Gold (1970) interviewed 522 youths between the ages of 13 and 16. He found that, even
by doubling the amount of reported fornication, this act only represent
11 percent of the girls' delinquent activity. Yes, boys were more active fornicators than girls. Gold (1970:64) suggests that we rethink
our traditional view of female delinquency.

> In sum, the question that should guide theorizing about girls' de-
> linquency is not "Why do girls rather than boys run away from
> home, commit sexual offenses, and seriously misbehave at
> home?"

Gold argues that the question we should ask if why boys commit
so many more delinquent acts than girls. In spite of the fact that boys

commit more status offenses involving sexual misconduct, girls are
more frequently adjudicated delinquent for those offenses.

Even though there are laws (and enforcement strategies) which
almost preclude the arrest of males for certain offenses, undeniably
fewer girls and women are arrested and sentenced to prison than men.

> ...although 1 in 6.5 arrests is a woman, and 1 in 9 convictions
> is a woman, only about 1 in 30 of those sentenced to prison is a
> woman (Simon, 1975:87).

Is part of the explanation of this discrepancy due to society's perception of the gender role of woman or male chivalry?

At least five major explanations for the differential arrest, sentencing, and incarceration of women exist (Phillips, et. al., 1976;
Simon, 1975). Male victims, police officers, and judges are more
lenient with women because women are perceived as being weak and
needing protection. The "sacredness" of motherhood is given as a
reason for not arresting or sentencing a female offender to prison.
The mother is needed at home; the social harm would be greater by
sending her to prison. Also, women like Poor Pitiful Pearl are less
capable than men. If a man and woman commit a crime together, the
men is seen as the "brains" of the operation. Often, a woman's co-
defendant will chivalrously shoulder all the blame. The public also
sees women as less dangerous than men; women are both less violent
and less apt to engage in lifelong criminal careers that will make them
menaces to society. Women are seen as more amenable to reform
and rehabilitation than men; women who "just got in with the wrong
crowd" can be set back on the right road; whereas a hardened male
criminal - that's another story. Finally, many people believe that a
woman is more stigmatized and harmed by a conviction than a man.
A man may elicit sympathy for reforming, but female ex-convicts receive at best pity - at worst, scorn.

Undoubtedly, many women are protected from the full consequences of their illegal acts; to what extent is unknown. Victims, prosecuting attorneys, and judges have been quoted as saying that they have
often shielded women from the consequences of their misconduct because women are "helpless," "mothers," "not responsible," or "weak."

Yet, the very impulse to protect women has led to differences in
the sentencing procedures between the sexes. The indeterminate
sentence was imposed on women because they were seen as more
easily rehabilitated; thus, women were thought to profit more than men
from incarceration (Armstrong, 1977). Recently, the imposition of
the indeterminate sentence for women only has been held unconstitu-

tional. Further, the paternalistic attitude of society toward women
is reflected in the treatment of young women. Girls are most apt to
be adjudicated delinquent for sexual activity than males of the same
age. Girls are sent to training schools to protect tham from "bad
influences" and "bad males."

Sex discriminatory statutes are being attacked on every front;
in some areas, i. e., the indeterminate sentence, the discriminatory
statutes are being eliminated gradually. All the same sex discriminatory statutes are being upheld, i. e., prostitution. The outcome of
constitutional challenges to sex-discriminatory laws is not yet clear.
The courts appear to be saying that for a sex discriminatory statute
to be upheld, it must be proved that there is something about the nature of one sex as opposed to the other which would call for a sex
discriminatory practice. Research into the biological and social differences between the sexes should aid the courts in making decisions
based upon knowledge rather than preconceptions.

Toward a Theory of Female Criminality

Any theory of female criminality must explain the following: the
sex difference in arrest rates; the increased participation of women
in crime; and the over-representation of women in some offense categories. The under-representation of women in arrest statistics may
be accounted for by biological differences between the sexes, the
differential socialization and opportunity structures, and societal protection of women.

Other than differences in size and strength, there are two other
factors which may account for sex differences in arrest rates. Men
are more aggressive than women and tend to stress power strategies
in their relations with others. The physiologically complex changes
which are required to produce a male fetus may, in turn, produce
long-lasting effects. Boys have more psychological adjustment problems with schools, families and communities than girls. These problems may lead either to delinquency or the appearance of delinquency,
i. e., the label of "bad boy." For example, a boy who is having reading difficulties in school may become a discipline problem to his teach-
er. He is labeled a "troublemaker"; this label may follow him through
his entire school career and negatively effect his future life chances.

Female socialization and opportunity structures tend to preclude
some criminal activities but not others. Also, the protective attitude
of society toward women may affect arrest rates. Studies of hidden
delinquency generally show that women and girls do commit many more

deviant acts than arrest records show; yet men and boys commit more
deviant acts than women and girls (Gibbens, 1970). Even though the
bulk of deviant and/or criminal acts go unreported, males commit
more of these than women; thus all the difference in arrest rates between the sexes cannot be due solely to chivalry.

Though the arrest rate for women has increased dramatically in
recent years, there is some disagreement concerning the implications
of this. Adler (1975) believes that women are engaging in more aggressive and serious crimes, yet the meanings of the term "serious,"
"violent," or "aggressive" are not clear (Norland and Shover, 1977).
These terms are used interchangeably, and there are very few reliable data on the actual roles of women in criminal acts.

What were the actual roles of women arrested for robbery? Were
they passive accomplices or active participants? Were female convicts
using drugs when they committed robbery or murder? A young woman
was sent to the State prison at fifteen for stabbing her grandmother to
death. She was under the influence of LSD at the time and had no memory of the act. Locally, some prostitutes are thought to be working
more aggressively as the number of assaults committed by prostitutes
has increased. A study of women prisoners shows that female robbers
are now more apt to work alone and use a gun than previously (Ward,
et. al., 1969); however, we do not have adequate studies of the actual
roles of women in serious crimes. Until this knowledge is available,
we cannot say whether or not women act significantly more aggressively or violently now than before. We can say, however, than women
are engaging in more property offenses; this suggests changes in the
opportunity structure as a key variable in explaining both changes and
types of female criminal participation.

The study of female criminality and the development of a theoretical perspective from which to view it should proceed from an investigation of new "scripts" available to women. Gagnon and Simon (1973:
20) define a script ". . . as an organization of mutually shared convictions that allows two or more actors to participate in a complex act
involving mutual dependence." A script defines the actors and the
situation, and plots the behavior. A typical recent traditional script
for women involved: learning as a child and adolescent to be pretty,
sweet, dependent and consumer-oriented; getting a job or going to
college until marriage; marrying and raising a family; and going back
to work only after the children were in school or for pressing financial reasons. This script called for women to be dependent, passive,
law-abiding, and non-assertive; this script called for women to be
confined largely to "female space" - the home, shopping center, and
office floor. There were, of course, counter-scripts; an example of

one was for the "bad girl" which called for early promiscuity, prostitution, and related minor offenses. Today many emerging scripts call for changes in both traditional attitudes and behaviors of women, plus the merging of men's and women's spaces. Studies of these new scripts and criminal activities associated with them point the way to a future understanding of female criminality.

THE FUTURE OF FEMALE CRIME

The extent of criminality in women is and will be dependent on two major factors: the types of scripts available to women and the laws which particularly affect them.

Emerging Female Scripts: Key Factors

The types of scripts available to women in the future depend upon many factors, most important of which is the future of women's roles in marriage and the family, especially the latter. If women still accept as their dominant goals getting married and raising children, then their criminal activities will be both limited and circumscribed by their locations in female space. If, however, women reject traditional marriage and especially child-rearing, then they will be able to engage in a wide variety of economic and leisure activities in male space with a consequent increase in opportunity for deviance and crime.

Although opportunities for living arrangements outside of marriage abound, most Americans are continuing to marry. More than 90 percent of both sexes marry eventually, and more than 90 percent of married couples have at least one child (Kenkel, 1977). However, the marriage rate is declining slightly, in part due to the decisions of both sexes to postpone marriage. Childlessness also seems to be increasing slightly among young women (Kenkel, 1977). Still, the majority of young men and women plan to both marry and have children sometime during their lives. Most women still play traditional roles in marriage; the egalitarian marriage is largly a myth. Poloma and Garland (1971) interviewed 53 highly educated professional women about their marital relations. Though it might be expected that these women would have egalitarian marriages, 20 marriages were traditional and 27 were neo-traditional; only one was egalitarian. In the neo-traditional marriages the wives' careers were considered important, but the women were still considered primarily responsible for home and child care. No strong evidence indicates that women in the future will abandon their husbands and children; nor is there any evidence that women will become significantly less nuturant, affiliative, and supportive than they have been in the past.

Women will, however, continue to work. Most women work because they or their families need the money. The majority of female The majority of female workers have jobs rather than careers, which require more committment in time and energy. Yet in the last ten years the admission of women to graduate and professional training programs has increased significantly (Tavris and Offir, 1977) so that more women will enter the professions and other better-paying and more prestigious occupations in the future. The continuation of this trend will depend on a variety of factors, including the vigor of government agencies monitoring professional schools.

In sum, women will likely continue to marry, raise children, and work outside the home. The distinctions between men's and women's spaces will disappear as women are employed in previously male-dominated occupations and men take more responsibilities for home maintenance. The opportunities for women to engage in certain types of crime should increase dramatically; more women will be arrested for the category of crime generally labeled white-collar, occupational or corporate. (5) In effect, in the future more women than ever will be following previously all-male scripts. As women adopt these scripts, their opportunities for crime should equal men's.

The Law: The Structure of the Future

It is a truism that the amount of crime in society is related to the laws of that society because no behavior is a crime unless it is made so by law. In regard to the relationship between law and female criminality, there are two categories of laws which are important. First, there are numerous laws and government regulations affecting racial and sex discrimination. The success of both laws and enforcement procedures are crucial in predicting the future of female criminality. If women, especially minority women, are given equal access to educational and training opportunities as well as jobs, there should be a decrease in some offense categories among women. For example, the absence of prostitution in Sweden is generally attributable to the absence of poverty there (Boles and Tatro, 1977; Linner, 1971). Prostitution, petty theft, and even murder and assault should decrease as women have more opportunities to earn a decent living. On the other

hand, opportunities for white-collar and occupational crime should
increase.

Two categories of criminal laws important to the study of the
female criminality are sex and drug-related laws. State and local
criminal statutes regulating such behaviors as solicitation for prosti-
tuion, mingling, B-drinking, topless dancing, etc., affect the arrest
rate of women. The elimination of these statutues will lead to a decrease in the number of women arrested. However, the trend, though
unclear, seems to be toward more laws and stricter enforcement of
those already on the books (Boles and Tatro, 1977). If Americans
are becoming more conservative, as some observers believe, then
we can expect the arrest rate for vice offenders among women to
increase.

The status of drug usage laws is also important. For example,
the decriminalization of marijuana, if it occurs, should lead to a drop
in the arrest rate of women. However, nothing indicates the usage
of such drugs as cocaine, heroin, LSD and others will be decriminalized in the near future, and women are abusers of these drugs as well
as alcohol.

Predictions of Things to Come

Forecasting the future is always risky because unforeseen events
can radically alter what was expected. We may suffer another depression; the energy crisis may worsen; a religious revival may sweep
the country. Innumerable unexpected events can alter even the best
of predictions. Nevertheless, based upon present trends and state of
knowledge, we believe the major trends in female crime are as follows:

1) the percent increases in arrest rates for women will begin
to stabilize. Part of the astronomical percent increases were due to
the effects of small numbers. For example, in the city of Atlanta in
1960 there were ten women arrested for murder; in 1975 there were
fifty. The percent increase is impressive, but the actual number increase is not that substantial.

2) the largest increase in arrest rates will be in larceny, embezzlement, and fraud.

3) the educational level of female offenders should rise.

4)   the rationales given by female offenders will change. Women will assume more responsibility for their crimes.

5)   More female robbers and burglars will act independently and use weapons.

6)   Both the public and court officials will be less protective of women.

7)   the number of murders and assaults by women will decrease slightly.

As more women are able to support themselves, they will be able to leave their husbands and lovers whenever those relationships prove unbearable. Thus, some of the murders and assaults committed by both men and women against each other in the heat of rage may be prevented. Men and women will no longer be trapped in a relationship which neither party cares to preserve.

8)   the number of child-beating cases will gradually decline as birth control information becomes more widely disseminated and supportive services are available for troubled parents.

9)   the number of women arrested for prostitution and related offenses will gradually decline as women are able to get better paying, more socially acceptable jobs.

10)   the number of young girls adjudicated delinquent will gradually decrease as more young women learn in school and through the mass media that there are futures open to them that were closed in the past.

PRESCRIPTIONS FOR THE FUTURE

If we wish to reduce female crime and help women lead lives that are as productive as possible, then several short and long range goals need implementing.

Short-range Goals: The Future is Now

We should strengthen and enforce all laws regarding equal employment and educational opportunities for women. Second, we should
evaluate the effectiveness of our sex and drug-related laws. Many of
these laws are of symbolic use only; their removal would not cause a
serious deterioration of any community's moral standards. We should
try creative new approaches to old problems. For example, Denmark
allows prostitution as long as the prostitute is otherwise employed.
This allows the woman to supplement her income and yet keeps her in
the legitimate work force.

We must improve the conditions and training programs in women's
prisons. Women's correctional facilities have been traditionally understaffed, and the training programs have been grossly inadequate. Most
of the vocational programs for women are in low-paying, sex-stereo-
typed occupations like housekeeping, food service, and cosmetology.
The following statement is from an inmate of Indiana's Women's Prison.

But what about those who are inside the prison walls? Where do
we go from here? What can we do about the neglect women suffer in penal institutions? She already has two strikes against
her. First she is a female and second she is an offender ...
if you care about us - If you are interested - Will you help?
After all we once lived in your communities, and we will be
back out there again someday and we don't want to become a
recidivist figure. My last comment to you is this - If you were
in my shoes, in my present situation, wouldn't you be wanting to
see improvements made to help for advancement (Short, 1977).

Long-range Goals: The Future is Tomorrow

Research from the biological and social sciences has contributed
to our knowledge of sex role behavior. Continuing efforts to understand the biological and social bases of gender identity and sex role
differences are needed. We also need studies of the actual roles played by female offenders during the commissions of their crimes.
Further, we must continue to monitor the goals, aspirations, and
interests of young people. Career aspirations and life-style plans
are important indicators of future crime rates.

Sex and career education are needed. Venereal disease and
illegitimacy rates are increasing; sexual experience is not synonymous

with sex knowledge. For a nation emphasizing work, we give young
people very little career guidance. If an individual begins his/her
work life at 21 and works until retirement at 65, that individual will
have spent approximately 88,000 hours at work. We leave young
people to find their own way through the maze of conflicting career and
educational tracks. Career education would enable young men and women to plan their work and educational experiences with a goal toward
maximizing their abilities and increasing their life satisfactions.

Finally, legal reform is needed. Laws which serve no real function should be repealed; discriminatory statutes should be amended,
and innovative deterrent strategies should be tested. These are tasks
to challenge the minds and energies of future lawyers, criminologists,
police officers, and all other criminal justice practitioners.

NOTES

1. The terminology used is adopted from John Money (Money and Tucker, 1975).

2. There is considerable research on the problems of individuals who, because of either birth injuries, accidents, or idiosyncractic sex assignments by parents, have difficulty with their gender identity (Money and Tucker, 1975; Green, R., 1975).

3. Simon (1975) points out that the percent of females arrested among all arrested for violent crimes has been between 10.33 percent and 13.51 percent between 1953 and 1972.

4. For excellent books about the participation of women in the labor force see Boulding (1977) and Howe (1977).

5. There are a variety of terms which are sometimes used interchangeably to indicate crimes committed by people during the course of their work. Some of these concepts are: white-collar, occupational crime, corporate crime.

BIBLIOGRAPHY

Adler, F. Sisters in Crime. New York: McGraw-Hill 1975.

Armstrong, G. "Females Under the Law- Protected but Not Equal," Crime and Delinquency 23 (2):109-20, 1977.

Balswick, J. and Ward, D. "Strong Men and Virtuous Women: A Concept of Sex Role Stereotypes," paper presented at Southern sociological meetings, Atlanta, Georgia, 1977.

Bardwick, J. The Psychology of Women: A Study of Bio-Cultural Conflicts. New York: Harper and Row, 1971.

Boles, J. and Garbin, A. P. "Stripping for a Living: An Occupational Study of Night Club Strippers." In Clifton Bryant, ed. Deviant Behavior: Occupational and Organizational Bases Chicago: Rand McNally, 1974.

Boles, J. and Garbin, A. P. "The Strip Club and Stripper Customer Patterns of Interaction," Sociology and Social Research 58(2): 136-44, 1974.

Boles, J. and Tatro, C. "Legal and and Extra-Legal Methods of Controlling Female Prostitution: A Cross-Cultural Comparison,"
paper presented at American Criminology meetings, Tuscon,
Arizona, 1977.

Boulding, E. Women in the Twentieth Century World. New York:
Wiley, 1977.

Cowie, J. V., and Slater, E. Delinquency in Girls. London: Heine-
mann, 1968.

Davidson, K., Ginsburg, R., and Kay, H. Sex Based Discrimination.
St. Paul, Minn.: West Publishing, 1974.

Deutsch, H. The Psychology of Women: A Psychoanalytic Interpretation, vol. 1. Grune and Stratton, 1944.

Erikson, E. H. "The Inner and Outer Spaces: Reflections on Woman-
hood," Daedalus 93:582-606, 1964.

FBI Uniform Crime Reports, U. S. Department of Justice. Washington, D. C.: U. S. Government Printing Office, 1976.

Gagnon, J. and Simon, W. Sexual Conduct: The Social Sources of
Human Sexuality. Chicago: Aldine, 1973.

Geis, G. "Not the Law's Business: An Examination of Homosexuality,
Abortion, Prostitution, Narcotics and Gambling in the United
States." Rockville, Maryland: National Institute of Mental Health
Center for Studies of Crime and Delinquency, 1972.

Gibbons, D. Delinquent Behavior. Englewood Cliffs, New Jersey:
Prentice-Hall, 1970.

Gold, M. Delinquent Behavior in an American City. Belmont, California: Brooks/Cole, 1970.

Goldberg, S., and Lewis, M. "Play Behavior in the Year-Old Infant:
Early Sex Differences," Child Development 40: 21-31, 1969.

Gray, D. "Turning Out: A Study of Teenage Prostitution," Urban
Life and Culture 1(4):401-35, 1973.

Green, R. Sexual Identity Conflict in Children and Adults. Baltimore, Maryland: Penguin Books, 1975.

Greene, N., and Esselstyn, T.C., "The Beyond Control Girls," Juvenile Justice, November: 13-19, 1972.

Greenwald, H. The Elegant Prostitute: A Social and Psychoanalytic Study. New York: Ballantine Books, 1970.

Gusfield, J. Symbolic Crusade: Status Policies and the American Temperance Movement. Urbana: University of Illinois Press, 1963.

Harris, A. "Sex and Theories of Deviance: Toward a Functional Theory of Deviant Type-Scripts," American Sociological Review 42(1):3-16, 1977.

Hoffman-Bustamante, D. "The Nature of Female Criminality," Issues in Criminology 8 (Fall):3-30, 1973.

Howe, L.K. Pink Collar Workers: Inside the World of Women's Work. New York: G.P. Putnam, 1977.

Kenkel, W.P. The Family in Perspective. Santa Monica, Calif: Goodyear Publishing, 1977.

Klein, D. "The Etiology of Female Crime: A Review of the Literature," Issues in Criminology 8 (Fall):3-30, 1973.

Konopka, G. The Adolescent Girl in Conflict. Englewood Cliffs, New Jersey: Prentice-Hall, 1966.

Koser, N. and Rigsby, C. "Is Crime a Man's World? Issues in the Explanation of Female Criminality," Journal of Criminal Justice 3(2):131-40, 1975.

Leventhal, G.S. and Lane, D.W. "Sex, Age and Equity Behavior," Journal of Personality and Social Psychology, 15:312-16, 1970.

Linner, B. Society and Sex in Sweden. Stockholm: The Swedish Institute, 1971.

Maccoby, E.F. and Jackson, C.N. The Longest War: Sex Differences in Perspective. New York: Harcourt Brace Jovanovich, 1974.

Money, J. and Tucker, P. Sexual Signatures: On Being a Man or a Woman. Boston: Little, Brown, 1975.

Norland, S. and Shover, N. "Gender Roles and Female Criminality: Some Critical Comments," Criminology 15(1):87-102, 1977.

Phillips, D. L., Nelson, L. Defleur, and Walters, G. "The Female Offenders and Public Opinion: Perceived Seriousness of Crimes and Recommended Dispositions," paper presented at American Society of Criminology meetings, Tuscon, Arizona, 1977.

Pollak, O. The Criminality of Women. Philadelphia: University of Pennsylvania Press, 1950.

Poloma, M. M. and Garland, T. N. "The Myth of the Egalitarian Family: Familial Roles and the Professionally Employed Wife," in A. Theodore, ed. The Professional Woman. Cambridge, Massachusetts: Schenkman, 1971.

Rock, S. "Imprisoned Women on the Rise-Why? How Can We Resolve This Problem?" Lincoln, Nebraska: Contact, Inc., 1977.

Simon, R. The Contemporary Woman and Crime. Rockville, Maryland: National Institute of Mental Health, 1975.

Simon, R. "American Women and Crime," The American Academy of Political Science and Social Science Annals 423 (Jan):31-46, 1976.

Smart, C. Women, Crime and Criminology: A Feminist Critique. London: Routledge and Kegan Paul, 1977

Tavris, C. and Offir, C. The Longest War: Sex Differences in Perspective. New York: Harcourt Brace Jovanovich, 1977.

Ward, D., Jackson, A. M., and Ward, R. F. "Crime and Violence by Women," in D. J. Mulvilhill and M. M. Tumin, ed. Crimes of Violence. A staff report submitted to the National Commission on the Causes and Prevention of Violence. Washington, D. C.: U. S. Government Printing Office, 1969.

Williams, J. Psychology of Women: Behavior in a Biosocial Context. New York: Norton, 1977.

V
Personnel in the Criminal Justice System: Anticipated Changes

14 Problems in Police Leadership

John T. O'Brien

Police leadership, even before the turn of the century, will differ radically from what it is today. This does not mean to reflect the normal change that can be expected in any field but it is to suggest the many traumatic influences that will be brought to bear. It is obvious that the police must be affected by changes in the forms of government, new theories of personnel administration, as well as new ideas of public accountability and control, to name but a few external influences. Internally, the organization will change as new types of people enter the field and as the model of policing evolves from the military to the social service paragon.

While there are many changing elements which will interact and thus bring further change, they must be looked at in isolation to gain any comprehension of their influence. It is believed that there will be ten major factors influencing police leadership in coming decades.

GOVERNMENTAL FORM

The increasing popularity of professional administrators in local government as exemplified by the council-manager and mayor-administrator forms bids fair to remove some of the onerous political pressures on some departments. The interposition of a nonpolitical administrator between the chief and the mayor and council should prove of great benefit. The direct rule by the chief executive has often militated against effective police service. The growth in these two governmental forms has been paralelled by decreasing popularity of the commission form of local government. This type of administration, which

285

combined the traditional executive and legislative branches, arose as
an answer to the demoralization resulting from a tidal wave which
struct Galveston, Texas in 1900. The efficiency in an emergency
situation, however, was often subject to abuse in normal times, as
shown by the Edward Crump machine in Memphis, Tennessee and the
Frank Hague organization of Jersey City. (1) The three forms of
government were alike in their search for economy and efficiency, a
quest which continues today at a time of rising costs and increasing
distrust of local government.

The increasing popularity of non-political executives bids fair to
insulate the police from the political influences of the past, but at the
same time it offers an opportunity for more community control in
policy making. The recognition that policy decisions, as to the use of
patrol dogs or lethal weapons or in guidelines governing close pursuit
and interrogations, are of paramount interest to the public is long overdue. This recognition, coupled with increasing legislative and judicial
scrutiny, will require police administrators to justify their decisions.
They must possess the administrative capability to deal with these new
responsibilities. Therefore, future police selection will reflect more
administrative ability rather than merely police experience in the past.
The in camera policy making by police administrators or the purely
political policy decisions of the executive will then be a thing of the
past. The governmental form will also be influenced by regional agreements and the consolidation of smaller units of government.

Unfortunately, the term consolidation has connotations indicating
either a loss of control by local government or the growth of a Leviathan
or megalopolis unresponsive to local needs. Responsible officials should
promote consolidation to attain economy and efficiency even though un-
warranted public fears exist. Consolidation is also opposed by those
who have applauded minority control of urban centers and who fear the
loss of such in any move toward consolidation with the suburbs.

The political differences in changing local government are well
known but voices calling for the realignment of local police will continue to effect changes in this area. Increasing consolidation coupled
with the growth of county government will result in much larger police
departments which will demand more competent leaders at the same
time that the greater size of such forces will permit a wider choice
of prospective applicants. (2)

THE POLICE MODEL

The great influence of the military on the police has been very apparent from the outward marks of both organizations, such as uniforms, rank, insignia, decorations, and organization. But the clear connection between the first modern police force and the military is pointed up in the organization of the London Metropolitan Police by Sir Robert Peel, who chose Lt. Colonel Sir Charles Rowan as its first commissioner because he felt that a military man was necessary. Rowan's obituary notice in The Times of London, May 24, 1852, stated:

Those who witness (and more especially when recently the eyes of the world were fixed on it) the usefulness of that body can little conceive the difficulties which had to be encountered and overcome in the engrafting of the discipline and efficiency of a military force on the heretofore constitutional but inefficient police constable, the apprehensions entertained of its impracticality, and of the constitutional prejudice it naturally had to overcome. (3)

The first model of American police was patterned after the English form laid down by the Metropolitan Police Act of 1839. The rise of both forces came about because of public disorder, urbanization and revulsion against enforcement of law by the military. Nevertheless there have been great differences in the orientations of the two models as follows: (4)

	ENGLISH	AMERICAN
STYLE	Formal	Informal
EMPHASIS	Legal	Political
ORIENTATION	Impersonal	Personal
SUBORDINATION	To law	To the people
PERSONNEL	Professional	Amateurish

The reform movement ushered in by the post-Civil War muckrakers had very great effects on local police because of the dominance

of such by the various political machines. It was this hegemony which
was responsible for many of the early police problems. (5) The early
reformers attempted to alleviate the problems through the utilization
of nonpartisan boards which were as inefficient as they were nonpolitical. The next remedy proposed was State control by rural, Republican, Protestant state legislatures apparently appalled by the actions
of urban, Democratic, Roman Catholic city executives; (6) but these
State boards were not responsive to the local public, so that after the
turn of the century most such departments reverted to local control.
There ie still some State control existing in cities such as Boston,
Baltimore, Kansas City and St. Louis.

For all of the evils surrounding the police of the 19th Century,
who were severely castigated by reformers who saw only politics and
corruption, we now realize they had some advantages. Not being bound
by a strictly law-and-order mentality permitted them a great deal of
discretion in which problems often could be mediated to general public
satisfaction. Whether due to humanity or venality, they were enabled
to ignore many of what we call today "victimless crimes." These early
police were interested in order rather than law, peace rather than morality and referral in lieu of arrest. (7)

While there was disagreement as to the remedy for police corruption, there was near-unanimity of opinion as to its cause being politics.
Therefore, there was general agreement as to the need to insulate the
police from local contact as much as possible. The Mugwumps, now
turned Progressives, stimulated by writers such as Upton Sinclair,
Ida Tarbell and Lincoln Steffins, (8) turned their ire on the cities.

The result was a new police model, but it was influenced by many
factors resulting from the desire to clean up the cities. There was
a recognition that science had a role in this as well as law and morality. It was soon recognized that the efforts to end corruption were often
as disappointing for as soon as the light of public scrutiny moved on
the rascals returned to the public trough. Therefore, the New York
Bureau of Municipal Research was founded in 1906 to bring a new
emphasis to bear on the problem.

In place of platforms, conventions and politics, it substituted the
painstaking research methods of natural science; in place of intui-
tive and rationalized programs of reform, it insisted upon an un-
biased observation of facts; in place of public attacks upon officials,
it devoted its time to analysis of the "system" which controlled
those officials. (9)

There was also a drive for economy and efficiency as a number of cities organized commissions to develop executive power, an executive budget, an organization pyramid and staff agencies to assist the chief executive.

Those forces of reform were also encouraged by the "scientific management" school of public and private administration, which employed, on the one hand, a works management movement consisting of time and motion studies, cost analysis, incentive pay, selective of employees, and finding the best method and functional foremen. (11) On the other hand, the school advocated an executive process of administrative management emphasizing broad principles of leadership. (12)

Lastly, there was reliance on non-political innovations such as civil service, the Australian and the short ballot, the initiative, referendum, proportional representation, the single tax and home rule. None of these proved to be a panacea but they all emphasized the oversimplified struggle between bosses and reformers which has characterized the urban scene since 1900.

The new emerging police model now shifted its emphasis from patronage and service to reform and crime. Ministerial enforcement of State law replaced the former maintenance of local order as the main purpose of the police. The local political authority was replaced by a hierarchal professional administration. The military virtues of order and discipline and discretion. The centralization of authority was the hallmark of police reform, as was true of the reform movement generally. (13)

The reformers concentrated on crime, centralization, mobility, specialization, efficiency and personnel selection through a merit system. Such personnel would be emotionally detached from the public and assure impartiality. In many departments the personnel were often rotated so as not to remain in any neighborhood too long. In general, the reform of the 1930s accentuated the military model to a greater degree than did the reform at the turn of the century.

This unfortunate military matrix which resulted from the presumed need for teamwork, instant obedience and high hazards obviously required a quasi-military organization. The birth of police in the civil disorder in England in the early 19th Century cast the mould which would endure in both countries down to modern times. In fact, disorders such as the Peterloo Massacre of 1819 initially resulted in a drastic increase in the British Army until public resentment forced a rethinking which resulted in the creation of a quasi-military force as a compromise.

The many similarities between police and military organizations, a number of which are readily apparent, have tended to hide the equal-

ly great differences between these two types of organizations. That
these similarities have been exaggerated has been made apparent by
those individuals who have entered police work after duty in the armed
forces, expecting the work to be very similar and finding that this is
not the case.

There have been many studies made of the armed forces of many
nations and recently research in the field of police administration has
become very popular. But this writer does not know of any work
which specifically compares the two vocations.

The police have profited from the experiences of the military
forces and have modeled themselves after the military. Recently, the
armed forces have become more aware that they can also profit from
the experiences of the police. The increasing emphasis on criminology,
espionage and intelligence have encouraged those units of the armed
forces specifically charged with these problems to establish liaison
with local police departments to profit from their knowledge.

This early reform was stimulated by moral reformers and public
administrators from without the police field, but by 1930, a new breed
of reformer had arisen from within the police ranks. They concentrated their efforts to upgrade the police on the same moral, ethical and
administrative principles as did the early reformers except that, working within the system, they were far more successful. But the new
reformers were even further removed from politics than were their
predecessors. Therefore, they created a police model almost entirely divorced from public contact and often even from public control.
The cry of "political interference" sent many chief executives scurry-
ing back to city hall. The recognized need for community interest,
involvement and control came into conflict with the divorce from political processes. (14) In time, this detachment from the community,
coupled with military centralization, mobility and authority often led
to the total isolation of the police from the community, with dire results for society.

Professionalization, which has been the major goal of modern
police administrators during the past two decades, has the effect of insulating the police from public pressures.... Yet we must
be wary since insulation from political influence without other
methods of integration, such as a positive relationship to the community, can mean insulation from all of us, and if the goals of the
police should vary from those of the citizens, it can become a
very serious problem. (15)

Most police reform has been beneficial and the debt owed to such men as Bruce Smith, August Vollmer and O. W. Wilson is very great indeed. But the cure has also proven to have had some dire side effects. Thus the uniform enforcement law has destroyed that discretion and equity which must ever be part of any rational system of justice and which the police must exercise in many cases. Law enforcement, no less than the courts, must temper justice with mercy and charity.

The rigid enforcement of the law has been one of the causes of tension with minority groups, perhaps even more than its counterpoise of corruption. The rush to motorization and the removal of footmen from the local community has severed the police from local contact and changed their role from that of social workers to that of soldier. Centralized headquarters and the closing of local stations have also removed a stabilizing influence from the community. Specialization has caused another evil resulting, very often, in the referral of complainants instead of the complaints. The impartial civil service system has resulted in a white police force in black neighborhoods, causing an estrangement which is one of the major problems affecting the cities.

The police have responded to these problems with a return to the community through minority recruiting, storefront offices and open acceptance of civilian complaints. The latter was often instituted primarily to offset demands for a civilian review board.

However, the military model continues to be the hallmark of police departments and it may be expected to continue as such for many years to come. This is especially so because the police themselves regard this as their proper role and continue to press for such through their unions. In fact, the police have returned to the politics which they foreswore many years ago. They now actively promote candidates partial to the military role.

Other models of police organizations have been described emphasizing community concerns, union orientations and administrative efficiency. (16) But the primary emphases have been the military model on one hand and the social service orientation on the other.

PUBLIC CONTROL OF POLICE

The great importance of police work to the average citizen requires that police agencies be responsive to public control and direction. Such control is effected internally, externally and sometimes by special commissions.

Internal direction requires not merely strong administrative leadership but also staff inspections and investigations by internal affairs units. The necessity for such has been pointed up many times in the past, (17) but unfortunately some police administrators are reluctant to take the proper action because of civil service requirements or fear of the union. (18) Because of this, internal police investigations are somewhat suspect. Some authorities have therefore criticized internal investigators as unrealistic and recommended external inquiries. (19)

It would appear that serious internal police investigations of the future will be conducted by outside agencies, including ad hoc commissions, special prosecutors and the Department of Justice where a violation of Federal law is in question. The danger of this removal of the control of police corruption from the administrator to special boards and commissions must be obvious and should be undertaken only in unusual circumstances where the department has obviously lost control of the situation.

At least one national commission has gone on record as specifically favoring external review of the police.

The Crime Commission Police Task Force reviewed the various external grievance procedures attempted to suggested in this country and abroad. Without attempting to recommend a specific procedure, our Commission believes that police departments should be subject to external review. (20)

Public control of the police also involves the formulation of public policy. Public desires will, of course, be affected by changes in values, technology, ecology, federalism, etc. (21) On the one hand, the increasing complexity of government will further divorce the citizen from public administration, but on the other hand, distrust of government will force an even greater accountability of government to the public. Government, including the police, may be expected to render greater responsibility to the public, who will have much more to say in the future as to developing public policies in the area of lethal weapons, high-speed chases, the use of dogs, terrorist mediation, etc. The day when these matters were almost solely within the purview of the chief of police is fast coming to a close.

The police must expect greater public interest in control of policy if for no other reason than that the public expects more. (22) The once passive role of government is a thing of the past. The average citizen expects his political leader to actively promote his welfare and happiness other than by merely protecting him from physical dangers.

The police leadership of the future must be aware of the social activist role. Thus, public desires will have a large role in uplifting police leadership of the future.

Despite the most aggressive and enlightened leadership, law enforcement cannot rise about the level set by the electorate. A condition precedent to the establishment of efficient, professional law enforcement in a community is a desire and a demand on the part of the residents for that type of service. (23)

The increasing popularity of private ombudsmen who hold public and private agencies to public accountability is a harbinger of increased future public interest led by consumer advocates, ecologists and other champions of the common man. These advocates have been granted a willing ear by the judiciary, thus further increasing their popularity. (24)

The American scene will continue to be influenced by the basic revolutionary ideas of Natural Law, Natural Rights, the compact theory of limited government and an open society permitting a verical pursuit of happiness. These early ideas have been modified by later forces of immigration and frontier individualism. They have forged a people who will continue to demand a responsive government form, one in which their police will be even more responsive to local control than in the past.

SOCIAL FACTORS

Police leadership will be further influenced, and moulded to some degree, by the social milieu. Change in the age and ethnicity of the general population, not to speak of the greater changes in the urban scene, will obviously affect police direction.

The social disorders of the 1960s would appear to be a thing of the past and Vietnam is now history. But the disorders of those periods have left the police with a reemphasized military model. In fact, the police were probably never closer to the military than in their riot control role of recent years. Even the Kerner Commission suggested the continued importance of such in asking for the improvement of "police and National Guard forces so that they can respond to potential disorders with more prompt and disciplined use of force. " (25)

The continued drive for minority rights will obviously result in greater female and ethnic representation in leadership roles in future

years. New York City already has a woman in command of one of its
police precincts.

At the present moment in police work there is a seller's market.
That is, the economic slump has resulted in keen competition for police positions. The depression brought many excellent candidates into
the system in the late 1930s. We are witnessing a similar development which promises to improve the leadership of the 1990s.

The continued worship of organization will undoubtedly influence
future police commanders to some degree so as to mould them into
the "organization man." (26) This must be especially guarded against
in police leadership, which must be imaginative, creative and dynamic.
The continued growth of scientific management, systems analysis and
operations research in criminal justice bids fair to stifle the police
chief, who must be aware of morals, traditions and values. The dangers of "managerism" must also be guarded against by an informed
public which makes its wishes known, thus preventing the rise of a
managerial class of police leaders. (27)

                         CRIME AND CRIMINOLOGY

Future criminal justice leadership must be affected by prevalent
theories of penology and criminology. The beliefs of experts in the
field coupled with community morals and mores will, of necessity, impact on police as well as courts and correction. The failure of the
criminal justice system as a whole in preventing crime have led to a
public outcry and alarm which is beginning to affect the basic theory
of the system.

The literature in the field suggests that there has been an over-
criminalization and society must revamp its penal codes to reclassify
much of present deviant behavior to reflect changes in mores as well
as recent research. (28) The new Critical school states that the
criminal law is the creation of elite groups which formulate law to
protect their property rights. (29) That there is some historical
basis for the theory cannot be doubted. One has but to look at the
development of the law of larceny (30) or that of vagrancy (31) to
realize there is some germ of truth in Critical criminology. The
new criminology bids fair to leave the police even more isolated
from the people, since it portrays them as guardians of private
rather than the public weal.

Of perhaps greater import are the pending changes in penology,
where the politicalization of the prison community will put greater

strains on the criminal justice system.

The rise of the new, radical, or critical criminology, as it is variously called, is a reflection of the times. (32) The aforementioned theory of elites proclaims the existence of some group in every government which protests its position by the promulgation of law. This iron law of oligarchy is as old as Socrates and Thrasymachus. (33) But it has achieved new heights with Marxian criminologists who have promulgated the new crimes of war, racism and imperialism while at the same time abolishing many of the more traditional crimes.

While much of the reasoning of the new school of criminology is beclouded by rhetoric, emotions and Marxist propaganda, there is some truth to radical arguments in that there are always groups in power which obviously strive to maintain their positions, whether in a democracy, republic, monarchy or dictatorship, and whether communist or fascist.

The politicalization of crime and criminals, on the one hand, suggests that this class is the victim of an elite which controls society and the police and should therefore be treated as such. On the other hand, there is a rising tide of feeling that correction has failed precisely because it has not held criminals to account and has disregarded the criminal's victim. It advocates just desert for the former and satisfaction for the latter. (34) This theory, whether looked at as private vengeance, official retribution or just desert, looks back to the crime rather than forward to future public safety, as with correction, deterrence and prevention. Thus, the theory is not claimed to be utilitarian, but it has arisen because of the failure of the system and a return to a belief in some degree of free will and responsibility. (35)

Police leadership will be challenged by this classical-radical mix of criminology and penology. Radical criminologists have confounded traditional deterministic sociologists by blaming crime not on the environment, but on an elitist property-oriented class, as Reasons has done. (36) The identification of the police with a repressive establishment and the identification of criminals with an exploited class will make police work even more difficult, as it seriously affects the police role and image.

Administrators will also be challenged by another force in criminal justice, the victims. The new victimology will bring to bear organized pressure groups to evaluate and monitor the system and its leaders to insure its responsiveness to public scrutiny. (37)

Future police leadership must also come to closer grips with the continued growth of organized crime. It may be that the Mafia or Cosa Nostra as such does not exist. In fact, one writer has gone to the extreme of suggesting that it exists only to the degree that it is part of the conspiracy theory endemic to American society, akin to the Proto-

cols of the Elders of Zion. (38)   But the existence of a national association to cooperate in the promotion of crime has not been in doubt since
the Apalachin, New York meeting in 1970. (39)
     The prosecution of organized crime has become even more diffi-
cult in recent years as a result of Watergate and the laws as to privacy. But the failure to implement many of the recommendations of
the President's Commission with regard to organized crime must also
be noted. (40) There has been a tendency by some in recent years to
regard organized crime as the province of Federal agencies, and yet
the burden continues to rest with local police. (41) In fact, the failure
of Federal agencies in this critical area has created a desire for them
to remove themselves from much of the responsibility for organized
crime. The decision of the Internal Revenue Service to discontinue
its Intelligence Division is a case in point, and was bitterly resented
by local police. (42)

                              LAW AND ORDER

     Police leadership must be influenced by any change in basic
philosophy. This is particularly true in the area of law and order.
One authority has stated that the terms are tautological and we shall
speak rather of law and disorder; (43) but in spite of possible redun-
dancy, there is an underlying difference of opinion as to what the law
is and to what degree it should be obeyed.
     Be that as it may, there are two schools of jurisprudence. One
emphasizes the law in its coercive aspects. This is the Positive
school, which looks to the power and might of the law. On the other
side are the natural law theorists, emphasizing rights and morality
existing beyond the law. The former emphasizes discipline and power,
while the latter espouses civil disobedience to unjust laws.
     In recent times we have seen undue reliance on both of these
schools. Many well-meaning people believe that the law is sacrosanct
and are not aware that as customs change so too must the law. Today's
avant garde is often tomorrow's conservative. Police administrators
must be able to perceive such change and deploy their efforts toward
community objectives which do not always coincide exactly with the
written law. On the other hand, there are those who demand rights,
duties and justice with little regard for that modicum of order without
which no one is safe.
     Unfortunately, American law has ignored philosophy and jurispru-
dence to a great extent. The Common Law tradition generally has been

antithetical toward a philosophy and science of the law. The English universities of early medieval times refused to teach the developing English law and instead taught the canon law of the Church. This forced the developing legal profession to develop the Inns of Court as a practical way of teaching the law as a kind of trade school, lacking the scholarly orientation of the university. (44) America's meagre contribution to the field has been with the Realistic school which emphasizes social science, technology and pragmatism. Justice Oliver Wendell Holmes was the champion of this emphasis, which believed that law is not a system of rules but rather a means of predicting what a judge may decide. This school rejects the traditions of Western civilization. (45) The continued growth of realistic jurisprudence espoused by John Chipman Gray, W. W. Cook, K. N. Llewellyn and Jerome Frank, in addition to Holmes, emphasizes that the law is what the judges say it is. This judicial absolutism has resulted in judicial activism and a lack of legal precedent.

The uncertainty and constant change in the law has made it very difficult for police administrators to understand and stay abreast of their field. However, recently we have seen a revival of the natural law which was overthrown in modern times with the rise of nationalism, capitalism, determinism and pragmatism. (46) Its revival is a result of the failure of modern society due to the lack of permanent values. The condemnation of the excesses of the modern Leviathans or superstates can be based only on the supremacy of natural laws. Thus the capture, trial and execution of Adolf Eichmann had no justification in any civil law, but rather depended on some code above and beyond the states.

This revival of natural law will be of great assistance to criminal justice, as was recognized some years ago by one outside observer who applauded this revival of order.

In recent years there has been a revival of natural law throughout the world. This revival has become well marked in the United States in the past decade... As both a creative ideal and as an ideal basis of criticism, under whatever name it is called and however we arrive at it, a picture of the purpose of the legal order must have a place of real importance in any system of science of law except in the hands of those who deny that there is any reality in systematic application of the force of politically organized society to the controversies and conflicting and overlapping claims and expectations of individuals or of those who consider law nothing but the holding down of the community by a socially or ecnomically dominant class in its own interest. For

those who hold such views there is no ideal element. Law is
merely organized force. (47)

TRAINING AND EDUCATION

The tremendous strides made in the training and education of police officers has blinded us to the fact that there are still many police
leaders whose primary qualification is seniority in the police service.
This liability will be overcome in time because of the pressing need
of the police for quality leadership. The vast amounts of funding and
the great number of scholarships bid fair to continually raise the level
of education. At the same time, the introduction of State training commissions and mandatory training programs will insure at least a minimum capability. Even the FBI Academy, however, does not fill the
void of quality training for police leaders. There is need for an institution of the calibre of the British Police College at Bramshill, which
has no equivalent in the United States. It has functioned for thirty
years to give a professional well-rounded training and education to
England's police superior officers.

The need for such an institution will continue to increase to such
an extent as to possibly seeing at least the groundwork for it by 1984.
(48) It may well be that the American Bramshill will be a broader
institution including all of the criminal justice system. Such an institution was urged by one writer, who asked for a West Point of Criminal Justice. (49)

In the education of our chiefs of police, there will exist the perennial problem of training the generalist or the specialist. There must
be a proper balance between police administrative expertise and societal moral values. For many years students of public administration
applauded the British generalist approach as opposed to the American
specialist emphasis. The former espoused the rank of the individual,
while the latter emphasizes the particular position that the individual
holds. Recently, however, Britain has been questioning the shortcomings of its own system. Yet there is a need for police chiefs,
indeed administrators generally, who have a knowledge of the broader
purposes of government in addition to their narrow professional specialty. (50) Thankfully, professional schools are now coming to realize
that many of their students will occupy positions outside of their narrow specialty and are amending curricula accordingly.

COURTS

The judicial system is exerting an ever more powerful influence on all phases of American life. The age-old legal problem of stability and precedent versus requisite change and progress has moved in the latter direction. The extension of the right of privacy, which privilege is not even mentioned in the Bill of Rights, will certainly affect police administration in coming years. (51) In addition, the judicial branch has become activist to the extent of becoming legislative and even executive in nature. For example, courts have literally taken over and also closed down schools. They have determined the staffing of mental hospitals, declared that cocaine is less harmful than tobacco or alcohol, decided on the amount and type of school discipline, etc.

The court takeover of schools, jails and hospitals has been through the use of the judicial power of contempt citation flowing from the Civil Rights Act of 1964 and the decision of the Warren Court. (52) This activism may be expected to continue, and police executives should expect it to affect police policy and operations. The judges openly admit that their judicial determinations are personal, based on conscience and gut reaction, which makes for difficulty in forecasting by administrators.

Class action suits may be expected to further influence police administrators. In a recent Philadelphia case the Federal court directed the setting up of machinery for police supervision and complaints. However, the United States Supreme Court determined that the judiciary cannot properly undertake such general operation of government. (53)

The multiple suits involving applicants for police positions have been determined by the job relatedness of the requirements. Police executives must have more than just a hunch or guess as to height, weight, age and sex requirements. They must be based on validated studies of operational necessity. (54) Psychological testing is another difficult area for the police and personnel administrators, where the job validation is even more difficult. (55) The perennial difficulty of public order versus individual security will, of course, continue to be a favorite subject of judicial decision.

All of the above indicates that police chiefs will require an ever-increasing knowledge of the law. The police executive must have some exposure to legal training or at least have available to him staff legal services of a calibre to deal with the changing judicial system.

ADMINISTRATIVE LAW

The police chief of the future will be more acquainted with the power of administrative law to achieve its criminal justice aim. The advantages of a system which emphasizes compliance with regulation through inspection rather than by criminal justice should be obvious.

Administrative law continues to grow as agencies proliferate and specialization continues. Since such agencies, unlike the courts, are not expected to be neutral arbiters but rather guardians of the public interest, the usual rules and procedures of the criminal courts do not apply. This permits more expeditious police action - the much-heralded proactive rather than reactive roles.

Knowledge of health, fire and building codes can be of great benefit to police administrators. Just as there are problem families in which many agencies of government must coordinate their efforts, so too there are problem locations in which various departments of an administration should cooperate.

The valuable executive tool of administrative regulation has been mostly ignored because of the compartmentalization of government, the specialization of knowledge and the desire not to take on too much; but has the public adopts a greater interest and knowledge of government, it will demand appropriate responses. In addition, as many areas of the law are decriminalized, there will be even greater demand for administrative regulation to prevent the development of public nuisances. The police chief of the future will be expected to have much greater knowledge and appreciation of this emerging management capability.

THE CHIEF

As in the business world, the trend in public administration is toward even larger departments. Even with the recent distrust of large impersonal organizations, whether political, academic or commercial, the trend is likely to continue. Therefore, managers of the future will require better education, particularly in the field of decision making. This will require some knowledge of systems analysis, organizational development and program evaluation and review techniques (PERT). (56) Computer technology will be available to chiefs of even the smallest departments in future years, but the police executive must have at least some knowledge of the capabilities and limitations of such technology. There will also be a greater need for knowledge in the social area in such subjects as psychology, human relations and behaviorism, as one observer noted a few years ago. (57)

The importance of the chief in any department has been perhaps greater than was formerly believed. The style of the chief is reflected in the type of organization and changes in policy. (58) The problem of police leadership, as with so many occupations, has been one of properly defining its role. Many chiefs have regarded themselves as the top cop and not as a criminal justice administrator, a misconception which is further confounded by the originally uncertain police model. Such chiefs want their subordinates to regard them as one embodying physical courage rather than administrative ability. (59)

Yet since the position of police chief is often one of political football, there is a need for some reasonable amount of tenure to bolster his courage in making administrative decisions. The serious ramifications of improper police leadership and the growing need for qualified people as agency directors has recently been further emphasized. (60)

The need for proper research to determine the proper relation be-between the chief executive and the police administrator is only becoming apparent apparent at the very moment that other forces are demanding a voice in police determination and decision making in criminal justice. (61) As between the chief and his superior, the guidelines as to policy should be determined at the time of the chief's selection. (62) This is not being done in most cases, but will be a practice in the future, as the present method which is dependent on local traditions and the personalities involved (63) can no longer be afforded.

While the qualifications of a police chief will depend on the size and needs of a particular department, there is general recognition of the need for broad education at the college level.

It can no longer be assumed that the affairs of a police department can be administrered effectively by a person whose single qualification is extensive police experience. With few exceptions, the completion of 4 years at a college or university is a minimum requirement for top administrative and staff positions in other branches of government. No less should be demanded of administrative and supervisory personnel in our police departments. (64)

The increasing importance of the police chief executive in the American community has recently been noted. The National Advisory Commission on Criminal Justice Standards and Goals recently recognized this position as the pivotal one to improve standards in the police field. (65) Thereafter, in 1973, the Police Chief Executive Committee was formed by the President of the International Association of Chiefs of Police, Francis B. Looney, to search for solutions to the problems confronting chiefs of police. The committee's mandate was to set guidelines for the selection of police chief executives and to develop further guidelines for the retention of those qualified. It was obviously necessary that such guidelines should apply only to future chiefs of police.

The importance of the eighteen standards promulgated by the committee suggests that there will be better and specific methods of selection with specific criteria as to personality traits, management skills, state standards, formal selection, adequate compensation, and determination of the relationship of the chief to his superiors in government.

The police chief of the future will emphasize values rather than technology. He will recognize that he is a decision maker rather than a police officer. He will concentrate on public service as opposed to law enforcement. His internal emphasis will be on employee relations as opposed to discipline. Lastly, his leadership will be innovative, responsible, honest and accountable.

NOTES AND REFERENCES

1. Charles N. Glaab and A. Theodore Brown, A History of Urban America (New York: Macmillan, 1967) p. 197.

2. The call for county government was echoed as early as 1946 by Edward W. Weidener, American Society for Public Administration The American County - Patchwork of Boards, Chicago, Illinois: (1946).

3. Charles Reith, A New Study of Police History (London: Oliver and Boyd, 1956), p. 251.

4. The difference between the two models is very well described by Patrick V. Murphy, President, Police Foundation, "The Development of the Urban Police," Current History, vol. 70, no. 417 (June 1976) pp. 245-48, 272-73.

5. Bruce Smith, Sr., Police Systems in the United States 2nd rev. ed. (New York: Harper and Brothers, 1960), pp. 105-106.

6. The myth of Catholic control of city corruption was exploded by Lincoln Steffens. His exposé of municipal corruption showed it to be under native American control for the most part. The Shame of the Cities (New York: Hill and Wang, 1960), p. 2-3.

7. Stephen M. David and Paul E. Peterson, ed. Urban Politics and Public Policy: The City in Crisis (New York: Praeger, 1973), pp. 238-47.

8. Upton Sinclair, The Jungle (Cambridge, Massachusetts: Robert Benchley, Inc., 1946). Lincoln Steffens, op. cit.

9. Luther Gulick, The National Institute of Public Administration: A Progress Report (New York: The National Institute of Public Administration).

10. See Harrington Emerson's "Twelve Principles of Efficiency," (The Engineering Magazine, New York, 1912).

11. Frederick Winslow Taylor, The Principles of Scientific Management (New York: Harper and Row, 1911).

12. Henri Fayol, Industrial and General Administration (London, 1930).

13. Samuel Walker, "The Urban Police in American History: A Review of the Literature," Journal of Police Science and Administration vol. 4, no. 3, pp. 252-60, 258.

14. Gene E. Carte and Elaine H. Carte, Police Reform in the United States: The Era of August Vollmer 1905-1932 (Berkeley and Los Angeles: University of California Press), p. 93.

15. William A. Westley, Violence and the Police: A Sociological Study of the Law, Custom and Morality (Cambridge, Massachusetts: The MIT Press, 1970), pp. 15-16.

16. See Louis Radalet, The Police and the Courts (Beverly Hills, Calif: Glencoe Press, 1973), p. 491. Also Michael J. Kelly, Police Chief Selection - a Handbook for Local Government, The Police Foundation, and International Management Association.

17. The President's Commission on Law Enforcement and the Administration of Justice, Task Force Report: The Police (Washington, D.C.: U.S. Government Printing Office, 1967), pp. 193-97.

18. Jerome H. Skolnick and Thomas C. Gray, ed., "ABA Standards for Criminal Justice Relating to the Urban Police Function," Police in America (Boston: Educational Associates, 1975), p. 292.

19. Herman Goldstein, Police Corruption - A Perspective on Its Nature and Control (The Police Foundation, 1975), p. 44.

20. Report of the National Advisory Commission on Civil Disorders, (Bantam, 1968), p. 311.

21. See Charles E. Gilbert, "The Shaping of Public Policy," The Annals, vol. 426 (July 1976), pp. 116-51.

22. Gary T. Marx, "Civil Disorders and the Agents of Social Change," Journal of Social Sciences, vol. 26 (1970), pp. 19-57.

23. The President's Commission on Law Enforcement and Administration of Justice, Task Force Report - The Police (Washington, D.C.: U.S. Government Printing Office, 1967), p. 62.

24. See "Symposium on Public Interest Representation" in Public Administration Review, vol. 37, no. 2 (March-April 1977), pp. 131-48.

25. National Advisory Commission on Civil Disorders, Report of the National Advisory Commission on Civil Disorders (Washington, D.C.: U.S. Government Printing Office, March 1968), p. 297.

26. William H. Whyte, Jr., in The Organization Man (Garden City, New York, 1956), clearly explains this problem.

27. The dangers of a managerial class were clearly pointed out by James Burnham, The Managerial Revolution (John Day Company, 1941).

28. Norval Morris, The Honest Politician's Guide to Crime Control (Chicago: University of Chicago Press, 1970).

29. Modern critical criminology, while Marxian, also continues the myth first propagated by Charles Beard that the Founding Fathers wrote the Constitution as a weapon favoring propertied interests in Economic Interpretations of the Constitution of the United States. For an exposition of the criminal theory see Richard Quinney, The Social Reality of Crime, (Boston: Little, Brown, 1970).

30. Jerome Hall, Theft Law and Society, 2nd ed. (Indianapolis: Bobbs-Merrill, 1952).

31. William H. Chambliss, "A Sociological Analysis of the Law of Vagrancy," Social Problems, Vol. 12, No. 1, Summer 1964, pp. 67-77 also C.J. Ribton-Turner, A History of Vagrants and Vagrancy (Montclair, New Jersey: Patterson Smith, 1972).

32. Gresham S. Sykes, "The Rise of Critical Criminology," Journal of Criminal Law and Criminology, vol. 65, no. 2 (June 1974), pp. 206-13.

33. The Republic of Plato, translated by Francis MacDonald Conford, (Oxford University Press, 1941), pp. 14-29.

34. The new penology has been advocated by Ernest van den Haag, Punishing Criminals (New York: Basic Books, Inc., 1975), and

Andrew von Hirsch, Doing Justice - the Choice of Punishments, Report of the Committee for the Study of Incarceration, (New York: Hill and Wang, 1976).

35.   Karl Menninger, M. D., Whatever Became of Sin? (New York: Hawthorne, 1973).

36.   Charles F. Reasons, "The Politicalization of Crime, the Criminal and the Criminologist," The Journal of Criminal Law and Criminology, vol. 64, no. 4 (December 1973), pp. 471-77.

37.   For an excellent review of victimology, see Chapter 10 of Stephen Schafer's Introduction to Criminology (Reston, Virginia: Reston Publishing Co., Inc., 1976).

38.   Dwight C. Smith, Jr., "Mafia: The Protypical Alien Conspiracy," The Annals, vol. 423 (January 1976), pp. 75-88.

39.   Donald R. Cressey, Theft of the Nation - The Structure and Operations of Organized Crime in America, (New York: Harper and Row, Harper Colophon Books, 1969), p. 22.

40.   The President's Commission on Law Enforcement and Administration of Justice, Task Force Report: Organized Crime, Washington, D. C.: U. S. Government Printing Office, 1967).

41.   National Advisory Commission on Criminal Justice Standards and Goals, Report of the Task Force on Organized Crime, (Washington, D. C.: U. S. Government Printing Office, 1976), p. 86.

42.   International Association of Chiefs of Police, The Police Yearbook, 1977 (Gaithersburg, Maryland, 1977), p. 342.

43.   Edward J. Bloustein, President of Rutgers University, in an address to the Annual Judges Dinner, Cherry Hill, New Jersey, September 1, 1972.

44.   Morris R. Cohen, Law and the Social Order (New York: Harcourt, Brace, 1933).

45.   The school is described by Denis Lloyd, The Idea of Law (Baltimore, Maryland: Penguin Books, 1964), pp. 213-17. It is critically evaluated by John H. Hallowell in Main Currents in Modern Political Thoughts (New York: Holt, Rinehart & Winston, 1950), pp. 358-67.

46.   Brendon F. Brown, The Natural Law Reader (New York:
       Oceana Publications, 1960).

47.   Roscoe Pound, Introduction, General Principles of Law, by
       Giorgio Del Vecchio, 1956, quoted by Brendon F. Brown, Ibid.,
       p. 21-22.

48.   The call for such an institution was recently sounded by Sam S.
       Souryal, "A Plausible Concept for Police·Leadership Education -
       The British (Bramshill) Model, " Journal of Police Science and
       Administration, vol. 4, no. 4, (1973), pp. 373-81.

49.   Roscoe Pound and Criminal Justice, ed. Sheldon Glueck, Nation-
       al Council on Crime and Delinquency (Dobbs Ferry, New York:
       Oceana Publications), Appendix by Glueck, pp. 255-58.

50.   The problem is treated very well by Don K. Price in American
       Public Administration, ed. Frederick C. Mosher (University,
       Alabama: The University of Alabama Press, 1975), pp. 238-43.

51.   The growing right of privacy has been fostered by four cases, in
       particular, in recent years.

           NAACP v. Alabama   357 U. S. 449 (1958)
           Griswold v. Connecticut   381 U. S. 479 (1965)
           Stanley v. Georgia   394 U. S. 557 (1969)
           Roe v. Wade   410 U. S. 113 (1973)

52.   New York Times, January 24, 1977, p. 50.

53.   Rizzo v. Goode, 96 S. Ct. 598 (1976).

54.   Thomas W. White, and Peter B. Bloch, Police Officer Height
       and Selected Aspects of Performance, Police Foundation and
       International Association of Chiefs of Police in cooperation with
       The Urban Institute, Police Foundation, (1975).

55.   John Furcon, Ernest C. Froemel, The Relationship of Selected
       Psychological Tests to Measures of Police Officer Job Perfor-
       mance in the State of Illinois, Industrial Relations Center (Chi-
       cago, Illinois: The University of Chicago, 1973).

56. Harry W. More, Jr., ed. Effective Police Administration: A Behavioral Approach, (San Jose, Calif: Justice Systems Development, Inc., 1975) passim.

58. Richard Quinney, The Social Reality of Crime (Boston: Little, Brown, 1970), pp. 118-20.

59. James F. Ahern, Police in Trouble (New York: Hawthorne, 1972), p. 78.

60. Introduction to The Police Chief Executive Report, A Report of the Police Chief Executive Committee of the International Association of Chiefs of Police (Washington, 1976).

61. The emerging public interest groups in criminal justice are well recognized, but not as apparent perhaps is the increasing militancy of police unions in demanding a voice in policy making.

62. The Police Chief Executive Report, op. cit., p. 63.

63. Michael J. Kelly, Police Chief Selection: A Handbook for Local Government, Police Foundation and International City Management Association, Police Foundation, 1975, p. 3.

64. The President's Commission on Law Enforcement and Administration of Justice, Task Force Report: The Police (Washington, D.C.: U.S. Government Printing Office, 1967), p. 127.

65. National Advisory Commission on Criminal Justice Standards and Goals, Police (Washington, D.C.: U.S. Government Printing Office, 1973).

15 Lateral Entry

William J. O'Rourke
James T. Nolan

Professions are singled out by their adherence to and embodiment of specific requirements. No matter how diverse the fields of professional endeavor are, they consistently come up to the following requirements.

1. A fund of knowledge.
2. Training facilities.
3. Admission standards.
4. Organization of Practitioners.
5. An ethical code
6. Self-regulation.
7. Mobility.

The fund of knowledge within a profession is usually the general knowledge of the area of endeavor. Within the general knowledge there are divisions of specialization, each comprising an integral part of the professional whole. There are areas of practice and research, but also areas of professional assistance. For example, within the medical profession there are specialists such as orthopedic surgeons, heart specialists and psychiatrists. There are also those who specialize in the research of medical problems, and those people who, through investigative research, are the providers of tools to assist the practicing specialists. Professionals are usually assisted by hordes of auxiliaries. Nurses, lab technicians, and x-ray technicians are the technical auxiliaries of the medical profession. The legal, business and military professions all have similar circumstances in regard to education and specialization. All professions are backed up by technicians or career assistants.

Training is one of the most fundamental aspects of a profession. It is that area where those entering the profession are initiated and trained in the area of general knowledge. Without a uniform training system any professional endeavor would cease to exist being professional. Expertise is highly developed and perpetuated by strict regimentation of intellectual exercise and expansive research.

Admission standards insure the high caliber of the professional elite. This elitism separates the various levels of a professional endeavor. Admission standards differ very much among doctors and nurses, lawyers and paralegals, officers and enlisted personnel in the military, and management and production personnel in business. Admission standards, along with training requirements, form a system of advancement into the upper echelons of any profession.

Organization of professional practitioners is extremely important in creating and maintaining the elitist upper echelons and forging unity throughout the profession. Without unity in training, admission standards and operations, professionalism would become fragmented into individual definitions of what the professional is in fact to be.

Ethics is the cement of all professional endeavors. It not only deals with the goals and aspirations of the profession, but also with the day-to-day activity of a functioning reality. However, ethics is written words, not actions, and words that are not acted upon are of no value. The action that makes ethics feasible is the self-imposed regulation of the individual practitioner, who by the force of his own will and dedication to the aspirations of the profession guarantees its continuance and success.

Mobility is, in all probability, the key mark of a professional. Mobility not only unifies professional application of a discipline, but enhances the discipline through varied experience and growth exposure. A doctor, lawyer or business administrator can work at or in their profession anywhere in the country at any time. There exist various systems of testing and licensing to act as a check on the qualifications of the mobile professional, such as bar exams, medical boards, and engineering boards. To the unqualified, these pose a great obstacle; to the qualified professional, they are a necessary hurdle.

Law enforcement is not a profession, despite all the high talk throughout the field. By the criteria set above, law enforcement falls far short of the established goal of professionalism. Growth of the law enforcement field has been sporadic, yet at certain levels in the field, there are those who approach the level of professionalism. But the overall fact is that there is no more professionalism in the law enforcement field than there exists a system within the Criminal Justice process. Those who have achieved a level of professionalism have done so on an individual basis. There is no uniformity or direction to what growth has occurred within the law enforcement field.

Law enforcement has been called a "profession" at all levels, from the police officer through the highest echelons of administration. Law enforcement has not yet - and seemingly refuses to - admit that there is a distinction between the "professional" and the "careerist" (tradesman) within the field. Police professionalism is the child of a rootless, half-hearted quest to upgrade the police service in the United States.

Let us now look at the criteria of professionalism as applied to law enforcement today.

1. Knowledge: There has been a growth in the number of Criminal Justice programs in American universities and colleges. Each curriculum however, is an independent entity, without an overall "discipline" or uniformity of approach. There is a dissimilarity in the overall scope of these programs, some being theoretical, others administrative or technical in nature.

2. Training Facilities: There are some training facilities established to go beyond the initial "police academy" training. The FBI National Academy, Southern Police Institute, Northwestern Traffic Institute all serve as examples of the trend toward more sophisticated police education.

    These higher educational facilities in the law enforcement field go beyond the "tradesman" level of police activity and into the managerial and administrative realms.

3. Admission Standards: In general, admission standards have been raised to varying levels, depending on the agency's requirements. Some agencies now require Bachelor degrees for initial employment or at least for promotion to upper administrative ranks. However, the majority of police agencies in the United States dictate their own requirements and most do not go much higher than the high school level.

4. Organization of Practitioners: In the field of law enforcement, many organizations have formed for various reasons. The International Association of Chiefs of Police, National Police and Prosecutors Institute, Eastern Armed Robbery Conference, Association of California Peace Officers and many others exist. However, no single organization is general in scope and embodies the entire law

enforcement field. Most are regional and limited to one area of
expertise, or are used as union type organizations for the benefit of the members.

5. Code of Ethics: In the law enforcement field, a more refined code
    of ethics seems to be evolving from various sources, including po-
    lice associations, departmental rules and regulations, and judi-
    cial and legal decisions.

6. Self-regulation: Due to the strict eye of public scrutiny and the
    organizational discipline, the self-regulation in law enforcement,
    which still being important, is minimized. This minimization is
    in large part the effect of the law enforcement field being a truly
    organizational endeavor, with virtually no individual practitioners
    existing independent of an organization.

7. Mobility: For the most part, mobility within the law enforcement
    field is limited to the high ranking administrators or to the lowest
    entry level. There is virtually no movement laterally within the
    middle management or specialized areas of the field without loss
    of accrued service time or benefits.

American law enforcement has grown up only since the late 1940s,
when the "professionals," of the caliber of Orlando W. Wilson first
instituted extensive training, education, and forward thinking into the
field. However, progress was exceedingly slow through the 1950s and
the early 1960s. With the advent of the civil rights movement, the police were not only thrown into the limelight, but were very much on the
spot. By 1965, urban riots erupted and continued to erupt through the
year 1969. The results of urban riots, the Vietnam war protest, and
a great amount of social upheaval was the panic of the people and the
loud lamenting behavior of the police and the politicians in the country.
money, money and more money was poured into the police system.
Money bought cars, tear gas, riot helmets and other hardware, of
which the police were in short supply. Also, the high talk of professionalism was spoken often and loudly. More and more police officers
earned college degrees, and several police departments required degrees for hiring and/or promotion. Yet the police and the critics of the
police missed the most vital point of the professional impetus, that
police work is not and cannot be "professionalized" without corresponding radical rearrangement of the police service in the United States.
    During the periods of upheaval, the quasi-professional police ad-
ministrator came into his own. Top flight professional leadership be-

gan to move, from department to department, from the field to the
ivory tower, from the closed police system into the working outside
world. Riot, disorder and demonstrations also pushed many men out
of the urban police world, with its stresses and strains to the less
strenuous conditions of the suburban and rural settings. Lateral entry was an idea that had been "kicked around" a great deal, but put to
little use except in some individual cases involving high ranking adminis
trators. The concept was originally put forward to bring the police out
of their closed society and into the mainstream of our democratic free
enterprise system.

The early police agencies were very often corrupt arms of the pre-
vailing political machines. The job of a police officer was a political
appointment used as a reward for faithful service to the party machine.
It didn't take long for the abusive system to fall prey to the reformers
of the day. The most durable reform that resulted from the purge was
the civil service system, which indeed cleansed many of the police hiring practices, but also perpetuated the closed system in which the police lived, a system so closed as to be almost feudal in nature.

Mobility, being a key mark of the professional, is also a strong
attribute of the tradesman in our free enterprise system. Americans
are the most highly mobile society in the history of mankind. This
mobility, and the constant change and influx of new blood, greatly
enhanced the growth of American law, industry and science. Yet,
amid the mobility and freshness of American life, a stale, stagnant
subsociety of police is charged with the awesome responsibility of protecting and serving the society as a whole.

Out of the turmoil of the 1960s and the sporadic growth of the law
enforcement field, one concept has especially been the most talked
about and least acted on, that being lateral entry. Lateral entry is
defined as "the appointment of administrative, professional and technical (A. P. T.) personnel at compensation levels above normal entrance
levels, from outside existing local, state and federal organizations."
Further defined by Title 11, Chapter 2 of the Administrative Code of
the State of California, (revised September 15, 1976), Section 1001
(K), "lateral entry" refers to the appointment of an officer whose appointment is based upon special qualifications and/or experience in
the law enforcement field.

The first definition presented is of a much wider scope than the
one put forward by the Administrative Code of California. Accordingly, under Professor Hewitt's definition, hiring a person "from outside existing local, state and federal organizations," could encompass
anyone of administrative, professional or technical expertise, not
necessarily in the law enforcement field, whereas the California Code

definition seemingly would be limited to those from the law enforcement field alone.

Therefore, it stands to reason that "lateral entry" can be used to
create mobility that would foster professionalism and open the doors of
a closed system, or that lateral entry can be used to fill a need for
personnel with certain expertise within a closed system. Despite all
the advantages that can be argued about lateral entry, those in the law
enforcement field must decide from the onset whether they desire "professionalism" or "careerism."

Later on in this chapter we will discuss the implications of professionalism that are advanced by the full, open use of lateral entry.
However, at this point, let us look at lateral entry, where it came
from, how it has been implemented, and its contemporary usage.

Literature on the subject of lateral entry is not abundant. The
main publications available are as follows:

1.   Report on Lateral Entry prepared by Professor William H. Hewitt,
     Sr., for "The President's Commission on Law Enforcement and
     the Administration of Justice," 1967.

2.   Professor William H. Hewitt, Sr., "New Directions in Police
     Personnel Administration," Lexington Books, D.C. Heath and
     Company, Lexington, Massachusetts, 1975.

3.   "Portable Police Pensions - Improving Inter-Agency Transfers,"
     by Geoffrey N. Calvert, (U.S. Government Printing Office), 1971.

4.   "Report of the National Commission on Criminal Justice Standards
     and Goals," Governor Russell W. Peterson of Delaware, Chair-
     man.

5.   "Lateral Energy for California Law Enforcement," a report by
     The Commission on Peace Officer Standards and Training, State
     of California, Glen E. Fine and Richard A. Baratta, authors,
     1969.

The above works deal in depth with lateral entry and its proposed
uses in American law enforcement. Professor Hewitt's works offer
the most definitive writing on the subject to date. Let us now briefly
summarize the above reports. Some of these explore in detail the
technicalities of law and finance that would have to be considered before implementing any plan that provided lateral entry in law enforcement.

A summary of Professor Hewitt's report on lateral entry to The President's Commission on Law Enforcement and the Administration of Justice reviews the history of police personnel administration, the spoils system, civil service, the reform movement, and the development of an open career police service. The report points out that 95 percent of all police executives have worked for only one unit of government. The possibility of using a career service similar to the military is mentioned. The Federal Government now permits Federal employees leave (without pay) to work in local and State posts. Temporary Federal employment is also provided for state and local employees. Obviously, this is a step to provide a more diversified experience for persons in local, State and Federal employ.

In 1961, the Public Personnel Association conducted research concerning lateral entry and mobility, to determine how many states had positive legislation relating to this problem. The findings were not encouraging, particularly in regard to lateral entry. The research committee reported that greater interchange should be encouraged to increase lateral entry and mobility. The advantages and problems involved in lateral entry, as reported by the committee, are listed as follows:

Advantages:

1. Enhances mobility of professional, administrative and technical personnel.

2. Mitigates inbreeding tendencies.

3. Increases opportunities of maximum individual development in service.

4. Encourages sharing of experiences and the search for solutions to common problems.

5. Provides a way to meet short term emergency needs for a particular skill.

6. Improves relations and creates a climate for cooperation between those within and without public service.

Problems:

1. Limited participation by public jurisdictions because of legal and/or policy obstacles.

2. Suspension or loss of employee rights and benefits.

3. Possible loss of promotional and other career opportunities.

4. Payment of travel, moving and other expenses and allowances.

5. Fear of having better employees "pirated."

6. Inability to perform official acts.

7. Disruption of work operations; also inertia of management.

In summing up the advantages and problems of an exchange program, Dr. William J. Ronan, former Secretary to the Governor of New York, had the following to say:

Despite the conviction on the part of most leaders in public personnel management that these employment interchanges are both useful and important, there is relatively little interchange. There are technical and housekeeping obstacles, but the biggest hurdle has been inertia on the part of management. Interchange as an abstraction is fine, but if it means disrupting the routines of personnel management it all too often has been avoided. What is needed is a genuine desire on the part of management to effect a workable program of exchange.

The report to the President's Commission stated that "Only through the achievement of a career corps of professional executives with a sound education, with a variety of experience, and with a government perspective, can law enforcement hope to cope with its tasks.

"The movement of career police personnel within and between jurisdictions is a vital element of the larger and urgent objective - the best possible staffing of a rapidly expanding police service."

The report lists over 28 leading police administrators who support the concept of lateral entry for law enforcement. Among those listed are the late O.W. Wilson, V.A. Leonard, and Clarence Kelly, former Director of the F.B.I. The committee did qualify its endorsement of lateral entry by stating in the report that lateral entry should be used only when and where necessary.

Mention is made of the fact that lateral entry is used in Europe, at least to the extent that non-police personnel are allowed to enter

the police service as lieutenants, captains, and chiefs. It is also mentioned that "closed" civil service systems tend to breed mediocrity, sterility, isolation, and insulation or self-protection.
The report cited the following advantages of lateral entry.

1. Attracts professional personnel
2. Develops a fresh point of view
3. Saves training time
4. Bolsters management and technical strength
5. Disturbs the status quo, thereby avoiding complacency
6. Is easier to measure executive performance
7. Creates better understanding of law enforcement affairs
8. Offers personal advantages to the individual

Obstacles to the adoption of lateral entry were also listed as follows:

1. Promotion from within - defense mechanism
2. Residence requirements - restrictive
3. Qualification standards - may be unrealistic
4. Veterans preference - disruptive
5. Lack of career planning
6. Fear of favoritism
7. Retirement rights
8. Lack of mobility in law enforcement
9. Pay (low, varied, etc.)
10. Low prestige
11. Limited opportunities for advancement
12. Diversity of employment systems
13. Conflict of interest statutes
14. Limited funds for personnel administration
15. Inadequate information on job opportunities
16. Discrimination
17. Inconvenience
18. Background investigation (out-of-towner, etc.)

The report continued to cite the opinions of many experts on public administration, all of whom advocated open systems that included lateral entry, mobility and a national career concept. Rotation, goal displacement, mobility, and lateral entry were discussed and opinions, both pro and con, on these subjects were offered.

Recommendations:

1. Recruitment at colleges with adoption of the military junior officer concept.

2. Positive nationwide recruitment for administrative, professional and technical personnel.

3. Financial assistance to those who move (paid by receiving agency).

4. Demand upon all American citizens for quality professional personnel to serve in their police agencies.

5. Withholding Federal funds from any law enforcement agency not engaging in positive lateral entry recruitment.

6. Interchange programs with other police agencies and universities.

7. Rapid promotion for degree holders to encourage lateral entry.

8. Elimination of all barriers to an "open" civil service system.

The recommendations and conclusions offered by Professor Hewitt on lateral entry and mobility were generally adopted by the President's Commission and incorporated into the commission's report.

The booklet, Portable Police Pensions - Improving Inter-agency Transfers, prepared by Geoffrey N. Calvert for the National Institute for Law Enforcement and Criminal Justice, dwells on one of the main obstacles to latery entry in law enforcement, namely the lack of reciprocity among police pension plans.

A number of states have created State pension systems, but only the State of Washington has swept aside all local pension plans and incorporated all law enforcement officers into one plan. This permits policemen to transfer from their present agencies to any other police agency within the State of Washington without loss of benefits. The authors conclude that this system should be adopted by the other 49 states. This would increase mobility within each state; however, there is still the problem of interstate transfers.

Several states, including New Jersey, New York, and Texas, have statewide pension systems; however, usually there is at least one large city that is not included in the State pension plan.

Various ways of resolving the problem are considered by Calvert, including improved vesting provisions, a central retirement system patterned after the Railroad Retirement system, a plan similar to the Teachers Insurance and Annuities Association (T. I. A. A.), and other solutions.

After detailed exploration of the various plans, the report recommended that the best solution would be a two-step plan that would have every state set up a retirement system for all enforcement officers within that particular state. The second step would be to set up a system of reciprocity between the 50 states.

The most noteworthy public comment on lateral entry was issued by the National Commission on Criminal Justice Standards and Goals. Former Governor Russell W. Peterson of Delaware was the chairman of the commission. The commission recommendations relating to lateral entry were summed up as the following by Crime Control Digest:

If the opportunity for lateral movement within the law enforcement profession were enhanced, manpower would be used more efficiently with commensurate benefit accruing to individual agencies and professions as a whole. Lateral entry is particularly promising in selecting the police chief executive and in adding minority officers to the ranks.

Before the full benefits of lateral mobility can be realized, certain dynamic changes must be made within the police service. Among the necessary changes is the elimination of the overly restrictive residency requirements and of civil service restrictions on eligibility for entry-level and advance positions. Additionally, state and national provisions must be made for transferring retirement pensions and other fringe benefits so that those who desire to move laterally do not suffer financially.

Personnel should be recruited for lateral entry at any level from outside police agencies when it is necessary to do so in order to obtain the services of individuals who are qualified for a position or assignment.

Now that we have reviewed these reports concerning lateral entry, it would be proper that we look into some statistical evidence of its use in the United States today.

Prior to looking into various surveys conducted on the subject of lateral entry, we shall look to the state of California. Lateral entry, however limited in application, is much better received in that state than anywhere else in the United States.

We have already stated that, in order to meet the aspirations of professionalism, certain definite characteristics must be met.

Historically, government has sought leaders from without to serve in special positions. The American people, in fact, laterally transfer men from civilian private leadership to government, such as representatives, senators, governors and presidents. The Presidential Cabinet is made up through lateral entrance as are city and town managers and a good number of various departmental heads.

In California, the first real moves to lateral entry began in the 1950s when California law enforcement was moving into an era where merit was becoming the rule rather than the exception. Farsighted police officers began the tedious job of improving the status, prestige and service of the police craft for the time where it would be accepted as one of the professions. They quickly realized that certain earmarks of a profession must be met. They saw that professions required adherence to a code of ethics, years of educational preparation, and a uniform set of standards against which the professional practitioner could be measured. They noted that professionals, once enlightened and accepted as such, were not limited to practice in any given geographic locality. Thus, lateral mobility was recognized early as a prerequisite for professionalization of the police service.

Peace officers from northern, central and southern California formed the Peace Officers Research Association of California, an organization dedicated to professionalizing the police service. Working with the California Peace Officers Association, they drafted a code of ethics for peace officers that has since been adopted by the police service throughout the nation. A program for the establishment of uniform minimum standards was taken to the legislature, and out of it the California Commission on Peace Officers Standards and Training came into being.

After establishing minimum standards for employment, the commission organized police science and related courses in educational institutions throughout the state. Jurisdictions were encouraged to participate in the P. O. S. T. (Peace Officer Standards and Training) program through reimbursements through the cities and counties for a portion of the trainees' salaries and other expenses. Certificates based upon education, training and experience were issued by the commission to individuals who qualify. The certificates constituted a recognized standard of achievement and removed what was once a very basic obstacle to lateral entry. There now exist standards which attest to a peace officer's standards for selection, his experience and his achievements in education and training. An experienced peace officer, who holds one of these P. O. S. T. certificates (basic, intermediate or advanced), may be presumed capable of performing the police job at a predictable level of proficiency.

When some of the early certificate holders moved from one police agency to another, the appointing authorities were pleased to discover that the certificate attested to certain levels of training and that they were saved the expense of retraining. These savings could be returned in the form of higher starting salaries. The higher starting salaries would be in turn used as a recruitment inducement. The police career attracts many qualified, capable men, but unfortunately, the capable and good men soon become disillusioned by the fact that there is no predictable career line within the police service. This lack of career satisfaction, assurance and advancement causes a great deal of frustration amongst those in the law enforcement field. This frustration, in turn, inhibits drive and in many cases compels some good men to leave the police service.

In the 1960-61 PORAC Survey it became quite clear that lateral entry other than on a loan basis was virtually nonexistent. What lateral movement did occur was limited to the higher echelon police managers and administrators. The second survey, conducted in 1966 by PORAC of peace officers in the state of California, is a look into the individual officer's attitude toward lateral entry. The survey did indicate that a majority of police officers felt that lateral entry would enhance the professionalization of the police service as well as that of the individual police officer.

The third survey, done by PORAC in 1969, of police administrators in California, indicated that lateral entry had in fact become somewhat of a reality in that state. In a letter to the Bureau of Police of Wilmington, Delaware from Glen E. Fine, Bureau of Chief, Special Project Bureau, California Peace Officers Standard and Training Commission, dated 9 June 1977, he stated "there is currently a great deal of lateral mobility in California at the police officer and chief of police levels. Mobility at the police officer level has steadily increased because of the standardized basic training requirements."

The Wilmington Bureau of Police, Wilmington, Delaware, conducted a sample survey throughout the United States in early 1977, the results of which indicate that outside of California and a few isolated locations, such as Mecklenburg County, South Carolina, lateral entry is a dormant subject.

These aforementioned surveys are an indication of the state of American police services and the governments that support them. The following comment, the author feels, will put light on the situation regarding lateral entry:

1. Lateral entry between police departments is very rare. It must
    be asked why. The answers are many-sided; however, the prin-
    cipal cause is a severe lack of leadership on the part of police
    administrators and government officials. The police, especially,
    are to blame for an ingrained protective attitude toward their
    field of endeavor. One of the "traditional" functions of the police
    is the maintain the status quo. This seems to rub off on a police
    service itself. The status quo of the police service is not being
    maintained, nor is the status of the police service progressing.
    Rather, it would appear that the police service in the United
    States is beginning to regress back to a time of laissez-faire ser-
    vice, lead by tenured seniorcrats and protective of its closed
    sheltered position.

2. Tradition is against lateral transfer. Police systems are closed,
    sheltered worlds, unto themselves. While hiring and promotion
    procedures were implemented to clean up and stabilize the police
    systems in the early part of the 20th century, they are in effect
    destroying any chance of advancement in the police service field.
    This stagnation will kill any idea of professionalism that exists in
    the hearts and minds of policemen. Traditionalism on the part of
    the American people also bears a great responsibility for the re-
    tardation of police service growth in the latter 20th century.
    Americans have always been traditionalists and have always be-
    come uneasy at innovations such as the income tax, the fulltime
    standing army and navy, increased overall federal power and
    social security.

3. Reluctance of the police to move has a negative effect on lateral
    entry. An individual officer might well be dissatisfied with his
    lot within the organization he belongs to, yet if given the oppor-
    tunity to move, he might not. This reluctance is due mainly to
    the loss of security and the fear of the unknown. Cloisterism is
    the death of initiative; security is the blanket of the grave into
    which the police service is burying itself. The fact that some or
    many officers will be reluctant to move is no reason for the main-
    tenance of a system that denies mobility. This is another key to
    unlocking the door of professionalism in the United States. Every
    officer, from patrolman to chief, is locked into the same system.
    We have failed to recognize and to take advantage of the differen-
    ces between movers and nonmovers.

4. The surrender of pension rights all but eliminates lateral entry
    possibilities. The police service, as we have already emphasi-
    zed, is a closed system to which pension rights is the key that
    locks the door. There are not many advantages to a police career,
    but one advantage does exist; that is the promise of an early re-
    tirement. The key of freedom in later years is also the enslaver
    of the in-service time for any police officer. Nothing short of a
    complete overhaul of the police pension system, to allow unifor-
    mity of application and mobility of personnel, should be maintain-
    ed by the police service in the United States.

5. An organization is no better than the people serving it. If the po-
    lice service, by its nature and regiment, retards personal growth
    experience and education, it stands to reason that the service it-
    self will suffer. The police service makes up a large part of
    governmental operation in the United States, yet with few excep-
    tions, no career development exists. Policemen have no direc-
    tion for their career aside from advancing in order to gain higher
    monetary rewards. The advancement is required regardless of
    qualifications, thus creating the realm of mediocrity in the ser-
    vice. Lateral entry would foster a system designed for the better-
    ment of the individual and the organization.

6. History has demonstrated promotion only from within does not pro-
    duce the quality needed among key administrative, professional
    and technical personnel. It would seem futile for a closed, in-
    bred, narrow-minded organization to attempt to deal with the
    dynamics and outlook of an open society. To simply lock educa-
    ted, forward-thinking and capable men into a closed system de-
    feats the purpose of higher educational requirements and initia-
    tive.

7. The average police executive has considerably less varied ex-
    perience than his counterpart in private business. Yet this po-
    lice executive bears some of the heaviest burdens of responsi-
    bility in the every day function of government and of society.
    The closed system is indicative of the closed minds that run it.
    A system of mobility and expanded growth experience would
    seemingly force new light into the world of law enforcement. A
    new light and perspective could work miracles for the efficiency
    of any police agency.

8. Whatever the possibilities of interchange of personnel among po-
    lice jurisdictions, the basic kind of mobility required is that which

leads to the development of career generalists within the police
service. Those in American law enforcement have failed to
recognize that necessary balance between generalists and specialists, operational and administrative functions, careerists and
professionals. Again they must fall back to a previous statement
about the severe lack of professional qualifications and career
development in the police service. These problems will remain
to plague the police service until it opens up to new thought, new
systems, and new freedom of development. Police jurisdictions
are very old, outmoded, inefficient, political subdivisions. The
police service concept of a closed society is equally outmoded.
Mobility, education, and experimentation will supply the initiative for the goal of reshaping and "growing up" of the police service.

9.   Law enforcement personnel problems will not be solved until
      the problem of low prestige of the police service is surmounted.
      Since law enforcement is wrapped up in a cocoon of protective
      isolationism, how the police see themselves is greatly distorted
      by how they are seen by others. Despite all the talk of raising
      salaries, raising expectations, and raising education in the police
      service, the prestige has peaked and now due largely to inaction
      on the part of the police, is slowly slipping back down. This
      slippage is also due to the relative calm of our time, the return
      to "normalcy" that has set in since the mid-seventies.

10.   Police personnel mobility will include all long term permanent
      interchange, as well as short term, special purpose interchange.
      The lateral entry concept not only makes leaving, or joining a
      police agency, more readily achieved, but extremely enhances
      interchange of people and ideas on a short term basis between po-
      lice agencies. Lateral "loan" would greatly benefit smaller agen-
      cies in obtaining help and advice where, when and how needed,
      from larger agencies which are more free to develop expertise
      among personnel.

11.   Current personnel practices of law enforcement prevent acquisi-
      tion of new blood at intermediate levels by rigid rules, archaic
      civil service regulations, and promotion from within on the basis
      of tenure rather than merit, thus pushing mediocre quality up-
      ward. An entirely new process for selection, training and ad-
      vancement in the police service must be created to meet the
      challenge of the future. The police officer, as well as the police

system, must be given a shot in the arm. A system that fulfills the needs of the service and of the individual must be created. New directions of career development must be initiated to draw upon the strengths and aspirations of the individual, and by so doing strengthen the organization and bolster it to more readily meet its aspirations and responsibilities. There is a noticeable lack of well-planned, forward-looking programs to secure and retain qualified personnel for the police service.

12. The mobility concept can be employed quite effectively as a training and development process with police employees, particularly so for lower and middle-level managers. As studies have shown, more lateral entry is employed at the police chief level. However, while many agencies actively seek higher echelon managers, few seek to train and develop middle management.

Looking beyond 1984, the surveys indicate that the concept of lateral entry will continue to make limited progress. It will take further professionalization or perhaps union pressure to make viable progress for a concept which will do much to improve policing in America.

16 From Minority Recruitment to Professionalization: New Directions in Criminal Justice

Linda L. Stabile

One of the main issues in the criminal justice system of today is that of minority recruitment. Yet given current progress in this area, minority recruitment, selection, and utilization beyond 1984, will be of lesser importance. The issue then will be one of professionalization. Reform leading to the achievement of a more efficient and effective criminal justice system will be found, not in personnel divisions, but in organizational administration and management.

For the past decade, the criminal justice system (namely, police, courts, and corrections) has been legitimately concerned with minority recruitment. The impact of the civil rights and women's liberation movements have made affirmative action a reality. This is demonstrated by the laws which are changing discriminatory employment practices. While white males still dominate the criminal justice system, increasing numbers of females and minorities are gaining entrance. The evidence indicates that eventual correction of the problem is inevitable. By 1984 or thereabouts, the problem will have been essentially solved - at least, it will not be an issue. The minority representation in all agencies of the criminal justice system will lead to the broader concern of professionalization - either on account of the influx of new ideas from these minorities or the need for new standards by which to select personnel.

Professionalization must be distinguished from professionalism. Professionalization is the development of a calling which requires specialized knowledge and intensive academic preparation, used for the purpose of serving others; in other words, professionalization is the "development" of professionals. Professionalism, on the other hand, is the "use" of professionals. In this paper, we make the case that professionalism is reflected by court and corrections treatment personnel,

and that professionalization is needed by police and corrections custody officers. Criminal justice professionalization will be essential
toward the end of the century because society will require it.

Society will be requiring a criminal justice system that has three
main components of positive relations with the community: representativeness, responsiveness, and efficiency. (1) The system has been
achieving "representativeness" where members of all ethnic, racial,
and sexual groups occupy all levels of positions in the organizations.
The system is also in the process of attempting to provide "responsiveness" to the various community demands; this is being accomplished by its increasing emphasis on more highly educated practitioners who can devise more realistic approaches to requests for service delivery. Beyond 1984, the issue will be that of "efficiency" or
improved organizational effectiveness. This will be achieved through
professionalization of the various organizations - of police, court,
and corrections. To develop the above themes, an examination of the
history of the acceptance of minorities is presented. From there, we
reveal the current state of professionalism and nonprofessionalism in
the criminal justice system. Finally, we view the future as the
achievement of total professionalization.

REPRESENTATIVENESS:
MINORITY RECRUITMENT

Minorities and women are constituting noticeable percentages of
criminal justice personnel: representativeness of the criminal justice system has been addressed above. Racial minorities and women
have been the last in line to enter these occupations, but they certainly have not been the only ones to experience the effects of discrimination. A brief review of history allows us to see the progress made,
however slow it may seem, in the achievement of the representativeness of the criminal justice system relative to the population being
served.

The history of minority groups in the criminal justice system
closely follows the political history of this country. In colonial times,
communities experienced little tension and few disputes over the administration of justice; the members of the communities were the
criminal justice system. The many different national groups immi-
grating to America settled in separate sections of the country. They
maintained close-knit societies bound together by agreed-upon standards and laws which were perpetuated in the moral and ethical pre-

cepts taught by family, church, and school.

However, in the early nineteenth century, the country changed from a predominantly rural to an urban society, causing an intermingling of the many different groups in the metropolitan areas. Consequently, tension arose between these ethnic groups and the dominant power structure. They rebelled against being treated as "second-class citizens," and despite the obstacles, the many nationalities (Irish, German, etc.) began to achieve status and prosperity in occupational and social spheres. Over time, they became assimilated into the national population. (2) They entered occupations in the criminal justice system, as evidenced by the predominance of some ethnic groups (particularly the Irish) in many police departments.

Although the various ethnic immigrants could change their names and lose their accents to become assimilated, other groups (notably blacks) have experienced, largely due to their color, more difficulties in transition. It has taken unified political action in the form of the civil rights movement, due to which, during the past thirty years, racial minorities have begun prospering in the political and economic realms of society. Increasing numbers of these minorities are being represented in all phases of the criminal justice system - as police officers and officials, as lawyers and judges, as probation officers, corrections officers, and superintendents (wardens). Yet this has not been without a struggle, much of which has been carried out in the courts.

A brief legal analysis of these court decisions summarizes equal opportunity gains not only for racial minorities, but also for women. The problems have been more acute for employment as police and corrections custody personnel who are nonprofessional than for employment as court and corrections treatment personnel who are professional. The latter solely rely on academic credentials, no matter what racial, ethnic, or sexual characteristics are displayed. However, the former rely on physical characteristics, many of which tend to exclude specific groups of people.

Title VII of the Civil Rights Act of 1964, as amended by the Equal Employment Opportunity Act of 1972, prohibits "discrimination on the basis of race, creed, color, sex or national origin with regard to compensation, terms, and conditions or privileges of employment." The 1972 amendments extended coverage of the act to public employers, including police departments and corrections institutions. Because of the technicalities involved in utilizing Title VII, attorneys for a plaintiff frequently rely on constitutional grounds as the basis for the suit. Individual jurisdictions have been feeling the impact of these suits and, as a result, have set hiring goals for blacks and for women.

Furthermore, the Law Enforcement Assistance Administration

(LEAA), created by the Federal government to provide financial assistance to police departments, courts, juvenile agencies, corrections
institutions, and drug treatment programs, prohibits its grant recipients from discrimination in hiring on account of race, creed, color,
sex or national origin. Sets of guidelines require that analysis be
made of representation of blacks and women in all job categories, including an assessment of recruitment and selection practices, seniority practices, promotion procedures, training programs, and a determination of whether employment is being hindered by "external factors."
     The resultant court decisions and LEAA regulations have caused
police and corrections agencies to change certain conditions for employment. Challenged, to date, have been written tests, particularly intelligence tests (on the grounds of discrimination against blacks); and
physical qualifications such as minimum height and weight requirements and physical agility tests of strength and endurance (on the grounds
of discrimination against women). (3)
     This history, simplified as it is, demonstrates that inroads have
been made on the problem of minority representation in the criminal
justice system. Although the system has become representative of
the community it serves, the various components still are faced, to
greater and lesser degrees, with their failure to adequately perform
their legitimate functions. Thus the issue becomes one not of minority
recruitment, but of organizational administration and management
directed toward the fostering of professionalization.

RESPONSIVENESS: A MOVEMENT
TOWARD PROFESSIONALIZATION

     While representativeness of the criminal justice system has al-
ready been addressed, responsiveness to the community (or society at
large) and the client (or the offender) is being undertaken in varying
degrees by the different agencies of the criminal justice system. At
first glance, there is an inherent conflict in a process designed to simi-
ltaneously provide societal safety and insure offenders' rights, but
under the American system, both must be done. Required is a professional approach to the seeming dilemma - that is, one of fair and impartial administration of justice by highly educated individuals interested in developing more efficient and effective ways to serve the general
public. This professionalism, at the present time, exists in the court
system and in a part of the corrections system (the treatment portion).
It does not exist for the police or for corrections custody personnel.
This section of the paper examines two issues: 1) the current level of

professionalism demonstrated by the court and by treatment corrections; and 2) the specific actions taken toward professionalization by
the police and by custody corrections.

Current Professionalism

Professionalism, at the current time, exists in the court system and in the treatment portion of the corrections system. Professionalism exists because of the level of training required, and the
flattened organizational structure which permits the various specialized personnel to interact on the same level.

Virtually all members of the court system are lawyers. Their
education, in the majority of states, consists of a minimum completion of three years of college work and graduation from a law school
approved by the American Bar Association or proper State authorities.
Admission to the bar of a state is generally achieved by passing a
written examination. (4) The effect of this educational experience is
exposure to the various constitutions, statutes, and cases which structure legal authority. Written law gives structure to activities as it
specifies that conduct which is criminal, the maximum and minimum
punishments to be imposed for such conduct, the procedures to be
followed by the formal criminal justice machinery in processing the
offender, and particular problems of interpretation of laws. Within
the confines of this structure, however, considerable discretion is
exercised by the various personnel.

As highly educated individuals, members of the court system
practice considerable discretion at many decision points in the administration of criminal justice. The prosecuting attorney has the
power to charge or not to charge the arrested individual with a crime.
The defense attorney has the power to present all the relevant facts
and circumstances in his client's defense and to maintain the obligation of privileged communication or a confidential relationship. The
judge governs the decisions and actions of others (victim, accused,
prosecutor, defense attorney, witnesses, jurors, spectators) by his
immediate rulings on all kinds of legal controversy and by his own
attitude toward particular crimes. He serves as the arbiter in the
process of trying and determining facts for the purpose of insuring
that the proceedings against the accused are conducted fairly and
within the rules of adjudicary process. (5)

A more recent trend is that of professional court administration,
the management of the nonjudicial business of a court or a system of
courts. Court administrators are usually appointed by the judges of

the court and have had legal training and prior court-related employment. These positions are obtained through career advancement and
by lateral transfer. (6)

While the court system employs professionals from one particular discipline, law, the corrections system employs professionals
from many disciplines. They are hired to perform a variety of
specialized functions, from maintaining specified living conditions to
providing personalized contacts with individual offenders. The maintenance of certain standards of living is provided by such diverse
specialists as psychiatrists, psychologists, social workers, rehabilitation counselors, recreation counselors, academic and vocational
teachers, lawyers, librarians, nurses, dentists, physicians, chaplains,
and vocational counselors. While graduate study achievements are a
prerequisite to such employment, completion of doctoral work and
even postdoctoral study is quite common. For the corrections manpower who work primarily with individual offenders, an undergraduate
degree is often acceptable. The positions include case managers,
institutional counselors, parole agents, and probation officers. The
preferred educational areas are psychology, sociology, social work,
education, public administration, and, in recent years, criminology
and criminal justice. (7) These various individuals, although each
performs a particular specialty, work together, exercising much discretion.

The psychologist is the dominant force in the classification process because intelligence tests and other measurements are aids in
classification and treatment decisions. The sociologist is especially
adept in identifying and developing the roles and structures of the prison subcultures and the administrative personnel. Many of the current research projects in prisons and other areas of corrections treatment are being directed by sociologists, the findings and recommendations of which are helping to push corrections back into the community.
Sociologists have also worked their way into administrative positions
in the agencies. The social work profession - as represented by the
caseworker, who is essential in the presentence investigation phase
as well as the probation and parole officers - has become more involved in institutional programs as the emphasis has shifted toward
treatment. (S)he has training to help the offender adapt to the prison
situation inside the walls by capitalizing on the constructive elements
in the prison experience. (8)

Rehabilitation is considered the ultimate goal of the corrections
institution. Various occupational specialties work together to develop
programs for the prison population in education, vocation, and individual counseling so that the criminal can return to society and a normal life. Supporting this effort are those probation and parole officers

who, outside the institution, assist persons on probation and parole
in readjustment to society. Their responsibilities are twofold: 1) to
investigate the background of offenders and to make these reports
available to the judge in the case of probation officers and to the parole
board in the case of parole officers; and 2) to counsel and supervise
persons on probation or parole, help them secure necessary education
or employment, and attempt to resolve any family problems they encounter. (9)

   For both the court and the corrections (treatment) systems, professionalism is required. The activities of the personnel are based
on specialized bodies of knowledge which are translated into courses
of action. The tasks are equally well-defined. Within this structure,
the professional is trusted to function as an individual. The same cannot be said for police and corrections custody personnel. Having no
accepted body of knowledge or professional status, their activities are
structured by organizational rules and regulations. Moreover, they
are closely observed by supervisors to insure their adherence to the
prescribed standards.

                        Current Nonprofessionalism

   There is a lack of professionalism, at the present time, in the
police department and in custody corrections. This exists noticeably
on the line officer level, that level where the greatest interaction occurs with the client. The following discussion examines the factors
prohibiting professionalization for both the patrol officer and the corrections officer, and then describes changes in these job factors,
particularly those of the police, that are breaking down the barriers to
professionalization. Such factors include the existent paramilitary
orientations, conflicting organizational goals, and bureaucratic supervision.

   The need for organized and effective control forces in prisons and
in the community at large has fostered a paramilitary approach in most
custody staffs and police personnel. The adoption of militaristic
organizational structures and procedures has made it easier to train
and supervise these forces, each of which has a limited background to
do a specific job. The paramilitary approach is apparent in the uniforms, titles, and procedures of custody and police personnel. Training for corrections officers is directed toward the mission of security
and for police officers toward the mission of enforcement, and little
if any emphasis is placed on interaction with inmates or citizens.
After a specified number of weeks of training and basic orientation,

they learn the ways of the "institution" or the "street" by working with
one or more officers in a modified apprenticeship program, which
often institutionalizes bad habits of the past. The models that emerge
are those of the aloof but efficient guard or police officer.

The work for corrections officers resembles that of a continuous
mass-production organizations, and the prison argot refers to inmates
being "worked," "fed," and "housed." The prison is, to a great degree, an institution isolated from the day-to-day exigencies of the outside world. With the exception of infrequent riots, few exceptional
happenings are likely to occur. The same problem of boredom exists
for patrol officers. Most of the time - usually more than half the
tour of duty - officers are on patrol, on foot or in a car. They walk
around and around or cruise over and over again in an assigned zone
of the city. For corrections workers and patrol officers alike, one
day's routine is like the next. Yet existing alongside these feelings
of boredom are feelings of stress. In the course of their work, they
experience fear and uncertainty. The tension in their relationship
with their clients often creates a threatening environment in which
assault or even riot may occur. They develop vigilance and alertness
lest the unexpected take them unaware. These feelings of boredom
and fear work only to increase the distance between the corrections
officer and the inmate and between the patrol officer and the citizen.

But this is only one side of their work. For corrections officers,
the goal is prevention of escape and riot by the maintenance of internal order and security. But another goal exists - that of the treatment
of each inmate as unique, having individual needs. This creates a
conflicting role where, under the rehabilitative ideal, the guard who
"restricts freedom" is to relax and act spontaneously, is to "understand" the inmates, and is to use formal disciplinary mechanisms as
infrequently as possible. The same conflict exists for patrol officers,
who not only pursue the goal of "enforcement of the law" by making
arrests, but also pursue that of "provision of community services" by
performing these noncrime, and often peacekeeping, services. Thus,
the authoritarian police officer who fights crime is also expected to
provide emergency medical, social-welfare, and psychological services
to various citizens. These conflicts create considerable personal and
institutional problems. Neither corrections nor police officers are
hired on their ability to work with people; they are hired on criteria of
physical condition. Furthermore, corrections and police officers are
not trained in personal intervention strategies or interpersonal communications, and they are not rewarded for performance in these areas.

In fact, the line officers in these paramilitary organizations are
under the same kind of scrutiny as the inmates or citizens under their

surveillance. Alleged corruption and brutality is held to justify intensive investigations and periodic inspections of line officers. Just as
guards are required to write disciplinary reports (tickets) on inmate
rule violators, and just as police are required to issue citations or
make arrests of civilian violators of the law, so too do superiors make
written reports on subordinates' infractions of the rules. The line officers, as a result, become as alienated from their supervisors as
they are from their clients.

The result of this paramilitary environment is that of subcultures
in which the officers share the same parochial and defensive world
view. United by common attitudes toward the general public, the offenders, and their supervisors, they share a high degree of solidarity.
This cohesion is also characterized by mutually reinforcing attitudes
about work and about organizational goals - about "fighting crime" or
"keeping criminals in their place." Because of their desire for secre-
cy, their odd working hours, and their strong brotherhood, they tend
to restrict their social contacts to other members of the force. (10)

There have been, in recent years, some signs of change or some
trends away from these problems. Police departments, in some respects, have moved ahead of corrections systems. Improvements
have been made in such areas as remuneration, educational qualifications, and advanced administrative and managerial techniques.

While corrections custody officers are still receiving inadequate
pay, adequate salaries for police officers are now the rule rather than
the exception. The resultant shortage of personnel and the high turnover rate (18 percent to 64 percent annually) plaguing corrections systems (11) is less a problem for police departments, many of which
enjoy a waiting list of qualified applicants. In fact, educational standards for police applicants (ranging from at least one year of higher
education to at least four years or a baccalaureate degree) as a condition of employment are becoming more common. So, too, are
educational incentive programs (addition of 2 percent to 5 percent or
more to the salary of those of a certain educational level). Furthermore, a few police departments provide for lateral entry: moving
from one employing agency to another when career advancement is
blocked, or when another agency appears more attractive for self-
improvement and advancement or offers the opportunity for more
meaningful work assignments. These departments have overcome
such complications as residence requirements and nontransferable
pensions. Corrections systems, on the other hand, have even fewer
instances of lateral entry, for there exists an additional barrier not
encountered in police agencies or the courts - lack of uniformity of
job titles in corrections, and the differing functions performed in

various jurisdictions under the same or similar job titles. As a result, most incumbents in the personnel categories of administrator and supervisor have won these positions in competition with other employees of a department or agency. Only in the very top executive positions has outside recruitment of administrators broken this overall practice of internal promotion to high level positions. (12)

Changes have been made not only to attract better qualified personnel, but also to utilize their capabilities as efficiently and effectively as possible. Changes have been made in redefining goals and in restructuring officer roles. Officers of the San Diego Police Department are assigned to particular beats for which they are held accountable - and they are encouraged to handle problemsolving on their own. They are trained to do a community analysis and to develop a profile of the community structure. Then, based on this knowledge of both criminal and social problems, they develop their own particular tactics and strategies. Their activities may include talks at community meetings, encouragement of citizen ride-alongs, utilization of local media, development of innovative approaches to handling parties and disturbances, and utilization of appropriate referrals. The officers then analyze their work and discuss the results with each other during roll call meetings. (13)

Another approach to improve managerial efficiency and to eliminate conflicting officer roles is taking place in Wilmington, Delaware. The patrol force is split into two sections: community service and crime prevention. In the former section, officers answer calls for service, and in the latter, they deter crime and make apprehensions. The officers become either "community service agents" or "crime fighters." With this program in effect, the department has realized improved officer morale and increased officer productivity. (14)

The programs undertaken by police departments reflect improvements in the utilization of personnel. Corrections, too, has developed a model that achieves closer interpersonal relationships among inmates, the treatment staff, and custody personnel. Known as the "integrated treatment team" concept, this model, employed by juvenile training schools and several Federal corrections institutions, serves to offset the negative consequences of the authoritarian approach. Custody personnel, after being trained in counseling and other rehabilitative techniques, work hand-in-hand with the paraprofessional treatment staff. They join treatment personnel in making the diagnostic decisions of prison management on such matters as the custodial security required of each inmate, the optimum program for his rehabilitation, and his readiness for gradual release. Additionally, inmates, security officers, and treatment staff meet regularly to dis-

cuss mutual problems and their possible solutions. Such an arrangement insures a model of a collaborative institution where lines of communication are continuously open between prisoners and staff and between treatment and security personnel. (15)

These changes, innovative as they are, still do not allow police
or corrections officers, no matter how educated or competent they
are, to exercise discretion as completely as court personnel and
corrections treatment staff. New channels of communication must be
opened between administrators and employees as well as between employees and clients. Ideally, the many layers in the hierarchy of such
bureaucratic structures should be eliminated so that line workers can
make decisions on their own.

REPRESENTATIVENESS, RESPONSIVENESS,
EFFICIENCY: THE RESULTS OF
PROFESSIONALIZATION

Beyond 1984, a trend toward provessionalization will revolution-
ize police departments and corrections custody systems. Efficiency
- increased quantity and quality of service delivery - will supersede
goals of representativeness and responsiveness. To accomplish this,
police and corrections agencies will be moving in line with the standards required by the courts' legal profession and by the professions
and paraprofessions composing corrections treatment. The characteristics they will strive to attain are as follows: 1) basis of a systematic theory or body of knowledge; 2) authority recognized by their
clientele; 3) broader community sanction and approval of this authority; 4) advanced educational requirements; 5) formal licensing authority; 6) code of ethics; and 7) formal professional associations. (16)
First let's take a look at the structure of police departments at a
point in time beyond 1984, and then let's examine that of corrections
custody. Finally, we shall discuss other possible changes - far beyond 1984.

Police Professionalization

The police, as has been demonstrated, reflect bureaucratiza-
tion, not professionalization. Today the administrators manage by
crisis, handling situations only as they arise; and the line officers
are no more than technicians taking orders. Decision-making is cen-

tralized and concentrated at the top of the organization; hence, any
outside professional specialists (e. g. , General Counsel, civilian advisors) are brought in at the staff level. Rarely is the patrol division
coordinated with any of the other units - investigative, administrative,
or support units. Patrol operations may not be consistent with or have
an impact on overall departmental goals. Patrol often exists as an
independent operation in which "management by crisis" occurs in reaction to various external or internal demands. The result is the accomplishment of numerous, diverse activities by individual police officers controlled only by isolated disciplinary actions. (17) Furthermore, the so-called professional police organizations and associations are indistinguishable from labor and craft unions; (18) and the
so-called professional code of ethics turns out to be many "proposed"
codes of ethics, often failing to even mention the concept of provision
of noncrime services. (19)

In the future, patrol officers will become "community managers"
and "monitors of social change. " They will work together with other
operations units (detective, vice, traffic, juvenile), coordinated by
service units (records, communications, laboratory, etc.) and supported by administrative units (planning and research, personnel and
training, public information, etc.). To accomplish this, there must
be professionalization through organizational change, the development
of a systematic theory or body of knowledge, and officer education.

Organizational change will involve, optimally, a flattening of the
pyramid by the elimination of many superfluous ranks or, minimally,
reliance on a matrix organization. The flattening of the usual hierarchical arrangement has led, as many studies point out, to improvements in management. The administrative distance from top to bot-
tom is reduced, permitting increased contact and improved understanding. The administrators can rely more on knowledge gained
from direct contact with line officers, and less on information filter-
ed upward through successive levels of supervision, which often becomes distorted in the process. (20) At the very least, the traditional organization will be arranged along the lines of a matrix organization. With a matrix organization, projects become the focal point
around which to organize the efforts of the department. A project is
undertaken by a team consisting of representatives with differing
ranks from the several divisions affected by the project. The team
works together only until the project is well under way, but during this
time, overcomes such problems of the traditional structure as inadequate communication, ineffective decisionmaking, and slow and inflexi-
ble responses to changing demands. (21)

The evolution of the paraprofessional police officer who exercises

considerable discretion in his everyday activities will come about
through the requirement of a four-year baccalaureate degree (at the
least) in the administration of justice from an accredited college or
university.

The development of particular theories is being undertaken, but
they have not as yet been pulled together into a comprehensive discipline. Research has been done in the areas of task analyses of officers' activities, crime analyses, resources allocation strategies,
tactical and strategic experimentation, and organizational and administrative configurations. (22) These, when further analyzed and refined,
will become the core of the police discipline.

The requirement of a four-year college degree is even now evident in certain jurisdictions. In these early stages, it remains just
another "requirement" for the job. In the future, however, it will
replace police training academies and serve as the basis for the academic preparation of police paraprofessionals. One further step toward professionalization will be the development of a formal licensing
authority; this requires the passing of a written examination of the degree candidate before (s)he is permitted to work as a police officer.
Such a step also necessitates the adoption of a universal code of ethics,
setting forth the standards to which a police officer must adhere, as
well as the organization of a formal professional association to promote the police standards.

With these changes, that insure the upgrading of standards, will
evolve a proficient force of officers who will be respected not only by
their clientele, (the recipients of their services), but also by the community at large.

Corrections Custody Professionalization

Corrections officers, as has been shown, presently function
within the same type of bureaucratic organization as police officers.
In fact, there exists a line organization of custodial ranks, such as
officer, sergeant, lieutenant, captain, to superintendent (warden), a
clear indication of the chain of command within the hierarchy. Yet
this line organization is separated completely from the staff (or non-
line) positions of treatment, training, and industrial personnel. In
fact, they exist as essentially separate organizations, each with its
own salary differentials and titles, that compete with each other for
resources and power. Corrections officers, as police, are rarely
allowed any part in the decision-making process. In addition, they
frequently are used as a convenient scapegoat for the lack of success

that has attended most efforts at rehabilitation.

Professionalization for corrections officers depends on their development of a specialized body of knowledge, or their borrowing portions of that body of knowledge from the treatment personnel. Required is the careful study of human attitudes and behavior and the development of particular approaches to effect changes. Task analyses have been done of the many specialized duties of the corrections officer (23) but more attention must be focused on interpersonal communications between guards and inmates and between inmates and inmates so that behavior changes can be effected.

The future of corrections officer professionalization will lie in one of two courses of action: either a movement toward paraprofessionalization, much as that outlined for police officers, or an elimination of the position altogether. In the latter instance, treatment personnel will assume the duties of corrections officers by providing security and routinizing activity.

In the first instance, corrections officers will add the duties of rehabilitation or treatment to their usual responsibilities. Yet before this can be accomplished, corrections (as policing) must undergo such changes as the elimination of paramilitary ranks for a flattened organizational structure, the requirement of a baccalaureate or master's degree in corrections (including sociology, psychology, criminology, and related courses) from an accredited college or university, the development of a formal licensing authority, the adoption of a code of ethics, and the establishment of a formal professional association.

The result of such a plan will be the merger of custody and treatment personnel into one entity. No longer are corrections officers merely turn-keys or guards; they now perform casework and classification services for inmates assigned to their custody. They develop special programs and monitor the progress of inmates under their care. The use of military uniforms and military titles and terms will be discontinued, and regimented behavior in all facilities, both for personnel and for inmates, will be abandoned. (24) This allows the prison environment to more closely resemble that of the community. Treatment than arises from face-to-face relations of line staff with small groups of inmates in the course of routine work, study, and recreation activities. Only when activities inside the walls relate to circumstances in the outside world will eventual reintegration take place.

CHANGES BEYOND 1984

Even after professionalization has been achieved for police officers and corrections custody personnel, other changes will take place in the criminal justice system. Technology and research will have devised testing that identifies those individuals with particular qualifications and skills needed for any specialized position within an agency (whether police, courts, or corrections). (25) Paraprofessional police officers will become specialists, opting for such positions as computer technician, crime analyst, dispatcher, traffic regulator, juvenile worker, and the like. Paraprofessional corrections officers will become cell house managers, security specialists, factory managers, and the like. In fact, university curricula will provide choices of courses enabling specialization.

Other concerns of the future will revolve around executive expertise. Administrators of all the organizations will be carefully selected and specially trained in administration and management. A planned methodological approach may be the development of two separate career types or paths. An individual chooses to pursue advancement opportunities within the area of the agency's various operational levels or chooses to pursue advancement within the area of the various managerial positions. This dual career ladder permits an employee to consider a professional career as a functional, or as a managerial, specialist. (26)

The achievement of professionalization for police and corrections custody personnel will take place over time. The matter is complex; there must be not only advancement in education of the individual officers, but also fairly radical changes in the organizational structures. Bureaucracies are difficult to change; but even now, there are indications of receptiveness to the altering of the organizations in either of two ways: 1) by flattening the organization with the removal of unnecessary ranks, or 2) by creating a dual career ladder with a functional tract and an administrative tract. Additionally, there remains the pulling together and refinement of a body of knowledge, and the development of agencies to uphold the standards of professionalization. Although a complex matter, it will be achieved beyond 1984.

CONCLUSION

Society is requiring, and will be demanding, more professionalized delivery systems. The accelerating difficulties of life and the

growing complexities of crime and disorder, as the nation advances
into the next century, will require far more productivity on the part
of the criminal justice system than has so far been demonstrated.

Good intentions and hard work no longer will be adequate. The
recent introduction of racial minorities and women in the police and
corrections custody systems has not been enough. Still to be addressed are issues of competence - competence to handle the complex
tasks of serving the public and administering justice. The integration of representativeness, responsiveness, and efficiency in the form
of professionalization will be the goal - and the achievement - of beyond 1984.

NOTES AND REFERENCES

1. Robert C. Trojanowicz and Samuel L. Dixon, Criminal Justice and the Community (Englewood Cliffs: Prentice-Hall, 1974), pp. 53-55.

2. Ibid., pp. 82-86.

3. Catherine Higgs Milton and others, Women in Policing: A Manual (Washington, D.C.: Police Foundation, 1974), pp. 49-57.

4. Ronald J. Waldron and others, The Criminal Justice System: An Introduction (Boston: Houghton Mifflin, 1976), p. 426.

5. Paul B. Weston and Kenneth M. Wells, Criminal Justice: Introduction and Guidelines (Pacific Palisades: Goodyear Publishing, 1976), pp. 205-21.

6. Ibid., p. 347.

7. Ibid, pp. 349-50.

8. Harry E. Allen and Clifford E. Simonsen, Corrections in America: An Introduction (Beverly Hills: Glencoe Press, 1975), pp. 416-17.

9. Waldron, op. cit., p. 423.

10. James B. Jacobs and Harold G. Retsky, "Prison Guard," The Sociology of Corrections: A Book of Readings, ed. Robert G. Leger and John R. Stratton (New York: Wiley, 1977), pp. 49-61.
    Jesse Rubin, "Police Identity and the Police Role," The Police Community: Dimensions of an Occupational Subculture, ed. Jack Goldsmith and Sharon Goldsmith (Pacific Palisades: Palisades Publishers, 1974), pp. 131-36.

11. Allen, op. cit., pp. 399-400.

12. Weston, op. cit., pp. 344-49.

13. San Diego Police Department, Community Profiling and Police Patrol: Final Staff Report of the Community Profile Development Project (San Diego: San Diego Police Department, 1974).

14. James M. Tien, An Evaluation Report of an Alternative Approach in Police Patrol: The Wilmington Split Force Experiment (Cambridge: Public Systems Evaluation, 1977).

15. Robert D. Pursley, Introduction to Criminal Justice (Encino: Glencoe Press, 1977), pp. 421-25.

16. Robert E. Blanchard, Introduction to the Administration of Justice (New York: Wiley, 1975), pp. 284-85.

17. Norman E. Kassoff, Organization Concepts (Gaithersburg: International Association of Chiefs of Police, 1973), pp. 29-30.

18. Albert J. Reiss, Jr., The Police and the Public (New Haven: Yale University Press, 1971), p. 128.

19. Blanchard, op. cit., pp. 287-88.

20. Kassoff, op. cit., pp. 19-21.

21. Richard A. Johnson and others, The Theory and Management of Systems (New York: McGraw-Hill, 1973), pp. 406-08.

22. Theodore H. Schell and others, National Evaluation Program Phase I Summary Report: Traditional Preventive Patrol (Washington, D.C.: Law Enforcement Assistance Administration, 1976).

23. Jacobs, op. cit., pp. 55-60.

24. Allen, op. cit., p. 398.

25. Ibid., pp. 400-401.

26. Weston, op. cit., pp. 345-46.

17 The Role of Police in Pollution Control

Marshall Stalley
Theodore B. Shelton
Barry Evan Kline

"In the early 1960s Congress, aroused by its constituents, awoke to the need for national legislation to conserve, protect and assess the resources of the nation. Man's interruption of the natural assimilative action of streams through overuse, overloading with pollutants, and destruction of the natural recharge areas, had brought the country to the point of widespread degradation of its water resources. The disruption of the capability for natural self-cleansing of the atmosphere by overloading with pollutants was bringing man close to poisoning the air and destroying life around him. Suburban sprawl around decaying central cities threatened remaining open space needed for the regeneration of air and water for urban centers." (1)

There is a comprehensive body of laws now available on the Federal, State and local levels designed to protect the environment. The streams of the nation have been legally protected from pollution by the Refuse Disposal Act of 1899. As a result of congressional action in the 1960s, a series of legislation was enacted, including: Water Pollution Control Act of 1961, 1965, 1966, the National Environmental Policy Act of 1969, and the Clean Air Acts of 1963-1967. These acts were followed in the 1970s by amendments of the older acts, as well as the Federal Safe Drinking Water Act, the Resource Recovery Act, the Noise Control Act (1972) and the Toxic Substances Control Act (1976), to mention just a few.

In response to Federal legislative action and public pressures, most states passed a flurry of legislation aimed at the protection of air, water and land from a multitude of physical insults. The intent of the legislative process is clear. A "clean environment" was expected. Unfortunately, the task proved too great for the limited resources of local health departments and State and Federal environmental protection agencies. These agencies have enlisted the help of the citizenry to direct their staffs to violations. Citizens are encouraged to report to the agencies apparent violations using a toll-free hot-line telephone number. Citizen activists have made significant contributions to programs such as the National Pollution Discharge Elimination System in identifying unlawful discharge. The role of the citizen is an important one; however, it has not been identified, defined and cultivated.

There is need for a more effective system to report violations of environmental protection laws. As one DEP administrator said, "Anything which can be done to improve the reporting system is bound to improve our effectiveness." Why should municipal and State police have a role to play in the detection, referral, and, at times, enforcement of this legislation?

The rationale for police involvement in this area is manifold. First, police are already trained for and engaged in law enforcement. Second, as existing public agencies with extensive field staff, the cost of their service would be substantially less than the cost of either creating a new agency or adding staff to existing agencies. Although there is little doubt that a highly skilled task force of environmental police officers, trained solely for the purpose of enforcing environmental protection legislation, could perform this role more effectively, there is much doubt that this could be accomplished at a price the taxpayer would accept. Third, the police already serve as an information and referral service. "The police are called because other agencies frequently are not available... however, they are systematically deprived of most professional resources. Thus they have to serve as an unauthorized and sometimes uninformed referral agency." (More, p. 87). The existing system would be strengthened by providing additional information to police and authorizing them to act on it. Fourth, police are already taking responsibility for certain aspects of environmental protection. An authorized role would enhance their effectiveness.

The characteristics of police organization are well suited for detecting, referring and enforcing violation of environmental regulations. These traits are a product of unique historical and social trends that have acted upon the police since the time of the "watch and ward." It is instructive to review this history.

The role of police as the "eyes and ears" of the community is rooted in the ninth-century English system of mutual responsibility, forerunner to American policing. At that time the crown dictated that "It was each citizen's duty to raise the 'hue and cry' when a crime was committed, to collect his neighbors and to pursue a criminal who fled the district" (More, p. 2). There were no policemen per se, only a hierarchy of accountability to ensure the reporting of crime. As villages grew into cities and were walled, the system developed into the "watch and ward." Each citizen was responsible to serve on the night watch to guard the city gates and apprehend law breakers. Thus, the night watch acted as the eyes and ears of the community, and served as a way of the citizenry's guarding themselves.

As industrialization developed, however, the system underwent a transformation. There were more important things to be done than stand night watch, and replacements could be had for a price. Those citizens who did not have time to guard themselves relied upon replacements to protect property from theft and fire. In 1636, the "watch and ward" system began in Boston (Savage). The trend of placing the responsibility of policing upon paid replacements continued. By the eighteenth century, there were regular municipal night watchmen in the large cities. Unfortunately, they did little to protect the city. Often they had daytime employment, as well, and were accustomed to sleeping through their tours of duty (Fosdick, pp. 62-65). This inefficiency was compounded by the lack of any hiring criteria, other than political ones. Nonetheless, the situation continued until the mid-nineteenth century.

The degree of diversification reflects the needs of an urbanizing population with access to the tools of industrial and technological advancement. From the crime-fighting specialties, such as detective work and fingerprinting, to animal control and traffic patrol, the police were quick to add to the list of their specialties and staff. Today, police are involved in a multitude of specialized technical areas to facilitate law enforcement and service-rendering responsibilities.

To pursue this, larger departments presently employ police with a variety of special abilities. Crime scene investigation requires specialists in chemistry, biochemistry, forensic medicine, photography and, at times, scuba diving. Criminal identification has created specialties in graphoanalysis, voice printing and fingerprinting. Suicide prevention, hostage negotiation and family dispute teams have been staffed with behavioral scientists. Computer specialists are utilized for planning, research, and record keeping. Other special areas include the emergency medical bureau, and the air and marine police.

Thus, there is historical precedence for the police accepting a wide variety of duties and pursuing them in depth. In certain fields, such as traffic, they have become the major agency in planning, research, and operations. In others, such as emergency medical assistance, they share responsibility with fire rescue teams and ambulance services.

Their technical abilities are proven. Educational levels of police are on the increase. One of the two more advanced departments (Nassau County, N. Y.) has an entrance requirement of two years of college, which may soon rise to a Bachelor's degree. Modern transport and communications equipment provide police with superior mobility, visibility, response and referral capabilities. Their 24-hour service is unmatched by other public inspection and patrol agencies. The police have a tradition of acting as the watchdog of the community - its "eyes and ears," so to speak.

These service characteristics relate in a unique way to pollution of the environment. Serious pollution, either purposeful or accidental, often remains unreported. In order for effective pollution control to be accomplished, enforcement officials must be on the scene. If pollution occurs in a swamp, or at 3:00 A. M., or while EPA or DEP inspectors are in another municipality, the damage may not be avoided. In essence the service characteristics of police department are well matched to the modus operandi of polluters.

The police are well-situated for environmental protection duties and for more than their technical abilities alone. The public views the agency as the public service organization. When a citizen with a complaint does not know where to turn, a call to the police is often the first step. In confirmation of this, one agency, the Middlesex County, New Jersey Health Department receives 90 percent of their complaints from police referrals.

From a legal perspective, police are somewhat limited in enforcement powers. Federal laws make no provisions for municipal or State police to enforce environmental statutes. On the State level, using New Jersey as an example, there are some provisions for enforcement in, for example, the State Sanitary Code (N. J. S. A. 26:1A-9). This includes many anti-pollution regulations normally handled by local health departments. The restrictions on police enforcement, however, have come as much from the traditional division of labor among public agencies, as they have from a lack of legal jurisdiction. Local ordinances are unique to municipalities, but often have provisions for enforcement by police.

In our view, the enforcement aspects of police participation in environmental protection are important, yet secondary to the role they could have in referral. In this connection, it may be helpful to review the ongoing enforcement and referral of environmental regulation by police in New Jersey and other states and to examine factors which affect their role. These include specifically the education and training of police, the information flow between the police and the DEP, EPA and health departments, the political climate, and the police executive and line officer's views on environmental protection.

There has been, and is today, direct enforcement by police in a number of areas related to environmental protection. Park police have had a traditional role of litter control and protection of the environment from what might be considered vandalism, e. g. damage to trees, animals and waterways. However, the major portion of their time - one environmental commissioner estimated 90 percent - is spent on patrol and with criminal work. They are not any more involved in environmental protection enforcement than are other police.

Auto emissions are regulated in New Jersey and may be enforced by local police. The enforcement has been characterized by police and DEP officials as "spotty." The reason for this is evident from the experience of one municipality which sponsored a crackdown of a Truck Diesel Emission Code (N. J. A. C. 7:27-14). Local officers, undertrained and using inaccurate measuring equipment, issued summonses which were challenged in court and overturned. More effective equipment is presently being developed which will enable police to give summonses which will be supported by accurate technical data in much the same way as a speeding ticket is now issued.

A similar problem exists in the enforcement of auto noise regulations. Most communities have adopted State regulations with specific limits on noise. Yet police are reluctant to ticket individuals if there are no technical records to support the officer in court. The chief of police of a suburban community stated his concern with regard to admissibility of subjective evidence in court. "What's noisy to you might not be noisy to me. If I asked my men I might get 80 different opinions. We don't have the equipment or the expertise." There are, however, police who do have the equipment and the expertise which would permit evidence to stand up in court. The California Highway Patrol has a special unit which monitors highway vehicle noise, operating in a manner similar to a speed trap. These officers have the technical capacity to effectively enforce noise standards.

In a recent pollution indictment, police proved their worth in the enforcement of water pollution statutes. A Newark police patrol discovered a "tanker... pouring 8, 000 gallons of toxic chemical wastes into a storm sewer" (New York Times, January 30, 1978). This is a common occurrence in New Jersey, a state with extensive chemical industries. The state's law enforcement officials have begun a drive to end the illicit dumping of toxic wastes onto streets and uninhabited lands and into sewers and waterways. It appears that local and State police forces could be crucial in detection and apprehension of illegal dumping.

The referral role of police generally has been one of forwarding

citizen complaints to the appropriate authorities. Although there are
no legal constraints on police to prevent their initiating an investigation, their role has remained reactive rather than proactive. Perhaps
because of a lack of awareness or personal discretion, most police
interviewed indicated they would rarely initiate a report of pollution.
The only proactive force contacted in this study was the Marine Bureau
of the Nassau County Police, New York State. This division regularly
initiated pollution referrals to the U.S. Coast Guard. In many cases
they were also involved in the followup investigation.

Concerning their role in environmental protection, police who
were interviewed related that they "don't know what they are looking
for." Investigation has discovered the reason. Formal information
pipelines between the police and all levels of environmental agencies
are nearly nonexistent, although this varies from state to state and
from one municipality to another. Some police departments have
cordial relations, and therefore an informal information flow, with the
health department. This appears to occur only when the individuals
involved take the initiative. In other departments, the only contact
was the result of police being asked to give physical protection to
health officials.

Another cause of uninformed police is the paucity of training programs. The New Jersey Police Academy conducts 10 to 20-week basic
training for police cadets of municipalities and for the State Police.
The subject of pollution or environmental law is never broached, and
there are no known in-house training classes on the subject; but there
may be a change occurring. The Nassau County police, New York
State, one of the highest salaried police departments in the country,
are kept informed of legal decisions, new laws and enforcement techniques for environmental statutes through training bulletins. The bulletins are distributed to all police in the county, including municipal
officers. New Jersey police have also been exposed to some pollution
control training. A 3-day course on noise pollution is offered by Cook
College, Rutgers University. Over the past two years, 35 police officers have taken the course after having been authorized by their municipalities with responsibility to enforce noise statutes. Generally,
however, there is little evidence of police training programs in the
area of pollution control.

Lax enforcement is partly due to insufficient training of, and legal
constraints on, the police. However, what seems to be of comparable
importance is the lack of pressure from mayors, town councils, and
police chiefs on the individual law officer and the personal discretion
of individual officers. A New Jersey patrolman discussed the situation in his department. "There is a lot of discretion out there. I
ticket them (vehicle smoke and noise violators) - especially the trucks,

because they should know better. The autos usually get a warning because of the cost of repairs (in the patrolman's view, the costs are prohibitive for motorists.)" The State and Federal law is unchanged from municipality to municipality; yet enforcement depends upon the personal attitudes of politicians in the town and those of the police officer. All police officials interviewed stated that they did not set administrative priorities for the enforcement of anti-pollution laws. The decision is left to each policeman's discretion.

The situation is that much of the legislation designed to control pollution is not being effectively enforced. Police are an appropriate agency to extend and improve enforcement. They are experienced in law enforcement; they have proven their ability to acquire technical skills; they are looked upon as a public service and referral agency; and their equipment and work routine are appropriate for the task. To date, however, they have done relatively little enforcement or referral. Areas where police departments appear to be deficient in enforcing violations of ordinances are those relating to auto emissions, auto noise levels, open burning and illicit dumping; they appear to be examples of pollution not especially difficult to detect. Although police do refer many citizen complaints, they have not extended their traditional role as the "eyes and ears" of the public to pollution control actions, and rarely initiate referrals.

A police agency performing significantly in pollution control is that of Stuttgart, Germany. There the police have a close working relationship with the Stuttgart Chemical Investigation Office (CIO), the local pollution control bureau. (2) The value of police in pollution control has been recognized. Police are oftentimes the agency contacted by citizens with complaints. Consequently, a team approach to the public problem has resulted in the study of environmental law by police cadets and involvement of police in environmental planning and design, together with the CIO. The work relationship has enhanced cooperation and respect between the two agencies, and therefore, more efficient service to the public.

The following recommendations are made to municipal and police officials interested in establishing an effective force to control pollution:

1. The institution of environmental education in in-house and academy training programs. This would improve a police officer's knowledge of environmental law and pollution and his technical competence with detection equipment. As a result, police may acquite a heightened awareness of environmental problems, and begin to view pollution as an act of vandalism against public property. They

might therefore be more proactive in enforcement and less discretionary. A better trained police officer would be more likely to recognize violations and have the technical competence to support his claims in court.

2. Provision of specialized training in a police academy, university or environmental agency for officers selected for special duty in dealing with violations of environmental law. These officers would act as liaison between the police, the health department, environmental commission, DEP and EPA. Such an arrangement would keep information up to date. In addition, fellow police could turn to these officers for advice 24 hours a day.

3. Establishment of priorities for police officers. The issuance of bulletins regarding environmental laws and regulations would inform officers that enforcement of such regulations is expected by police superintendents and other public officials

4. Establishment of formal relations with environmental protection agencies. This would help provide police with the necessary legal and technical information to assist in the apprehension of lawbreakers. In addition, a multi-agency approach is likely to be a more efficient and effective approach to enforcement than dependence upon only environmental agencies.

Ever since the establishment of police services, new roles have been added to the traditional roles of protection of property and crime control. The protection of the environment and the control of illegal pollution practices as a police function represents an extension of traditional activities, not a radical new departure. Police services respond to changing societal needs. The control of pollution and the protection of the environment are now well-accepted public policy by public officials and the citizenry alike. Police have a unique role to play in this new dimension, and are already showing evidence that the challenge will be accepted beyond 1984.

NOTES AND REFERENCES

1.   Association of N.J. Environmental Commissions, introduction to
     "Tools and Rules... Federal Environmental Protection Programs,"
     February, 1977.

2.   Conversation with Mr. G. Arno Loessner, University of
     Delaware.

BIBLIOGRAPHY

Fisk, James G. The Police Officer's Exercise of Discretion in the Decision to Arrest. Institute of Government and Public Affairs, 1974, no. 188.

Fosdick, Raymond B. American Police Systems. Montclair, New Jersey: Patterson Smith, 1969.

Janson, Donald. "Jersey Hunts Dumpers of Toxics," New York Times, Monday, January 30, 1978, p. A1, B3.

More, Harry W., Jr., ed. The American Police: Text and Readings. St. Paul, Minnesota: West Publishing, 1976. p. 2 from: The President's Commission on Law Enforcement and Administration of Justice, Task Force Report: The Police. Washington, D.C.: U.S. Government Printing Office, 1967, pp. 3-7. p. 87 from Clarence Schrag, "Police Discretion," Crime and Justice: American Style. Maryland: National Institute of Mental Health, 1971, pp. 145-50.

Price, Barbara Raffel. Police Professionalism: Rhetoric and Action. Lexington, Massachusetts: Lexington Books, 1977.

Savage, E.H. Police Records and Recollections. Boston, 1865. Savage quote in Fosdick, p. 59.

Vollmer, August. The Police and Modern Society. College Park, Maryland: McGrath Publishing, 1969. Reprint of Bureau of Public Administration, University of California, 1936.

Walker, Samuel. A Critical History of Police Reform. Lexington, Massachusetts: Lexington Books, 1977.

Index

About the Contributors

JOHN T. O'BRIEN is Associate Professor at the New York Institute of Technology. Most recently he was the director of the Northern Virginia Police Academy. He served for twenty years in the New York City Police Department, attaining the rank of deputy inspector. Thereafter he served for four years as director of the New Brunswick, New Jersey Police Department.

MARVIN MARCUS is the Acting Chief of the Training Section Federal Protective Service Division, General Services Administration. He has been a professor of criminal justice both at Georgia State University and at Old Dominion University. Mr. Marcus previously served with the New York City Police Department.

ELINOR OSTROM is Co-director of the Workshop in Political Theory and Policy Analysis and Professor of Political Science at Indiana University.

ROGER B. PARKS is Associate Director of the Workshop in Political Theory and Policy Analysis, Indiana University, and Co-Principal Investigator for the Police Services Study.

GORDON P. WHITAKER is Assistant Professor of Political Science at the University of North Carolina at Chapel Hill.

JOHANNES F. SPREEN is sheriff of Oakland County, Michigan. He served 25 years with the New York City Police Department and as Police Commissioner of Detroit, Michigan.

WILLIAM CONNELIE became Superintendent of the New York
State Police after a 29-year career in the New York City Police Department.

DAVID J. FARMER is Director of the Police Division in the
National Institute of Law Enforcement and Criminal Justice.   He was
formerly Director of Operations Management and Special Assistant
to the Police Commissioner of the city of New York.

ROBERT A. HAIR is a retired New York City Police Department
Deputy Inspector and is now a professor at John Jay College of Criminal Justice.

JOHN W. POWELL, a Certified Protection Professional, is a
graduate of Dartmouth College.   He entered the FBI in 1943 and served
for over seventeen years.

JOSEPH J. O'BRIEN is a twenty-two-year veteran of the New York
Police Department, where he has spent seventeen of his years
assigned to its Intelligence Division.

RALPH F. SALERNO has been involved in combating organized
crime for more than thirty-two years.   He retired from the New
York City Police Department after serving for twenty years.

FREDERICK J. CAVANAGH is an Associate Professor and
Chairperson at Northwestern Connecticut Community College, Winsted, Connecticut.   After retiring from the New York City Police Department, he served as Chief of Administration in the New Brunswick
New Jersey Police Department.

HARVEY SCHLOSSBERG, Ph. D., is presently practicing as a
psychologist and consultant to police departments on psychological
problems in police work.   He is retired from the New York City Police Department, where he was the Director of the Psychological
Service Unit.

NEIL C. CHAMELIN is the Director of the Florida Police Standards and Training Commission and Director of the Standards and Training Division, Florida Department of Criminal Law Enforcement.   He
has been Administrator of the Police Science Division, Institute of
Government, University of Georgia.

VERNON B. FOX is a director of the School of Criminology, Florida State University. His first book, <u>Violence Behind Bars</u>, was based on his experiences in breaking the Michigan prison riot in 1952, when he was Deputy Warden at the State Prison of Southern Michigan.

JACQUELINE BOLES, Ph. D. , is Associate Professor, Sociology Department, Georgia State University. She is book review editor of the <u>Criminal Justice Review</u>.

CHARLOTTE TATRO, Ph. D. , has written and conducted work shops on women in prison as well as in management. She is the director of the Institute for Women of the Department of Community Affairs, Florida State University.

WILLIAM J. O'ROURKE is the Secretary of Public Safety for the State of Delaware. After retiring from the New York City Police Department, he was appointed the Commissioner of Public Safety for the City of Wilmington, Delaware.

JAMES T. NOLAN is a retired captain of the Wilmington Bureau of Police, Delaware. Mr. Nolan is currently an executive assistant in charge of grants administration for New Castle County, Delaware.

LINDA L. STABILE is a professor of Criminal Justice at Prince George's Community College and has served as a Law enforcement officer in the Metropolitan Police Department, Washington, D. C.

MARSHALL STALLEY is Professor of Environmental Resources and a Specialist in the Cooperative Extension Service of Cook College, Rutgers University.

THEODORE B. SHELTON is Associate Specialist in Water Resource Management of the Cooperative Extension Service and a member of the Department of Environmental Resources of Cook College, Rutgers University.

BARRY EVAN KLINE served as a Teaching Assistant in the Department of Environmental Resources of Cook College.

Pergamon Policy Studies